CHRISTUS
LUX MUNDI

Cambridge studies in medieval life and thought

Edited by WALTER ULLMANN, LITT.D., F.B.A.
Professor of Medieval History in the
University of Cambridge

Third series, vol. 10

THE CHURCH AND POLITICS IN FOURTEENTH-CENTURY ENGLAND

CAMBRIDGE STUDIES IN MEDIEVAL LIFE AND THOUGHT

THIRD SERIES

1 *The King's Hall within the University of Cambridge in the Later Middle Ages.* ALAN B. COBBAN

2 *Monarchy and Community.* A. J. BLACK

3 *The Church and the Two Nations in Medieval Ireland.* J. A. WATT

4 *The Spanish Church and the Papacy in the Thirteenth Century.* PETER LINEHAN

5 *Law and Society in the Visigothic Kingdom.* P. D. KING

6 *Durham Priory: 1400–1450.* R. B. DOBSON

7 *The Political Thought of William of Ockham.* A. S. MCGRADE

8 *The Just War in the Middle Ages.* FREDERICK H. RUSSELL

9 *The Two Italies: Economic Relations between the Norman Kingdom of Sicily and the Northern Communes.* DAVID ABULAFIA

10 *The Church and Politics in Fourteenth-Century England: The Career of Adam Orleton c. 1275–1345.* ROY MARTIN HAINES

11 *The Staffords, Earls of Stafford and Dukes of Buckingham, 1394–1521.* CAROLE RAWCLIFFE

THE CHURCH AND POLITICS IN FOURTEENTH-CENTURY ENGLAND

THE CAREER OF ADAM ORLETON

c. 1275–1345

ROY MARTIN HAINES

CAMBRIDGE UNIVERSITY PRESS
CAMBRIDGE
LONDON · NEW YORK · MELBOURNE

Published by the Syndics of the Cambridge University Press
The Pitt Building, Trumpington Street, Cambridge CB2 1RP
Bentley House, 200 Euston Road, London NW1 2DB
32 East 57th Street, New York, NY 10022, USA
296 Beaconsfield Parade, Middle Park, Melbourne 3206, Australia

First published 1978

Printed in Great Britain by
The Eastern Press Limited
London and Reading

Library of Congress Cataloguing in Publication Data
Haines, Roy Martin.
The church and politics in fourteenth-century England.
(Cambridge studies in medieval life and thought; 3d ser., v. 10)
Bibliography, p. .
Includes index.
1. Adam of Orleton, Bp of Winchester, d. 1345.
2. Statesmen – Great Britain – Biography.
3. Bishops – England – Biography.
4. Great Britain – History – Edward II–III, 1307–1377.
I. Title. II. Series.

DA231.A3H34 942.03′6′0924 [B] 76-54062

ISBN 0 521 21544 7

TO

HILARY FRANCES

CATHERINE ELIZABETH

HELEN MARY

CONTENTS

PREFACE

It was while I was working on a D.Phil. thesis in the late 1950s that Adam Orleton first came to my notice as one of the Worcester bishops. At the time I found no reason to dissent from the opinion commonly held of him – that of Stubbs and Tout – which has been generally adopted with scarcely a reservation. On a number of occasions I found myself returning to various stages of Orleton's career; editing his Worcester register, examining his tenure of the great see of Winchester, transcribing the 'defence brief' directed against his accusers of 1324, and reading papers about him in places as far apart as Durham and Kalamazoo. It soon became clear that the evidence used to convict him of moral turpitude – and worse – was in need of re-examination. Something of the kind was attempted by Canon Bannister, but in his anxiety to rehabilitate Orleton he adopted a number of Geoffrey le Baker's erroneous assertions and made of his 'hero' a political schemer in the Mortimer interest; in fact, for Bannister, the Mortimer connection provided the motivation for Orleton's adult life. Since the publication of Bannister's introduction to Orleton's Hereford register the reign of Edward II has been the subject of meticulous study and reinterpretation by scholars, notably T. F. Tout, J. Conway Davies and Bertie Wilkinson, and, more recently, J. R. S. Phillips and J. R. Maddicott. None of this work has had the least impact on Orleton's reputation, but it has done much to illuminate virtually every aspect of the reign and hence the context into which this biography – if biography it is – can be fitted.

Orleton's career falls naturally into three compartments: his diplomatic missions, his activity as ruler of three English sees, and his involvement in politics at the national level. With respect to the first I have been guided in my interpretation by the published works of such scholars as D. Queller, H. S. Lucas, G. P. Cuttino and P. Chaplais, who have elucidated the intricacies of diplomatic process and protocol as well as the role of the negotiators concerned. My debt to these men and to those who have written about the political aspects of the reigns of Edward II and Edward III is amply demonstrated in the footnotes and bibliography. I have, of course, been at pains to relate their findings to Orleton's particular circumstances and have gone back to the manuscripts wherever he has been involved.

My own particular interests have been in ecclesiastical history – especially that of the English episcopate. None the less, I have tried to avoid over-emphasising the work of Orleton as diocesan, although it is copiously documented by his three registers and other subsidiary material. I hope, too, that I have avoided the assumption that competent administration necessarily stems from moral principle.

Over thirty years ago Miss Kathleen Edwards wrote a stimulating article on the political importance of the bishops during Edward II's reign. By and large her conclusion was that (following the death of Archbishop Winchelsey) the chroniclers rightly found the bishops guilty of a combination of futility and self-centredness. Nowadays Edward's foibles and eccentricities may be better understood, so too his unsuitability for kingship and the oppressive nature of the last few years of his reign. Against this background it is possible to view more favourably the attitude of those bishops who – breaking their oath of fealty – readily deserted Edward II for the cause of Isabella.

There are many who doubt whether it is feasible to undertake the biography of a medieval figure. In Orleton's case it is true that we can discover a great deal about his actions, but very little indeed about the motives which inspired them. Much remains dark, but it is hoped that a more realistic and open-minded examination of Orleton's life will help to change the monster of Baker's chronicle into the semblance of a human being beset by exceptional problems and divided loyalties: a man who in more settled times might have come down to us as a loyal servant of the monarch; a gifted administrator and diplomatist.

R. M. H.

Dalhousie University
March 1977.

ACKNOWLEDGEMENTS

Research for this book has been undertaken under the auspices of the Canada Council. To that body I wish to express my most sincere thanks. A grant from the Dalhousie University Research Development Fund provided welcome help at the writing-up stage.

Those who have given me assistance in the various archives are too numerous to mention individually, but I gratefully acknowledge their patient and friendly help, in some cases rendered over a number of years. I have also been assisted by the prompt execution of orders for photographic copies of manuscripts and of printed material unavailable in Canada. Here I thank in particular the officers of the British Library, the Public Record Office, the Hampshire Record Office, the Hereford and Worcester Record Office (St Helen's, Worcester), Hereford Cathedral Library, the Joint Record Office at Lichfield, and the Central Reference Library, Birmingham.

Professor C. W. Dugmore, editor of the *Journal of Ecclesiastical History*, has kindly consented to the reprinting of the substance of my article on Orleton's Winchester episcopate.

Unpublished Crown Copyright material is reproduced by permission of the Controller of H.M. Stationery Office. For permission to print the documents in the appendixes I thank the Bishop of Worcester, the Right Reverend Robin Woods, the Lichfield Diocesan Registrar, the Hampshire County Archivist and Diocesan Record Officer, and the British Library Board.

As usual, my wife has removed some of the infelicities of style which so readily arise from too close a proximity to the intractable phrases of the original sources. I am also much indebted to the staff of the Cambridge University Press for the care which has gone into the preparation of the typescript for publication.

ABBREVIATIONS

In the footnotes the authors of articles and books are given together with abbreviated titles. Full details can be found in the Bibliography, where abbreviations for printed chronicles and episcopal registers are likewise extended.

B.I.H.R.	*Bulletin of the Institute of Historical Research.*
B.J.R.L.	*Bulletin of the John Rylands Library.*
B.L.	British Library.
Biog. Cantab.	A. B. Emden, *A Biographical Register of the University of Cambridge to 1500*, Cambridge 1963.
Biog. Oxon.	A. B. Emden, *A Biographical Register of the University of Oxford to 1500*, 3 vols. Oxford 1957–9.
C.C.R.	*Calendar of Close Rolls.*
C.Ch.W.	*Calendar of Chancery Warrants.*
C.F.R.	*Calendar of Fine Rolls.*
C.P.L.	*Calendar of Papal Letters.*
C.P.P.	*Calendar of Papal Letters, Papal Petitions.*
C.P.R.	*Calendar of Patent Rolls.*
C.Y.S.	Canterbury and York Society.
Cal. P.M.R.	*Calendar of Plea and Memoranda Rolls . . . of the City of London, 1323–1364*, ed. A. H. Thomas, Cambridge 1926.
D.N.B.	*Dictionary of National Biography.*
E.E.T.S.	Early English Text Society.
E.H.R.	*English Historical Review.*
Excusaciones	of Archbishop Stratford in 1341: see *Birchington*, pp. 27–36.
Foedera	*Foedera, Conventiones, etc.*, ed. T. Rymer, 3rd edn, 10 vols. The Hague 1739–45.
G.E.C.	G. E. Cokayne, *The Complete Peerage*, 12 vols. London 1910–59.
H.B.C.	*Handbook of British Chronology*, ed. F. M. Powicke and E. B. Fryde, 2nd edn London 1961.
H.C.M.	Hereford Cathedral Muniments.
H.M.C.R.	*Historical Manuscripts Commission's Report.*
H.M.S.O.	Her Majesty's Stationery Office.

Abbreviations

H.R.O.	*Hereford Register Orleton*. (Cited both from the MS. and from the printed edition.)
J.E.H.	*Journal of Ecclesiastical History*.
Le Neve	*John Le Neve, Fasti Ecclesiae Anglicanae 1300–1541*, 12 vols. Inst. Hist. Res. London 1962–7.
Lit. Cant.	*Literae Cantuarienses*, ed. J. B. Sheppard, 3 vols., R.S. 1887–9.
M.	*Magister* (Master). (With respect to other university degrees I have followed Emden's abbreviations in *Biog. Oxon.* and *Biog. Cantab.*)
M.G.H. SS.	*Monumenta Germaniae Historica, Scriptores*.
N.R.A.	National Register of Archives.
O.H.S.	Oxford Historical Society.
P.R.O.	Public Record Office.
Responsiones	of Bishop Orleton in 1334: see Twysden, *Historiae Anglicanae Scriptores Decem*, London 1652, cols. 2763–8; Lambeth MS. 1213, pp. 300–6.
R.S.	Rolls Series.
Rot. Parl.	*Rotuli Parliamentorum*. (See Bibliography.)
S.C.H.	Studies in Church History.
T.R.H.S.	*Transactions of the Royal Historical Society*.
V.C.H.	*Victoria History of the Counties of England*. (As individual volumes are readily identifiable from the abbreviated titles they are not included in the Bibliography.)
W.A.M.	Westminster Abbey Muniments.
W.H.S.	Worcestershire Historical Society.
W.R.O.	*Worcester Register Orleton*. (Cited by both the folio number of the MS. and the number of the entry in the calendar to be published by H.M.S.O.)
Win.R.O.	Winchester Register Orleton (MS.).
Worc. Admin.	R. M. Haines, *The Administration of the Diocese of Worcester in the First Half of the Fourteenth Century*, London 1965.

All the Calendars and the Rolls Series (Chronicles and Memorials of Great Britain and Ireland during the Middle Ages) are listed in *Government Publications, British National Archives*, sectional list no. 24, H.M.S.O. 1974.

Chapter 1

APPRENTICESHIP

Of Adam Orleton's background and early education we know virtually nothing. That by 1301 he was both beneficed and a master of arts [1] points to his having been born about 1275 – certainly no later than the early 1280s.[2] Even his place of birth is uncertain, though John Leland, writing in the sixteenth century, may have been accurate in his bald assertion that Adam was born in Hereford,[3] rather than his name-place Orleton, a township close to the Mortimer seat at Wigmore.[4] In a number of documents of the early fourteenth century he is called either 'M. Adam de Orleton *seu* de Hereford' or, more simply, 'M. Adam de Hereford',[5] descriptions which lend support to Leland's opinion.

[1] First mention of him as *magister* in the printed sources comes during the Worcester vacancy following Bishop Giffard's death, when he was granted letters dimissory for the diaconate (Emden, *Biog. Oxon.*, *s.v.* Orleton wrongly has 'all holy orders') 27 March 1302: *Worcester Reg. Sede Vacante*, p. 77 (fo. 33ʳ). Emden gives *Hereford Reg. Swinfield*, p. 532, as the earliest reference, though in fact the editor does not record the title in this or other instances in the abstract of institutions. The MS. register does so (fo. cxxxiᵛ, *al.* 130ᵛ). Orleton was instituted to Turnastone on 4 February; his successor, Nicholas Talbot, on 31 October 1301. *Op. cit.* pp. 532–3 (fos. cxxxiᵛ, cxxxiiᵛ, *al.* 130–1).

[2] *Licet canon* (*Sext* 1, 6, c. 14) laid down a minimum age of twenty-five for the rule of a parish church. Under the terms of the new constitution *Cum ex eo* (*Sext* 1, 6, c. 34) it was possible to secure a benefice as early as the eighteenth year, the minimum age for the sub-diaconate according to *Clement.* 1, 6, c. 3. In 1302 Orleton was in subdeacon's orders, and so was lawfully entitled to hold a benefice without taking further orders for the time being, provided he held a *Cum ex eo* licence for study. No licence for Orleton earlier than 1304 has been recorded, and in any case he *did* secure letters dimissory for orders beyond the sub-diaconate. For details of *Cum ex eo* and its operation see Boyle, 'Constitution *Cum ex eo*'; Haines, 'Education of the English Clergy'.

[3] Leland, *Itinerary*, 5, pp. 161–2, 184. For Leland himself see McKisack, *Medieval History*, ch. 1.

[4] Cf. *H.R.O.*, pp. i–ii.

[5] S.C.1/50/29 (formerly 27); *Foedera* 1, iv, p. 192; *Treaty Rolls 1*, no. 494; *C.P.R.* 1313–17, pp. 200, 573, and cf. *ibid.* p. 90. He is also called 'de Hereford' in *Winchester Reg. Woodlock*, p. 592. In the appendix to *Biog. Oxon.* 3 Emden lists an 'Adam de Hereford D.Cn.L.' of whom it is recorded only that he was envoy to Philip IV in 1311 and that in 1316 he was granted protection for two years. This man is in fact Orleton. A possible pointer to Adam's origins is provided by his

Orletons were certainly conspicuous in the affairs of Hereford at about this time,[6] but the name is also to be found in some other towns, notably Ludlow.

From Orleton's subsequent association with the two Roger Mortimers, uncle and nephew, of Chirk and Wigmore respectively, the editor of his Hereford register conjectured that he was a protégé of that family and subsequently took the hypothesis for fact.[7] It is true that Orleton's sympathetic relationship with these men, which brought him little but misfortune, argues either remarkable loyalty or strong identity of interest. The latter is arguably nearer the mark, but may have been a later development. After all, the Mortimers were prominent parishioners of the bishop of Hereford – which position Orleton was to occupy – and their goodwill would be looked for by the diocesan.

What is certain is that no evidence has yet been produced to show that Orleton's early career benefited from Mortimer patronage, but there may have been a local benefactor, hitherto virtually overlooked, in the person of M. Robert le Wyse (or LeWyse) of Gloucester.[8] A canon of Hereford as early as 1279 and member of Bishop Cantilupe's *familia*,[9] Robert became diocesan official first of Hereford, then of Worcester diocese.[10] From 1299 until his death during Orleton's tenure of the Hereford see [11] Robert was

testimony (in 1321) that he had known William Penk, a monk of Tintern born in St Martin's parish in Hereford, from the latter's early youth (*H.R.O.*, pp. 185–6).

6 *H.R.O.*, p. ii and index *s.v.* Orleton. William de Orleton was an especially prominent Hereford citizen in Edward II's reign, acting as bailiff for many years. On occasion he used the same proctor in the royal court, Hugh de Farndon, as did Adam himself and also Henry de Orleton. Henry, and after his death William, occur from time to time in the *Curia Regis* rolls: K.B. 27/251–63 (1322 x 1326). See also Just. 3/116/2[v] (Hereford gaol delivery 18 Edward II). Henry, Thomas and William de Orleton were returned to parliament as Hereford burgesses 1307 x 1324: *Parliamentary Writs*, 2, iii, p. 1246. A Reginald de Orleton was one of Adam Orleton's attorneys in 1314: *C.P.R.* 1313–17, pp. 90, 200. Clemence (wife of Walter), Henry, Reginald, Thomas, Walter and William, together with Adam and his brothers John and Thomas, occur in H.C.M.

7 *H.R.O.*, pp. i–ii, xiii.

8 For a biographical sketch see *Biog. Oxon.*, *s.v.* Gloucester.

9 *Hereford Reg. Cantilupe*, index *s.v.* Gloucester.

10 Emden does not mention his appointment as official of Worcester on 25 October 1297 under Bishop Giffard or his work in that diocese, for which see *Worcester Reg. Giffard*, p. 489 (fo. 414[v]), and index *s.v.* Gloucester, Robert of. The Robert of Gloucester at p. 135 of the register is the chancellor's relative, for whom see n. 11 below.

11 He died 1 March 1320 x 31 January 1322. At the earlier date his relative M. Robert of Gloucester was made co-administrator of his affairs by Orleton. *H.R.O.*, pp. 127–8, 209.

chancellor of the cathedral church there and an energetic canvasser for Thomas de Cantilupe's canonisation, a process brought to a successful conclusion by Orleton himself. In 1302 the fledgling *magister* was in the chancellor's *familia* and one of his brothers, Thomas, was at his instance being helped to a pension from Worcester Priory by their mutual patron.[12] Shortly afterwards Adam is to be found acting with Robert le Wyse, among others, as executor of the troublesome testament of Godfrey Giffard, bishop of Worcester.[13]

Notices of Orleton's academic career are sketchy. He has been numbered among the alumni of Oxford University[14] and although there is no direct evidence of his having studied there, the probability is heightened by his subsequent concern with the affairs of that institution and his anxiety for its welfare.[15] Having achieved the status of *magister*, Orleton turned his attention to the higher faculty of law – a discipline which at the time was attracting ambitious clerks and one which his patron had also pursued. In 1304 he obtained a three-year licence to be absent from his Gloucestershire rectory of Wotton from Michaelmas, for the purpose of studying at a university in England or abroad.[16] Where he went is obscure, but it could have been to the continent as there is no further reference to him in English records for the duration of the licence. On his reappearance in 1307 he is described as 'utriusque iuris peritus' and three years later as doctor of canon law.[17]

For seculars engaged in the expensive pursuit of higher education benefice income was often essential, and in itself provided a measure of the worldly success of an aspiring clerk. Orleton's first benefice was the Herefordshire parish of Turnastone with its subordinate chapel of St Leonard, to which he was presented early

[12] *Worcester Reg. Sede Vacante*, p. 44 (fo. 17^{r}): 'ad instanciam dilecti nostri clerici magistri Ade de Orleton'. Robert was collated on 16 September and installed on 29 September 1299: Hereford Reg. Swinfield, fo. cxxvi^{r} *al.* 124. Thomas succeeded him in his Westbury canonry and in the chancellorship of Hereford: *C.P.L.* 1305–42, p. 185; *H.R.O.*, p. 387. From at least 1305 Thomas was also receiving an annual pension from the Hereford chapter: H.C.M., nos. 2591, 2663, 2716.

[13] *Worcester Reg. Gainsburgh*, pp. 195, 197, 203, 207–8, 215. These citations concern debts due to the king.

[14] *Biog. Oxon.*, *s.v.*

[15] See below, pp. 7, 60–1, 187.

[16] *Worcester Reg. Gainsburgh*, p. 84 (fo. 25^{v}).

[17] *Foedera* 1, iv, p. 103. The first mention of him as D.Cn.L. appears to be in *Bath & Wells Reg. Drokensford*, p. 35 (2 September 1310).

in 1301 by the precentor of Hereford cathedral, John de Swinfield, a nephew of the bishop, Richard Swinfield.[18] This rectory he held for less than nine months, probably because in the interval he had been instituted to Wotton-under-Edge on the authority of the neighbouring Worcester diocesan, Godfrey Giffard.[19] Then in 1304 the bishop of Bath and Wells, Walter de Haselshaw, presented Orleton to Ashbury church in Berkshire. Without papal dispensation he could not have held this in addition to Wotton, so Simon of Ghent, in whose diocese of Salisbury it lay, granted him the commend for the canonical period of six months, and this allowed Orleton to make use of the revenues.[20] It could be that Ghent, well known for his interest in rising scholars, was anxious to assist him towards the cost of his university studies. In the event, another clerk who was to be closely associated with Orleton, M. Gilbert de Middleton, was instituted after only two months.[21]

Orleton's subsequent promotions coincide with his newly-won status of doctor, just as his earlier ones marked his completion of the arts course. Clement V provided him to a canonry and prebend of Wells in 1310,[22] and in the following year he is first mentioned as canon of Hereford.[23] Walter Reynolds, bishop of Worcester, in whose service Orleton was at the time, dispensed him from the plurality regulations by virtue of a grace from Pope Clement. A further dispensation, not implemented because of Clement's death but reiterated by his successor, John XXII, enabled Orleton to hold the rectory of Acle in Norwich diocese as well as his other rectory (Wotton) and both canonries, but he had to surrender the first-fruits of Acle as subsidy for the mooted crusade.[24] Reynolds

18 *Hereford Reg. Swinfield*, p. 532 (fo. cxxxi^{v} *al.* 130).

19 *Worcester Reg. Giffard*, p. 543 (fo. 464^{r} *al.* cccclxix). This is a commission of 1 May 1301 to institute Orleton ('clericus noster'). The institution itself is not recorded, but presumably took place shortly afterwards. The abbot and convent of Bristol (Augustinian) were patrons and appropriated the church in 1313, but failed to gain possession on Orleton's relinquishing it when promoted bishop (1317). *Worc. Admin.*, pp. 246, 256, 265.

20 *Salisbury Reg. Gandavo*, p. 629. According to the canonical regulation (Lyons II, c. 14: *Sext* 1, 6, c. 15) the beneficiary had to be in priest's orders and of age to hold a benefice (i.e. twenty-five). See *Worc. Admin.*, pp. 197–9.

21 *Salisbury Reg. Gandavo*, p. 631.

22 *Bath & Wells Reg. Drokensford*, pp. 35, 59; *H.R.O.*, p. v.

23 In letters of credence dated 10 October 1311: *Foedera* 1, iv, p. 196. Cf. *Worcester Reg. Reynolds*, p. 29 (fo. 37^{v}).

24 Walter Reynolds's dispensation is dated 30 January 1312 (I read 'iii' rather than

also favoured him with a grant of the sequestration of the Worcester archdeaconry, only to revoke it within a fortnight. The reason for this abrupt change of plan seems to have been that news of the papal reservation and appointment to the archdeaconry had reached the bishop meanwhile.[25]

In such manner Orleton financed himself, his studies, and to some degree his other activities, until his promotion to a bishopric in 1317. By the standards of his day this amount of benefice accumulation was moderate, certainly less extensive than that of his contemporary, Thomas de Cobham, with whom he has been unfavourably contrasted.[26]

Two careers were now opening up before this able cleric: diocesan administration and diplomacy. His qualifications fitted him for either, and for a time he made it his business to interest himself in both.

The precise means by which Orleton came so quickly to the notice of Edward II, who succeeded his father in July 1307, can only be surmised. The context was provided by the new king's anxiety for the canonisation of Bishop Thomas de Cantilupe, partly perhaps from motives of filial piety, for Edward I had set the matter in train towards the end of his life.[27] A man beneficed in Cantilupe's former diocese and with experience in the household of the Hereford chancellor, who moreover had served as one of the chapter's proctors in the cause of the prospective saint, clearly had a strong claim to Edward's attention. At any rate, it was as envoy to the pope in this business that Orleton is first

'iv Kal. Feb.'). Orleton may have had a Hereford prebend early in 1311, if we can judge from an erased memorandum (rubric: 'Preb' collata magistro Ade Orleton') in Hereford Reg. Swinfield (fo. clxi^{r} *al.* 170) noted by Bannister (*H.R.O.*, p. vi, n. 1). In November 1316 he was granted further prebends at Wells and Hereford by Pope John XXII, on condition that he surrendered his former ones. These papal letters were presented to Bishop Swinfield on 22 February 1317 by Orleton's brother and proctor ad hoc, Thomas. *C.P.L.* 1305–42, pp. 133–4; *Worcester Reg. Reynolds*, p. 84 (fo. 42^{v}); *Hereford Reg. Swinfield*, p. 523 (fo. ccviii^{r} *al.* 206). He was instituted to Acle, Norfolk, on 22 February 1312, in the person of his proctor Roger de Badyngton, the monks of Tintern being the patrons (Norwich Reg. Salmon, fo. 46^{r}). In 1317 Acle passed to his brother Thomas by papal provision (*ibid.* fos. 72^{v}–73^{r}; *C.P.L.* 1305–42, p. 160). We know that he held Hanwell church, Oxon., because in 1317 he acknowledged his obligation to pay annates for it. *H.R.O.*, p. 43; cf. Lunt, *Financial Relations* 1, pp. 494–5.

25 *Worcester Reg. Reynolds*, p. 154; *Worc. Admin.*, p. 33, and for *custodia sequestri*, *ibid.* pp. 202–4.

26 See *Biog. Oxon.*, *s.v.* Cobham, Thomas de.

27 *Foedera* 1, iii, p. 51.

designated 'king's clerk'.[28] After that he eludes observation until 1309, when he is to be found travelling on royal service in the entourage of Walter Reynolds, the king's treasurer.[29] As we shall see, diplomatic missions interrupted his association with Reynolds's diocese of Worcester, but in December 1311 he is numbered among those of the bishop's *familia* in London, where he was deputed to examine and confirm the election process at Wroxall Priory.[30] The episcopal register provides few glimpses of him thereafter.[31]

It is testimony to Adam Orleton's reputation for administrative and legal expertise that in August 1312 Henry Woodlock, bishop of Winchester, appointed him official. He seems to have continued in office at least until 30 October 1315 [32] when, because of his absence *in remotis*, a deputy was appointed to hear the consistory court cases and to carry out the official's additional duties of enquiry, correction and punishment with respect to the bishop's subjects.[33] Even between those dates his professional activities are scantily recorded; in fact he is mentioned only twice by name: in September 1312, and again in April of the following year, when he was present with M. Gilbert de Middleton at the bishop's manor of Southwark on the south bank of the Thames opposite London.[34] Pressure of legal business in the consistory is conceivably the reason for Orleton's lack of employment in day-to-day diocesan business as recorded by Bishop Woodlock's registrar. A more convincing explanation is that he was busy elsewhere, as he certainly was for much of 1314. His absence would not have occasioned much embarrassment since continuity was maintained by his assessor M. Peter Poleyn *alias* 'de Worldham', the commissary-general and a clerk experienced in the diocesan's service.[35] It may be a mark of Orleton's methodical character that he kept his commission of appointment and in 1330, as Worcester

28 *Foedera* I, iv, p. 103.

29 *C.P.R.* 1307–13, p. 103.

30 *Worcester Reg. Reynolds*, pp. 29–30 (fo. 37v).

31 *Ibid.* pp. 59, 96, 119.

32 *Winchester Reg. Woodlock*, p. 584. He could even have continued as nominal official until early in 1317, the end of the episcopate.

33 *Ibid.* p. 645.

34 *Ibid.* pp. 592, 631.

35 See, for instance, *ibid.* p. 655: appointment (3 January 1316) jointly with M. Adam de Capel to deal with vacant benefices in the bishop's absence. *Pace* the editor this does not appear to be a general commission for vicars-spiritual. See also the index to this register *s v.*

diocesan, made use of its preamble in the commission for his own official, Robert de Worth.[36]

In May 1313 Orleton, jointly with a fellow canon of Hereford, Richard de Bello, the reputed author of the *Mappa Mundi*, was appointed Bishop Swinfield's proctor for the provincial council summoned to St Paul's for the morrow of the Ascension (i.e. 25 May).[37] Not much more is to be gleaned about his employment in England at this time, except that in a document dated 9 November 1313 he is named as proctor of M. Gilbert de Middleton, one of four arbitrators in a dispute between the University of Oxford and the Friars Preachers.[38] Years later, as bishop of Worcester and in his capacity as conservator of the privileges of the Franciscans, Orleton was to write a warning letter to the chancellor about what seems to have been a recrudescence of this conflict between secular and regular masters.[39]

Meanwhile – and this was to be crucial for the future – Orleton had created a favourable impression at the papal Curia. Doubtless this arose from his effectiveness in the despatch of business there and at the Council of Vienne in 1311. It was about the time of the council that Clement V made him a papal chaplain.[40] Clement's successor, John XXII, promoted him auditor of causes in the Sacred Palace. He was one of three such auditors to be advanced by Pope John to the English episcopate.[41]

The signs were auspicious for a man who had gained the approbation of pope, king and a number of diocesan bishops: one of these last, Reynolds, had in 1313 become archbishop of Canterbury. But Orleton's interests had turned decisively in the direction of the king's diplomatic service and his experiences in that sphere between 1307 and 1321 and, in the reign of Edward III, between 1327 and 1336, will be the subject of the following chapter.

36 *Worc. Admin.*, p. 112.

37 *Hereford Reg. Swinfield*, p. 491 (fo. clxxxvi^r *al.* 184). The editor gives the date wrongly as 16 August. Cf. *H.R.O.*, p. vi, n. 7. For Bello see Denholm-Young, 'Mappa Mundi', pp. 74–82, esp. 77–8.

38 *Collectanea*, pp. 264–72, esp. p. 266.

39 *W.R.O.* 2, fo. 49^v [898].

40 The first mention of Orleton as papal chaplain seems to be in Clement V's letter of 18 October 1311 to King Philip: Lizerand, *Clément V et Philippe IV*, p. 470. See also Edward's letter of 16 December 1311 to Clement: *Foedera* 1, iv, p. 202.

41 Cerchiari, *Capellani Papae*, pp. 24–7. The other two were Rigaud d'Assier and John de Ross.

Chapter 2

THE DIPLOMATIC ENVOY

IN EDWARD II'S SERVICE 1307–1321

It was in December 1307, less than six months after Edward II's accession, that Adam Orleton, described as the king's chosen clerk skilled in civil and canon law, was despatched to Pope Clement V to promote the canonisation of Bishop Thomas de Cantilupe. The mission marked the beginning of a highly successful diplomatic career.

As the young monarch pointed out in his letters to pope and cardinals, Cantilupe's sanctification had been the subject of representations by his late father, of whose council the bishop had been a member, and the lengthy process of assessing the candidate's credentials was far advanced.[1] The papal commissioners, William Durandus, bishop of Mende, Ralph Baldock, bishop of London, and William Testa, archdeacon of Aran, had been hard at work examining witnesses and pursuing other enquiries. They spent the summer and autumn months of 1307 at Hereford; indeed they did not complete their investigations in the city until mid-November, at which point they returned to London and despatched a letter to Clement V in which Orleton and Thomas de Guines are named as the Hereford chapter's proctors.[2] Thus Orleton went to the Curia in a double capacity. Quite when he returned is unknown, though the king in a letter of 15 April 1308, reiterating his wishes with respect to Cantilupe, implies that the envoy was still abroad.[3]

While Orleton was at the papal court, which had not yet moved

[1] *Foedera* 1, iv, p. 103: 12 December 1307. 'Et dilecto clerico nostro magistro Ade de Orleton, utriusque juris perito (qui, pro hujusmodi negotii promotione, ad vestram beatitudinis praesentiam accedit).'

[2] *Acta Sanctorum mensis Octobris* 1, p. 592. Cf. H.C.M., no. 1443. Also Yates, 'Fabric Rolls of Hereford Cathedral', pp. 80–1, quoting Douie, 'Canonisation of St Thomas', p. 277.

[3] *Foedera* 1, iv, p. 117.

to Avignon,[4] the vacancy of the see of Worcester precipitated the first of many struggles between Edward II and the papacy on the subject of promotion to English bishoprics.[5] Royal instigation was clearly behind the election by the Worcester chapter on 13 November 1307 of Walter Reynolds, the king's treasurer. This was some two months after the death of Bishop Gainsburgh at Beauvais, while travelling back from the Curia.[6] Pope Clement promptly claimed the reservation of the see, a move which Edward (with some inconsistency) denounced as an unheard-of encroachment on free capitular elections. The outcome was a compromise: the elevation of the royal candidate by papal provision on 12 February 1308.[7] What part, if any, Orleton played in the affair can only be surmised; he was, after all, still a novice in the intricacies of curial practice and politics. All the same, it may not be wholly coincidental that we next encounter him in Reynolds's *familia*.

The occasion was the embassy which set out for Avignon in March 1309. At its head were two prelates, Walter Reynolds and the Norwich diocesan, John Salmon, and two nobles, John of Brittany, earl of Richmond, and Aymer de Valence, earl of Pembroke. Some specially secret business, which touched the king closely, was entrusted independently to Reynolds and the earl of Richmond.[8] The main purpose of the embassy was to secure a reversal of Archbishop Winchelsey's excommunication of Piers Gaveston, the king's unpopular favourite. Among the clerks of the bishop of Worcester's party enumerated in the royal letters of protection were Orleton and M. William de Birston, whom Reynolds had recently made archdeacon of Gloucester and who was to function as his auditor and commissary-general.[9]

4 Most of the papal letters of this period are dated from Poitiers. E.g. *C.P.L.* 1305–42, pp. 22–49.

5 On this topic see Smith, *Episcopal Appointments*, chs. 1–2.

6 *Worc. Admin.*, p. 77.

7 *Ibid.* pp. 77, 323; Smith, *Episcopal Appointments*, pp. 11–13. Edward wrote of Reynolds: 'Virum utique consilii maturitate conspicuum, discretione providum, quem vitae conversatio, morum honestas, laudabiliaque decorant gratiarum munera et virtutum, quemque in spiritualibus novimus et temporalibus circumspectum, cujus etiam probata fidelitas ipsum nobis et populo regni nostri gratum reddit multipliciter et acceptum. . .' *Foedera* 1, iv, p. 98.

8 *Foedera* 1, iv, pp. 136–7; and see Phillips, *Pembroke*, p. 29.

9 For Reynolds's entourage see *C.P.R.* 1307–13, pp. 103, 107; and for Birston, *Worc. Admin.*, index *s.v.*

According to a rubric in his diocesan register Reynolds set out on Palm Sunday (23 March), having appointed M. Benedict de Paston his vicar-general seven days previously.[10] It can be assumed that Orleton travelled with him. Amongst his effects he carried a petition to the pope with covering letters from Walter de Bedewynde, the treasurer of York.[11] These were intended for Bedewynde's clerk, William de Ros, who notes that he received them on 4 May, which must have been some time after Orleton's arrival at Avignon. In his reply Ros enigmatically remarks of his principal's advice to consult Orleton about his affairs, that because the latter and Andrea Sapiti, the king's permanent proctor at the Curia,[12] were of one mind in all things, such a course would serve no useful purpose.[13] William de Ros's letter is dated 10 May, and he adds a postscript to the effect that on the previous Monday Edward's envoys had delivered to the pope money and other items to the value of 30,000 florins.[14] This can be taken as a conspicuous mark of the king's gratitude for the success of the negotiations: the bull for Gaveston's absolution from excommunication is dated 25 April, and another bull of 18 May directed the bishops of Lincoln and London to resume their collection of the papal tenth, three-quarters of the proceeds of which were to be paid to the king.[15]

The principals of the embassy moved off towards the end of

10 *Worcester Reg. Reynolds*, p. 7 (fo. 9^v).

11 S.C.1/50/29 (formerly 27). What follows comes from Ros's reply to Bedewynde. This is dated 10 May from Avignon and can with a measure of confidence be ascribed to 1309. Bedewynde, the royal appointee as treasurer of York, was disputing the dignity with Francesco Gaetani. *C.P.R.* 1301–7, p. 467; *C.P.L.* 1305–42, p. 344; *Le Neve* 6, pp. 12–13. The ramifications of the case are discussed by Smith, *Episcopal Appointments*, pp. 62–4, 66. Bedewynde was to die *pendente lite*.

12 For whom see Kirsch, 'Andreas Sapiti'; P.R.O. 31/9/17A (transcript of his register of petitions).

13 S.C.1/50/29. 'Item continebatur in eisdem [litteris quod?] magister Adam impenderet auxilium suum et consilium circa expedicionem dicte peticionis dubito quod non foret sanissim[um] [con]silium multum cum eodem conferre super negociis vestris nam ipse et Andreas Sapiti sunt unanimes in omnibus unde absque ipso negocium vestrum occasione predicta melius expedietur.' (Some tears in the MS. A version is given by Langlois, 'Documents', pp. 76–7.) Does this stem from professional jealousy?

14 Ros promised to keep his principal informed: 'Adhec domine mi reverende qualiter nuncii regis Anglie negocia pro quibus venerunt . . . expedient et quid facient vos celeriter certificare non omittam. Ex parte regis presentarunt pape in pecunia et in aliis usque ad valorem xxx millium florenarum auri die Lune ante confeccionem presencium.'

15 *Hereford Reg. Swinfield*, pp. 451–2; Lunt, *Financial Relations* 1, pp. 384–5.

May.[16] There were other matters outstanding, not least the disturbed state of England and the king's treatment of the Church there. In a letter of 26 May Pope Clement gave some fatherly encouragement to Edward and promised to send special legates in the near future.[17]

Reynolds was back in his old rectory at Sawbridgeworth in Hertfordshire by 22 July 1309, when he received the registers of his see (those of Bishops Giffard and Gainsburgh) at the hands of a clerk despatched by his vicar-general. One would expect Orleton to have returned with Reynolds's other clerks, but the records are silent on the point.[18]

It was the early summer of 1311 before Orleton found further diplomatic employment. At that time Edward sent three *nuncii*,[19] M. Thomas de Cobham, the distinguished scholar much in demand at this time as a diplomat, Sir Gilbert Pecche, later seneschal of Gascony, and Orleton – here called M. Adam de Hereford – to Philip IV of France to discuss Gascon affairs.[20] This constituted a further incident in the lengthy negotiations of a basically legal character collectively termed the Process of Périgueux. By such means the English and French sought to determine what remained to be implemented of the treaties concluded between 1259 and 1303, as well as to settle the many border disputes and conflicts of jurisdiction which had subsequently arisen.[21] Philip's answers to the problems raised on this occasion are dated 13 August from St Ouen near St Denis.[22]

These negotiations broadened Orleton's experience, though he was certainly the junior colleague. Gascon affairs were notoriously complex and required negotiators versed in the ramifications of the respective treaties and the subsequent lines of argument and diplomatic manoeuvring. The same negotiators were reappointed time and again. Orleton was to have much more experience of Gascon and French affairs – indeed he became a trier of Gascon

16 The certificate of Valence's expenses covered the period 6 March to 17 July: E.101/373/23. See Phillips, *Pembroke*, p. 29 (and n. 3).

17 *Foedera* 1, iv, p. 142.

18 *Worc. Admin.*, p. 4, n. 3; *Worcester Reg. Reynolds*, pp. 10–11 (fo. 12^{r}).

19 For a discussion of the titles *nuncius*, *procurator* and ambassador see Queller, *Office of Ambassador*, chs. 1–3.

20 *Foedera* 1, iv, p. 192; *Treaty Rolls 1*, no. 494.

21 See Cuttino, *Diplomatic Administration*, pp. 87–100, and for many documents concerned with these and subsequent negotiations, B.L. Cotton MS. Julius E. 1.

22 *Treaty Rolls 1*, p. 197, n. 1.

petitions[23] – but his principal expertise initially lay in curial diplomacy.

Once the French negotiations were out of the way, Orleton was directed to turn his energies to preparations for the general council summoned to meet at Vienne in the autumn. The English representatives included William Greenfield, archbishop of York, Walter Stapledon, bishop of Exeter, various laymen and half a dozen experienced clerks. All of these were summoned to appear in London within three weeks of the Nativity of St John the Baptist (24 June) before Gilbert de Clare, custos of the realm while Edward was engaged with the Scots in the north,[24] and Walter Reynolds, the king's chancellor. This constituted a briefing of the *nuncii* in the presence of the royal council. About the same time Edward informed the pope that he had deputed Orleton to arrange for the housing of the English delegation.[25]

This last assignment was not easy. We know that the Aragonese expressed irritation at the unsatisfactory conditions and the difficulty of finding accommodation in so small a town, and that one of the English proctors at the Curia, Henry Fykys, sent a memorable letter in which he complained similarly of Vienne's inadequacy.[26] These conditions were aggravated by the style which the participants, including the English, thought it necessary to maintain.[27] We can imagine that Orleton spent many wearisome hours on this intractable business, though we learn nothing of the details. By the end of September the pope himself had arrived at Vienne after a leisurely journey from Avignon.[28]

At this juncture (10 October) Edward found it necessary to appoint a further delegation to Pope Clement. Those named were

23 In 1320 and 1321. *Parliamentary Writs* 2, ii, p. 221; *Rot. Parl. Inediti*, pp. 92–3.

24 He succeeded Henry earl of Lincoln: McKisack, *Fourteenth Century*, p. 11.

25 *Foedera* 1, iv, pp. 190, 192.

26 Müller, *Das Konzil von Vienne*, pp. 65–6. For the proceedings of the council see also Lizerand, *Clément V et Philippe IV*, ch. 6; *Conciliorum Collectio*, cols. 367–426. Henry Peters or Petri of 'Ayssele' (Ashill, Norfolk?), called 'Fykys', was a clerk of Norwich diocese who was made a notary in 1310 (*C.P.L.* 1305–42, p. 65). His letter is printed (from S.C.1/58/16) by Langlois, 'Documents', pp. 73–6. Addressed to John (Salmon), bishop of Norwich, whose proctor he was, it is dated 27 December 1311.

27 *Foedera* 1, iv, p. 191. In this request for safe conduct of his representatives through France Edward mentions the *nuncii* and their *familiae* 'cum equis, jocalibus, vasis, moneta, quam secum deferent, et aliis rebus suis versus dictum concilium'. The *iocalia* were not mere ostentation; the royal wardrobe accounts show that they were a regular source of gifts and *douceurs*.

28 Müller, *Das Konzil von Vienne*, p. 63, n. 5.

Archbishop Greenfield and Bishop Baldock, Otto de Grandisson, Amanieu d'Albret and lastly Orleton. Special messengers were despatched with their new instructions.[29] The move was prompted by the publication of the baronial Ordinances, which Edward protested should be annulled in the event of their proving prejudicial to his dignity.[30] Orleton returned to England not long after the advent of this fresh commission, making his report to the king's council on 18 November.[31] At the beginning of the following month he is to be found in London with Bishop Reynolds. On 16 December Edward wrote to tell Clement that his envoys, Sicaud de Lavaur and Orleton, had duly delivered their messages viva voce and that for the time being he intended to retain the latter by his side.[32]

One further incident concerned with Orleton's stay at Vienne is worth mentioning. While there he took the opportunity of employing a scribe to copy the decretals of Gregory IX with the apparatus of Innocent IV.[33] Marginalia suggest that the volume may subsequently have been used at Worcester.[34]

29 *Foedera* I, iv, pp. 196–7; Müller, *Das Konzil von Vienne*, pp. 66–8. Clement V, in a letter to Philip dated 18 October 1311, which Lizerand transcribed from a MS. in the Archives Nationales (*Clément V et Philippe IV*, pp. 467–71), states that he is sending his chaplains Sicaud de Lavaur, canon of Narbonne, and Orleton back to England. The evidence at this point is somewhat confusing. Robert de Newenton and William de Loughborough were despatched from England with instructions for the new delegates (including Orleton and with the addition of Henry Woodlock, bishop of Winchester, and John de Halton, bishop of Carlisle), and were paid expenses for the period 12 October to 20 November. They must have taken the protestation (see n. 30 below) with them. Cotton MS. Nero C. VIII, fo. 55r. However, the king in his letter of 10 October to Greenfield and Baldock expressed the hope that his *nuncii* – so long delayed – would arrive at the council by St Martin's day (11 November), and intimated that Woodlock and Halton were already there.

30 Cotton MS. Nero C. VIII, fo. 55v (I owe the reference to Phillips, *Pembroke*, pp. 40–1). On 13 October in London three notaries were paid a mark each for drawing up public instruments in triplicate 'de quadam protestacione facta per regem de revocacione ordinacionum . . . si que earundem fiant in aliquo in preiudicium regis aut corone sue'.

31 Bodleian Tanner MS. 197, fo. 44v. In April 1312 an arrangement was made with him (on the king's order) by Walter Langton (as treasurer) and the royal council for payment at the rate of 200 marks a year. He was therefore allowed half that sum for the period 20 May to 18 November 1311, 183 days. As will be seen below, this allocation was to be recovered as custodian of the lands of Grey of Rotherfield. For the various methods used in such cases see Larson, 'Payment of Fourteenth-Century English Envoys'.

32 *Worcester Reg. Reynolds*, pp. 29–30 (fo. 37v); *Foedera* I, iv, p. 202.

33 Bodleian New College MS. 187. 'Explicit hoc opus factum per me Nicholinum de Cauill' Januen' Et scriptum apud Viennam tempore generalis concilii ad instanciam reverendi viri et discreti magistri Ade de Orleton canonici Herefordiensis per manus W. de Birthou clerici pontificatus domini Clementis pape quinti anno sexto.'

34 E.g. fo 66v.

Orleton seems now to have proved his worth, for he did not remain unengaged for long. At the beginning of April 1312 the king wrote from York to the papal penitentiary and to other cardinals requesting assistance in expediting his business at the Curia, details of which were to be expounded verbally by Orleton. Edward was unstinting in praise of his envoy: he was diligent about the affairs of the Roman Church in the realm and had served him with helpful counsel and unremitting endeavour.[35]

Orleton left England on the brink of civil disturbance. In defiance of the Ordainers Gaveston had returned from exile at the end of 1311. Archbishop Winchelsey, searching for a peaceful solution, summoned a council of prelates and secular lords to meet at St Paul's in March 1312. This deputed the earls of Pembroke and Surrey to seek out Gaveston and was instrumental in preventing Walter Langton, who had been appointed treasurer contrary to the Ordinances, from taking up his duties at the Exchequer.[36]

The king's letter of recommendation to Cardinal Bérenger Frédol, the penitentiary, is dated 1 April 1312 from York, so Orleton's departure must have been roughly coincidental. There is a note in Reynolds's Worcester register against a record of sequestration to the effect that this was at the instance of Orleton and the bishop of Hereford, but such a matter could readily have been arranged beforehand.[37] Towards the end of April Orleton was granted custody of the person and lands of John Grey of Rotherfield until he should recover the hundred marks – a considerable sum – due to him for six months in the king's service during the previous year.[38] But again this is not evidence that Orleton was still in England.[39]

35 *Foedera* 2, i, p. 1. 'Ac praefatum magistrum Adam (qui circa negotia ecclesiae Romanae in regno nostro diligenter intendens commoda et honores ejusdem sollicitis studiis procuravit, et nobis, per utilia consilia, et exequia non remissa, velud minister intelligens, se carum reddit et acceptum) vestrae gratiae speciali recommendamus.'

36 *Salisbury Reg. Gandavo*, pp. 418–19; Edwards, 'Importance of English Bishops', p. 323; Phillips, *Pembroke*, p. 32. Cf. n. 31 above for his action at York. According to *H.B.C.* he was treasurer from 23 January 1312.

37 Worcester Reg. Reynolds, fo. 46^{r}: 'Relaxacio sequestri de Morton et Waddon ad instanciam Herford' episcopi et magistri Ade de Orleton.'

38 *C.P.R.* 1307–13, pp. 468–9, 517. The lands were said to be worth £21 0s 1½d a year.

39 He did not retain the custody after the following December. It was transferred to another royal clerk, William Ayrminne. *Ibid.*

The moment of Orleton's return in 1312 is equally elusive, but he must surely have been back well before 23 August 1312, the date of his appointment as official of Winchester.[40] We may also assume that Bishop Woodlock would have been chary about entrusting Orleton with so important an office had his plans involved absence in the immediate future. At the same time, as we have noted, the new official left little trace of his activity in the diocese, so that this part of his career remains even more of an enigma than his diplomatic comings and goings.

That there was a reason for Orleton's temporary abandonment of diplomacy is suggested by a letter of Walter Reynolds, by then archbishop of Canterbury, to Cardinal Arnaud de Pellegrue. This is undated, but its position in the archiepiscopal register suggests that it was written prior to 16 March 1314. Reynolds declared that although some unfortunate things (' quedam sinistra ') about Orleton had come to the ears of pope and cardinals, his innocence had been demonstrated to the king and *maiores* of the realm. He went on to ask the cardinal to recommend Orleton to the pope, so that in view of his good services in the past he might be restored to that grace from which he had been cut off by the poisonous insinuations of the envious (' venenosa suggestio emulorum ').[41] Apparently nothing more can be learned of this singular episode, but at the beginning of 1314 Orleton was recalled to diplomatic duties. His safe-conduct until the following year is dated 18 February, and on 4 March he was granted protection for a year. Woodlock's register shows that he was still *in remotis* at the end of October 1315.[42] It is possible, of course, that he made visits to England in the interval, and a cancelled appointment of attorneys on 22 November 1314 may indicate something of the kind.[43]

While he was abroad momentous events took place which were to change the course of his life. Clement V died on 20 April 1314, and after an extended election process, accompanied by much confusion, lobbying and no little violence, his successor,

40 *Winchester Reg. Woodlock*, p. 584. Woodlock probably had some experience of Orleton's capacity at Vienne.

41 Canterbury Reg. Reynolds, fos. 33^{r}, 44^{r} (duplicated). The regular response to accusations of this kind is that they stemmed from ' emuli '.

42 *C.P.R.* 1313–17, pp. 89, 90; *Winchester Reg. Woodlock*, p. 645.

43 *C.P.R.* 1313–17, p. 200.

Jacques d'Euze or Duèse, cardinal-bishop of Albano and formerly bishop of Avignon, was finally elected on 7 August 1316 as John XXII.[44] Although Orleton had prospered under Clement's regime and might well have been elevated to the episcopal bench in any case, it was John XXII who regarded him with special favour, advancing him from one see to another and standing by his appointee in the teeth of Edward II's wrath.

It is quite conceivable, as suggested by Canon Bannister, that Orleton witnessed the solemn entry of the new pope into Avignon on 2 October 1316; he was assuredly there in December, when Edward directed him and other clerks at the Curia to give every assistance to an embassy he was about to send. Among the leaders of this prestigious deputation were the bishops of Norwich and Ely (John Salmon and John Hothum respectively), the earl of Pembroke and Bartholomew Badlesmere. It reached Avignon early in March 1317 bearing rich gifts.[45] The delegates secured papal assent to the postponement of Edward II's projected crusade,[46] and to the diversion by way of loan of the proceeds of a papal tenth already being levied for that purpose on the English clergy.[47] Pope John also deputed Cardinals Gaucelme d'Eauze and Luca Fieschi to negotiate a settlement with the Scots and he himself proclaimed a truce between the two countries: neither move was effective.[48] The author of the *Vita* says that an object of the embassy was to overthrow the baronial Ordinances; [49] if so, that too was not achieved.

There remained the long-standing obligation of tribute which Edward II had hoped to circumvent, but upon which Pope John now insisted. It was towards the end of the mission that Aymer de Valence, Badlesmere and other royal agents gathered in the chamber of Cardinal Arnaud de Pellegrue, where they proceeded

44 See Mollat, *The Popes at Avignon*, pp. 9–11, and in more detail *idem*, 'L'election du Pape Jean XXII'. The king's letters on the topic of the election are in *Foedera* 2, i, pp. 67, 71, 74.

45 *H.R.O.*, p. viii (cf. *Murimuth*, p. 24); *Foedera* 2, i, p. 106; *Murimuth*, pp. 25–6.

46 *Foedera* 2, i, pp. 109–10.

47 *Foedera* 2, i, pp. 117–18; *C.P.L.* 1305–42, pp. 138–9. For the sexennial tenth decreed at Vienne see Lunt, *Financial Relations* 1, pp. 395ff and, for the names of the collectors, *ibid*. p. 636. The proceeds of the first year and an additional tenth were granted to the king on 28 March 1317. For the latter see *ibid*. pp. 404–5, 636–7.

48 *Foedera* 2, i, pp. 108–9, 115–6; *C.P.L.* 1305–42, p. 444.

49 *Vita*, pp. 78–9. See the discussion of this point in Maddicott, *Lancaster*, p. 199.

to excuse their master for his failure to pay the thousand marks' annual tribute and to promise payment of the 24,000 marks outstanding. This sum was to be discharged in four instalments due at Michaelmas. Orleton is mentioned as one of the witnesses to the arrangement.[50] It was during his return journey from Avignon that the earl of Pembroke suffered the indignity of being waylaid at Étampes and held to ransom.[51] Orleton, however, remained in the Curia as the king's agent.

The new regime in Avignon soon brought its rewards. Orleton received papal bulls of provision and dispensation in November 1316[52] and, as has been shown, was appointed a papal auditor. Soon a far greater opportunity arose: on 15 March 1317 Richard Swinfield, bishop of Hereford, died. Exactly two months later Pope John, claiming the reservation of the see, appointed Adam Orleton in his place. Edward had another man, Thomas Charlton, in mind for this bishopric and had already petitioned the pope for his advancement. Once Swinfield's anticipated demise became a fact the king asked Pope John to promote his candidate. Not only were Charlton's personal qualifications a recommendation, he argued, but also he came from a family with many connections in the Welsh March, which was in a disturbed state and hence in need of the stability which such an appointment might ensure.[53] News, or at any rate rumours, of Orleton's provision to Hereford reached the king by 6 May, when he wrote from Windsor to declare that he would not tolerate anything of the kind.[54] He forbade Orleton under threat[55] to accept the promotion, which he maintained was derogatory to the crown, and despatched M. John de Hildesle post-haste to make his attitude absolutely clear. He also wrote at greater length both to the pope and to the cardinals, expanding his reasons for wanting Charlton as bishop.[56] However, it is probable that neither the letters nor

50 *C.P.L.* 1305–42, pp. 140, 443–4; *Foedera* 2, i, p. 123; Kirsch, 'Andreas Sapiti', p. 591. For the context see Lunt, *Financial Relations* 1, ch. 3, esp. pp. 165–72.

51 Phillips, *Pembroke*, pp. 110–17.

52 *C.P.L.* 1305–42, pp. 133–4.

53 *Foedera* 2, i, p. 119. For the whole business see Smith, *Episcopal Appointments*, pp. 27–8.

54 *Foedera* 2, i, pp. 124–5. A letter from Orleton to the king (Avignon, 12 May 1317) records the appointment ('in mea presencia') by Cardinal Raymond de Farges, dean of Salisbury, of attorneys to act on his behalf in English courts. S.C.1/34/150.

55 'Promotio ad ecclesiam supradictam, vos assensum vestrum in tanto discrimine nullatenus praebeatis, sicuti vestri et amicorum vestrorum tranquillitatem diligitis et profectum.' *Ibid.* p. 125.

56 *Ibid.*; C.70/3/m. 1.

the personal messenger reached their destination before Orleton's consecration by the cardinal-bishop of Ostia on 22 May.[57] Another diplomat of longer standing, Thomas de Cobham, was consecrated bishop of Worcester at the same time.[58]

Meanwhile as a counter-stroke on 9 May Edward had urged the Hereford chapter to elect Charlton.[59] A committee of clerks, comprising Orleton's colleagues Gilbert de Middleton, John Stratford and John de Hildesle, was formed to investigate the matter. With some venom Edward made the point that English prelates were members of his council, concerned with affairs of his crown and kingdom, whereas Orleton had behaved in an unseemly manner by revealing his counsel whilst in the court of Rome.[60] This accusation should not be considered in isolation. When writing to Pope John in December 1316 on the question of William Melton's candidature for the York archbishopric, Edward had urged that men beneficed in England, both cardinals and others, were acting in contempt of the king's wishes.[61] In the latter case, however, the royal nominee secured the see. Edward's view of episcopal promotion was limited by his own interests as he perceived them. English clerks were caught on occasion between the loyalty due to the papacy in such matters, and that which they owed to the monarch. Their less successful colleagues (and some of the chroniclers) were eager to attribute promotion by the papacy in contravention of royal wishes to ambition coupled with malpractice. As for those who were successful by such means, as was Orleton, it would be misleading to argue that obedience to the papacy and a respect for canon law were untainted by the desire for personal advancement. It would be equally misleading to jump to the conclusion, as has often been done, that the selfish pursuit of gain was the sole determinant of their conduct.

57 *H.R.O.*, pp. x–xi; *Le Neve* 2, p. 1; *C.P.L.* 1305–42, p. 150.

58 *Worcester Reg. Cobham*, p. x; *Annales Paulini*, p. 280.

59 *C.C.R.* 1313–18, p. 467.

60 *C.Ch.W.* 1244–1326, p. 468.

61 *Foedera* 2, i, p. 107: 'Intelleximus quod nonnulli in sancta Romana curia, tam cardinales quam alii beneficiati in regno nostro, nescimus quo spirito ducti . . . nedum negotium electionis [magistri Willielmi Melton] . . . odio atque exquisitis coloribus impetere ac impugnare quinimmo provisiones et electiones singulas ecclesiarum regni nostri quae ad examen Romanae curiae, juxta statuta canonica deducuntur, machinatione malivola impedire, ac destruere moliuntur, personas electas, et eis adhaerentes . . . nimis inhumaniter, in contumeliam nostri nominis pertractantes.'

Despite the strength of his remonstrance, Edward did not press his opposition in Orleton's case to extremes and the envoy was able to return home. According to a later papal dispensation Orleton was severely ill about the time of his promotion, which could mean that he was not as active in his own interests as has been thought. However that may be, he left Avignon so precipitately that he omitted to take the customary oath of fealty to the pope.[62] On 30 June, the feast of the Commemoration of St Paul, he made his profession of obedience to the archbishop – though Reynolds himself was absent – before the high altar of Canterbury cathedral. He then made his way to Lambeth where, on 2 July, Reynolds granted him livery of the spiritualities and informed Stephen de Ledbury, his official sede vacante, that he had done so.[63] Before the end of July the guardian of the temporalities had the king's order to deliver them to the new bishop.[64]

Edward's anger soon subsided, and his irritation at Orleton's conduct was so far forgotten as to enable the envoy to return to diplomatic duty. At this stage Orleton graduates from being one of several proctors at the Curia,[65] or a professional negotiator on a par with half a dozen others, to the leadership of a minor diplomatic mission, a status commensurate with his new office of bishop. His first assignment in this capacity was a temporising one. In June 1318 he was appointed jointly with John Abel, knight, and M. Richard de Burton to take the oath of fealty to Philip V, the new king of France, for the duchy of Aquitaine.[66] For this purpose on 12 June letters of protection valid until St Peter ad Vincula (1 August) were issued.[67] But the taking of the

[62] *C.P.L.* 1305–42, p. 195.

[63] *Canterbury Professions*, p. 93, where Richter gives the date wrongly as 29 June; *H.R.O.*, p. 1.

[64] *C.P.R.* 1317–21, p. 3: 24 July 1317, Nottingham. Letters sent to the custos Robert Broun and to M. John Walwayn, escheator this side Trent.

[65] See Behrens, 'Office of English Resident', who suggests (pp. 642–3) that it was from the time of the 'Avignonese Captivity' that most states maintained proctors more or less permanently at the Curia.

[66] *Foedera* 2, i, p. 153; *Treaty Rolls 1*, no. 575; *C.P.R.* 1317–21, p. 162. Philip V had summoned Edward II to attend his coronation at Rheims in 1316, and in the following year urged that homage should be done for Gascony. See Chaplais, 'Le Duché-Pairie de Guyenne', pp. 149–50.

[67] *C.P.R.* 1317–21, p. 162. Abel accounted for the period from 18 June (London) to 20 July (London), reckoned as thirty-two days; Burton ('assignato per dominum regem et consilium suum una cum domino Hereford' episcopo et domino Johanne Abel milite') for the period from 18 June to 15 August (Northampton) [Nottingham?],

oath had to be postponed because Philip found that the envoys had come without letters patent setting out the precise terms of homage. He asked that the necessary documents be brought to him by the beginning of September.[68] Edward demurred on the grounds that he was engaged against the Scots, and that in any case letters of that kind could not be issued until the parliament due to meet after Michaelmas had given the matter its attention.[69]

Orleton must have been on his way back from the French court when on 29 July at Rue, near Abbeville in Ponthieu, he had a document drawn up appointing M. Adam de Murimuth, Andrea Sapiti and Roger de Breynton his proctors at the Curia. Breynton was separately deputed to perform the neglected oath of fealty on Orleton's behalf.[70] The bishop then resumed his journey to England, arriving in time to append his episcopal seal to the Treaty of Leake at the beginning of August. His involvement in such political events will be dealt with later (' The path of the mediator ', ch. 4). By 18 October he is known to have been in London.[71]

In the interval, the question of homage to Philip V had been temporarily overshadowed by the encroachments of that monarch's officials in Gascony, brought to Edward's notice by his seneschal. To cope with this situation Orleton was again sent to France at the end of August with his former associates, Sir John Abel and M. Richard de Burton,[72] both of whom had already spent much of the year on the continent.[73]

The following year, 1319, Orleton returned to the task with which he had inaugurated his diplomatic career – the sanctification of Thomas de Cantilupe. The process was in its final stages and Orleton had acquired an additional qualification for advocacy as the incumbent of Cantilupe's former see. Associated with him in this mission to the Curia were M. Robert de Worksop, an Augustinian friar and doctor of theology, and two knights. Orleton's letters of protection until Michaelmas are dated 18

reckoned as fifty-nine days, only twenty-seven of them abroad, London, Society of Antiquaries MS. 121, fos. 9^v–10^r.

68 *Foedera* 2, i, p. 157. See Chaplais, ' Le Duché-Pairie de Guyenne ', pp. 150–1.

69 *Foedera*, *loc cit.*; *Treaty Rolls 1*, no. 576. The parliament met at York.

70 *H.R.O.*, pp. xi, 77–8.

71 *H.R.O.*, p. 78.

72 *Foedera* 2, i, p. 159; *Treaty Rolls 1*, nos. 577–8.

73 Society of Antiquaries MS. 121, fos. 7^v, 8^r, 9^v, 10^r.

January from York and extend to seven members of his *familia*.[74] There was some delay in getting started. The bishop was still in England on the last day of February, when from Dover he appointed officers to confer benefices in his absence.[75] We catch sight of him at Avignon in early May, and he remained abroad until February of the following year.

It was on 24 May that Orleton was once again deputed to do homage in Edward's name for Aquitaine, this time in association with Walter Stapledon, bishop of Exeter, and two clerks, M. Robert Baldock and M. Richard de Burton. Details of his participation in the mission are lacking, but this is hardly significant, for once again the act of homage was postponed.[76]

Back in Avignon Orleton was empowered, in conjunction with John de Neville, knight, to grant a pension of twenty-five marks to some 'discreet person' who would further the king's business in the Curia.[77] It was at this time that he came into contact with a noted Benedictine scholar and doctor of theology of Paris known as Laurence 'the Englishman', whom the Hereford register describes as Laurence Bruton of Chipping Norton, nephew of the John of Gloucester, abbot of Hailes, who in 1328 was to attend Orleton's enthronement as bishop of Worcester. They may already have met during the sessions of the council at Vienne, which Laurence certainly attended. At any rate in November 1319 he lent Orleton a number of books, including the *Summa* of Thomas Aquinas and Anselm's *De Similitudinibus*, and the bishop promised to return them in England or to pay compensation. In view of the aspersions on Orleton's character and the strictures on borrowers made by the contemporary bibliophile Richard de Bury, it is worth mentioning that all were duly given back, for they appear among Laurence's effects at the time of his death.[78] Of interest also is the fact that Orleton's studies, despite a crowded life, were by no means confined to canon law.[79]

74 *Foedera* 2, i, pp. 168–9; *C.P.R.* 1317–21, p. 265; *H.R.O.*, p. 107; S.C.1/36/15.
75 *H.R.O.*, p. 109.
76 *Treaty Rolls 1*, nos. 597ff; *Foedera* 2, i, p. 175.
77 *Foedera* 2, i, p. 179.
78 *H.R.O.*, pp. 119–20; *Biog. Oxon.*, *s.v.* Orleton and Housom *alias* Gloucestre, Laurence de; also *ibid.* 3, Additions and Corrections, p. xxix. Laurence was admitted D.Th. of Paris, completing his regency in 1318. For his effects, mainly books, see H.C.M., no. 565; Charles and Emanuel, 'Notes on Old Libraries', pp. 354–5.
79 Apart from Anselm's work and Aquinas's *Summa* (in four volumes) the books borrowed by Orleton were: Aquinas's commentary on the fourth book of Peter

The bishop returned to England early in February 1320 and reported to members of the king's council at Loughborough. He carried with him no fewer than eight papal bulls, six of which were delivered on the 20th to the chamberlain for safe-keeping in the treasury. Two of these six bulls were concerned with the papal tenth, the third contained the cardinals' process against Robert Bruce, the fourth was for the citation of certain Scottish prelates to the Curia, while the fifth, addressed to the English archbishops and bishops, provided for the excommunication of those who invaded the English realm or who gave such invaders help or encouragement. It was this bull, so it would seem, that Reynolds was to republish at the time of Isabella's 'invasion' in 1326. The sixth bull, addressed to the archbishop of York and the bishops of Durham and Carlisle, was for Bruce's excommunication for the killing of John Comyn. The remaining two bulls were directed to the papal arbitrators, Cardinals Gaucelme d'Eauze and Luca Fieschi, and contained instructions for proceeding with their sentences against Bruce. As the cardinals had already left the realm, these two bulls were entrusted to Robert Baldock, the recently-appointed keeper of the privy seal, so that they could be taken with the king to France and restored at a later stage to the treasury.[80]

Orleton then wrote to Archbishop Melton and sent copies of two of the bulls for execution.[81] These the archbishop transmitted to his suffragan Louis de Beaumont, on the grounds that as bishop of Durham he was nearer to Scotland. Orleton's letters suggested that the papal plan for the citation of Bruce and the Scottish prelates was at the wish of the English king and his council. When Melton returned his certificate of execution to the king it included the tenor of Orleton's letters to that effect. The royal council, meeting in London during April, repudiated the suggestion, declaring that the scheme was the pope's entirely, and that therefore Melton's certificate should be amended and

Lombard's *Sentences*, the *Historia Scholastica* (Peter Comestor), Aristotle's *Rhetorica*, a rhetorical work of Cicero's (*De Inventione*?) and a book of geometry with commentary.

80 *H.M.C.R.* 15, app. X, p. 3; E.159/93/77. The first two bulls enabled the king to collect a papal tenth for the defence of the realm (raised in 1320–1): Lunt, *Financial Relations* 1, p. 409.

81 I.e. the third and fourth bulls.

addressed to Orleton as the papal agent rather than to the king. Bishop Salmon, the chancellor, conveyed this view to Melton, accompanying his observations with the draft of a revised certificate. Melton replied that the alterations suggested could not be made, since they modified the tenor of Orleton's letters and those of the bishop of Durham sent in response to his own mandate, which would be a contradiction of the earlier certificate. However, he did issue simplified letters for despatch to Orleton. These omitted both the offending clauses and the texts of the letters concerned, but none the less incorporated the substance of the matter. The choice of certificate was left by Melton to the chancellor's discretion.[82] It appears that we have here another instance of conflict between papal and royal policy, which placed Orleton, as the agent of both, in an ambivalent position. That the affair did not damage his credibility with the government is shown by the fact that almost immediately he was sent on yet another embassy to the French court and the Curia.

In a letter to his neighbour, Bishop Cobham, Orleton expressed dismay at the prospect. He was wearied by his long-sustained labours, grievously affected by the death of much-loved friends in the Curia and the serious illnesses of others of his *familia*, as well as by an intolerable burden of expense and a train of mental anxieties. Time was too short to restore his depleted *familia* or even to make proper arrangements with those who were to exercise authority in the diocese during his absence. He longed to be able to cast aside worldly cares, which entailed laborious days and sleepless nights, and instead to join Cobham in the agreeable duty of pastoral care. Such could not be; the king's majesty was adamant.[83]

The ostensibly reluctant Orleton travelled on this occasion with the elder Despenser and Bartholomew Badlesmere, men particularly close to King Edward, in order to make arrangements for a meeting of the French and English monarchs, at which the latter might render the long-promised homage in person.[84] The same envoys, but with the addition of the king's half-brother Edmund

[82] *Letters from Northern Registers*, pp. 300–4 (from Archbishop Melton's register).
[83] *Worcester Reg. Cobham*, pp. 80–2. The letter should probably be dated *c.* 29 February x 20 March 1320.
[84] *Foedera* 2, i, p. 194; 15 March 1320; *Treaty Rolls 1*, pp. 610–1. See Phillips, *Pembroke*, p. 188.

of Woodstock, were also given letters of credence to the pope.[85] The Bardi advanced 1,500 marks for the royal expenses at the Roman Court, which sum was delivered to Orleton.[86]

While in London and prior to setting out for the coast, Orleton issued a forty days' indulgence for the king's benefit in honour of the Virgin and of King Ethelbert, the Hereford patron. Clearly he was at this juncture high in Edward's favour.[87] On 20 March, at Dover, he appointed attorneys before making the channel crossing.[88] By 1 April he reached Paris, where he was to fix a date for the homage and, by the beginning of May, Avignon, where he handed over the annual tribute of 1,000 marks.[89]

On the surface Orleton's most urgent task at the Curia was to press the claim of M. Henry Burghersh, the under-age nephew of Bartholomew Badlesmere, to the bishopric of Lincoln. To the king's chagrin Burghersh had already failed to secure Winchester. This time he was to prove more fortunate. But according to the continuator of Trivet's chronicle the underlying purpose of the mission was to persuade John XXII to absolve Edward from his oath to observe the Ordinances; a task, he suggests, which was duly achieved by the personal petition of Edmund of Woodstock.[90] Orleton's part in the affair does not transpire, though he is named in the papal letters which informed the king of the

85 *Foedera* 2, i, p. 194. Henry of Canterbury accompanied the party ' cum litteris instrumentis et aliis memorandis domini regis ducatum [Aquitanie] predictum tangentibus ', claiming expenses 22 March to 13 August: B.L. Add. MS. 17362, fo. 12^{r}. Letters of credence for Despenser, Badlesmere and Orleton were sent to various cardinals (dated 28 February): S.C.1/32/78–82.

86 *C.P.R.* 1317–21, p. 436.

87 *H.R.O.*, pp. 129–30.

88 *H.R.O.*, p. 130.

89 *H.R.O.*, pp. 130, 131–2; S.C.7/25/7 (acquittance dated 27 May 1320); cf. Kirsch, ' Andreas Sapiti ', p. 591. While at Avignon he received 400 florins from the Bardi purchased for 100 marks sterling. Of the embassy's reception Dene writes: ' per regem Francie transeuntes magnifice sunt recepti et in curia Romana honorificencius magnificati '. This chronicler (who calls Orleton M. Adam de Hereford) assumes the mission to be primarily concerned with Burghersh's appointment. Cotton MS. Faustina B. V, fo. 34^{r}.

90 Cotton MS. Nero D. X, fo. 110^{v}: ' Ad presenciam pape deductus est a quo impetravit absolucionem domini regis Angl' et optinuit a iuramento prestito super ordinacionibus observandis alias factis per comites et barones.' Maddicott, *Lancaster*, pp. 255–6, draws attention to this point. Yet Murimuth, who ought to have been well informed, cynically observed (*Murimuth*, p. 31) that despite an expenditure of £15,000 nothing was achieved save Burghersh's promotion and he was to prove ungrateful.

success of his petitions.[91] As for Burghersh, his bulls of provision were issued on 27 May – the day of Cantilupe's canonisation ceremony – and on his return journey Orleton joined Bishops Salmon and Stapledon for the consecration of the new bishop at Boulogne in the king's presence.[92] This took place on 20 July, the envoys having earlier found King Edward and Queen Isabella at Amiens, where on the last day of June they attended the long-deferred ceremony of homage to Philip V who, as it turned out, was to die some eighteen months later (3 January 1322).[93] The whole party then recrossed the channel, a ship and accompanying barge being placed at the disposal of Orleton and his familiars.[94]

To contemporaries by no means the least important outcome of this mission was the issue on 17 April 1320 of Cantilupe's bull of canonisation – the culmination of years of effort and vast expenditure. Edward was much pleased by this and his other diplomatic successes. In a cheerful letter to Pope John he wrote of his special affection for Orleton and of his intention to be present at the forthcoming translation of the new saint.[95]

One further diplomatic errand remains to be considered, again to the French court. This time Orleton was associated with Amaury de Craon, seneschal of Gascony, and M. Richard de Burton, his colleague on previous occasions. Their principal concern seems to have been Gascon affairs.[96] The letters of protection

[91] S.C.7/56/11; *C.P.L.* 1305–42, p. 445 (undated). There is no warrant for suggesting that Orleton's reluctance to go abroad on this occasion was prompted by the nature of the business he would have to transact.

[92] *Foedera* 2, i, p. 198; *Annales Paulini*, pp. 289–90; Cotton MS. Faustina B. V, fo. 34r. For the official view of Burghersh's qualifications see *Foedera* 1, i, p. 190, and for Cobham's laudatory opinion, *Worcester Reg. Cobham*, pp. 46–7. An account of the Lincoln appointment is in Smith, *Episcopal Appointments*, pp. 35–6.

[93] Cotton MS. Faustina B. V, fo. 34r; Phillips, *Pembroke*, p. 192; Chaplais, 'Le Duché-Pairie de Guyenne', pp. 152–3. The *Winchester Chartulary* (pp. 62–4, no. 127; cf. pp. 64–5, nos. 128–9) records the five acts of homage from that of Henry III to St Louis in 1259 to that of Edward II at Amiens.

[94] Orleton's expenses for the mission (19 March to 22 July 1320, 126 days) totalled £336. Add. MS. 17362, fo. 11r (also at fo. 70r: £15 for part payment of £400 due to him *per billam garderobe* for 11–12 Edward II). Edward himself was abroad from 19 June to 22 July: *Foedera* 2, ii, pp. 3–4.

[95] *H.R.O.*, p. xviii; *Foedera* 2, ii, p. 15. At the time Roger de Breynton was travelling to the Curia on matters concerning the church of Hereford. In the event Cantilupe's translation had to be deferred and it was Edward III who attended it. See *Polychronicon* 8, app. p. 355; Douie, 'Canonisation of St Thomas', pp. 278, 286.

[96] Orleton and Craon despatched a letter from Paris (20 March 13[21]) with a petition from Guy de Rochefort for settlement of a long-standing dispute which he

are dated 22 February 1321 and the bishop was back in England by 24 April.[97] By that time the country was fast approaching civil war. The envoys had difficulty in finding anyone to whom they could report; the king was some four days' journey from London and only when his chancellor (Bishop Salmon) and treasurer (Bishop Stapledon) returned to the city was it possible for Orleton and Burton to be instructed as to their best course of action. As Burton plaintively remarked in his report to Amaury de Craon, decisions on Gascon problems, such as the dispute about the castle of Blanquefort, could not be reached in the absence of those closest to the king: the earl of Pembroke, the younger Despenser and M. Robert Baldock.[98]

Not before the middle of June is Orleton to be found in his diocese.[99] By the year's end the bishop was implicated in rebellious activity. He never recovered the king's confidence and his diplomatic work was only resumed in the following reign, but his continued interest in matters of this kind is attested by copies of letters from the French king, Charles IV, which are entered in his Hereford register.[100]

A CAREER RESUMED 1327–1336

Before Orleton could resume his diplomatic career momentous events intervened: the deposition and death of Edward II and the coronation of his son Edward III under the aegis of Queen

and Isabelle de Moulon had maintained against Geoffroi, lord of Mortagne-sur-Dordogne, 'super avoacione terre de Chasaco [Guy was "administrator et gubernator" of the heir] quam dominus Gaufridus de Chasaco . . . avoavit se tenere a vobis [i.e. Edward] in preiudicium dicti domini de Mauritania'. The writers request the king to confirm an arrangement ('pro vestro comodo, quam ex racione equitate et de rigore iuris'), whereby Guy was absolved 'ab avoacione et iuramento fidelitatis', subject to the payment of twenty livres Tournois [a year]. S.C.8/237/11825.

97 *Foedera* 2, ii, p. 9; *C.P.R.* 1317–21, pp. 564–5; *Treaty Rolls 1*, no. 621. M. Roger de Breynton, the bishop's agent, accounted for the period 21 February 1321 (when Orleton crossed from Dover to Wissant) to 24 April (the date he reached the sea again); 63 days at four marks a day. He was allowed £168 plus £5 for the sea-crossings. Two particularly experienced men were also involved in these negotiations: M. Henry de Canterbury, who was with Orleton and Burton between February and April, for which service he claimed £12 on 11 May, and Elias Joneston. See E.404/484/29; Add. MS. 9951, fo. 9^v.

98 S.C.1/54/139. The contents of the letter speak strongly for Burton's authorship (Orleton being mentioned as his colleague); Craon, likewise, must surely have been the recipient. Neither is named in the copy.

99 *H.R.O.*, fos. 52^v–53^r, p. 197.

100 *H.R.O.*, pp. 334–7.

Isabella and her paramour Roger Mortimer, shortly to become earl of March. The bishop's part in this revolutionary upheaval will be discussed later ('Isabella's triumph', ch. 4); for the present let it suffice that so far as we know Orleton was content to relinquish the treasurership, which he had held under the new regime for barely two months, and to return to his former peripatetic occupation.[1] By doing so he may have enhanced his chances of further ecclesiastical advancement, for the reign of Edward II and the early years of that of his son show that the kings' political weakness made it relatively easy for a strong-willed pope to advance the candidates he preferred to English bishoprics in disregard of royal wishes.[2] We have no means of knowing whether Orleton made a deliberate calculation of this kind. It could be simply that he found diplomacy congenial – despite earlier protestations to the contrary – or that he had no wish to engage in the struggle for power which soon developed at home.

Orleton's first mission of the new reign was to Avignon. Associated with him were Bartholomew Burghersh and M. Thomas de Astley, canon of Hereford and a distinguished secular clerk;[3] letters of credence were directed to the pope and dated 24 March 1327 from Westminster.[4] The declared aim of the embassy was to secure dispensation for the marriage of the young king and Philippa of Hainault; a necessary formality indeed, but there must have been a more general commission to acquaint Pope John with the details of recent happenings and to gain his sympathy for the new regime.[5] In fact the pope wrote to his nuncio, Hugh d'Angoulême, and after commiserating with him about the wretchedness of the English climate, expressed his eagerness for Orleton's arrival so that he could learn the state of affairs and give advice accordingly.[6] For this purpose Orleton was

[1] He was treasurer 28 January to 24 March 1327, being succeeded by Henry Burghersh, bishop of Lincoln. For his activities as treasurer see *Calendar of Memoranda Rolls 1326–1327*, index *s.v.* Orleton; E.403/226 (issue roll temp. Orleton).

[2] See Smith, *Episcopal Appointments*, chs. 1–2.

[3] For a summary of Astley's career see *Biog. Oxon.*, *s.v.* Emden (*loc. cit.*) says that he was a clerk of Orleton's, but this seems to be a misreading of *H.R.O.*, p. xlii. He acted as advisor to the Worcester chapter at the time of Bransford's election to the see in 1339. See *Worcester Reg. Bransford*, p. xiii.

[4] *Foedera* 2, ii, p. 184.

[5] According to Baker Orleton went to the Curia 'pro negociis propriis et matris regis'. *Chronicon*, p. 42.

[6] *C.P.L.* 1305–42, p. 484. The date of this letter is 13 July; on the 14th the pope wrote in response to the requests brought by the envoys.

an excellent choice; having borne the brunt of Edward's displeasure, not to say vindictiveness, and played a notable part in the 'revolution', he was well qualified both as advocate and apologist.

The bishop's pre-eminence is reflected in the size of his entourage. He was accompanied by seventy men and 46 horses, as against the thirty-two men and 22 horses in Bartholomew Burghersh's party. Leaving London on 30 March, a few days after Burghersh, he made the regular crossing from Dover to Wissant in the Pas-de-Calais on 5 April. As his account for expenses shows, he was absent for 299 days from the time he left the English court at Westminster until he returned to the king's presence at York on 22 January 1328.[7]

The principals of the embassy kept in touch both with the home government and with the count of Hainault. Orleton sent his trusted clerk William de Culpho from Wissant to Count William at Valenciennes, but the count moved away and Culpho had to follow him to Middelburgh in Zeeland before setting out to rejoin his master at Avignon.[8] It is said to have been the bishop's plan to send not one but two messengers from the Curia to England with the pope's initial response, so that if one were held up for any reason the other could carry on alone.[9] This initial response was unfavourable, but the difficulties proved only temporary and the required bull was issued on 30 August.[10]

While the king's marriage was being discussed at Avignon,

[7] E.101/309/38; E.372/175/46. Cf. Mirot and Déprez, 'Ambassades anglaises', p. 556, who wrongly give the return date as 22 February. With respect to the number of those with Orleton on this and later occasions, it should be remembered that in the normal course bishops travelled abroad with rather more attendants than lay barons did.

[8] E.101/309/37. Ralph de Brok was sent to the count of Hainault and thence to Paris. This clerk (though 'eiusdem' could be read as 'cuiusdam') then journeyed via Dover, carrying the bishop's letters to the king at Stamford. On the return journey to Paris he joined some merchants for the Dover–Wissant crossing 'propter periculum malefactorum'.

[9] E.101/309/37. 'Et in expensis duorum nunciorum cum primo responso domini pape de Avynion' usque Ebor' unanimiter missorum per consilium et avisamentum domini [dicti?] episcopi Hereford' ut unus eorum litteras dicti episcopi et ipsius Bartholomei cum omni qua poterit festinacione ad regem deportasset si alius eorum infirmitate vel aliquo alio casu impeditus fuisset, pro vadiis suis per xvi dies et passagio maris quod tunc erat difficile lxx s.' Despite the date (13 July) of the papal letter mentioned in n. 6 above, the payment of 200 marks' pension on 20 June to Cardinal Bertrand de Montfavèz could mean that Orleton was by then at the Curia: E.101/309/37–8. [10] S.C.7/24/5; *C.P.L.* 1305–42, p. 484; *Foedera* 2, ii, p. 196.

Orleton's neighbouring diocesan at Worcester, Thomas de Cobham, died on 27 August 1327. This was not unexpected; the bishop had been ailing for some time and even in the thick of the troubles of 1326 had been searching for medical treatment in London, though barely able to maintain himself in the saddle.[11] The Worcester chapter grasped this rare opportunity to elect their prior, Wolstan de Bransford, in his stead. On receiving the election decree (10 September) Archbishop Reynolds issued his commission for the subprior to act as official sede vacante and on 3 October confirmed the election. The report of Cobham's death probably took somewhat less than three weeks to reach the Curia where Pope John, acting with despatch, provided Orleton to the vacant see by bulls dated 28 September.[12] Rumours of papal reservation had been current in England much before this. Letters in the king's name to the pope and cardinals dated 6 September mention it but point to Bransford's election and the fact that he was already seeking confirmation and consecration at the hands of the metropolitan. A special letter was rushed to Andrea Sapiti, the king's proctor at Avignon; at home preparations were set on foot for the consecration ceremony. The bishop-elect and -confirmed proceeded to take the oath of fealty and received livery of the temporalities. Reynolds was repeatedly urged to consecrate, but knowing the pope's intention he continued to procrastinate. As an alternative the subprior of Worcester was pressing Henry Eastry, the Canterbury prior, to approve an archiepiscopal commission which would permit Bransford to be consecrated elsewhere than at Canterbury. Eastry tartly replied that he had not seen any such commission and therefore it would be improper to give his approval.[13] The harassed archbishop was only rescued from this predicament by his timely death on 16 November, whereupon the government put pressure on the Canterbury chapter to act by virtue of its right to metropolitan jurisdiction during vacancies. Both the Worcester and the Canterbury monks

[11] *Worcester Reg. Cobham*, pp. 204–6.

[12] For this election see Haines, 'Wolstan de Bransford', pp. 104–5; *Worcester Reg. Bransford*, pp. xii–xiii.

[13] *Lit. Cant.* 1, pp. 241–2. The editor has confused the issue by stating that it was Orleton who was seeking consecration. He was of course already a bishop. Moreover, it was the subprior of Worcester who was petitioning; the prior was Bransford, the bishop-elect (*op. cit.* p. 241, rubric).

were warned to do nothing prejudicial to the elect under pain of being accounted violators of the crown's rights and contemners of royal mandates.[14] As late as December Bransford's proctor 'Master Nicholas'[15] was still urging Prior Eastry to do something, but by that time Charlton's bulls of provision to Hereford (reciting Orleton's release from the see) had reached Canterbury and he himself had taken his profession to the future archbishop and his successors.[16] On 12 December a strongly-worded letter was sent to Orleton himself, reiterating the doctrine of election said to be customary in the realm.[17] The bishop was told that his conduct smacked of ambition ('non absque ambitionis vitio'), and further reminded of his oath of fealty and allegiance. In conclusion there came a threat of forfeiture were he to act to the detriment of the king's authority.[18] Since all this proved unavailing, Orleton was summoned to answer before the parliament due to meet at York in February 1328 and expressly forbidden to publish his bulls meanwhile.[19]

Only the outcome of the proceedings at York is known. Orleton must have returned home with some trepidation, mindful of an earlier summons of this kind, and it says something for his courage and accurate assessment of the situation that he argued his case in person and carried the day. All was over by the end of February when the bishop gave orders for his bulls to be published. Early in March he left York with his temporalities restored.[20] A fortnight later he was holding an ordination in his new diocese at Cirencester.[21] He had ridden out the storm.

14 *Foedera* 2, ii, pp. 196–7, 202–3.

15 The identity of this person is obscure, but he was Bransford's proctor, not Orleton's as stated in *Lit. Cant.* 1, p. 259, rubric.

16 *Lit. Cant.* 1, pp. 256–8, 259; *Canterbury Professions*, pp. 97–8. Charlton took his profession on 30 November. He would have been carrying the bulls with him; Eastry's letter-book notes their receipt on the 29th.

17 It is recapitulated in the letters to the Canterbury and Worcester chapters. In the case of 'cathedral churches of royal patronage' the process was said to be as follows: (1) electors seek royal licence to elect; (2) election by chapter; (3) royal assent to the election; (4) signification to pope in case of churches immediately subject to him, or to the metropolitan having right to confirm; (5) notification of confirmation to king; (6) elect does fealty to king; (7) restoration of temporalities.

18 *Foedera* 2, iii, pp. 3–4.

19 This was summoned for 7 February 1328. Orleton was at York from 22 February until 5 March.

20 *W.R.O.* 2, fo. 4^{r-v} [502–3]; *C.P.R.* 1327–30, p. 245. The temporalities were restored on 2 March.

21 *W.R.O.* 1, fo. 1^{r} [1].

Who or what lay behind the opposition to Orleton's promotion can only be conjectured. His rival Bransford was a worthy candidate but a political nonentity. The treasurer, Bishop Burghersh, was in Queen Isabella's confidence and with reason considered a close friend of Orleton's; he had certainly been a companion in adversity. The chancellor, John Hothum, bishop of Ely, had held similar office before 1320 and been associated with Orleton during episcopal attempts at political mediation in 1321.[22] But the real power lay behind these men. Queen Isabella was probably favourably disposed towards Orleton; it was the bishop's praiseworthy service in her cause that allegedly prompted the restoration of his temporalities.[23] This leaves Mortimer, who was surely party to the policy adopted, not necessarily on personal grounds, but because no government could afford to let the papacy trespass on what were considered to be regalian rights. To have taken the conflict further would have been foolhardy. Nothing was to be gained by the pope's alienation, and as the near future was to show, Orleton's services as a negotiator were not yet dispensable.

Following the death of the French king, Charles IV, his successor Philip VI was crowned at Rheims on 29 May 1328. It was Orleton and Roger Northburgh, bishop of Coventry and Lichfield, who were at Paris on the morrow to press the claims of Edward III through his mother, Isabella.[24]

For about a year and a half after this Orleton was free to address himself to the administration of his diocese. Then, early in 1330, he became involved once more in French affairs as member of an extremely important embassy. Apart from Orleton its leaders were William Ayrminne, bishop of Norwich, Henry earl of Lancaster and William lord Ros of Hamlake, a northerner who makes an isolated appearance on the diplomatic scene at this point.[25] They were supported by two experienced men, M. John Walwayn the younger[26] and M. John de Schordich.[27]

22 Hothum was treasurer in 1317; chancellor in 1318 and 1327.

23 *W.R.O.* 2, fo. 4^{r-v} [503].

24 See Perroy, *Hundred Years War*, pp. 80–1; Déprez, *Les préliminaires*, p. 36 (where 'Chichester' is written for 'Chester', i.e. 'Coventry and Lichfield'). The decision to send the two bishops was taken in April at the Northampton parliament according to *Cal. P.M.R.*, p. 78.

For footnotes 25 to 27 see p. 32.

The purpose of the embassy was threefold: to arrange a double marriage linking the English and French royal houses,[28] to clarify the loosely-worded oath of homage for Gascony which Edward III had used at Amiens in June 1329,[29] and to continue the quasi-legal processes of Montreuil and Périgueux. The ambassadors' terms of reference with respect to the last and most tedious of their assignments are set out at great length, and range over the whole field of conflict between the English and French crowns.[30]

Orleton crossed from Dover to Wissant on 10 February. Once again he travelled in some state, this time with two ships carrying sixty-eight men and forty-four horses. He accounted for fifty-four days between 31 January and 25 March 1330, on which day he arrived back at Reading to deliver a report which was far from encouraging.[31] There was no opportunity to attend to his diocese: on 10 April he was at the royal manor of Woodstock and there appointed with Bishop Ayrminne, Walwayn and Schordich to resume the negotiations, in particular those for the marriage of Edward III's sister Eleanor and John, eldest son of King Philip VI.[32] On this occasion the mission was to last fifty-two days from the time of Orleton's leaving Woodstock on 11 April until his return there on 1 June. He was at Dover on 21 April with a smaller company than usual, fifty-seven men, and back there on the eve of Whit Sunday.[33] The marriage schemes came to nothing; two years later Eleanor married Reginald II, count of

25 *Foedera* 2, iii, pp. 36–7: 5 February 1330. William lord Ros was a northern baron. In 1317 the family castle of Wark-on-Tweed was being exchanged with Edward II for other lands (*C.P.R.* 1317–21, pp. 29, 32). Cuttino suggests that the reason he did not serve after 1330 was that he was a partisan of Queen Isabella (*Diplomatic Administration*, p. 136).

26 To be distinguished from the elder John Walwayn, who died before July 1326 and was possibly the author of the *Vita*. Both Walwayns are in *Biog. Oxon.* 3, app. *s.v.*

27 Schordich had been a councillor of Edward II. A D.C.L., he subsequently became a knight and married. He was long associated with French affairs. See *Biog. Oxon.*, *s.v.* Shordich; *The War of Saint-Sardos*, index *s.v.*; and for details of his famous response in the Curia on the topic of papal provisions and his murder, *Murimuth*, pp. 143–6, 149, 171, 229–30.

28 Between John, eldest son of King Philip VI, and Eleanor, Edward's sister, on the one hand, and between John of Eltham, Edward's brother, and Marie, daughter of Philip, on the other. *Foedera* 2, iii, p. 35: 17 January 1330.

29 *Foedera* 2, iii, p. 36: 5 February 1330. Edward took the oath in the choir of the cathedral on 6 June: *ibid.* p. 27.

30 *Foedera* 2, iii, pp. 36–7.

31 E.101/310/8; E.372/175/46. Cf. E.101/310/7.

32 *Foedera* 2, iii, p. 42.

33 E.101/310/14.

Guelders.[34] However, the convention of Bois de Vincennes, sealed on 8 May 1330 by Orleton, Ayrminne and Schordich, provided a temporary settlement of some outstanding (principally Gascon) issues. Edward confirmed it at Woodstock on 8 July.[35]

After this achievement Orleton spent much of the summer of 1330 at his manor house of Beaumes in Berkshire, possibly taking a part in discussions preliminary to the despatch of a further embassy to France in which his place was taken by Bishop Northburgh.[36] This was no time for Orleton to be abroad, for his earlier close association with Mortimer and Isabella placed him in potential jeopardy. Edward III was finding their tutelage increasingly irksome, just at the moment when Mortimer's marked acquisitiveness and quasi-judicial murder of the earl of Kent rendered him particularly vulnerable. Orleton's itinerary suggests that he was at the Nottingham assembly during the course of which Mortimer was arrested, and that after a brief visit to his diocese he journeyed to London for the November parliament which condemned the earl, who was hanged at Tyburn shortly afterwards.[37]

As it turned out, Orleton's situation did not deteriorate noticeably as a consequence of these political upheavals: authority for him to undertake further discussions with the French was given by letters patent of 16 January 1331. In this embassy continuity of personnel was provided by Orleton, Ayrminne and Schordich, while the secular clerk, Thomas Sampson, was a relative newcomer and two laymen, Henry Percy and Hugh Audley, were fresh recruits.[38]

Orleton's account covers the period from 23 January to 25

[34] See *Foedera* 2, iii, pp. 74–6, and for a subsidy raised on this account, *ibid.* pp. 87–9. When asked to contribute, the prior of Winchester demurred, but the king brushed aside his excuses: *Winchester Chartulary*, p. 75, no. 153 (12 February 1333). An account book of Princess Eleanor's expenses on the occasion of her marriage survives in two copies: E.101/386/7; B.L. Add. MS. 38006. See Safford, 'Expenses of Eleanor', pp. 111–40.

[35] *Foedera* 2, iii, pp. 46–8; C.47/28/8 m.14. The three signatories are termed 'messagers et procurours du roy d'Engleterre'. For a narrative of events see Déprez, *Les préliminaires*, pp. 57–8ff.

[36] *Foedera* 2, iii, p. 48. The credentials permitting the envoys to treat are dated 8 July from Woodstock. Orleton was there at the beginning of June and possibly on the 17th, though a duplicate entry has 17 *July*. *W.R.O.* 2, fo. 35^r [770]; cf. 1, fo. 20^v [117].

[37] He was at Ilkeston, Derbys., on 21 October and in London from before 1 December. *W.R.O.* 1, fos. 21^r [121–2], 35^{r-v} [308ff]. For Mortimer see *G.E.C.* 8, pp. 440–2

[38] *Foedera* 2, iii, p. 56, and see Déprez, *Les préliminaires*, pp. 71–3.

March 1331 – the date of his return to the king at Westminster. He made the crossing from Dover to Calais on 28 February and sailed back by the more usual route from Wissant.[39] The embassy was seeking a solution to some of the problems which had been under discussion the previous year. Negotiations culminated in the Paris agreement of 9 March 1331 in which Edward III gave way on the principal issue and agreed to perform liege homage.[40] The precise words to be used at future ceremonies were set out and published as letters patent on 30 March.[41] This agreement, Déprez says, was nothing more than a complement of the convention concluded at Bois de Vincennes in the previous year.[42]

There followed a pause of rather more than a year, during which interval Orleton busied himself about the affairs of his neglected diocese. Then, at the end of April 1332, a new embassy was formed. This time Orleton was associated with John Stratford, bishop of Winchester and now royal chancellor, William de Clinton – one of the men fast rising in the favour of the young Edward – and the well-tried Schordich.[43] The relative status of the leaders is reflected in the sums paid to them by the Exchequer: Stratford received £100, Orleton 100 marks (£66 13s 4d), Clinton £40 and Schordich £20.[44] Other mandates issued at this time to Orleton and a number of professional clerks and laymen provided for the continuation of those interminable processes of Montreuil and Périgueux.[45]

The ambassadors were sent to the French court to discuss the

39 E.101/310/16.

40 The text of the oath is given in *Foedera* 2, iii, p. 61; *C.P.R.* 1330–34, pp. 90–5. See also Déprez, *Les préliminaires*, p. 73, n. 3; Cuttino, *Diplomatic Administration*, pp. 15–16.

41 Cuttino, *Diplomatic Administration*, p. 16 (cf. p. 5), points out that it was seventy-two years after the Treaty of Paris (1259) had stipulated that Henry III should perform liege homage. Contemporaries were also aware of the fact: at Winchester the various forms of the oath of homage were carefully recorded. *Winchester Chartulary*, pp. 62–5, nos. 127–9. For Philip's interpretation of the matter and some measures which followed the agreement see *Foedera* 2, iii, pp. 63ff.

42 *Les préliminaires*, p. 72.

43 In execution of a writ of privy seal, dated September [1331], Schordich (on the treasurer's instruction) directed Elias Joneston, the *custos processuum* (for whom see Cuttino, *Diplomatic Administration*, ch. 2), to see that the processes and copies of all letters which might serve the king's case were to be made available for the use of the chancellor, Stratford. C.47/28/2 m.9 (cf. m.8) and cf. Cuttino, *op. cit.* pp. 52–3.

44 *Foedera* 2, iii, p. 77.

45 C.47/28/2 m.28 (cf. m.27): 2[4] April 1332. See also n. 43 above.

projected crusade with King Philip, to establish a perpetual alliance, to make arrangements for a meeting of the two monarchs, and to settle details of the marriage proposed between Edward's infant son and Joan, daughter of the French king. The crusading project was dear to John XXII's heart and had the added advantage that it might be the means of reconciling the kings of France and England and of providing an outlet for the adventurous spirit of the martial Edward. But hopes for the alliance, the marriage and the crusade were all ill-founded.[46]

These weighty matters occupied Orleton for forty-one days from the time he left London on 27 April until 6 June 1332 when he rejoined the king at his manor of Woodstock.[47]

Orleton's final mission as bishop of Worcester commenced with his return to the capital in the first week of November 1332. There, together with Bartholomew Burghersh, Sir William Trussell and William de Cusancia, he was charged with a variety of matters: a marriage between Edward's brother John of Eltham – who was to die within four years – and Joan, daughter of the count of Eu; synchronisation of the departure of the French and English contingents for the crusade; and once again, the settlement of outstanding differences about Gascony.[48]

The bishop left London on 11 November and after an extremely stormy passage to Calais arrived in Paris some eight days later. He was to remain at the French court until 22 February 1333, when he received fresh instructions which took him to Avignon. Quitting the Curia on 10 September he travelled back to Paris, finally returning to the king at Wallingford on 9 January 1334.[49]

46 *Foedera* 2, iii, pp. 77–8. In 1331 Pierre de la Palu, patriarch of Jerusalem, was vigorously counselling John XXII to send a force to the Holy Land. The pope responded by ordering the preaching of a crusade. Philip's intention to take part seems to have been genuine and Edward brought the matter before parliament. Déprez, *Les préliminaires*, pp. 83–7; *Lit. Cant.*, 1, pp. 438–40; Lunt, *Financial Relations* 2, pp. 88–94.

47 E.352/126/38. The outward journey was by way of Calais, but Orleton returned via Wissant and Dover.

48 *Foedera* 2, iii, pp. 89–90; *C.P.R.* 1330–34, pp. 359, 361, 373, 413, 466–7, 472.

49 E.101/310/28; E.372/178/42; E.352/126/38. See also Michelmore, 'Expenses of Adam Orleton', who gives an English version of one of the Yorkshire Archaeological Society's MSS. (MD 4/1), apparently the original account. Its total, £157 23d, is corrected to £156 16s 10d in E.101/310/28 and it is the latter sum which is entered on the chancellor's and the pipe roll. I am indebted to H. M. G. Baillie, assistant secretary of the Royal Commission on Historical Manuscripts, for this reference.

During Orleton's sojourn abroad Archbishop Simon Mepham died (12 October 1333). The Canterbury chapter elected John Stratford, bishop of Winchester, as his successor (3 November). The king informed the pope of the fact, requesting his assent and the forwarding of the pallium.[50] Pope John, however, seems to have made up his mind in advance of his receipt of Edward's letters, for Stratford's provisory bulls are dated 26 November.[51] For once there seems to have been unanimity between chapter, king and pope.

Stratford's promotion created a vacancy at Winchester, which the king seems to have earmarked for Simon de Montacute, younger brother of the William de Montacute (Montague) prominent in Mortimer's overthrow whom Edward was to create earl of Salisbury in 1337. That at any rate is the credible view of Adam Murimuth, Orleton's sometime diplomatic colleague, of the Durham chronicler Graystanes, and of the cardinals at Avignon. As the Winchester vacancy had been created by translation, Pope John claimed the right to fill it, and did so by moving Orleton from Worcester early in December.[52] Within a few days Montacute was assigned the consolation prize of Worcester,[53] from which he shortly secured translation to Ely.[54] Murimuth declares that Orleton owed his translation to the intervention of the French king whom he had served better than his English master. Edward, he adds, was piqued by the success of the king of France in English domestic affairs.[55] Baker's passage is more elaborate; it includes a derogatory jingle, a denunciation of the French 'usurper', and the allegation that someone promoted by him could readily be turned into a traitor.[56] Such jingoism should not be taken too seriously. If Philip did make some representation, as he may well have done, it was not at the time

50 *Foedera* 2, iii, pp. 102–3; *Concilia* 2, pp. 564–9. The king's letters are dated 18 November.

51 *C.P.L.* 1305–42, pp. 405, 512.

52 *Murimuth*, p. 70; *Graystanes*, pp. 671–2; *Winchester Chartulary*, p. 111, no. 244; *C.P.L.* 1305–42, pp. 405, 512; Win.R.O. 1, fo. 1r (rubric). The bulls bear dates 1 and 8 December, the former being taken as that of appointment in the Winchester register.

53 *C.P.L.* 1305–42, *loc. cit.*; Worcester Reg. Montacute 1, fo. 11r; Thomas, *Survey*, app. 95, pp. 109–10. Bulls are dated 4 and 11 December; the latter was copied into the episcopal register.

54 *C.P.L.* 1305–42, p. 540; *Foedera* 2, iii, p. 160.

55 *Murimuth*, p. 70, and cf. *Annales Paulini*, p. 360.

56 *Chronicon*, pp. 54–5.

particularly reprehensible. It is far more likely that the initiative came from the pope himself; it was certainly not at variance with his inclination. As Orleton's bulls followed hard on Stratford's there was not much time for lobbying. It is worth noting in this connection that there had been comparable backbiting and demonstration of official disapproval in the past. When Stratford was provided to Winchester in 1323 Edward II had branded him 'pseudo-nuncius', yet within five months of the restitution of his temporalities the bishop was being sent back to France.[57] Ayrminne's integrity was impugned for similar reasons, but this imputation has been rebutted by a modern champion, who has little difficulty in demonstrating the chroniclers' inconsistency, not to say inaccuracy.[58]

Pope John wrote in strong terms to the newly-appointed archbishop on behalf of Orleton. He deplored the fact that the king, influenced by the bishop's rivals ('emuli'), had not permitted the translation, that he had retained the temporalities, and what was even worse, had directed Orleton's subjects not to accept him as diocesan. According to the pope's information, Stratford himself had failed to give assistance to his suffragan; indeed had refused to acknowledge him as such, and under colour of a royal gift had received the fruits and temporal rents, and even denied to Orleton the seal of the Winchester officiality and the registers. If such was the case, John concluded, he was astonished: the archbishop was to do his best to intercede on the bishop's behalf.[59] What effect this letter had is not known, but official disapproval kept Orleton waiting for his temporalities until 23 September 1334, although he had entered his diocese towards the end of March.[60] Even more pointed was Edward's neglect to summon him to parliament as bishop of Winchester until the March of 1336.[61] In that year he

[57] *Foedera* 2, ii, pp. 78–9, 82–3, 89–91, 101 (temporalities restored 15 June 1324), 119–20 (sent to France 12 November). The charges against Stratford on this occasion were very serious; allegedly he had refused to give an account of his mission.

[58] Grassi, 'William Airmyn', *Vita*, p. 141 (where Ayrminne is considered a protégé of the king of France).

[59] Lambeth MS. 1213, pp. 307–8. In *Winchester Chartulary*, p. 110, no. 243b, this letter is dated 20 June 1334. M. William Inge, archdeacon of Surrey, is also alleged to have opposed the translation: Win.R.O. 2, fo. 15r.

[60] Win.R.O. 1, fo. 1r.

[61] See the detailed note on this point in Plucknett, 'Parliament', p. 94, n. 2. To what is said there might be added that Stratford, who was summoned to the parliament

seems to have been fully restored to favour, and consequently set out on his final embassy.

The council which met at Northampton in June 1336 determined that *nuncii* should be sent to the French court.[62] Various matters demanded immediate attention. In accordance with their instructions the envoys were to make detailed plans for the crusade, arrange another meeting of the two monarchs, discuss the threat posed to the English by David Bruce and his adherents, and deal with the disputes and litigation in Gascony – a never-ending source of altercation. Apart from Orleton the leaders of the embassy were Richard de Bury, bishop of Durham, a man high in Edward's esteem because of his part in the coup d'état which dislodged Mortimer, Sir William Trussell and M. Richard Bentworth, a doctor of civil law.[63]

This embassy was clearly intended to be an impressive one, as we see from Orleton's expense account. He sailed with a small flotilla of two ships (three on the return journey) and four barges, which served to transport his *familia* of 113 persons and their accompanying horses. Leaving London on 21 July 1336, he returned there on 5 September to retail the disappointing outcome of his efforts and those of his colleagues. Richard de Bury, who both started earlier and returned later, was absent some five weeks longer than Orleton. His account illustrates how, by means of a series of messengers, the two bishops kept the king and council informed at each stage of the negotiations.[64] But things went badly: the French king was reported to be aiding the Scots with ships and men. So serious was the situation that parliament was summoned to discuss it at the end of September. Orleton's diplo-

of February 1334 as bishop of Winchester rather than as archbishop, *was* the king's candidate. It was the manner in which the pope carried out these promotions that irritated.

62 *Foedera* 2, iii, p. 150; Déprez, *Les préliminaires*, pp. 130–1, 132, n. 5. Orleton was at Northampton on 28 June: Win.R.O. 2, fo. 55^r. For this council see Morris, *English Government at Work*, intro. pp. 34–5.

63 *Foedera* 2, iii, pp. 149–50.

64 E.101/311/21. Cf. E.372/181/31 (expenses of Henry de Canterbury while with the bishops of Durham and Winchester); E.372/184/45 (enrolment of Orleton's account presented by his attorney Elias de Wadeworth). On 20 August [1336] at Paris Orleton acknowledged the receipt of 100 marks from the merchants of the Peruzzi as part payment of his expenses. E.43/100 (endorsed: 'Allocatur secundo die Septembris anno decimo ').

matic career therefore concluded on a note of failure: the Hundred Years' War was imminent.[65]

As will be evident from what has been written above, our knowledge of the intricacies of diplomatic negotiations and the part played in them by individuals is severely limited by the nature of the materials available. We know much about the formal and less formal documents, the comings and goings of envoys and the expenses they incurred, but are quite unable to apportion praise or blame for the outcome of particular negotiations. It must, of course, be kept in mind that the authority of *nuncii* was strictly limited by the instructions they received from the government at home.[66] There are instances of blame being attached to individuals for specific policies, but they are scarcely reliable. Thus the unpopular Scottish treaty, the 'turpis pax' of Northampton (1328), was set at the door of Isabella and Mortimer, to whose names the chronicler Baker gratuitously added Orleton's.[67] One account records that Orleton himself berated Stratford for fabricating an oath of homage without consultation,[68] and the archbishop in similar vein sought to incriminate the sponsors of the mission undertaken by Orleton and Northburgh in May 1328.[69] Claims and insinuations of this sort are infrequent and invariably generated by political heat. In Orleton's case it can be argued that his continued employment in the diplomatic sphere bespeaks a measure of success, but also of political compatibility: he exhibited a remarkable capacity for survival. We see him rubbing shoulders with the older generation of diplomatists, represented by such men as William Ayrminne, John Stratford and John de Schordich, as well as with Bartholomew Burghersh, who saw much service from 1327,[70] and the newcomers to political influence in the post-Mortimer era: William de Montacute, William de Clinton and, among the bishops, Richard de Bury.

65 *Foedera* 2, iii, p. 150; Chaplais, 'Le Duché-Pairie de Guyenne', pp. 159–60.

66 On this topic see particularly Lucas, 'Diplomatic Intercourse', pp. 302–5.

67 *Chronicon*, pp. 40–1.

68 *Birchington*, p. 40. Stratford subsequently swore that he was innocent of any such fault: *Winchester Chartulary*, pp. 219–20, no. 518.

69 *Birchington*, p. 29: 'Quae quidem legatio maximam guerrae praesentis materiam ministravit.' Some of Stratford's other comments on the origins of the war are instructive.

70 The bishop of Lincoln's brother, imprisoned by Edward II in 1321, for whom see Cuttino, *Diplomatic Administration*, pp. 137–8.

It will be noticed too that in this later period of his career Orleton's principal area of operation shifted decisively from the Curia to the French court, where hindsight reveals a steady drift towards war, however camouflaged by projects of matrimonial alliance and perpetual peace, or somewhat impractical gestures in the direction of crusade.

Orleton's retirement from diplomacy in 1336 is probably to be attributed as much to the onset of old age and its concomitant debility as to any loss of confidence in the value of his services.[71] He may have been as old as sixty and his eyesight was failing; the strenuous journeys to and from the continent were becoming too much for him. Instead, he turned belatedly to the diocesan work which his other commitments had for too long crowded out. Even then it is clear that his energies were by no means exhausted.

[71] On Orleton's health at about this time see Haines, 'Orleton and Winchester', pp. 2–3.

Chapter 3

THE DIOCESAN BISHOP

HEREFORD 1317–1327

Adam Orleton's was no ordinary episcopate. As we have seen, its early stages were disrupted by frequent missions abroad, and when these came to an end with the bishop's alleged involvement in rebellion, there ensued the loss of his temporalities and some lengthy periods of exile at the Hereford chapter's rectory of Shinfield in Berkshire. In the circumstances it is remarkable that so much routine business was accomplished and equally remarkable that we know what we do about it, for the episcopal records were carried off by an over-zealous royal yeoman, John of Towcester – a fact which may account for some of the irregularities in the latter part of the register which has come down to us. More than twenty years later the then bishop, John Trillek, who had been only too well aware of his uncle's misfortunes, returned a royal writ to the effect that he did not have access to Orleton's registers, which had been stolen and never recovered.[1] This despite the fact that Orleton had issued a commission – to be found among the entries for 1325 – for the absolution of the perpetrator of this sacrilege.[2]

Having made profession of obedience at Canterbury and received his spiritualities, Orleton presented his bulls of promotion to the king at Nottingham. Despite his earlier irritation, Edward

[1] *Hereford Reg. Trillek*, p. 91 (3 December 1346): 'Ad manus non habemus.' On 17 August 1348 Trillek was still complaining of the loss of Orleton's muniments: 'cujus registra fuerunt ablata et deperdita et nunquam sibi nec successoribus suis restituta' (*ibid.* p. 317). In this instance the Thomas Dobyn enquired about does not appear in the extant register anyway. Trillek was able on 2 November 1349 to certify that he had successfully searched the register (*ibid.* pp. 325–6: cf. *H.R.O.*, p. 388). It is interesting to note that Trillek, as Orleton's executor, was in possession (29 April 1347) of his Worcester register also (*ibid.* pp. 297–8).

[2] *H.R.O.*, pp. 323–4. The commissary was Gilbert de Middleton. Orleton had himself been in possession of at least the ordination lists, now lost, on 27 November 1326 (*not* 1327), *ibid.* p. 371.

is said to have received him cordially (' benigne ') and writs for the livery of the temporalities were issued on 23 July 1317.

Instead of hastening to take up his charge the new bishop travelled to Thame in Oxfordshire. There he dedicated five altars in the prebendal church, which about this time underwent extensive alterations to the south wall of the chancel and the north and south aisles of the nave. At first sight his action appears strange, but the newly appointed prebendary was M. Gilbert de Middleton – a fellow envoy at the Council of Vienne – who was to be named in the archdeacon of Canterbury's commission for Orleton's enthronement.[3] So it was not until the third week in September that Orleton crossed the borders of the diocese to his enthronement in the cathedral church on Sunday 2 October.[4] It is unlikely to have been mere coincidence that this date was shortly to be officially allocated to the feast of St Thomas de Cantilupe. Almost at once the bishop received an urgent summons to the king's council. Hastily appointing M. Richard de Vernon his vicar-general[5] he set off for the capital, which he reached by the first week in November.[6] Almost three months elapsed before his return.[7]

Within the diocese Orleton's most pressing problems were of a jurisdictional and financial character. Complaints were flooding in concerning the improper activities of Archbishop Reynolds's sede vacante agent, one Gilbert de Sedgeford,[8] a bigamist[9] who had lodged his wife in Hereford, where many of the bishop's subjects had felt obliged to bring her gifts! Orleton composed a polite but vigorously-phrased letter to the archbishop and ex-

3 *Le Neve* 2, p. 1; *Canterbury Professions*, p. 93 (*recte* 30 June); *H.R.O.*, pp. 8, 9, 16, 21–2, 32. Orleton collated the prebend of Hinton to Middleton in the following year after removal of the pluralist claimant, William de Knapton. *Ibid.* pp. 79–81, 83–4.

4 *H.R.O.*, pp. 26–7, 31–3.

5 *H.R.O.*, pp. 43–4: 28 October 1317.

6 *H.R.O.*, p. 43.

7 He was at Awre on 20 January 1318; at English Bicknor on 25 January, *H.R.O.*, fo. 16^r.

8 *H.R.O.*, pp. 23–5, 29–30. The archbishop's sede vacante appointments are in Canterbury Reg. Reynolds, fo. 88^{r-v}. M. Adam Carbonel was deputed to carry out visitation (27 March 1317) and to act as official (same date). He was replaced by M. Stephen de Ledbury (28 April). M. Walter de Penebrugg' (Pembridge) was made sequestrator (27 March and 13 April). Sedgeford received Carbonel's oath of faithful administration on behalf of Reynolds. Only Sedgeford was not a ' local man '.

9 *H.R.O.*, p. 29: ' Quendam bigamum ministrum detestabilem.' This was in the medieval sense of someone who married a second time.

pressed his intention of following it up with a personal interview at the forthcoming convocation.[10] He invoked the topical example of Bishop Cantilupe who – faced with similarly unjust mandates – had not scrupled to make a personal appeal to the Holy See, the justice of his case being amply demonstrated by signs and miracles. Reynolds's initial reaction was to accuse Orleton of fostering resistance to the payment of his lawful dues, but once the full facts became known he suspended their collection and then promised redress in a cordial and mollifying letter. It could have been as much for Reynolds's information as his own that Orleton instructed the rural deans to discover what portion of Gilbert's exactions had been used for the archbishop's purposes, and what portion for his own. And so the matter ended with a show of goodwill on both sides.[11]

The bishop's introductory exchange of pleasantries with the dean of Hereford [12] rapidly gave way to the more serious business which earlier in 1317 had been Orleton's concern at Avignon. Arrears of two papal tenths [13] had to be collected and the proceeds passed to the king as a loan. In addition Cardinals Gaucelme d'Eauze and Luca Fieschi, in England on an abortive peace-making mission to the Scots, were pressing for their procurations.[14] Dean John de Aquablanca urged that this threefold task of collection was an intolerable burden. Cardinals' procurations, he declared, had always been a matter for the bishop's officials, not for the chapter. What was more, he argued, the rural deans and other clergy would not obey him, which in view of the penalties involved might prove extremely dangerous. The bishop admitted the practice of collection by the official but claimed that the circumstances were peculiar in that there had been no time to set up his administration. In a well-articulated answer, fortified

10 *H.R.O.*, pp. 29–30: 'Adeo quod multi nostri subditi collatis muneribus uxori sue, quam secum in Herefordia tenuit, vexacionem suam redimere sunt exacti.' The reply is dated 28 September [1317].

11 *H.R.O.*, pp. 35–6, 37–8. The mandate to the rural deans is dated 17 October 1317. In it the archbishop's agent is described as the *tabellio* (notary) of the official.

12 *H.R.O.*, pp. 1–2.

13 *H.R.O.*, pp. 2–3 (writ dated 10 June 1317 for the continued collection of the first year of the sexennial tenth on the king's behalf), 17–18. In fact the additional tenth of 1317 was not in arrears, being due for payment in 1318. Lunt, *Financial Relations* I, p. 405.

14 *H.R.O.*, pp. 9–14, 17–20, 28, 44–6; H.C.M., nos. 1366–7, 1854; *C.C.R.* 1313–18, pp. 479–80.

by a mixture of law, precedent and common sense, he deftly swept away the dean's arguments one by one and at the same time repudiated the suggestion of innovation on his own part. Here again acrimony is lacking, but the chapter had none the less to comply with Orleton's wishes.[15]

In the case of the annual tenth of 1317 the dean and chapter acted as deputy collectors for the whole diocese, but for securing the proceeds of the sexennial tenth imposed at the Council of Vienne they were associated with the abbot of Wigmore. The latter was responsible for the archdeaconry of Shropshire, but whether from negligence (as Orleton averred), or from the difficulties of collection (as the abbot claimed), he failed to raise even a quarter of the amount due.[16] But the king's needs were urgent and his merchant creditors were demanding their money.[17] November 1317 saw Bartholomew Badlesmere's messengers kicking their heels in Hereford, while the allowance for their return journey dwindled to nothing. They had been promised £300, yet by June of the following year only £100 had been delivered by the dean and chapter and a niggardly £17 by the abbot of Wigmore; all this despite the bishop's repeated admonitions.[18] In addition to all the other taxes Peter's Pence were being levied and Rigaud d'Assier, the papal collector, threatened to proceed against the bishop if they were not paid at his London house by the feast of St Martin (11 November). Copies of Rigaud's mandate were promptly despatched for execution by the long-suffering dean of Hereford and the two archdeacons.[19]

As soon as circumstances permitted Orleton took up the task of visitation. At the end of March 1318 he commissioned his official to correct the offences discovered in three rural deaneries of the

15 *H.R.O.*, pp. 17–18: 25 August 1317.

16 *H.R.O.*, pp. 53–4, 55–6. The sum outstanding for the archdeaconry of Shropshire was £114 2s 11½d.

17 See, for instance, *C.C.R.* 1318–23, pp. 33–4.

18 H.C.M., nos. 1366–9, 1854 (cf. *C.C.R.* 1313–18, pp. 479–80). Acquittances were issued as follows: 3 February 1318, £300; 1 May, £80; 18 February 1321, £12 and £312 (i.e. the original £300 + £12); *C.P.R.* 1317–21, pp. 77, 136, 560, 562.

19 *H.R.O.*, pp. 40–1; cf. pp. 298–9, 302. Orleton himself acted as Rigaud d'Assier's commissioner for the collection of annates in Hereford and the four Welsh dioceses. On 6 November 1317 in London he contracted (under obligation of his personal goods and those of his see) to pay the first-fruits due on his own account. See Lunt, *Financial Relations* 1, pp. 494–9, and *Papal Collectors*, pp. 5–6; *H.R.O.*, pp. 43, 64, 68–70.

southern archdeaconry – Hereford.[20] The bishop's personal involvement was suspended between mid-May and the end of October by reason of his diplomatic duties. On his return Orleton empowered M. Richard de Sidenhale to proceed to the correction of *comperta*.[21] This points to a winding up of the visitation process, although one piece of evidence suggesting that it continued elsewhere is Orleton's subsequent letter claiming that he was too busy in the northern part of his diocese to attend the consecration of Stephen Gravesend, the bishop of London.[22]

At Hereford it was not customary for the bishop to visit the cathedral chapter because of the latter's long-standing immunity, but it looks as though Orleton intended to break the tradition. While at the Curia he secured a bull from Pope John, dated 14 January 1320, authorising him to visit and correct the chapter and choir clerks, notwithstanding the compromise made in the time of Bishop Peter d'Aigueblanche almost seventy years before.[23] More pacific counsels must have prevailed, there being no evidence of an attempt to implement the bull.[24] However, minor indications of parochial visitation in both 1320–1 [25] and 1324–5 [26] suggest that Orleton tried to maintain the triennial obligation.

It was as a monastic reformer that Orleton proved especially active. Pope John entrusted him with the reformation of St Mary's Priory, Abergavenny, in Llandaff diocese, the parlous state of which had brought complaints from the patron.[27] The bishop completed the process by securing the appointment as prior of the distinguished Worcester monk–scholar Richard de Bromwich.[28] His efforts to revitalise the priory of St Guthlac at Hereford, a cell of St Peter's, Gloucester, earned him the permanent hatred of its head, William Irby, a man defamed for his dissolute life in

20 *H.R.O.*, pp. xix, 68, 82–3.
21 *H.R.O.*, pp. 81–2.
22 *H.R.O.*, p. 87: 'in remotioribus partibus nostre diocesis prope Salopiam.'
23 *C.P.L.* 1305–42, p. 196. Bishop Aigueblanche's arrangement is printed in *Hereford Cathedral Charters*, pp. 95–101 (22 February 1253). In 1427 Bishop Spofford was also to contemplate a visitation of the chapter. See K. Edwards, *English Secular Cathedrals*, p. 132; Bannister, *Cathedral Church of Hereford*, pp. 176–80.
24 Though in April 1325 Orleton acknowledged the receipt of eight marks as visitatorial procurations (for 1324) from the dean and chapter's churches of Baysham and Diddlebury. H.C.M., no. 1374.
25 *H.R.O.*, pp. 172–4, 180.
26 *H.R.O.*, pp. 287–8, 339 [?]; H.C.M., no. 1374.
27 *C.P.L.* 1305–42, pp. 186, 211.
28 *H.R.O.*, pp. 151–5, 190–4.

the company of seculars and his wastage of the priory's goods.[29] Here too he had paved the way by securing a bull which overrode the privileges claimed by St Peter's with respect to its dependent houses.[30] It would seem that Orleton sought to replace Irby by Thomas de Burghill and that Irby appealed to the king on the grounds that the priory was in royal patronage. Irby was granted protection for two years on 23 December 1321.[31] For the Mortimer foundation of Wigmore Abbey Orleton drew up detailed regulations and entrusted its government to the prior of Wormsley, whose position he also filled. The former abbot, Philip le Galeys, resigned in the bishop's presence and that of both Mortimers.[32] When Philip of Montgomery, the prior of Chirbury, failed to respond to Orleton's monitions, he too was removed.[33] As a disciplinary measure the diocesan made particular use of the regulation whereby religious could be removed from one house to another of the same order, and for this purpose Orleton enlisted the aid of neighbouring bishops. Cobham, bishop of Worcester, co-operated readily enough; not so John Droxford, the Bath and Wells diocesan, who was so far reluctant to induce the abbot of Keynsham to comply that Orleton sought papal assistance, whereupon John XXII directed the archbishop to see that the canon-law regulation was obeyed.[34] But rigour could be tempered with forgiveness, as in the instance of the penitent monk, Henry Cays, whom Orleton asked the abbot of Flaxley to receive as a prodigal son.[35]

Action with respect to parochial benefices was almost equally vigorous. In 1318, following his primary visitation, Orleton directed his commissary-general, M. Richard de Sidenhale, to require all benefice holders to be resident within two months and to put their buildings in a proper state of repair.[36] The portionists of Westbury church who had neglected to proceed to the necessary holy orders were declared to have thereby forfeited their

29 *H.R.O.*, pp. 199–200, 258–9, 275–7, 285–6 and index *s.v.*

30 *C.P.L.* 1305–42, p. 196: 14 January 1320.

31 *C.P.R.* 1321–24, pp. 41, 49.

32 In December 1318. *H.R.O.*, pp. 90–4, 99–102 and index *s.v.* Wigmore.

33 *H.R.O.*, pp. 172–3, 212, 215–16, 226–7, 228–9.

34 *H.R.O.*, pp. 94–5, 98–9, 103–4, 107–8.

35 *H.R.O.*, pp. 204–5.

36 *H.R.O.*, p. 86. Cf. pp. 134–5 for a rarely-recorded process against a vicar absent in violation of his oath of residence.

portions.[37] Various entries in Orleton's episcopal register argue energetic implementation of the constitution *Execrabilis*[38] against plurality[39] and of the diocesan's obligation to provide for the cure of souls when neglected by an appropriator, an absentee incumbent, or one past the age of personal ministry.[40] Other entries betoken a careful use of the regulation *Cum ex eo*, enabling rectors to be temporarily absent for study,[41] and of *Super cathedram*,[42] which provided for the licensing of friars to preach and hear confessions.[43] The ordination lists are missing, which precludes us from knowing the extent to which the bishop carried out this task in person.[44] Overall Orleton's regimen, as one might expect of a canonist, is marked by a determination to ensure that ecclesiastical law was known and obeyed.

Orleton's register contains surprisingly few of those complex processes engendered by the appropriation of parish churches or the foundation of chantries. In fact only two appropriations of rectories within the diocese are entered[45] – those of Avenbury to

37 *H.R.O.*, p. 180. There was no personal animus in Orleton's action; he promised help to Richard de Ludlow, one of those deprived, should he visit the Curia again. *Ibid.* p. 184.

38 *Extrav. John XXII*, t. 3, c. 1 [1317]; *Extrav. Commun.* 3, 2, c. 4.

39 E.g. *H.R.O.*, pp. 59, 382–3.

40 *H.R.O.*, pp. 57, 62, 172, 173–4, 224, 267, 281–2, 352, 364.

41 *H.R.O.*, pp. 31, 352–3 and the table of dispensations at pp. 390–2. An interesting case (*ibid.* pp. 293–4) concerns M. Hugh de Barewe who when in his eighteenth year had been instituted to the church of Aston Ingham and then, after ordination to the sub-diaconate within a year (as the canon required), enjoyed its fruits (apart from those allotted to a vicar) for five years on the basis (' pretextu ') of a *Cum ex eo* licence. Having resigned the church he was directed by the papal penitentiary to repay the fruits when his circumstances permitted. On the other hand, Richard Baret, vicar of Bromyard (and hence ineligible for the *Cum ex eo* licence[s?] granted by Swinfield), was absent for fourteen years while studying at Oxford, and though made to resign his vicarage was allowed to keep the income he had received. *C.P.L.* 1305–42, p. 197; *Hereford Reg. Swinfield*, p. 545; *Biog. Oxon.*, *s.v.* Baret. The date of Baret's dispensatory bull (14 January 1320) suggests that Orleton had a hand in the matter.

42 *Clement.* 3, 7, c. 2 *Dudum* (incorporating *Super cathedram*); cf. *Extrav. Commun.* 3, 6, c. 2.

43 The register contains a variety of forms for use in such cases: *H.R.O.*, pp. 338–9.

44 He seems to have held his initial ordination ceremony at Bromyard, 24 September 1317. *H.R.O.*, pp. 17, 27. He held several ordinations at Reading during his ' exile ', e.g. *H.R.O.*, pp. 350, n. 1, 350–1, 352–3; *Hereford Reg. Trillek*, p. 91. See also *H.R.O.*, p. 325, for ordinations elsewhere.

45 The Shinfield (Berkshire) process is entered (*H.R.O.*, pp. 158–61, 162–3) and the appropriation by the bishop of London of Bedfont church to the Trinitarians of Hounslow (*ibid.* pp. 161–2). The latter was apparently intended as an exemplar for Shinfield.

the Cistercian monks of Dore [46] and Wolferlow to the nuns of Aconbury [47] – and no chantry foundations. It would seem that the bishop kept an eye on appropriators; for instance, he commissioned his official to enquire into the report that the prior of Llanthony had neglected to provide for the cure of souls at Orcop,[48] and the rector of Dorstone to ascertain whether the prioress of Aconbury had assigned a sufficient portion for the newly-appropriated church of Bridge Sollers.[49]

The highlight of the episcopate was undoubtedly the canonisation of Thomas de Cantilupe, which Orleton himself had done much to set forward. This protracted undertaking [50] culminated in the issue of John XXII's bull of canonisation, a formal *inspeximus* of which took place in Orleton's presence early in September 1320. Before the end of the month the good news was circulated to the diocese with details of the papal indulgences, to which the bishop added one of his own.[51] Preparations were already well in hand for the construction of a new shrine to which the body of the saint could be translated with appropriate ceremony.[52]

Ironically, popular devotion to Cantilupe had reached its peak some years earlier, perhaps in 1307 when the papal commissioners were engaged in sifting the evidence for his sanctity.[53] Substan-

46 *H.R.O.*, pp. 174–6, 197, 202–4.

47 The Hereford official in an undated document ordered the rural dean of Frome to execute Orleton's mandate (Canterbury, 13 March 1320) for enquiry as to the value of Wolferlow: S.C.1/49/109 (180v). See also *H.R.O.*, p. 276.

48 *H.R.O.*, p. 62.

49 *H.R.O.*, p. 254. The church had been appropriated in Swinfield's time. See *Hereford Reg. Swinfield*, pp. 505–6.

50 Seven hundred folios are said to have been transcribed from originals: H.C.M., no. 1443. For the whole process see *Acta Sanctorum mensis Octobris* 1, pp. 539–705.

51 The bull is printed in *Hereford Cathedral Charters*, pp. 190–4; cf. *C.P.L.* 1305–42, p. 199. The notarial instrument attesting the *inspeximus* at Bosbury is dated 3 September 1320 (H.C.M., no. 1445). Orleton informed the archbishop on the same day and his diocese on the 20th (*H.R.O.*, pp. 139–40, 142–3). Various indulgences were issued by other bishops including Roger Martival of Salisbury (H.C.M., no. 1429; *Hereford Cathedral Charters*, p. 194); John Langton of Chichester (H.C.M., no. 1430); John Droxford of Bath and Wells (H.C.M., no. 1428); and Archbishop William Melton of York (H.C.M., no. 1431). See also H.C.M., no. 3214, for later indulgences. Reynolds exhorted his province to help the agents of the Hereford bishop and chapter in their quest for funds towards the shrine of St Thomas and the cathedral fabric (H.C.M., no. 1444); the king likewise ordered his bailiffs to render them every assistance (H.C.M., no. 1435; *C.P.R.* 1317–21, p. 526).

52 *Hereford Cathedral Charters*, pp. 195–6; H.C.M., nos. 1436–7, 1440.

53 *Acta Sanctorum mensis Octobris* 1, p. 592. This argument is advanced by Yates, 'Fabric Rolls of Hereford Cathedral', pp. 80–1.

tial funds were required for the cathedral fabric: bishop and chapter were engaged in an extensive building programme, a legacy from the previous century.[54] Because the masons or architects had pronounced the ancient foundations sound, a superstructure had been erected at a cost of 20,000 marks. Only when this was built did the defective nature of the foundations become evident; allegedly the whole building was threatened with collapse.[55] Such was the burden of the petition which in 1320 determined Pope John to appropriate Shinfield church in Berkshire to the Hereford chapter. In the long run the income it provided was to be of more benefit to the fabric fund than the offerings at Cantilupe's tomb.[56] As some return for his labours in the cause of both canonisation and appropriation, the tithes of Shinfield were leased to Orleton for £20 a year, with the obligation to keep the fabric in repair.[57]

The temporalities of the bishopric gave rise to some serious concern. In the early stages of his episcopate Orleton petitioned the king and council for the restoration of three vills, appurtenances of his manor of Bishops Castle, which Hugh Audley the elder claimed as belonging to his castle of Montgomery; this despite the fact that the previous bishop, Swinfield, had held them, and on his death the royal escheator, M. John Walwayn. On 1 March 1318 Walwayn was ordered to recover the lands and to restore them to the bishop.[58] Four years later, when Orleton was away at the York parliament, a band of marauders raided his manors of Ross and Upton, drove off stock, removed crops, and burnt timber for charcoal in his woods.[59] Worse was to come.

The whole complexion of the episcopate was changed with the confiscation of the temporalities in 1324. In March of that year the bishop's old adversary, William Irby, prior of St Guthlac's, was granted custody jointly with the royal escheator, John de Hampton.[60] Even Shinfield passed for a time into the hands of John of Towcester.[61] But the custodians by no means had it all

54 Yates, *op. cit.* p. 84; *H.R.O.*, p. 158.

55 *H.R.O.*, p. 158; *C.P.L.* 1305–42, p. 196. These constitute the arguments in the chapter's petition for Shinfield's appropriation.

56 See Yates, *op. cit.* pp. 79–80.

57 H.C.M., nos. 2269–70; *Hereford Cathedral Charters*, pp. 207–8.

58 S.C.8/203/10138ᵛ; *C.C.R.* 1313–18, pp. 529, 588.

59 *H.R.O.*, pp. 227–8, 231–3.

60 *C.P.R.* 1321–24, p. 398.

61 *C.F.R.* 1319–27, p. 269.

their own way. A group of the bishop's friends and associates, including his clerical brothers Thomas and John, were deemed responsible for driving off stock from the episcopal manors. In May 1324 a commission of oyer and terminer was set up to try them.[62] The fact that as late as 12 October John Inge was deputed to survey the lands of the bishopric and to appraise the crops and stock suggests that possession was not easily obtained.[63] A further raid, this time on the manor of Bishops Castle, occurred early in the following year, 1325, when forty brood mares were driven off.[64]

The activities of the custodians were almost certainly responsible for the insertion in the episcopal register of Archbishop Winchelsey's hard-hitting mandate of 1298, which declared excommunicate all who encroached upon ecclesiastical property or placed violent hands upon clerical persons. Significantly it is closely followed by a mandate for use against those carrying off ecclesiastical muniments.[65]

Open conflict erupted when Orleton attempted to visit part of the diocese in the spring of 1324. He was celebrating mass for the feast of St George in Ross parish church[66] when William Irby and his associates broke in uttering blasphemous words and disrupting the process of visitation – or so it was alleged. Orleton excommunicated him on the spot and asked Bishop Cobham to publish the sentence also, for Irby was a monk of St Peter's, Gloucester, within Worcester diocese.[67] The case is an interesting one. Irby made tuitory appeal to the Court of Canterbury[68] but unsuccessfully, for the case was remitted to the diocesan, who renewed his denunciation.[69] As there was no opportunity for further legal process, Irby sought out Orleton in London and asked for absolution. The bishop could not refuse a penitent willing to obey the Church's mandates, so he issued a commission

62 *C.P.R.* 1321–24, p. 452.

63 *C.P.R.* 1324–27, p. 33.

64 *Ibid.* p. 137.

65 *H.R.O.*, pp. 288–93.

66 The rector of Ross was James de Henley, canon of Hereford, who was implicated with Orleton in the 1321–2 revolt. See *H.R.O.*, pp. 42–3.

67 *H.R.O.*, pp. 285–6. Irby rendered his account as sacrist of St Peter's for 1314–16 and early in 1316 is mentioned as cellarer. *Cartularium Gloucestriae* 1, pp. 152–3; 3, pp. 272–3.

68 *H.R.O.*, pp. 297–8, 305.

69 *H.R.O.*, pp. 305–6: 2 August 1324.

for that purpose on 17 August. At the same time he made it clear that he could do nothing about any excommunication which Irby had incurred ipso facto; from such only the pope could absolve him.[70] As some of those named in Orleton's mandate were absent, its execution was delayed. Irby complained of this to the Court of Canterbury, thus forcing Orleton to issue a further mandate to the same effect from London.[71]

The vindictiveness of Orleton's opponents is vouched for by contemporary accounts. The Bridlington chronicler's version of the sentence against the younger Despenser charges him with the spoliation of the goods not only of Orleton, but also of Burghersh, Hothum and Ayrminne, bishops of Lincoln, Ely and Norwich respectively.[72] Knighton also records the charge.[73] Blaneforde gives a graphic description of the bishop's plight – his goods thrown into the highway to be looted by passers-by. All of this, he says, Orleton suffered with patience.[74]

Whatever Despenser's responsibility may have been, there can be no question about the culpability of the 'custodians', though it was only after a considerable interval that a royal writ addressed to John Inge, William Irby and John of Towcester inhibited their proceedings. It had come to his notice, the king declared, that under cover of their commission they had removed episcopal ornaments and sacerdotal vestments, prohibited the dean and chapter, as well as others, from communicating with Bishop Orleton, and forbidden anyone to receive him as a guest, to provide him with food or drink, or even to confess their sins to him. They were instructed to restore all the items which pertained to the spirituality and to desist from interfering with the bishop in the performance of his spiritual office.[75]

70 *H.R.O.*, pp. 307–8.

71 *H.R.O.*, pp. 308–9: 11 [not 12] November 1324.

72 *Bridlington*, p. 88. This accords with the Chancery version (in French): C.49/roll 11.

73 *Knighton*, p. 439 (French). Taylor, 'Judgment on Hugh Despenser', pp. 72–5, collates the Pipewell Chronicle's version with five other MSS. (including two of Knighton). A further MS., from Durham, has been edited by Holmes, 'Judgement on the Younger Despenser', pp. 264–7.

74 *Blaneforde*, p. 142.

75 *Salisbury Reg. Martival* 3, pp. 155–6, nos. 537–8. For Inge, a supporter of the Despensers, see Fryde, 'Edward III's Removal of His Ministers', p. 158. Orleton himself blamed Edward's 'Herodiana sevicia' for orders to prevent the bishop's subjects from communicating with him. B.L. Cotton MS. Vitellius E. IV 9.

In circumstances such as these regular diocesan work became impossible. The bishop spent many months of 1324 in London, and from about the end of May until November of 1325 he seems to have been chiefly at Shinfield, of which he regained possession in April.[76] Even there he was not at rest. Early in 1326 the bishop of Salisbury directed none other than William of Pagula, the learned author of the compendious *Oculus sacerdotis*, to sequestrate the goods belonging to Shinfield and its chapel of Swallowfield on account of notorious defects. An enquiry revealed that the cost of putting everything to rights would amount to over £40. Technically Orleton, as the lessee, would appear to have been responsible, but it was the dean and chapter of Hereford who undertook to remedy the defects in the chancel by Pentecost and those of the rectory and its buildings by the feast of St Michael.[77] This enabled the archdeacon of Berkshire to relax the sequestration.[78]

Quite apart from his own statement of them,[79] there is ample evidence of Orleton's financial difficulties. At the beginning of his episcopate he had surrendered his claim to dilapidations in his manors and had agreed to pay £744 for stock to the executors of his predecessor, Richard Swinfield. After Orleton's death Swinfield's executors were still owed £500, and it was claimed that on account of the delay the real loss was double that amount.[80]

76 He was in London for most of March 1324 and for the beginning of April (*H.R.O.*, fos. 75^{v}–76^{v}, pp. 277–9, 281). He is to be found at Thame (not 'Stane' as in the printed edition) in mid-July (*ibid.* fo. 82^{r}, p. 305). He was in London on 17 August and at the end of October (*ibid.* pp. 308, 311) and still there in mid- and late-November (*ibid.* fos. 83^{r}, 84^{r}, pp. 308–9, 312). For May–22 October 1325 see *H.R.O.*, fos. 90^{r}–91^{r}, pp. 326ff; for December, *ibid.* p. 320. Mandate for Shinfield's release: *C.C.R.* 1323–27, p. 92.

77 *H.R.O.*, pp. 318–9: 3 January 1326. Pagula's certificate (*ibid.* pp. 348–9) is dated 13 February from Winkfield. Orleton is not mentioned, but the dean and chapter were represented by M. Thomas de Boleye.

78 Martival, on the promise that the defects would be remedied, relaxed the sequestration on 15 February 1326: *H.R.O.*, p. 353. The archdeacon issued his mandate for that purpose to Pagula on the following day (*ibid.* p. 354).

79 In his letter to Cobham early in 1320 he speaks of the 'expensarum intollerabilium onera': *Worcester Reg. Cobham*, p. 80. See also *H.R.O.*, pp. 58–9, 64–5.

80 H.C.M., no. 1378 (*c.* 1345). According to this document Orleton on 27 March 1318 bound himself at Sugwas to certain named canons for the sum of £100, and then on 1 February 1320 (*recte* 1321?) at Shinfield for a further £400. Roger de Breynton, one of Swinfield's executors, produced the original evidences but agreed to forego the additional loss. The earlier part of Orleton's Hereford episcopate coincided with a period of economic depression. See Ian Kershaw, 'The Great Famine

Shortly before Queen Isabella's landing Orleton appeared once more in his diocese, to officiate at the burial of the elder Roger Mortimer who had died a prisoner in the Tower. In November 1326 he returned in triumph to his cathedral city, and lodged the queen in his episcopal palace and the troublesome Irby in the adjoining gaol.[81] His sojourn in the wilderness was over.

WORCESTER 1327–1333

Orleton's tenure of the see of Worcester was not bedevilled either by misfortune or by political disgrace, but was none the less abnormal in certain respects. His frequent absences necessitated the issue of no fewer than five commissions to vicars-general [1] and in one instance he was away for well over a year at a stretch.[2] No other Worcester bishop could claim to have celebrated orders in the dioceses of Paris and Soissons; few can have spent so much time in London and its neighbourhood – at the episcopal house in the Strand, the manor of the Worcester bishops at Hillingdon, or some private manor, as Orleton's at Beaumes in Berkshire.[3]

As a consequence of the contemporary, or near-contemporary jingle which Henry Wharton copied into his *Anglia Sacra* and which is also to be found in the Harleian MS. copy of Murimuth's chronicle,[4] Orleton's progression from Hereford to Worcester and then to Winchester has been universally stigmatised as a measure of his cupidity. This is misleading. It should be remembered that within a few years so respected a pastoral bishop as John Thoresby was to follow a similar course, moving by way of

and Agrarian Crisis in England 1315–1322', in *Peasants, Knights and Heretics*, ed. R. H. Hilton, Cambridge 1976, pp. 85–132 (esp. p. 124).

81 *Wigmore Chronicle*, p. 351; *C.P.R.* 1324–27, p. 337; *C.C.R.* 1323–27, p. 620; *Knighton*, p. 437.

1 Enumerated in *Worc. Admin.*, p. 324, and with some discussion, *ibid.* p. 103, n. 4.

2 He was abroad from shortly after 11 November 1332 until 3 December 1333.

3 Beaumes had formerly belonged to the elder Despenser and was the first-fruit of Isabella's gratitude. Orleton's appointment of John de Bromfield as custodian is dated 9 November [1326]. See *H.R.O.*, p. 371, where the editor did not extend the 'B' of the MS. Beaumes was particularly convenient because it lay in Shinfield parish.

4 'Trigamus est Adam, ductus cupidine quadam./Thomam neclexit, Wolstanum non bene rexit,/Swithinum maluit. Cur? Quia plus valuit.' B.L. Harleian MS. 3836, fo. 50r (added at the foot of the folio). Cf. *Chronicon*, p. 54 (which has the last two lines). The first line in *Anglia Sacra* 1, pp. 533–4 ('ex archivis castri de Belvoir') runs: 'Trinus erat Adam: talem suspendere vadam.'

St David's (1347–9) and Worcester (1349–52) to York (1352–73). Unfortunately for Orleton's reputation double translations were a novelty in his day, but the practice is more justly attributable to papal policy – in particular that of John XXII – than to individual ambition, although personal influence in such matters cannot be wholly disregarded. Only Orleton's final move to Winchester can be looked upon as generous promotion and by that time, in the autumn of his days, he was content to play the part of a diocesan bishop almost to the exclusion of other matters.[5]

There is no doubt that the move to Worcester was of financial benefit: it could hardly have been otherwise. The official figures suggest that in normal times it would have been only marginally so,[6] but in this instance the Hereford temporalities had suffered at the hands of their hostile custodians and on resuming possession Orleton had been forced to borrow towards the repair of the buildings. The pope gave instructions that he was not to be molested for dilapidations that were no fault of his,[7] but Orleton's Worcester register shows that he was attempting to raise five hundred marks from the sale of his goods and chattels to reimburse Thomas Charlton, his successor at Hereford, and that he borrowed £160 from a Salisbury cloth merchant.[8] Secular business and that of his church proved an additional expense: one of the

[5] Thoresby's successor at St David's, Reginald Brian, likewise moved to Worcester and thence to Ely. Prior to John XXII's pontificate there were only twenty-one provisions to the seventeen English sees. The development of reservation and translation enabled John to provide bishops to English dioceses on eighteen occasions. For papal policy in this matter see Smith, *Episcopal Appointments*, esp. ch. 1. As for Orleton's financial position at Winchester, Titow shows (from the Winchester pipe rolls) that, as it turned out, the period of his episcopate was a bad one from the point of view of the yields of wheat, barley and oats. See *Winchester Yields*, esp. graph on p. 145. Moreover, the papal *servicia* were particularly heavy: Lunt, *Financial Relations* 2, pp. 752–3 (where 1,200 florins is a slip for 12,000), 826.

[6] The temporalities of Worcester and Hereford were assessed in the 1291 *Taxatio* at £485 and £449 respectively (not including certain 'immobilia et mobilia'). In the fourteenth century the *servicia* due for Worcester amounted to 2,000 florins, for Hereford 1,800. The situation was substantially altered by 1535 when in the *Valor* Worcester was assesed at £1,049, Hereford at £768. See Lunt, *Financial Relations* 1, p. 499; 2, app. 2, pp. 721ff; *Hereford Reg. Swinfield*, pp. 281–6; *H.R.O.*, p. xliv.

[7] *C.P.L.* 1305–42, p. 280; *Lettres communes Jean XXII*, no. 30267. The pope's letter was directed to the abbots of Dore and Evesham and to the prior of Llanthony. Orleton was not to be molested on account of his temporalities 'quae per secularis potestatis negligentiam et malitiam ministrorum (qui per multos annos illa injuste detinuerunt occupata) sine culpa ipsius episcopi, aliqualiter deteriorata sunt'.

[8] *W.R.O.* 2, fos. 6^{r} [522], 12^{v} [583]. The 500 marks were for stock and each bishop was supposed to leave that sum for his successor. See *H.R.O.*, p. 39.

reasons advanced for the appropriation of Blockley to the episcopal *mensa* was the cost of journeying to and from London for such purposes.[9] But the heaviest and most immediate obligation was the sum promised to the pope and cardinals at the time of Orleton's translation. Half of it had to be met by 1 November 1328, the other half by 1 June of the following year. Payments of this kind were, of course, a regular feature at times of papal provision to the episcopate.[10] In the short term, then, the move to Worcester furnished no financial panacea; indeed Orleton even resorted to the expedient, unusual among Worcester bishops, of levying a charitable subsidy from the diocese.[11]

A problem which soon confronted the new diocesan was Archbishop Mepham's demand that he renew the profession made to his predecessor Reynolds. Orleton quite properly declined, drawing attention to the precedent established at the time of the similar claim by Archbishop Becket with respect to Gilbert Foliot on his translation to London (1163). In that instance Pope Alexander III had ruled that the initial profession remained binding. Orleton's opinion was the same as that of Prior Eastry, whom Mepham also consulted, although the prior did not cite the appropriate canonical authority.[12] The matter seems to have ended there.

Orleton's Worcester episcopate presents a number of difficulties, because the register is in some respects at least as defective as his Hereford one.[13] It is, for instance, far from explicit about the bishop's activity in the business of correction. It is possible that Orleton rushed through some sort of primary visitation following his enthronement at Worcester on 19 June 1328. Certainly he made an extensive sweep of the diocese during the

9 Worcester Reg. Montacute 1, fos. 11^{v}–12^{r}.

10 *H.R.O.*, p. 381. At Avignon, on 9 October 1327, Orleton promised 1,000 florins to the pope and a like sum to the cardinals – fourteen out of sixteen of whom were present – for the 'common services' and 357 florins 8s 5d for the five 'petty services'. Cf. Lunt, *Financial Relations* 1, ch. 5 and p. 681.

11 *W.R.O.* 2, fo. 9^{r} [550].

12 *W.R.O.* 2, fo. 10^{v} [559: undated]; *Lit. Cant.* 1, p. 276; *Canterbury Professions*, pp. lxxxv–lxxxvi (the author was not aware of this instance).

13 The first volume contains forty-three folios, the second fifty-seven (followed by two blank leaves). The ordination lists preface the first volume – an unusual arrangement. The quire of royal writs has slipped out and there is much duplication between the volumes.

following month, penetrating as far south as Gloucester. While in that area he visited Winchcombe Abbey, but ostensibly by specific request rather than in the regular process of visitation.[14]

A number of entries from 1329 suggest that the southern archdeaconry was undergoing visitation at that time. Injunctions were issued on 12 July for Winchcombe Abbey,[15] and a general mandate to the Gloucester archdeaconry may date from this period.[16] Muniments from the exempt abbey of Evesham were being scrutinised in July;[17] those of St Augustine's, Bristol, and of Horsley Priory late in the same year.[18] That Orleton visited Fairford deanery appears from his examination of the affair of Marston chapel where – to the detriment of the parish church – men from the curia of the lord, John de Meysey, had joined with other inhabitants for the celebration of mass and the sacraments. Orleton placed the chapel under an interdict but raised it on the intervention of his colleague Bishop Burghersh, who seems to have been a friend of John de Meysey's.[19] A commission for correction issued early in 1330 refers to Bristol deanery,[20] and the bishop's enquiry there could explain why Archbishop Winchelsey's mandate about St Giles's chapel is entered in the register.[21] Citation on 18 November of M. Nicholas de Gore, an absentee prebendary of Westbury, followed visitation of that college, from which procuration was being demanded on the 29th.[22]

Visitation was again under way during 1331. In July a mandate directed to the Bristol deanery could have been occasioned by Orleton's own observation, as it was issued from his nearby manor of Henbury.[23] If so, the Worcester archdeaconry must have been visited subsequently – an unusual if not unprecedented arrangement.[24] At any rate on 15 September the bishop dedicated

14 *W.R.O.* 2, fo. 8^v [544]: 29 July 1328.

15 *W.R.O.* 2, fos. 31^v–32^v [744].

16 *W.R.O.* 2, fo. 15^{r-v} [605: undated]. This concerns violation of the rector of Withington's close.

17 *W.R.O.* 2, fo. 15^r [603]: 16 July 1329.

18 *W.R.O.* 2, fo. 17^r [618]: 8 December 1329, citation of objectors to their privileges; *ibid.* fo. 12^r [578]: 11 December, commission for examination of witnesses.

19 *W.R.O.* 1, fo. 36^r [325]: 28 January 1330.

20 *W.R.O.* 2, fo. 34^v [764]: 8 January 1330.

21 *W.R.O.* 2, fo. 12^r [577]: among entries for 1329.

22 *W.R.O.* 2, fos. 16^{r-v}, 17^v [610, 614, 619].

23 *W.R.O.* 1, fo. 37^{r-v} [357]: 26 July 1331.

24 The normal arrangement was for the bishop to visit first his cathedral church, then the churches of the city, then the northern archdeaconry, and finally (usually in more cursory fashion) the southern one.

an altar at Alcester, celebrated mass there, and preached in the vernacular. The following day he dedicated the newly-built church at Sedgeberrow,[25] and marked the feast of St Clement, 23 November, by visiting half the Droitwich deanery in Tardebigge church.[26] Nothing more of this visitation transpires: the bishop was at either Ripple or Hartlebury during the month of December and left for London by way of Gloucestershire early in the new year.

Of Orleton's attention to monastic reform, of which we learn so much at Hereford, as well as at Winchester, there is scarcely a trace. Apart from the usual contact at times of ordination, visitation, or the election of heads of houses, the sole indication of his concern is provided by lengthy injunctions for Winchcombe Abbey, to which were attached the detailed regulations of Abbot Idbury for the distribution of income from the appropriated church of Enstone, assigned to the pittancer.[27]

The only conclusion that can safely be drawn from such fragmentary evidence seems to be that Orleton was by fits and starts active in reform, the determining factor being his commitments outside the diocese.

Fortunately the Worcester ordination lists have survived – unlike those of Hereford – to show that between 1328 and mid-1332 ordinations were conducted by Orleton in person. Thereafter he may have deputed a suffragan, but if so there is no trace of him. Three minor ordinations were celebrated at Beaumes in Berkshire, one in Paris, and two more at the abbey of Nogent l'Artaud in Soissons diocese.[28] At other times the number of orders conferred was extremely large, twice surpassing four hundred and on a third occasion three hundred.[29] The most notable ordinand was the scholar and future archbishop of Canterbury, Thomas Bradwardine, who was ordained priest to the title of the warden and 'scholars' of Merton at Pershore Abbey.[30] It so happens that this

25 *W.R.O.* 1, fo. 37v [366–7].

26 *W.R.O.* 1, fo. 38r [375].

27 *W.R.O.* 2, fos. 31v–32v [744].

28 *W.R.O.* 1, fos. 14r–15r [27–30].

29 More than four hundred were ordained on 17 June 1329 in Tewkesbury Abbey and 25 May 1331 in Campden parish church; 323 were ordained in the ordination of 24 September 1328 in St Mary's, Gloucester.

30 *W.R.O.* 1, fo. 13v [26p]. This was not known to Emden and the entry is worth quoting in full: 'Thomas le byer dictus de Bradwardyn ad titulum Roberti de Trenge custodis domus scolarium de Merton in Oxon' per dimissorias Cicestr' episcopi.'

was the last ordination before the bishop's final journey to Paris and Avignon, from which he was to return as bishop of Winchester.[31]

There was other business of an arduous and protracted nature. During Orleton's time at Worcester eight churches were appropriated, one of them, Blockley, to the bishopric or episcopal *mensa*, the remainder to religious houses, four of which – Llanthony, Cookhill, Tewkesbury and the cathedral priory itself – lay within the diocese.[32] The formal process of Duntisbourne's annexation to Dore Abbey is not in the episcopal register, although the Worcester chapter's assent is duly noted.[33]

No fewer than five of the eight appropriations were effected by papal bull, but in each case the bishop was executor.[34] In three instances – Dodderhill, Fairford and Longdon – papal authority was invoked to overcome episcopal intransigence. In Longdon's case Orleton was allegedly trying to barter consent to its union with Westminster for a restoration of diocesan authority over the abbey's dependent priory of Great Malvern, despite the fact that the Worcester bishops had already received a quid pro quo in the manor of Knightwick.[35]

Blockley's appropriation was Orleton's intimate concern. It had been held by papal provisees for some thirty years and at this time was in the possession of Jean Raymond de Comminges, cardinal-bishop of Porto.[36] To break this chain was not only in Orleton's interest but also in that of the Worcester bishops in general. The appropriation took place in 1333, for which year the register is blank, but a transcript is to be found in that of his successor.[37]

[31] The ordination was held on 13 June 1332. The next ordination in the register took place in Paris, on 19 December 1332: *W.R.O.* 1, fo. 14^{r}. There was no opportunity for holding further ordinations in England.

[32] See the list of appropriated churches in *Worc. Admin.*, pp. 255–7. Outside the diocese appropriations were as follows: Tetbury to Eynsham Abbey; Duntisbourne [Rous] to Dore Abbey; Longdon to Westminster Abbey.

[33] *W.R.O.* 2, fos. 16^{r-v}, 34^{v} [611, 616, 636, 767].

[34] See *Worc. Admin.*, pp. 244, 256. The churches appropriated in this way were Tetbury (1331), Blockley (1333), Dodderhill (1333), Longdon (1334), Fairford (1334). The date is that of effective appropriation.

[35] See Haines, 'Appropriation of Longdon Church', pp. 42–3; *Worc. Admin.*, pp. 29–30; *W.R.O.* 2, fo. 10^{r} [556–7].

[36] *Worc. Admin.*, pp. 216–17.

[37] Worcester Reg. Montacute 1, fos. 11^{v}–12^{r}; *C.P.L.* 1305–42, p. 382.

One extraneous appropriation found its way into Orleton's register, that of Bishopsteignton church to the *mensa* of John de Grandisson, bishop of Exeter. It is entered because Orleton was executor of the papal bull concerned.[38]

Canon law required that in cases of appropriation vicarages were to be assigned by the diocesan. Five such 'ordinations' are entered in Orleton's register. At Snitterfield the bishop had enquiry made as to the church's real value and then revised the astringent arrangement of Bishop Cobham who had resolved that the appropriators, the prior and convent of the Holy Sepulchre, Warwick, should reap as little advantage as possible from an annexation he had striven to prevent.[39] Another church appropriated by Cobham, St Andrew's, Pershore, had a vicarage portion set aside.[40] Of the churches appropriated in Orleton's own time, Tytherington, Duntisbourne and Fairford were provided with perpetual vicarages, though in the case of the last – appropriated by papal decree – the portion is laid down in the appropriation document.[41] At Astley, where the monks of St Taurin had been cited by various bishops from Reynolds onwards on account of their encroachment on the exiguous vicarial portion, Orleton attempted to ensure that the decisions of his predecessors were not flouted.[42]

Much of this was routine work, but the careful oversight of the bishop can be detected at a number of points. At first glance his action in particular cases, notably that of Snitterfield, suggests partiality for the religious, but it is more likely that he was attempting to administer the law as he, an expert, knew it. Longdon was a different matter; here the long-term interests of the see were felt to be at stake and Orleton did his utmost to be as obstructive as possible, in this following his predecessors at Worcester.

The bishop's register is complete enough to enable some deductions to be made about general trends. For instance, the record of institutions is instructive for the period 1328 to 1332. During that time remarkably few university graduates were instituted,

38 *W.R.O.* 2, fo. 55^{r-v} [944].
39 *Worc. Admin.*, p. 263; *W.R.O.* 1, fo. 22^{r-v}; 2, fo. 39^{r} [136, 804].
40 *W.R.O.* 1, fo. 39^{r-v} [397].
41 *W.R.O.* 2, fos. 43^{v}, 48^{v}; 1, fo. 39^{r}; 2, fos. 54^{v}–55^{r} [837, 884; 396 (838); 942].
42 *W.R.O.* 2, fos. 8^{v}–9^{r} [545].

in fact only four, one of them being the bishop's brother Thomas. Concurrently Orleton sought to improve clerical qualifications by implementing the relatively new constitution *Cum ex eo*, whereby a university education could be acquired subsequent to institution, the benefice providing the student's income subject to safeguards for the performance of his parochial duties by deputy.[43] Although forty-seven benefices were affected by such licences, Orleton was less generous in this respect than the previous bishop, Cobham, or his own successor, Montacute, and that despite his experience as a beneficed student. Viewed in perspective however, the falling-off in the number of licences granted appears as part of a long-term trend. A later bishop, Wolstan de Bransford, who as a monk may in any case have been less sympathetic towards the aspirations of secular clerks, granted fewer licences for study over a period roughly twice as long.[44]

The record of institutions also throws light on the mobility of the clergy, which was much increased by the practice of exchanging benefices. In fact so widespread was the practice at this time that exchanges accounted for almost a third of recorded institutions.[45] So far as the bishop was concerned these were administrative details and we know nothing of his personal views as to their effect on pastoral care.

By no means all the business which engaged Orleton outside the diocese was secular. His earlier connection with the affairs of Oxford University, when he had acted as Gilbert de Middleton's proctor,[46] was resumed in 1328 with the commission of Cardinal Bertrand de Montfavèz, which directed him, jointly with Bishop Martival of Salisbury, to cite the chancellor and masters on account of their dispute with the archdeacon of Oxford, Cardinal Gailhard de la Mothe, who was claiming jurisdiction over wills and corrections in the town. The case continued in the Curia until in 1330 the pope, to whom the king had complained about the strife, associated Orleton and Bishop Burghersh with Cardinal Gailhard as commissaries for securing a settlement with the uni-

43 For the working of this constitution see Boyle, 'Constitution *Cum ex eo*'; Haines, 'Education of the English Clergy'.

44 See *Worcester Reg. Bransford*, p. xxxiii; app. I a. and b. below.

45 App. I c. below.

46 See ch. 1 above.

versity.[47] Two years later, as co-conservator of the Minorites' privileges, Orleton was writing to the Oxford chancellor about the recrudescence of conflict between mendicant and secular masters, concluding his letter with a veiled threat: the situation might well lead to a curtailment of university privileges.[48]

Another issue with a long and unedifying history comes to the surface again at this time: the disagreement between the metropolitans of Canterbury and York about the latter's elevation of his cross within the southern province. As the northern primate did not return to his jurisdiction by way of the Worcester diocese, Orleton was not called upon to put Archbishop Mepham's strident mandates into effect.[49]

For the final year or so of his episcopate Orleton was bishop in little more than name. It was at Winchester that he was to resume his pastoral cares and with far less interruption by affairs of state.

WINCHESTER 1333–1345

The circumstances of Orleton's promotion ensured an inauspicious start to his episcopate. By the time his bulls of translation were issued he was returning from Paris and may actually have crossed the channel. Certainly he was at Dartford in Kent on 3 December 1333; six days later he named proctors to receive the apostolic letters.[1] Orleton was only too aware of Edward III's opposition to his translation, which was doubtless reiterated face to face when he reported on his diplomatic mission at Wallingford early in January. Not only had the pope disposed at his will of one of the wealthiest of English bishoprics, but Edward's own candidate, Simon de Montacute, had been relegated to Worcester. But behind the king Stratford's shadow may be discernible. At

[47] *W.R.O.* 2, fo. 12^{v} [584]; *Salisbury Reg. Martival* 2, pp. 582–9. Earlier (in 1325) Reynolds had been ordered to cite various masters (including Bradwardine), but had certified (18 January 1326) that he had been unable to do so: *Concilia* 2, pp. 526–8, from Canterbury Reg. Reynolds, fos. 145^{v}–146^{r}. Orleton and Martival in their turn certified that they could not execute Cardinal Bertrand's mandate in the time available because those to be cited were away from Oxford during the long vacation. S.C.1/37/126 is a draft (*c.* 1330) of a letter from Edward III to Cardinal Bertrand on this topic.

[48] *W.R.O.* 2, fo. 49^{v} [898]: undated, but between two entries from 1332.

[49] *W.R.O.* 2, fos. 31^{r-v}, 37^{r} [738, 742, 793]. Cf. *Foedera* 2, iii, pp. 27–8; *Concilia* 2, p. 525; also the earlier mandates in Worcester Reg. Maidstone, fos. 30^{v}–31^{r}.

[1] *W.R.O.* 1, fo. 28^{r} [187]; 2, fo. 54^{v} [941]; *Lettres communes Jean XXII*, no. 63898.

the time he was royal chancellor and in process of becoming archbishop of Canterbury; the nature of the accusation levied against Orleton was calculated to shift the responsibility for the revolutionary happenings of the previous reign from his own shoulders. Be that as it may, a nonentity called John Prickehare – or something of the kind [2] – described as a *literatus* of Winchester diocese, was put up to appeal against Orleton's translation on the grounds of his activities at the time of Edward II's deposition. As we shall see, Orleton had little difficulty in gainsaying the charges and his sponsor John XXII, well briefed long before on the matters in question, had no intention of putting him to the trouble and expense of personally contesting the case in the Curia.[3]

On 13 February 1334 Orleton wrote from Stanton-St-John, Oxfordshire, to thank the Winchester prior for his congratulations, explaining that he would have to defer the presentation of his bulls. He asked for the convent's prayers in a cause supported by 'a pure conscience, justice and truth'. The bishop had been in his diocese less than a fortnight when the galling charade of the appeal was enacted on 2 April within his cathedral church in the full glare of publicity.[4] Government support for the appellant is indicated by the presence of the sheriff of Hampshire, John de Scures, and of John de Schordich, newly created a knight,[5] who broke his journey at Winchester while en route for France on the king's business.[6] The mayor and other citizens of Winchester were present as well as a throng of clergy and people.

Despite this disturbed atmosphere, Orleton remained in his cathedral city until about the beginning of July. He was in London or its neighbourhood for much of August and at Shinfield and Southwark during September, obviously awaiting developments.[7] The king's disapproval found varied expression. The temporalities were of course retained, and lands of the

[2] John Pebrehave in *C.P.L.* 1305–42, p. 409.

[3] *C.P.L.* 1305–42, p. 409: 28 May 1334; *Winchester Chartulary*, p. 110, nos. 243^{a} (21 May), 243^{c} (cardinals to Edward III). Cf. Lambeth MS. 1213, p. 306 (John XXII to Edward).

[4] *Winchester Chartulary*, pp. 104–5, 105–7, 109–10, nos. 233–4, 242–3. Prior Heriard attempted to enlist the aid of John de Warenne, earl of Surrey. The appeal is discussed below, 'The Stratford affair and its prelude', ch. 4.

[5] *C.P.R.* 1330–34, pp. 398–9; *C.C.R.* 1333–37, p. 170.

[6] See *Foedera* 2, iii, pp. 108ff for various commissions issued to him at this time.

[7] Win.R.O. 1, fos. 4^{v} ff, and see Itinerary, app. 3 below.

Hastings family, custody of which had been granted to Bishop Orleton during the minority of the heir as recompense for the money owed him by the king, were resumed by the royal escheators.[8] A royal writ was withheld from Orleton ' who claims to be bishop of Winchester ',[9] and only in the spring of 1336 was he summoned to parliament. Moreover, as we have seen, there was a deliberate attempt to which Stratford seems to have been party to prevent his spiritual ministrations. The sheriff of Hampshire received instructions to inhibit all in his bailiwick, under pain of forfeiture, from rendering obedience to the soi-disant bishop, enquiries being subsequently held to discover those who had flouted the order.[10] Naturally Orleton's diplomatic commissions were not renewed. But in the long run there was little the king could do but accept the situation. It was said to have been the bishops assembled in the Westminster parliament of September 1334 who finally persuaded Edward to restore the temporalities, and this was authorised on the 23rd.[11] Great rejoicing ensued when the news reached Winchester a few days later. The monks were directed to peal the bells and to offer a solemn *Te Deum* with organ accompaniment. Could it have been on this occasion, rather than in 1338, that Prior Alexander Heriard provided an entertainment in his hall for the bishop, during which a celebrated minstrel named Herbert sang of how Guy of Warwick slew Colbrond the Danish giant under the walls of Winchester and Queen Emma walked unscathed over glowing ploughshares in the cathedral? [12]

[8] *C.P.R.* 1330–34, p. 106; *C.C.R.* 1333–37, pp. 258, 272–3, 311. In 1331 he was owed over £658 and he had some difficulty in recovering this amount before the coming of age of Laurence Hastings. As a result he asked for a compensatory grant. See S.C.8/146/7285, and for the Hastings pedigree Phillips, *Pembroke*, p. 2.

[9] *C.P.R.* 1330–34, p. 574.

[10] Plucknett, ' Parliament ', p. 94, n. 2, and see above, ' A career resumed ', ch. 2; *Winchester Chartulary*, pp. 108–9, nos. 237, 239–41. In a letter of 21 May 1334 John XXII told the king that he had been misled by Orleton's rivals (' emuli ') into thinking ill of someone whom he had formerly held in the highest esteem. Lambeth MS. 1213, p. 306. He wrote in similar vein to Archbishop Stratford, William de Montacute, Queen Isabella, Queen Philippa and several bishops. *Ibid.* pp. 307–8; *C.P.L.* 1305–42, p. 513; 20 June 1334.

[11] *Murimuth*, p. 70; *Annales Paulini*, pp. 360–1; *C.P.R.* 1334–38, p. 21. In a later petition (C.81/276/14100) Orleton pointed out that although the king had held the temporalities from 5 February to 23 September 1334 demands for £297 15s 5d were being made for the tenth payable during that time.

[12] *Winchester Chartulary*, p. 118, no. 260; Cassan, *Lives* 1, p. 186; Thomas Warton, *The History of English Poetry*, 3 vols. London 1840, 1, p. 81 and n. Warton's

In any case, celebrations were short-lived: the bishop's health was failing, the times were troubled, and there was much to be done in the diocese. Orleton's final diplomatic mission was accomplished in 1336. Two years later, at the beginning of 1338, he wrote of the defective sight in his left eye.[13] In September of the same year he excused himself from personal attendance at the Canterbury convocation because of a serious bodily infirmity.[14] An entry in his register for March 1340 reiterates his ailing condition [15] and in July 1341 Archbishop Stratford ordered the Winchester chapter to provide him with coadjutors in compliance with Boniface VIII's regulation.[16] Orleton was a step ahead, having already taken the precaution of choosing for himself two trusted associates, William de Edington, whom he had made master of St Cross hospital, and who was to succeed him as bishop, and John de Usk, the diocesan official, who had previously served in his Worcester administration.[17]

The bishop's movements – or lack of them – seem to corroborate these indications of declining vigour. His itinerary shows that he was at Farnham Castle, just under thirty miles from Winchester, uninterruptedly between November 1339 and May of the following year.[18] After a short stay at Bishop's Waltham, his manor to the south-east of the cathedral city, Orleton returned to Farnham in July 1340, apparently remaining there until January 1341.[19] His emergence to take part in the 1341 attack on

reference is to a parchment register of the priory in the archives at Wolvesey. For the story of Colbrond see *Thomae Rudborne*, *Historia Major Wintoniensis*, *Anglia Sacra* 1, pp. 211–12, and for that of Emma, *ibid.* pp. 233–5. The incident of the ploughshares is described by the editor of *Encomium Emmae Reginae* as one of the 'mere foolish stories' attached to the queen's name (p. 1). Emma died in 1052 and was buried at Winchester beside her first husband, Canute, in the Old Minster (*ibid.* p. xlix).

13 Win.R.O. 2, fo. 20^{v}: 28 January 1338.

14 Win.R.O. 2, fos. 65^{r-v}, 66^{r}. The council was summoned for 1 October 1338 at St Bride's, London, 'verum quia propter gravem infirmitatem corporis quam patimur dictis die et loco personaliter interesse non valemus'.

15 Win.R.O. 1, fo. 87^{r}; 3 March [1340]: 'gravi infirmitate corporis prepediti'.

16 *Winchester Chartulary*, p. 223, no. 525: a reference to *Sext* 3, 5, c. 1 *Pastoralis officii*.

17 *Winchester Chartulary*, p. 223, no. 526. This is the response of the prior and chapter to the archbishop's mandate (*ibid.* no. 525: see n. 16 above). For Usk see *Worc. Admin.*, index *s.v.* It would appear that the archbishop later attempted to appoint coadjutors unacceptable to Orleton, who secured a bull (28 April 1343) empowering him to remove them: *C.P.L.* 1342–62, p. 52.

18 Win.R.O. 2, fos. 78^{r}–85^{v}.

19 Win.R.O. 2, fos. 34^{r}, 84^{r}–86^{v}.

Stratford is notorious, thanks to the detailed account by the archbishop's biographer.[20] Thereafter, with only a few interludes, Orleton was regularly at Farnham, being permanently resident there from November 1343 until his death in July 1345.[21]

Interesting confirmation of the bishop's plight and of his whereabouts is provided by Etienne Robo in his book on medieval Farnham. According to him it was in 1339 that Orleton 'caused two doors to be opened in the east wall of his chamber [in Farnham Castle] "towards the fields" and had two bridges made to cross the ditch'. The implication, he suggests, is that the bishop, threatened with blindness, had by that date settled upon Farnham for his last years and this alteration facilitated exit and entrance to his quarters. Moreover, the chapel next to Orleton's chamber is said to have been built about the same time, presumably with similar considerations in mind, and in 1343, by which time, as we have seen, Orleton had been forced to confine himself to Farnham, workmen were making ready a room for his coadjutor.[22]

But it was not merely ill-health that troubled the new diocesan. The countryside was very disturbed. The relative degree of lawlessness and violence is always hard to determine, but that it was high during Orleton's episcopate is suggested both by entries in his register and by Archbishop Stratford's provincial legislation of 1341–2 which sought to curb widespread encroachments on church property and ecclesiastical immunity.[23]

From Wisley church thieves stole a breviary worth four marks, and in the same month, August 1336, carried off stock from the rectory and its outbuildings.[24] At Broughton three local men dug up a leaden coffin, threw aside the body and made off with the lead. But they were caught, ordered to provide seventy masses on behalf of the dead man's soul, whose burial they had violated, and condemned to carry expensive wax candles as penitents. As for the lead, it was to be sold and the proceeds distributed to the poor for the spiritual profit of the deceased.[25] Early in 1339 the

20 *Birchington*, pp. 38–9. See below, 'The Stratford affair and its prelude', ch. 4.

21 Win.R.O. 2, fos. 101^{r}–107^{v}.

22 Robo, *Mediaeval Farnham*, p. 141.

23 *Concilia* 2, pp. 675–8, 696–702, 702–9; Bolton, 'Council of London'.

24 Win.R.O. 1, fo. 42^{r}. For a similar case involving theft of a breviary see *Worcester Reg. Bransford*, pp. 9–10.

25 Win.R.O. 1, fo. 50^{v}.

deans of Guildford and Alton were ordered to see that satisfaction was made to a man and his family whose house had been broken into, its occupants treated with wolfish ferocity, and forty marks' worth of whose property had been stolen.[26] At Godshill in the Isle of Wight Walter Norreys was intruded into the vicarage and offerings and other things were diverted from their rightful owner, the lawful vicar.[27] Stratford's recent constitution *Immoderate temeritatis* was certainly infringed by the parishioners of Crondall who carried off the wax candles offered at the feast of the Purification.[28] Some fracas at Ford had seemingly resulted in the pollution of church or churchyard, while at Bedhampton a fee of five marks was exacted for the 'reconciliation' necessary after a similar violation.[29] At Winchester itself *nobiles* had to be deterred from tourneying in the cathedral cemetery and Carmelite friars taken to task for pursuing a youth as far as the priory cloister, where he was barely saved from serious injury by the monks' intervention.[30]

Despite the magnitude of the offence in canon law and its commensurate penalty, the clergy were by no means immune from violence, though some of this was fratricidal. John de Bornham, the parish chaplain of Ringwood, if we are to believe his version of the incident, unsheathed his sword to counter the threat of a drawn bow. But the sword did not injure those who menaced him but another chaplain, John de Newhall, who tried to intervene for the sake of peace and was wounded for his pains.[31] The parish priest of Wherwell, near Andover, was assaulted by two men.[32] A similar fate befell the parish chaplain of Warblington, who was badly hurt. The latter's attackers would in the normal course have had to seek absolution from the apostolic see, but because of the hostilities with France they secured a respite from this obligation.[33] At Merrow, near Guildford, there occurred a

26 Win.R.O. 1, fos. 70v–71r (Binsted): 'dictum Johannem uxorem et familiam suam ferocitate lupina irruentes contumelias plagas et vulnera gravia inhumaniter intulerunt'.

27 Win.R.O. 1, fo. 96r.

28 Win.R.O. 1, fo. 124r. See the similar incident in the contemporary *Worcester Reg. Bransford* (p. 104).

29 Win.R.O. 1, fo. 98v.

30 Win.R.O. 1, fo. 120v: 'ad ostentacionem virium suarum et audacie'.

31 Win.R.O. 1, fo. 62r.

32 Win.R.O. 1, fo. 64v.

33 Win.R.O. 1, fo. 100Ar.

most unclerical free-for-all. A priest, John atte Putte, who exercised the parochial cure, lived in the rectory together with William Frye, a layman who was the rector's son (' qui pro filio naturali alis et tenes '). The priest had only just celebrated St Bartholomew's mass when, according to his account, he was attacked by the rector with a stick. In self-defence and without motives of revenge – the usual formula adopted by the defendant in such cases – he drew a knife and inflicted a shoulder wound on the rector's son. In trying to wrest the knife from the priest's grasp the rector in his turn was slightly wounded in the hand.[34] Details of yet another attack on a priest are lost because the entry was left unfinished at the foot of the folio.[35]

The victims of these attacks – except for the last, about which there is inadequate information – were men actually engaged in the cure of souls in the parishes, the unbeneficed clergy. Yet even the bishop was not immune. His quarrel with M. William Inge, the archdeacon of Surrey,[36] arose from a jurisdictional dispute as least as old as the mid-thirteenth century and the episcopates of William Raleigh and Aymer de Valence.[37] Sometimes the affair degenerated into a personal attack. On one such occasion, Orleton, arrayed in pontificals, was observing the feast of the Holy Cross in Farnham parish church with the celebration of mass, confirmation of children and a sermon on a crusading theme,[38] when he was noisily interrupted by Inge, who persisted in his behaviour despite the bishop's repeated warnings to desist on pain of excommunication. Having concluded the divine office, Orleton and the clergy processed with difficulty through the churchyard, saying prayers for the dead as they went. Pressing forward with what was described as a large band of armed men Inge, with total disregard for the episcopal office, shouted insults and laid sacrilegious hands upon him.[39] At that moment Orleton may well

34 Win.R.O. 1, fo. 4^{r}.

35 Win.R.O. 1, fo. 100D^{v}.

36 Inge had been given the archdeaconry by Edward II by virtue of the vacancy of the bishopric of Winchester. *C.P.R.* 1317–21, p. 136: 10 April 1320.

37 The points at issue have been copied into Pontissara's register: *Winchester Reg. Pontissara*, pp. 1–2. A composition was eventually arranged between Bishop Edington, Orleton's successor, and the then archdeacon of Surrey, M. Richard Vaughan: Winchester Reg. Edyndon 1, fos. 12^{r}–13^{v}.

38 ' . . . verbum Dei super passagio ultramarino de mandato apostolico publice predicaret '.

39 Win.R.O. 2, fo. 15^{r-v}. There are some thirty entries in the register concerned with the Inge dispute.

have recollected the similar scene at Ross during his days at Hereford.

To add to these attacks on the secular clergy and the diocesan himself are a number involving the religious and their property. Geoffrey, abbot of the Cistercian house at Quarr in the Isle of Wight, was assaulted by a John de Lisle, whom Orleton summoned before him at Winchester, but with what result does not appear.[40] Malefactors fired woods belonging to the abbot and convent of Chertsey, allegedly destroying their fuel supply,[41] while at Bermondsey Priory in the north-east corner of the diocese, thieves sneaked in under cover of festivities for the Purification and made off with a hawk lodged on holy ground, adjoining the cloister, by that Simon de Montacute, now bishop of Ely, whom Orleton had displaced at Winchester.[42] At Waverley, a Cistercian house in Surrey, the monks complained that their outbuildings, manors and granges had been broken into and goods stored there carried off. The same fate befell building and other materials (' lapides, saxa, palos et sepes ') lying in the close of Beaulieu Abbey.[43]

One supposes that ' normal ' conditions entailed disturbances of the kind sketched above, but the number of incidents argues exceptional times.[44] The upheaval of war contributed to the situation, bringing fresh disorder of its own. The southern part of the diocese, Hampshire and the Isle of Wight, was exposed to imminent threat of invasion. When Portsmouth suffered at the hands of a French raiding party, the bishop and his Farnham tenants went to the assistance of the men of the neighbourhood, only to have Farnham Park broken into during his absence.[45]

40 Win.R.O. 1, fo. 54^v^.

41 Win.R.O. 1, fo. 78^v^.

42 Win.R.O. 1, fo. 57^v^: ' aucipitrem eiusdem patris infra monasterium de Bermondeseye infra claustrum eiusdem in loco sacro et eciam dedicato in pertica sua sedentem '. In ' Orleton and Winchester ' (p. 5) I followed R. E. Latham, *Revised Medieval Latin Word-List from British and Irish Sources*, London 1965, in calling this a sparrow-hawk; most late-medieval Latin–English glossaries give it as a goshawk.

43 Win.R.O. 1, fos. 88^v^, 50^r^.

44 Some of the problems have been studied in the context of Sir William Shareshull's career. See Putnam, *Sir William Shareshull*, esp. chs. 4–5 on legislative measures and law enforcement.

45 *C.P.R.* 1338–40, p. 134: 4 July 1338. Cf. *C.C.R.* 1337–39, p. 619. A commission of oyer and terminer, which included Shareshull, was appointed on Orleton's complaint. The fact that John de Ambresbury, clerk, is named as one of the alleged

Another French incursion saw the firing of wooden buildings adjacent to St Michael's, Southampton, and the desecration of the church itself.[46] Armed men occupied Farnham church and proceeded to fortify it, their activities interrupting the ministrations of the vicar and his clergy.[47] An urgent royal writ of March 1339 required the diocesan to assemble his clergy, both regular and secular, for the purpose of raising armed men.[48] But although Orleton busied himself with such warlike preparation, he had cause to complain about over-zealous commissioners of array who demanded a quota of two soldiers for coastal defence from his manor of Dogmersfield.[49] Various commissions urged the raising of arms and men in the Isle of Wight from parsons, vicars and other ecclesiastics,[50] and throughout the episcopate a constant stream of writs demanded increasingly onerous war taxation.[51]

It is against this background of ill-health and social disturbance that we must view Orleton's efforts to administer the diocese. His primary visitation was launched, in line with canonical practice, by an investigation of the cathedral priory, which took place on the morrow of All Souls (i.e. 3 November) 1334.[52] This

intruders suggests Inge's complicity, for John is known to have acted as his official in the Surrey archdeaconry (e.g. *C.P.R.* 1345–48, pp. 423–4). Orleton had excommunicated him in 1335: Win.R.O. 1, fo. 48^{v}. Portsmouth was plundered and burnt in March 1338. See *V.C.H. Hampshire and the Isle of Wight* 5, p. 363.

46 Win.R.O. 1, fo. 70^{r}: 'homicidio et sanguinis effusione ut dicitur pollutam cuius eciam lignea edificia per violenciam et hostium externorum incursum voracis incendii flamma in parte sunt combusta'. Cf. *V.C.H. Hampshire* 3, p. 530; 5, p. 363.

47 Win.R.O. 1, fos. 31^{v}–32^{r}, 6 February 1336: 'Mandatum contra incastellantes ecclesiam de Farnham.' Later (21 May 1340) Orleton petitioned against a similar situation at Godshill (Isle of Wight): 'nuper cum vario armorum genere violenter ingredientes ipsam ecclesiam vi armata contra sacrorum canonum prohibicionem et sanctorum patrum constituciones in hac parte editas per non modica tempora occupare ausu sacrilego temere presumpserunt ipsamque adhuc potestate laicali detinent occupatam'. S.C.8/237/11831; Win.R.O. 1, fo. 88^{v}.

48 Win.R.O. 1, fos. 153^{r}–154^{r}; and cf. fos. 163^{v}, 175^{r}.

49 Win.R.O. 1, fo. 157^{v}: 'Arraiatoribus hominum pro custodia terre maritime in comitatu Suthampton' [rubric]. 'Et licet idem episcopus circa arraiacionem predictam diligenter intendat et homines et familiares suos ac alios de retinencia sua arraiari et muniri fecerit et cum toto posse suo quanto potencius potest super custodia terre maritime in partibus illis moretur, vos nichilominus ipsum episcopum ad inveniendum duos homines ad arma racione manerii sui de Dogmersfeld in dicto comitatu Suth' pro custodia terre maritime facienda graviter distringi et multipliciter inquietari facitis minus iuste.'

50 Win.R.O. 1, fos. 154^{r}, 168^{r}–169^{r}.

51 Cf. *Worcester Reg. Bransford*, pp. l–li.

52 Win.R.O. 1, fo. 10^{r-v}; *Winchester Chartulary*, p. 75, no. 155.

betokens speedy preparation, for the bishop's position had only become stabilised in late September with the assumption of his temporalities, and warning of impending visitation was despatched on 21 October.[53] In the meantime his itinerary would have been planned and the various local officers apprised of his intentions.

There were two archdeaconries in this as in Orleton's former dioceses: Winchester in the south, Surrey in the north. Visitation of the southern archdeaconry occupied the month of November. From the cathedral priory Orleton proceeded to the nearby religious houses of the Newminster (Hyde) (7th)[54] and St Mary's, Winchester (9th), where he preached to the nuns in French, as was customary.[55] Southwick Priory (14th),[56] St Denys near Southampton (22nd),[57] Mottisfont (26th)[58] and the nuns of Romsey (28th)[59] were visited in quick succession, while at Titchfield, a Premonstratensian abbey exempt from episcopal visitation, the bishop examined muniments relating to the canons' appropriated churches and licensed the recall to the monastery of a disobedient canon who was serving the vicarage of Titchfield.[60] Of the ten deaneries of the archdeaconry, the bishop is recorded to have visited only three – Winchester, in the cathedral church (12 November),[61] Droxford, by halves in the churches of Southwick and Titchfield (17th–18th),[62] and Southampton, in the church of St Mary there (24th).[63] This done, on 27 November he commissioned his official, John de Usk, to enquire into, correct and punish the *comperta* of his visitation.[64]

The second part of the visitation, in the northern archdeaconry, was launched by a mandate of 31 January 1335 addressed to M. William Inge, the archdeacon of Surrey. This outlined Orle-

53 *Winchester Chartulary*, p. 118, no. 260.
54 Benedictine abbey. Win.R.O. 1, fo. 10ᵛ: Cf. *V.C.H. Hampshire* 2, p. 119.
55 Benedictine abbey (nuns). Win.R.O. 1, fo. 10ᵛ. Cf. *V.C.H. Hampshire* 2, pp. 123–5.
56 Augustinian priory, Win.R.O. 1, fo. 10ᵛ. Cf. *V.C.H. Hampshire* 2, pp. 165–6.
57 Augustinian priory. Win.R.O. 1, fo. 11ʳ. Cf. *V.C.H. Hampshire* 2, p. 162.
58 Augustinian priory. Win.R.O. 1, fos. 11ʳ, 12ʳ. Cf. *V.C.H. Hampshire* 2, p. 173.
59 Benedictine abbey (nuns), Win.R.O. 1, fo. 11ʳ. Cf. *V.C.H. Hampshire* 2, p. 128. Orleton stayed there at his own expense.
60 Win.R.O. 1, fo. 12ʳ.
61 Win.R.O. 1, fo. 10ᵛ.
62 Win.R.O. 1, fo. 11ʳ.
63 *Ibid.* On 19 November he had preached in the church and celebrated mass there.
64 Win.R.O. 1, fo. 11ᵛ, Mottisfont 27 November [1334].

ton's plans for visiting all three deaneries of Guildford, Ewell and Southwark, and at the same time cited the archdeacon before him at Guildford to show by what title he held his archdeaconry,[65] which from what we know of their relationship must have been something more than a formality.

According to memoranda in his register, Orleton visited Guildford deanery in the churches of Holy Trinity (20 February 1335) and St Mary's (23rd), as planned, yet on 21 February 'ex causis legitimis impediti' he deputed the official to visit and correct both that deanery and those of Ewell and Southwark.[66] The commission must have been largely if not wholly nugatory, for Orleton is stated specifically to have visited Ewell deanery, again in two parts, at Kingston on 25 and 27 February, on the earlier occasion 'excellenter predicando' – a rare observation from a scribe of a diocesan registry.[67] There is mention of a visitation having taken place in Southwark deanery, but whether this was effected in person or by deputy is uncertain.[68]

Visitation of religious houses was a long-drawn-out process and the evidence gives the distinct impression that Orleton gave it serious attention. Merton Priory was visited in March 1335,[69] as was Chertsey Abbey,[70] while Tandridge Priory received the bishop in the first week of September,[71] Selborne and Monk Sherborne in February of the following year (1336),[72] Twynham (Christchurch)[73] and Breamore[74] in the same month of 1337. It was not in the May of 1337, as the register states, but of 1336, that Orleton visited both Southwark[75] and Newark[76] priories.

A further visitation was launched on 12 May 1337:[77] the

65 Win.R.O. 1, fo. 15^r.

66 Win.R.O. 1, fo. 15^v.

67 Win.R.O. 1, fos. 15^v–16^r.

68 Win.R.O. 1, fo. 31^r.

69 Win.R.O. 1, fo. 16^v, 6–8 March 1335.

70 *Ibid.* 13 March 1335.

71 Win.R.O. 1, fo. 28^v, 4 September 1335.

72 Win.R.O. 1, fo. 33^r, 21 and 23 February 1336. Cf. *V.C.H. Hampshire* 2, p. 177 (Selborne).

73 Win.R.O. 1, fo. 50^r, 9 February 1337. Cf. *V.C.H. Hampshire* 2, p. 156.

74 Win.R.O. 1, fo. 50^r, 13 February 1337. Cf. *V.C.H. Hampshire* 2, pp. 170–1.

75 Win.R.O. 1, fo. 37^v, 7 May 1337 (*sic*) with corrections on the 13th (8th?). This corrects my statement in 'Orleton and Winchester', p. 23.

76 Win.R.O., *loc. cit.* 15–16 May.

77 Win.R.O. 1, fo. 54^{r-v}: warning to cathedral priory, Farnham 26 April 1337. According to the editor of *Winchester Chartulary* (p. 50, no. 106) there was a mandate dated 1 May [1337] with Monday after St Dunstan (i.e. 26 May) as the day of visitation. This is somewhat of an enigma, but may refer to some other year, possibly 1340, though there is no sign that the cathedral priory was visited then.

register provides few details, a not unusual state of affairs. There are no direct indications of any visitation of rural deaneries, and among religious houses only the cathedral priory, Hyde and Wherwell abbeys, and the nuns of St Mary's, Winchester, would seem to have received their diocesan in person.[78] Commissaries were appointed to visit St Elizabeth's College in Winchester,[79] as well as Newark [80] and Tandridge priories,[81] while the official was instructed to follow up the *comperta* at Twynham.[82] Not much more of the visitation programme can be unearthed and it would probably be accurate to assume that advancing ill-health dictated that such arduous business was not resumed on any scale during the remainder of the episcopate.

Orleton's concern with the religious and their reformation has been noted in his work at Hereford. His Winchester register affords some insight into the state of monastic life both during visitation and at other times,[83] although as usual this evidence is of a fragmentary and negative kind. The Augustinian priories of Breamore, Merton, Selborne, Southwark, Tandridge and Twynham all required some amendment, but at Mottisfont the bishop reported 'omnia honeste et cum ordine'.[84] Violence and mismanagement were recurring faults. At Selborne a canon who drew blood from one of his fellows had to seek absolution from the papal penitentiary,[85] while two Southwark canons who brawled in 1343 incurred excommunication ipso facto as determined by the regulation *Si quis suadente diabolo*.[86]

Following Orleton's visitation of Selborne in 1335 the prior was ordered to restrain one of his canons who engaged in secular pursuits and who, despite the diocesan's warning, had returned like a dog to his vomit ('tanquam canis ad vomitum rediens'), refusing to surrender his money to the prior.[87] For reason unknown Prior Walter de Lisle resigned his office some years later, when the bishop, who was patron of the house, appointed the

78 Win.R.O. 1, fo. 54^{r-v}.

79 Win.R.O. 1, fo. 74^{r}.

80 Win.R.O. 1, fo. 80^{r}, 6 September 1339.

81 *Ibid.*

82 Win.R.O. 1, fo. 56^{v}, 5 July 1337.

83 Much of this material is omitted from the relevant sections of *V.C.H. Hampshire* and *V.C.H. Surrey*.

84 Win.R.O. 1, fo. 11^{r}.

85 Win.R.O. 1, fo. 97^{v}.

86 Win.R.O. 1, fo. 121^{v}: *Extra* 5, 39, c. 26.

87 Win.R.O. 1, fo. 35^{v}.

subprior in his stead (6 November 1339).[88] At the time there were seventeen canons, including the retiring prior, a somewhat larger number than the usually-accepted figure of fourteen.[89]

At Tandridge Priory the troubles were inadvertently of the bishop's own making. At his visitation in 1335 the prior, John Hausard or Hansard, had resigned owing to bodily infirmity, whereupon Orleton provided Philip de Wokyngham in his place, bringing him from another Augustinian house, Newark, for the purpose.[90] Yet in 1341 Prior Philip had to be deprived for non-residence.[91]

About Twynham there are no specific details, but in 1337 the official received a mandate to correct the inmates, and to this was attached a schedule of *crimina et excessus*, which unfortunately was not copied into the register.[92] Two years later he was deputed to make further enquiries.[93] In 1343 two of the canons had penances relaxed which were described as having been imposed during a visitation by John de Usk and John de Wolveley, the diocesan official and chancellor.[94]

Orleton closed his 1335 visitation of Merton Priory by excommunicating in advance any clerk or secular person who should presume to take reprisals against those who had revealed irregularities.[95] The prior died within a month and the bishop subsequently advised his successor, Thomas de Kent, to remedy the sorry state of indebtedness said to be a consequence of previous neglect and careless administration.[96]

From Breamore one of the canons had to be sent for a period

88 Win.R.O. 1, fo. 82r.

89 *Ibid.* for a full list of the canons. Cf. Knowles and Hadcock, *Medieval Religious Houses*, p. 153 n.

90 Win.R.O. 1, fo. 28v. Hansard had been such a 'bad prior', according to *V.C.H. Hampshire* 2, p. 113, that Bishop Stratford had interdicted his interference with the temporalities and appointed Laurence de Rustington to act as coadjutor.

91 Win.R.O. 1, fos. 108r–109r.

92 Win.R.O. 1, fo. 56v. Richard de Buteshorn had been elected prior in March 1337. According to *V.C.H. Hampshire* 2, p. 156: 'There was clearly some great irregularity about this prior, for in July 1337, after a rule of only a few months, the bishop ordered the subprior to administer the affairs of the priory.' But this seems to be mistaken. There was a commission to follow up the bishop's visitation (Win.R.O. 1, fos. 50r, 56v), but the mandate issued to the subprior followed Buteshorn's death (*ibid.* 1, fo. 58v, 2 May 1338).

93 Win.R.O. 1, fo. 77r.

94 Win.R.O. 1, fo. 120v, 23 May 1343. This must refer to a visitation held between 1339 and 1343; the latter would seem likely to have been the actual date.

95 Win.R.O. 1, fo. 16v.

96 Win.R.O. 1, fo. 100v.

to do penance at Selborne. This was a measure adopted by Orleton at Hereford, as we have seen, and was enjoined by the chapter *Hoc quoque volumus* of the Council of Oxford (1222), duly quoted in this instance.[97] The penance which Orleton imposed for an unspecified offence on Andrew Wylton, also a canon of Breamore, was subsequently relaxed – a lenient or compassionate attitude to be found elsewhere in the Winchester register.[98] In the same year, 1338, another chapter of the Council of Oxford was invoked to bring the canons to a proper performance of their almsgiving functions.[99]

It should be no cause for surprise that religious life was disrupted in the alien Benedictine priories of Carisbrooke, in the Isle of Wight,[100] and Sherborne (Pamber), even before the arrival in 1338 of the royal mandate – following the French raid on Portsmouth – which ordered the removal to larger Benedictine houses on the mainland of all French monks and others who owed allegiance to abbeys in France.[101]

Oddly, it is for Sherborne alone of all the religious houses that visitation injunctions have survived, dated 30 April 1336. The bishop admonished the monks not to exceed their accustomed complement of twelve. They were forbidden to be absent from church or chapter without good cause and appropriate licence, and to ensure this a proper means of telling the time (' orologium ') was to be provided as soon as possible. Three chalices and silver cruets (' tres calices ac eciam phiales argenteas '), lost by the prior or through his carelessness, were to be restored, and candles, lamps and other necessities made available. The prior was prohibited from selling tithes or other goods belonging to the house and proper accounts were to be kept by him and other officers for annual presentation to the community. Women were outlawed from the monastery precincts and it was forbidden to visit them elsewhere. The monks were not allowed to keep birds, horses or other property.[102]

97 Win.R.O. 1, fo. 61^r; Council of Oxford c. 53. See *Councils and Synods*, p. 123.

98 Win.R.O. 1, fo. 68^r.

99 Win.R.O. 1, fo. 61^r; Council of Oxford c. 50 *Omnem etiam . . . interdicimus*. See *Councils and Synods*, p. 122.

100 Win.R.O. 1, fo. 56^r. An infringement of the canon *Si quis suadente diabolo*: Decretum C. 17, Qu. 4, c. 29; *Extra* 5, 39, c. 26.

101 Win.R.O. 1, fo. 145^v.

102 Win.R.O. 1, fo. 38^v.

There is little information about the other male Benedictine houses of the diocese. The abbot of Chertsey, though, had to defend himself against charges of maladministration and waste,[103] and a renegade friar-preacher of Guildford managed to intrude himself into Hyde Abbey by means of forged papal letters, only to be discovered and excommunicated.[104]

The disturbing economic and moral condition of the large Benedictine nunnery of St Mary's, Winchester, came to the bishop's notice. It appears that the abbess, prioress and others in authority had been so remiss in their duties that several nuns, unmindful of their sex, had resorted to the dwellings of seculars and other undesirable places and had even admitted persons of doubtful character into the convent itself. Two commissions for correction were issued in 1336.[105] At Wintney, a Cistercian house, the incursion of laymen and clerks, who on St Mary Magdalene's feast engaged in all the rumpus of a market and fair even to the singing of lewd songs ('cantica inhonesta canere sunt temere assueti'), seriously disquieted the nuns.[106]

Another facet of monastic economy which intimately involved the bishop, or by delegation the official,[107] was the appropriation of parish churches. During Orleton's episcopate negotiations were in train for the annexation of at least ten such churches: Kingsclere to William de Montacute's new foundation of Augustinian canons at Bisham;[108] Dorking, St Michael's, Southampton, and Leatherhead to the canons of Reigate,[109] St Denys[110] and Leeds

[103] Win.R.O. 1, fo. 39v.

[104] Win.R.O. 1, fos. 61v, 64v.

[105] In the first of these commissions (Win.R.O. 1, fo. 29*v, undated, but possibly of January 1336), those deputed to investigate were: M. John de Usk, the official, William de Edington, master of St Cross hospital, John de Nubbelegh (Nibley), treasurer of Wolvesey, and the chancellor, John de Wolveley, rector of Arreton. The other commission (*ibid.* 1, fo. 41r–v, 21 July 1336) recites the nuns' shortcomings. Cf. *V.C.H. Hampshire* 2, pp. 123–4.

[106] Win.R.O. 1, fo. 62v.

[107] The official's involvement in appropriation was in part to present the facts to the cathedral chapter on the bishop's behalf, and to secure its assent or dissent – on the rare occasions that diocesan or chapter took a stand against a particular annexation. One commission authorised the official (John de Usk) to treat of three appropriations at the same time: those of Compton, St Michael's, Southampton, and Froyle (Win.R.O. 1, fo. 85v). For further details see Haines, 'Orleton and Winchester', pp. 12–13.

[108] Win.R.O. 1, fos. 59v, 71r.

[109] Win.R.O. 1, fos. 19v, 57[ii]v. Cf. *V.C.H. Surrey* 3, p. 149.

[110] Win.R.O. 1, fo. 85v. Cf. *V.C.H. Hampshire* 3, p. 530.

(Kent)[111] respectively – the last at the promotion of Queen Isabella; Herriard to the Cistercian nuns of Wintney;[112] Compton-by-Guildford to the Premonstratensian canons of Durford (Sussex);[113] Froyle to the Benedictine nuns of St Mary's, Winchester;[114] Stoneham to Hyde Abbey;[115] and Wonston to the cathedral priory – by papal bull.[116] It was the bishop himself who, in return for the right to present one of the chaplains, granted the advowson of All Saints *supra solarium* in Thames Street, London, to the new collegiate foundation of the city merchant John Pulteney in the church of St Laurence (Poultney), Candlewick Street.[117] The episcopal register is not informative about the final outcome of most of these negotiations[118] or the concomitant establishment of vicarages – although there is something to suggest that Orleton was industrious in such matters.[119]

Once again Orleton showed diligence in enforcing residence on incumbents. By a mandate of 7 June 1340 he required the

111 *Winchester Chartulary*, pp. 59, 217–18, nos. 118, 119, 510–13. The petition mentions the damage caused by the siege of Leeds Castle in 1321. See below, 'The path of the mediator', ch. 4.

112 Win.R.O. 1, fos. 54^{v}–55^{r}. Cf. *V.C.H. Hampshire* 3, p. 369.

113 Win.R.O. 1, fo. 85^{v}.

114 Win.R.O. 1, fo. 122^{v}. After Orleton's death there was an attempt to overthrow the appropriation on technical grounds: *C.P.L.* 1342–62, pp. 112, 225; *C.P.P.* 1342–1419, pp. 56, 122.

115 Win.R.O. 1, fos. 15^{r-v}, 18^{v}, 22^{r}; 2, fos. 46^{v}–47^{r}; *Winchester Chartulary*, p. 176, no. 414.

116 *V.C.H. Hampshire* 2, pp. 197–8; 3, pp. 460–1.

117 Win.R.O. 1, fos. 41^{r}, 45^{v}–46^{v}. For a lengthy note on Pulteney see *French Chronicle*, pp. 64–7.

118 Churches effectively appropriated seem to have been Stoneham, Dorking, Herriard, Kingsclere, All Saints (All Hallows-the-less), London, and Leatherhead. For Froyle see n. 114 above. Orleton successfully resisted the appropriation of Wonston. St Michael's, Southampton, according to *V.C.H. Hampshire* 3, p. 530, was not appropriated until 1405. The proposed annexation of Compton to Durford does not appear to have taken place, nor that of Crondall to the cathedral priory. A papal mandate for the latter (1 April 1334) is in *C.P.L.* 1305–42, p. 400.

119 The ordination of Kingsclere vicarage (1338) is in the register (Win.R.O. 1, fos. 71^{v}–72^{v}; cf. 77^{v}). At Empshott Orleton attempted to regularise a long-standing situation which had been under review in Stratford's time (*ibid.* 1, fo. 47^{r}; *V.C.H. Hampshire* 3, p. 19). He reordained the vicarage of Shorwell (not mentioned in *V.C.H. Hampshire* 5, p. 284), appropriated to Carisbrooke Priory: Win.R.O. 1, fo. 57^{r-v}; 1335. A recension of the Malden vicarage ordination (1279) is registered; also the judicial settlement (1340) of the burdens to be borne by the vicars and appropriators respectively. The latter were the 'scholars' of Merton Hall, Oxford. *Ibid.* 1, fos. 110^{r}–111^{r}. The register also contains Godfrey de Lucy's amplification (29 March 1192) of the Hambledon vicarage settlement of his predecessor, Richard of Ilchester (1174–88): *ibid.* 2, fo. 31^{r}.

official to admonish all rectors to reside in their benefices, or if licensed to be absent, to show their dispensations.[120] A further commission in September of the same year associated the sequestrator-general of the Winchester archdeaconry, Richard de Haylinge, with the official for ascertaining the names of non-residents and punishing them.[121] On other occasions isolated action was taken against individuals, such as the incumbents of Hamble,[122] Warnford [123] and Esher.[124] The last case is of special interest. The rector of Esher, John de Bercheston, had acquired the benefice in exchange for his family's church of Barcheston in Worcester diocese. At the time of the exchange the regular enquiry held in the rural deanery of Kington revealed that Bercheston had been a persistent absentee.[125] Small wonder that he sought to continue the malpractice at Esher. But Orleton would have none of it. A strong contingent of familiar clerks – Nicholas de Caerwent, Adam de Aylton, Geoffrey de Upton and John de Beautre, the notary – accompanied him to Esher, where he threatened the absentee rector, in the person of his familiar, Richard de Alcester, that if he did not reside by mid-Lent he would incur the penalty of the law.[126] We are not told of the outcome.

It may have been the general tightening-up in this matter of residence that prompted the royal writ in favour of John of Askham, rector of Abbotstone, which pointed out that he was a chancery clerk and so not bound to stay in his benefice.[127] This firm line of Orleton's was to be followed by his successor, William de Edington, although by that time the mortality of clergy during the Black Death had created an entirely different situation.[128]

A corollary of this attitude to non-residents was the provision for those incumbents who were too old or ill to perform their office. Orleton had been careful about this before and there is evidence of his continued concern at Winchester. The neces-

120 Win.R.O. 1, fo. 89v.

121 Win.R.O. 1, fo. 96v.

122 Win.R.O. 1, fos. 88v, 89v, 90r–v. The prior of Hamble, Br. Richard de Beaumont (Bello Monte), was also rector of the church, which he had left and farmed to a layman.

123 Win.R.O. 1, fo. 89v.

124 Win.R.O. 2, fo. 46r.

125 Win.R.O. 2, fo. 44v.

126 Win.R.O. 2, fo. 46r.

127 Win.R.O. 1, fo. 170v.

128 E.g. Winchester Reg. Edyndon 2, fo. 22v: 'Monicio generalis ad residendum', 9 April 1350; *ibid.* fo. 23v: 'Mandatum ad compellendum presbiteros ecclesiis parochialibus et curis animarum deservire', 10 July 1350. But this was after the initial visitation of the Black Death.

sity to support such men with a pension from the income of the benefice had to be balanced by the maintenance of the rights of future incumbents. This could be effected with the co-operation of parishioners prepared to stand surety for the temporary chaplain, who was put on oath to maintain the benefice's value while discharging its obligations.[129]

There was at the same time a substantial amount of licensed absence from benefices. During the eleven and a half years of Orleton's episcopate his register records a total of some 165 licences, an average of roughly fourteen a year. The two principal categories are licences for study and those for attendance on prominent laymen or clerks. There were some eighty-four or eighty-five licences for study,[130] involving about 190 years of absence, sixty-seven or sixty-eight for attendance, seven for undefined absence, and a further six which permitted the farming of the profits.

While at Worcester, between 1328 and 1332, the five years for which recording is more or less normal, Orleton conceded ninety-five licences involving some 164½ years, an average of nineteen a year. This was substantially more than his average at Winchester. When licences for study are considered by themselves we find that Orleton's dispensations averaged 7.4 a year at Winchester against 11.5 at Worcester.[131] Of course these figures are only approximate, for we have no means of telling the accuracy of registration. In any case comparisons over different decades should be treated with caution because the long-term trend at Winchester has not been examined: it was almost certainly, as at Worcester, a declining one.[132] What can be claimed is that within the prevailing administrative framework Orleton appears to have been sympathetic to scholars and willing to grant licences for relatively

[129] See, for instance, the arrangements at Heckfield (Win.R.O. 1, fo. 10^{v} [1334]); St Michael's in Jewry, Winchester (*ibid.* 1, fo. 34^{r}, 1336); Calbourne (*ibid.* 1336); Tatsfield (*ibid.* 1, fo. 51^{r-v}, 1337); Stratfield Turgis (*ibid.* 1, fo. 90^{v}, 1340); Froyle (*ibid.* 1, fo. 96^{r-v}, 1340); Blendworth (*ibid.* 1, fo. 109^{v}, 1341); Stoke-by-Guildford (*ibid.* 1, fo. 119^{v}, 1344).

[130] One licence is for study *or* service.

[131] See app. 1 a. and b. below. At Winchester the breakdown of licences for study is as follows: 6 for the canonical maximum of seven years, 3 for five years, 2 for four, 10 for three, 31 for two, and 33 for one year.

[132] This notion of a falling trend is derived from a study of some individual dioceses and an analysis of the licences cited by Emden, *Biog. Oxon.* See Haines, 'Education of the English Clergy'.

long terms – at Winchester six are for seven years, the canonical maximum under *Cum ex eo*.

Orleton was also solicitous for the education of the monks of his cathedral priory in accordance with the Benedictine statute *De studiis*[133] and Boniface XII's recent constitution *Summi magistri*.[134] In pursuance of the former the official was instructed to provide a teacher of the elementary sciences of grammar, logic and philosophy for those monks apt to profit.[135] Some two years after the publication of Benedict's constitution on 20 June 1336 Orleton deputed his chancellor and official, in co-operation with the Winchester chapter, to select eight monks from among whom one for every twenty inmates of the priory could be chosen for despatch to the *studium generale* at Oxford.[136] There were probably some sixty monks in the priory at this time.[137]

Study of Orleton's Winchester register must mitigate the traditional impression of a grasping careerist neglectful of his diocesan responsibilities. At many points Orleton is to be found personally engaged in pastoral, judicial and administrative activity. He would appear to have been a diligent preacher, at any rate at times of visitation, and many of his sermon themes were noted by the registrar. Frequently present for the probate of wills of important laymen and clerics,[138] he took a lively interest in the rights of his see, defending them against king,[139] archbishop,[140]

133 For the operation of *De studiis* see *Documents of the English Black Monks*, index of subjects *s.v.* Benedict XII, and esp. 2, pp. 84–5.

134 Benedict's constitutions are printed in *Concilia* 2, pp. 588–613. Part of *Summi magistri*, containing the 'one in twenty' provision, is printed in *Chartularium Universitatis Parisiensis* 2, pp. 463–5. See also D. Knowles, *The Religious Orders in England*, 3 vols. Cambridge 1948–9, 2, ch. 2.

135 Win.R.O. 1, fo. 67^{v}, 30 October 1338.

136 Win.R.O. 1, fo. 67^{r-v}, 15 October 1338.

137 According to a note on a blank leaf of Bishop Pontissara's Winchester register (fo. 143) there were sixty-four monks in 1325: *V.C.H. Hampshire* 2, p. 111.

138 There are a large number of instances in the register. See Haines, 'Orleton and Winchester', p. 20, n. 8.

139 He received confirmation of the church of Winchester's liberties in 1338: Win.R.O. 1, fos. 144^{v}–145^{r}. He vigorously petitioned against defence measures which interfered with ecclesiastical rights (e.g. at Godshill: Win.R.O. 1, fo. 88^{v}; S.C.8/237/11831) and against unjust demands for payment of taxes (C.81/276/14100). He may well have been in sympathy with Archbishop Stratford's stand against the erosion of the Church's liberties, and the 'reformanda in concilio provinciali' (of October 1341) were put down for discussion by the Winchester clergy. See Win.R.O. 1, fol. 107^{v}; *Birchington*, pp. 26–7.

140 E.g. in response to Stratford's action in the Twynham election (Win.R.O. 1, fos. 93^{r}–95^{v}) and the appointment of coadjutors (*C.P.L.* 1342–62, p. 52). In 1343

and most notably against the virulent archdeacon of Surrey. Some of these affairs may seem trifling to us, as, for instance, the precise status to be accorded to the Winchester diocesan by virtue of his position as acting dean of the Canterbury province during the vacancy at London consequent upon the death of Richard Bentworth in 1339.[141] But to the men of those times – and they are hardly alone in this – the defence of privilege and prerogative was essential, and no one in an official position could safely neglect it.

There are some unexpected personal touches, such as the picture of the bishop on the high road between the villages of Oxenford and Elstead, preoccupied with the confirmation of children, warning the trouble-seeking minions of William Inge to permit him to finish his task.[142] Then again, that of Orleton hearing the confession of Matilda, the wife of Robert le Coupare of Stoke-by-Guildford, who had committed adultery. After granting absolution he commuted her public penance for one less severe, calling to mind as he did so Christ's action with respect to the woman taken in adultery.[143] There is another aspect too: the assurance of the trained lawyer in his round condemnation of the 'motivum sophisticum' of the dean of the Court of Arches in denying proof of the pension anciently due from the Surrey archdeacons.[144]

As he grew older and weaker Orleton had to seek the help of suffragans. In 1341, 'corporalibus molestiis prepediti', he informed the diocese of his commission of episcopal functions to Richard Francis, the bishop of Waterford;[145] earlier in the same year he had made use of the services of that stormy petrel, Richard Ledred, bishop of Ossory.[146] But once again there are no ordina-

Orleton secured the renewal of a papal bull of exemption for himself and his diocese in the same form as that granted to the Exeter diocesan, Grandisson. This was directed against the metropolitan. *C.P.L.* 1342–62, p. 112; *C.P.P.* 1342–1419, p. 59.

141 Win.R.O. 1, fo. 83v.

142 Win.R.O. 1, fo. 28v.

143 Win.R.O. 1, fo. 2v.

144 Win.R.O. 1, fo. 24r–v.

145 Win.R.O. 1, fo. 99r, 25 July 1341. Just before Easter 1342 Orleton informed the cathedral prior that the bishop of Waterford would be coming 'pro sacri confeccione crismatis et aliis que pontificalem requirunt presenciam': *ibid.* 1, fo. 111r, 26 March 1342. Some years earlier (5 November 1339) both the bishop of Waterford and Robert Stratford, bishop of Chichester, had been with Orleton at Farnham. *Ibid.* 1, fo. 81r.

146 Win.R.O. 1, fos. 42v–43r, 15 September 1336. He was appointed to celebrate orders on Ember Saturday, 21 September. Later (22 January 1337), he was authorised to

tion lists and hence no means of telling how much of this work Orleton had performed himself in the earlier years.

One of Orleton's last public acts was to assist at the consecration of his nephew John Trillek as bishop of Hereford. This took place on 29 August 1344 and it was doubtless for Orleton's convenience that Waverley Abbey, just outside Farnham, was chosen for the ceremony. The other bishops participating were Ralph Stratford of London, probably the archbishop's nephew and his staunch supporter in 1341, Robert Wyville of Salisbury, Martival's successor, and Wolstan de Bransford of Worcester, whom Orleton had ousted from that bishopric in 1327.[147] Any grudges that may have been harboured were by this time either forgotten or set aside. Trillek returned to Hereford for his enthronement on 24 October, but in March 1345 he is to be found at Farnham giving assistance to his uncle. He remained there until after Orleton's death on 18 July.[148]

It had been a busy episcopate beset by problems, some of them conspicuously out of the ordinary; so far as it is possible for us to judge Orleton has acquitted himself in a manner of which he could have no reason to feel ashamed.

ORLETON'S ADMINISTRATION AND 'FAMILIA'

By English standards all three of Orleton's dioceses were of moderate size, each being divided into two archdeaconries.[1] One distinction between them arose from the fact that Hereford cathedral was served by a secular chapter, whilst both at Worces-

dedicate the rebuilt church of Ockley ('Hokkeleye'), and in 1341 (4 May) to confirm children, to dedicate, consecrate or reconcile churches or altars, to confer the first tonsure and to hear confessions: *ibid.* 1, fos. 49^{r}, 104^{v}. Ledred's career is summarised by Colledge in his introduction to *The Latin Poems of Richard Ledrede*. Clarke, *Fourteenth Century Studies*, pp. 24–5, associates him with the 'Mortimer faction' in Ireland, opposed to the 'Despenser faction' of Arnold le Poer, seneschal of Kilkenny, Ledred's antagonist. For some years before 1321 Mortimer had been Justiciar of Ireland. It is doubtful whether this had anything to do with Orleton's choice of him as suffragan. After all, Ledred also served Hamo de Hethe.

147 *Hereford Reg. Trillek*, pp. i, 21. The editor gives the date as 24 June 1344, confusing the Nativity with the Decollation of St John the Baptist.

148 *Hereford Reg. Trillek*, pp. 21, 23ff. Entered in this register are Trillek's letters testifying to Orleton's death on 18 July 'inter horam dormicionis postprandie consuetam in Anglia et horam vesperarum ejusdem diei' (*ibid.* p. 55).

1 For Worcester diocese see *Worc. Admin.*, map facing p. 1 and ch. 2; for Winchester, Haines, 'Orleton and Winchester', p. 9.

ter and Winchester there was a house of Benedictine monks of which the bishop was nominal abbot – though on account of a jealously-preserved independence this fact was seldom emphasised. From the diocesan's point of view the former arrangement was more practical, for the secular chapter comprised clerks, usually university trained, with a wealth of experience in business, legal and diplomatic affairs – men whom Orleton found both congenial and useful. Strictly speaking, the monks of a cathedral priory, inhibited by their rule of claustral stability, were neither readily available nor particularly suited to the tasks for which the bishop required assistance, though in practice he did make limited use of some few of them.[2] However, Orleton's *familia* comprised only secular clerks some of whom, as we shall see, served him for long periods and accompanied him from one diocese to another.

Little is remarkable about the administrative system at Hereford. The bishop's principal legal and administrative officer was the official, and as soon as he reached the diocese Orleton deputed M. Richard de Vernon to serve in that capacity.[3] Vernon, the son of Sir Ralph de Vernon, a Cheshire knight, was completing his studies in canon law at Oxford when summoned to Orleton's service. The bishop rewarded him with a canonry and, helped by the king, secured licence from the university chancellor to enable him to cut short his regency.[4] Vernon continued to be active as official – though not always named as such in the register – until towards the end of 1324;[5] thereafter he could have been largely absent from Hereford. Either at that time, or shortly afterwards, he returned to his native diocese and secured a canonry of Lichfield, where he died in 1334 without having continued his administrative career.[6] No successor as official is traceable.

2 Orleton, for one, made very little use of the Worcester monks, but at Winchester he appointed Prior Alexander Heriard vicar-general on several occasions: see below and Haines, 'Orleton and Winchester', pp. 9–10. He also commissioned the subprior, John de Ford, to execute mandates directed to himself or his official: *ibid.* p. 11, n. 4; Win.R.O. 1, fo. 1r: 22 March 1334.

3 *H.R.O.*, pp. 31, 43–4.

4 *H.R.O.*, pp. 108–9, 216–17, 385 (Vernon was prebendary of Inkberrow); *C.C.R.* 1318–23, p. 121 (dispensation sought at the king's request because Orleton was engaged in his service, 18 January 1319). For a summary biography, though with some omissions, see *Biog. Oxon. s.v.*

5 E.g. *H.R.O.*, pp. 67, 94, 107, 130, 237, 239, 267, 307, 308.

6 *Biog. Oxon. s.v.*

At Hereford, and this is somewhat unusual,[7] the commissary-general was appointed merely as the official's assessor, although it could be, as in other dioceses, that he specialised in the correction of the bishop's subjects: we cannot be sure.[8] We do know that at this time commissaries were authorised to act 'in the official's absence' and with corresponding powers.[9] M. Richard de Sidenhale became commissary on 10 May 1318[10] and was reappointed some two and a half years later together with M. William Russell of Fownhope in Herefordshire.[11] Activity by Sidenhale is not evident after February 1321 and this later commission may mark the phasing out of his duties. His colleague Russell, who did continue to act,[12] was reappointed on 19 May 1326, this time with M. Nicholas de Caerwent and M. Thomas Boleye as his assistants.[13] Sidenhale's disappearance is unexplained: he later became archdeacon of Shropshire and vicar-general of Thomas Charlton, the king's nominee for Hereford in 1317 and Orleton's successor there.[14]

The offices of receiver and administrator and of episcopal treasurer were filled by two of Orleton's closest associates, Walter Carles[15] and Roger de Breynton.[16] Breynton was one of Bishop Swinfield's executors and like Carles destined to perform the same function for Orleton himself.[17] Early in the episcopate he handed to the new bishop the breviary which had been passed on from Cantilupe to Swinfield.[18] We have already noticed that he was appointed Orleton's proctor at the Curia, together with Muri-

7 Though the same practice obtained at Winchester. See below and Haines, 'Orleton and Winchester', pp. 14–15.

8 *Worc. Admin.*, pp. 128–33; Haines, 'John Carpenter', pp. 17–19.

9 E.g. *H.R.O.*, pp. 74, 85, 86, 157–8, 225.

10 *H.R.O.*, p. 74.

11 *H.R.O.*, pp. 157–8: 15 November 1320.

12 *H.R.O.*, pp. 233, 272, 283, 295–6, 311, 343, 361.

13 *H.R.O.*, p. 361.

14 *Le Neve* 2, p. 7; *Hereford Reg. Charlton*, *s.v.*; *Worcester Reg. Bransford*, pp. 4, 193.

15 Carles was rector of Broadway (Worcester diocese), subsequently of Cradley (Herefs.), and a canon of Hereford. His full title was 'receiver and administrator of the bishop's temporalities and spiritualities'. *H.R.O.*, pp. 119, 178, 387; *W.R.O.* 2, fo. 6r [522].

16 He was rector of Monnington, later of Rock (both Hereford diocese), and a canon of Hereford. See also *Worc. Admin.*, index *s.v.*; Haines, 'Orleton and Winchester', p. 17.

17 *H.R.O.*, pp. 58, 383–4; *Hereford Reg. Trillek*, pp. 53–4, 133–5.

18 *H.R.O.*, p. 40.

muth and Sapiti, and that his chief purpose at Avignon was to perform the new bishop's oath of fealty.[19] Breynton was employed in diocesan affairs until early in 1322: in March of that year he secured Orleton's licence to leave his benefice of Rock and to study abroad for five years.[20] This is the last we hear of him until after the bishop's translation to Worcester.

Apart from these regular officers the bishop's absences necessitated the appointment of vicars-general at frequent intervals. Seven such appointments of M. Richard de Vernon were made, the last jointly with Thomas de Pembridge, treasurer of the cathedral church.[21] Following the appointment of M. Thomas de Chaundos, archdeacon of Hereford, on 13 August 1322, no further commissions of the kind were issued until 28 March 1327, at which date Orleton resumed his travels at the behest of the new government and deputed M. Henry de Shorne, Adam de Herwynton and M. William Russell to act for him in the diocese.[22]

Whenever he left the country Orleton, in line with current practice, deputed attorneys as well as commissaries – one of whom was almost invariably the vicar-general – to fill the benefices in his collation.[23] John de Bromfield was one of the regular attorneys:[24] in 1317 Orleton had named him among those deputed to receive livery of the temporalities, and in August of the same year he became steward, the highest temporal office.[25] Bromfield was prominent in the locality and from time to time served on royal commissions to investigate complaints about land and property.[26] In 1319 he was associated with some of Orleton's most trusted officers, Vernon, Breynton and Carles, and with the bailiff of Bromyard, to audit the accounts which were to be

19 *H.R.O.*, pp. 77–8.

20 *H.R.O.*, p. 391; 17 March 1322. Until that time he had been acting as the bishop's treasurer: *ibid.* pp. 181, 214.

21 *H.R.O.*, pp. 43–4, 61, 67–8, 106–7, 124, 180, 241–2. They are dated, respectively, 28 October 1317, 13 February* and 28 March 1318, 19 February 1319, 1 March 1320*, 26 January 1321, 25 June 1322*. The dates marked with an asterisk indicate commissions omitted by Emden, *Biog. Oxon.*, *s.v.*

22 *H.R.O.*, p. 374.

23 E.g. *C.P.R.* 1317–21, pp. 265, 427, 564–5; *C.P.R.* 1327–30, pp. 61, 269; S.C.1/36/15.

24 *C.P.R.* 1317–21, pp. 265, 427, 564–5; *H.R.O.*, p. 107.

25 *H.R.O.*, pp. 8–9, 16. His appointment as steward is dated 21 August 1317.

26 E.g. *C.P.R.* 1317–21, pp. 298–9, 374, and cf. 483, 547; *C.C.R.* 1318–23, pp. 14, 37, 65, 133.

rendered by all deans, bailiffs and other ministers for the whole period from the livery of the spiritualities until that time.[27] Like the bishop's marshal, Tristram, he was implicated in the Mortimer rebellion. In 1326, after Edward II's flight, he acted as proctor for receiving the elder Despenser's manor of Beaumes.[28]

For the smooth running of diocesan business an efficient notary was essential – probably more than one. During the early part of Orleton's time at Hereford – that is until about 1320 – this work, and perhaps the office of registrar, fell mainly on the shoulders of M. Richard de Eastnor, who was a Herefordshire man.[29] The vacancy of his benefice reveals that he had died by September 1322[30] and it is not clear who took his place, for although various notaries, some of them no doubt in the chapter's service, were active in the diocese, no single one is dominant.[31] But the hand of M. John de Radenhale, identifiable from notarial instruments among the Hereford muniments, is to be discerned in Orleton's episcopal register,[32] and the subsequent career of John de Beautre, one of the notaries whom Orleton created, argues that he may also have served in the Hereford registry at this time.[33] Another notary, Reginald de Munslow, who drew up the *inspeximus* of the bull for Cantilupe's canonisation, was involved in a violent scuffle in the chapel of the bishop's manor of Bosbury, during the course of which he injured William de Wigton, one of Orleton's familiar clerks.[34] He was apparently the aggressor, for

27 *H.R.O.*, p. 119.

28 *Parliamentary Writs* 2 (app.), p. 218; *H.R.O.*, p. 371, 9 November [1326]. Orleton subsequently petitioned the king for redress because hay from meadows belonging to the manor had been carried off: S.C.1/37/95.

29 E.g. *H.R.O.*, pp. 84, 92, 93–4, 97–8, 110, 137, 149, 153, 160; H.C.M., no. 1445.

30 He became rector of Eaton Bishop by episcopal collation on 24 January 1321: a new appointment was made on 20 September 1322 following his death. *H.R.O.*, pp. 386, 388.

31 Among them were John de Radnor, John de Beautre, Reginald de Munslow, Walter de Leominster, Richard Berde of Ledbury and Richard Hervi. Notarial instruments drawn up by some of these are to be found among the Hereford Cathedral muniments. See the index to the 'Calendar of the Earlier Hereford Cathedral Muniments' and Emanuel, 'Notaries Public', pp. 147–63.

32 E.g. *H.R.O.*, fos. 6^r, 9^{r-v}, 72^r–78^r (top); H.C.M., nos. 770, 3006.

33 Beautre was to become Orleton's registrar at Worcester and possibly at Winchester too. See below and *W.R.O.* 1, fos. 31^v–32^v (one of his notarial instruments), Win. R.O. 1, fo. 55^r; W.A.M., no. 21262 (in which he is entitled bishop's notary); H.C.M., no. 1069 (dated 1340 at Farnham).

34 H.C.M., no. 1445; *H.R.O.*, pp. 233–4, 245–6. He fled to Worcester diocese where Orleton sought Cobham's help in declaring him excommunicate.

having taken an oath of good behaviour he repeated the offence some seven months later, after which we hear no more of him among the bishop's familiars.[35]

The identification of office-holders far from exhausts the list of those closely concerned with the bishop and his affairs. Both Adam de Aylton and Nicholas de Rock were termed *capellani episcopi* – apparently in the sense of domestic chaplains – when the Hereford chapter selected them to take possession of the newly-appropriated rectory of Shinfield.[36] This is surprising in Nicholas's case; admittedly he had served Bishop Swinfield for many years, but his early contact with his successor proved unfortunate. As portionist of Ledbury, besides being the non-resident and inadequately-ordained vicar of Stretton, he fell foul of the bishop's punctiliousness in implementing the plurality regulations and was for a time excommunicated for contumacy.[37] In fact Nicholas is scarcely to be found in the bishop's company and any permanent association may be discounted. Adam de Aylton or Aylington is a different case, for he was in frequent attendance on the bishop until late in 1320 when he temporarily disappears from view.[38]

Some other clerks warrant special mention. Among those with legal expertise were M. John Rees, M. Henry de London[39] and M. Henry de Shorne.[40] Orleton appointed Rees and London his proctors in the Court of Canterbury.[41] Shorne, whom Orleton had caused to resign from the archdeaconry of Hereford,[42] was

35 *H.R.O.*, p. 246.

36 *H.R.O.*, p. 162.

37 *H.R.O.*, pp. 86–7, 89, 105, 110–11.

38 E.g. *H.R.O.*, pp. 1–2, 41–2, 59, 97–8, 137, 149, 153, 160, 162. He had been one of Bishop Swinfield's clerks: H.C.M., no. 1030.

39 In 1334 Rees is termed 'doctor of decrees' i.e. D.Cn.L. (Win.R.O. 1, fo. 3^r), and could therefore be the man noted in *Biog. Oxon.* 3, app. *s.v.*; cf. *Biog. Oxon.*, *s.v.* Rys, John D.Cn.L. He later became John Trillek's vicar-general at Hereford: *Worcester Reg. Bransford*, pp. 107–8, 222. London is not mentioned in either *Biog. Oxon.* or *Biog. Cantab.*, but there are a number of references to him in Orleton's Worcester register. He also occurs in the Winchester one and in W.A.M., no. 21262, where he receives the same fee as the chancellor, viz. 6s 8d.

40 Shorne was an old associate of Orleton's. Both had been proctors of the Hereford chapter for securing Cantilupe's canonisation: *Acta Sanctorum mensis Octobris* 1, p. 599; H.C.M., no. 1443. *Biog. Oxon. s.v.* omits his appointment as vicar-general in 1327.

41 *H.R.O.*, pp. 242–3. London (like Radenhale) was to perform the same office for Orleton as bishop of Worcester. *W.R.O.* 2, fo. 8^v [537, 538].

42 *H.R.O.*, p. 60. He had contravened the new canon *Execrabilis* (1317) against plurality.

an Oxford doctor of civil law, who not only concerned himself with diocesan matters but also accompanied Orleton on some of his diplomatic missions.[43]

With M. Thomas de Guines, described on one occasion as 'dilectus socius noster', the bishop clearly had a close relationship. As long before as 1307 they had both been proctors of the Hereford chapter for forwarding Cantilupe's sanctification. Guines continued to be much concerned with the business of the saint – arrangements for the celebration of his feast and the erection of a new shrine in his honour.[44]

It is difficult to write specifically of the Hereford canons in Orleton's regular or occasional service simply because so many of his clerks in the ordinary course received recompense, indeed their means of support, by promotion to canonries: Vernon, Breynton and Carles all obtained them, while Shorne was already a canon prior to Orleton's episcopate.[45] It is noteworthy however that the bishop singled out Canons Adam Carbonel,[46] John de la Felde[47] and Richard de Hamenasch[48] for the purgation of criminous clerks lodged in the episcopal gaol at Hereford, while Adam Murimuth was commissioned to confer benefices in Orleton's gift and to admit the resignations of incumbents.[49] Somewhat after, in 1322, Canon Thomas de Pembridge is to be found performing these latter functions and acting as vicar-general.[50] Gilbert de Middleton, a canon with whom Orleton had almost a lifetime association, was likewise deputed to fill episcopal benefices.[51]

We may deal lastly with the bishop's relatives. Of his brothers Thomas and John, both canons of Hereford,[52] the former was by

43 *C.P.R.* 1317–21, pp. 265, 427.

44 *Acta Sanctorum mensis Octobris* I, p. 592E; *C.P.R.* 1317–21, p. 526; *H.R.O.*, pp. 139–40.

45 *H.R.O.*, pp. 385, 388, 389; *C.P.L.* 1305–42, p. 195. Surprisingly Aylton did not receive a canonry.

46 *H.R.O.*, pp. 5, 14, 37, 209, 372–3.

47 *H.R.O.*, pp. 5, 37, 312–13, 372–3. He was one of Swinfield's executors: see, for example, *ibid.* pp. 58, 384.

48 *H.R.O.*, pp. 14, 26–7. He was also an executor of Bishop Swinfield.

49 *H.R.O.*, pp. 36–7, 124, 130.

50 *H.R.O.*, pp. 237–8, 241. He was treasurer of the cathedral.

51 *H.R.O.*, p. 124.

52 Both are entitled *magister*, though only John has an entry in *Biog. Oxon.* See also *W.R.O.*, index *s.v.*

far the more active in Adam's administration and in 1322 succeeded Robert of Gloucester as chancellor of Hereford cathedral.[53] On the other hand Orleton's nephews John and Thomas Trillek, future bishops of Hereford (1344–60) and Rochester (1364–72) respectively, were still very young, and even when the pope provided them to Hereford canonries in 1327 neither could have been much more than eighteen and Thomas may have been somewhat younger than that.[54]

So far our concern has been chiefly with members of Orleton's *familia* engaged in diocesan business, but when the bishop went abroad in 1319, 1320 and 1321 royal grants of protection enumerate seven or eight men who accompanied him, and in 1327 as many as eleven.[55] Some of these, such as Breynton, Guines, and the brothers John and Thomas Orleton, are familiar names, but there were others. Among those who travelled with Orleton more than once are Thomas de Hompton, rector of the Worcestershire parish of Redmarley,[56] Howel le Waleys, a layman and among those whom the bishop was accused of sending to Mortimer's aid in 1321, and Thomas de Bishopston, elsewhere described as a clerk of Canterbury diocese.[57]

When Orleton moved to the neighbouring diocese of Worcester he found the administrative system substantially the same.[58] Again the most important officer was the official, three of whom are mentioned during the episcopate. The first, M. William Russell, brought with him experience of a similar office at Hereford and with M. John de Radenhale, whom we have already

[53] *H.R.O.*, p. 387. In October 1332 Adam Orleton, then bishop, described him as 'germanus noster senio gravatus et morbo': Worcester Liber Albus, fo. cli^{r}.

[54] *H.R.O.*, p. 389, and for short biographies *Biog. Oxon.*, *s.v.* In 1330 John Trillek is said to have obtained canonries of Bromyard and Westbury 'being in his twentieth year', as well as a prebend of Hereford, of which he had been deprived. *C.P.L.* 1305–42, p. 316.

[55] *C.P.R.* 1317–21, pp. 265, 427, 564–5; *C.P.R.* 1327–30, p. 62.

[56] In 1339 he and others acknowledged in the Exchequer that they owed £530 to Queen Isabella (*Worcester Reg. Bransford*, p. 297 and index *s.v.*). A man of this name, said to be a clerk, was steward of Roger Mortimer and responsible for prisoners in Pembroke Castle at the time of Mortimer's arrest (1330). In 1336 the bishop of Hereford was ordered to distrain him to produce records concerning certain of the prisoners. Charlton returned that he had no benefice. The rector of Redmarley had formerly held the church of Sapey (Hereford diocese). *Hereford Reg. Charlton*, p. 61; *C.P.R.* 1317–21, p. 265.

[57] In 1329 Orleton was executor of a bull of provision in his favour. *W.R.O.* 1, fo. 36^{r} [323]; *C.P.L.* 1305–42, p. 280.

[58] See *Worc. Admin.*, esp. ch. 3.

met as a notary, enthroned Orleton at Worcester on behalf of Hugh d'Angoulême, the archdeacon of Canterbury.[59] Russell occurs initially as official in May 1328,[60] continuing to act in that capacity until January 1330, at which point the dean of Worcester was empowered to assign days for the hearing of cases in the consistory court because business elsewhere prevented the official from so doing.[61] At a later stage – the first half of 1332 – Russell reappears as official.[62] His successor in September 1330, M. Robert de Worth, is the only official whose commission of appointment is to be found in Orleton's episcopal register.[63] He was still acting in January of the following year[64] and in 1333 became vicar-general of the bishop of Salisbury, thereby returning to the diocese from which he had come.[65] The third official, John de Karseleye, rector of Kidderminster, is first mentioned as such in October 1332 when he apparently succeeded the reappointed Russell.[66]

Again, as at Hereford, diplomatic activity necessitated Orleton's issuing repeated commissions to vicars-general, and there are five of these.[67] The first nominated Adam de Herwynton,[68] who less than three months later was reappointed, this time jointly with the official, William Russell.[69] In the third commission[70] Herwynton is associated with Robert de Worth, at the time official, and with Roger de Breynton, shortly to become archdeacon of Gloucester.[71] Herwynton is joined with Russell – once again acting as official – in the fourth commission,[72] and in the final one with Roger de Breynton.[73] In the nature of things Herwynton, a busy royal clerk, must often have been unavailable for

59 On 19 June, the feast of the martyrs SS. Gervasius and Prothasius. *W.R.O.* 2, fos. 6^v–7^r [528–9].

60 *W.R.O.* 2, fo. 6^v [526].

61 *W.R.O.* 2, fo. 12^r [579].

62 *W.R.O.* 1, fos. 25^{r-v}, 26^r [160, 167, 174].

63 *W.R.O.* 2, fo. 12^r, September 1330 [581]; printed *Worc. Admin.*, pp. 331–2.

64 *W.R.O.* 2, fos. 39^r, 40^v [803, 811].

65 See *Biog. Oxon.*, *s.v.*

66 *W.R.O.* 1, fos. 27^v, 42^r [181, 467]; *ibid.* 2, fo. 52^r [925].

67 Enumerated in *Worc. Admin.*, p. 324, and with some discussion, *ibid.* p. 103, n. 4.

68 For whom see *Worc. Admin.*, index *s.v.* Herwynton [Harvington]; *Worcester Reg. Bransford*, index *s.v.* M. Hodgetts, 'Adam of Harvington, Prelate and Politician', *Trans. Worcs. Archaeological Soc.* 36 (1959), pp. 33–41.

69 *W.R.O.* 1, fos. 3^v, 6^v [499, 526]: dated 29 February and 15 May 1328.

70 *W.R.O.* 2, fo. 39^r [803]: 18 January 1331.

71 *W.R.O.* 1, fo. 31^r [208–9], and see *Worc. Admin.*, *s.v.*

72 *W.R.O.* 1, fo. 40^r [414]: 20 April 1332.

73 *W.R.O.* 1, fo. 27^r [179]: 9 November 1332.

diocesan business, but in any case evidence for vicarial activity is slight apart from a few institutions effected by Russell.[74]

A commissary-general first appears in February 1328, when William Russell is so described.[75] On the 29th of that month Orleton deputed him to hear causes and to enquire into, correct and punish the offences of his subjects.[76] Seemingly Russell's task was to secure the spiritual jurisdiction pending the bishop's advent and the appointment of a permanent official – a post which he was himself to occupy a few months later.[77] Some years afterwards M. John de Usk is to be observed acting as commissary during the official's absence[78] – an arrangement surely copied from Hereford practice.

In Worcester diocese the sequestrator – later to be styled the commissary-general – was one of the principal members of the episcopal administration; but at Hereford, as has been shown, there was no officer of that name.[79] Even so, we may presume that Nicholas de Caerwent's previous experience as deputy-commissary there proved of value when he came to be appointed as the Worcester sequestrator (29 February 1328) – an office which, so far as we know, he continued to hold for the remainder of the episcopate.[80] Like other sequestrators Caerwent was engaged in correction ex officio, but following Orleton's visitation in 1329 or 1330 he was specifically deputed with the official and M. John de Usk to deal with *comperta* at Bristol, and perhaps elsewhere.[81] He also acted as collector of Peter's Pence[82] and the sphere of his work was further expanded by additional commissions.[83]

This time the episcopal register does reveal the name of Orleton's scribe or, as he was later to be called, registrar. He was the

74 *W.R.O.* 1, fos. 16^{v}–17^{r} [46–8]; *ibid.* 2, fo. 24^{r} [666–8].
75 *W.R.O.* 2, fo. 13^{r} [586]: 22 February 1328.
76 *W.R.O.* 2, fo. 4^{r} [500]: 29 February 1328.
77 See *W.R.O.* 2, fo. 3^{v} [498].
78 *W.R.O.* 2, fos. 37^{v}–38^{r} [797]: 18 December 1330.
79 It is to be noted, however, that sede vacante the archbishop appointed M. Walter de Penebrugg (Pembridge) sequestrator eo nomine. Canterbury Reg. Reynolds, fo. 88^{r-v}.
80 *W.R.O.* 2, fo. 4^{r} [501]. For the office see *Worc. Admin.*, pp. 114–24. For details about him see Haines, 'Orleton and Winchester', pp. 17–18. That he is sometimes termed *magister* may be because of his position as notary; he does not appear to have been a university graduate.
81 *W.R.O.* 1, fo. 36^{v} [331]; *ibid.* 2, fo. 34^{v} [764].
82 *W.R.O.* 2, fo. 11^{r} [565].
83 E.g. for the appropriation of Duntisbourne church to Dore Abbey: *W.R.O.* 2, fo. 16^{r} [611].

John de Beautre, a clerk native to Worcester diocese, whom we have already noticed at Hereford. Thanks to a notarial instrument of his preserved elsewhere [84] Beautre's hand can be identified in the episcopal register.[85] Other notaries who may have assisted him were Richard Hervi and Richard called ' Berde ' of Ledbury.[86] The latter was to remain at Worcester as the scribe of Orleton's successor, Bishop Montacute,[87] which suggests some earlier experience in the registry.

The nucleus of Orleton's Worcester administration was thus formed by Russell, Breynton, Caerwent and Beautre – all of whom he had brought from Hereford – with the addition of John de Usk, a native of Llandaff diocese and a newcomer to the *familia*. Usk was a canon lawyer [88] and for occasional legal business the bishop could turn to his former aides London, Rees and Radenhale. London, for instance, again acted as proctor-general in the Court of Canterbury, this time in association with Radenhale.[89]

Three men are specifically termed *capellani* or domestic chaplains: John de Mere,[90] William de Leamington,[91] and William de Wigton, who survived his ill-treatment at Munslow's hands.[92] To them as members of the *familia* should be added John de Loughborough,[93] William de Breynton brother of Roger,[94] William de Culpho [95] and Geoffrey de Upton.[96] Loughborough,

84 H.C.M., no. 1069. His notarial sign embodies a pun on his name.

85 *W.R.O.* 2, fo. 57^{v}. He was collated to St Helen's, Worcester, in 1332: *ibid.* fo. 50^{r} [901]. See also Haines, ' Orleton and Winchester ', p. 18; *Worcester Reg. Bransford*, pp. 61, 361.

86 Both clerks of Hereford diocese. For Hervi see *H.R.O.*, pp. 110, 115. Orleton by apostolic authority appointed Berde a notary on 2 September 1320: *ibid.* pp. 147–9.

87 *Worc. Admin.*, pp. 10, n. 4, 134, 253; W.A.M., nos. 21266, 21267.

88 In a petition of 1343 for provision he is described as a B.C.L. ' skilled in canon law ': *C.P.P.* 1342–1419, p. 58.

89 *W.R.O.* 2, fo. 8^{v} [537–8]. He was authorised to deal with specific matrimonial cases: *ibid.* fos. 20^{v}, 36^{r} [639–40, 784].

90 *W.R.O.* 1, fo. 25^{v} [166]. A licence, dated 1335, for three years' absence from his benefice (Worcester Reg. Montacute 1, fo. 15^{r}) shows that he continued in Orleton's service at Winchester.

91 *W.R.O.* 2, fos. 37^{v}–38^{r} [797], where he is termed ' capellanus noster familiaris '. Cf. *H.R.O.*, pp. 376, 378.

92 *W.R.O.* 1, fo. 28^{r} [187]; *H.R.O.*, pp. 233–4, 245–6, 378.

93 *W.R.O.* 2, fos. 9^{r}, 13^{v} [546, 593]; *H.R.O.*, pp. 376, 378.

94 H.C.M., nos. 12–14; *W.R.O.* 2, fo. 9^{r} [547]; *H.R.O.*, p. xxviii, n. 2; *C.P.R.* 1327–30, p. 269.

95 *W.R.O.* 2, fo. 32^{v} [744]; *H.R.O.*, p. 376; *C.P.L.* 1305–42, pp. 100, 264, 281, 388. He received dispensation for illegitimacy and plurality, Queen Isabella petitioning on his behalf.

96 *W.R.O.* 1, fo. 28^{v} [191]; Haines, ' Orleton and Winchester ', pp. 18–19.

William de Breynton and doubtless others are found doing duty as episcopal *nuncii.*[97] In addition there ought to be included Adam de Aylton, later to become non-resident dean of Westbury on the grounds that he was in Orleton's service,[98] the bishop's brothers and his nephews, the Trilleks, all of whom can be presumed to have given aid or counsel even though their presence is seldom recorded.

Once more the lists of those who accompanied Orleton on his continental journeys [99] include men who had served him in the diocese, for example Aylton, Roger de Breynton, Culpho, Mere, Upton and Loughborough, but also several others, among them Robert Petyt [100] and the layman John le Rous of Imber, Wiltshire, whose association with Orleton might otherwise have escaped notice.[101] The inclusion for the first time in 1332 of the physician John de Boys may be an early indication of the bishop's anxiety about his own health.[102]

The Worcester register is somewhat unusual in the amount of information it contains about custodians of the bishop's temporalities – lay members of the bishop's *familia*. Richard de Bikerton was initially deputed to receive seisin of the temporalities and then appointed to the principal office of steward.[103] In the spring and autumn of 1332, and again in October 1333, he was one of those named attorney during Orleton's absence on the continent. The bishop rewarded him with land in his manor of Northwick by

97 E.g. *W.R.O.* 2, fo. 9^r^ [547].

98 *Worc. Admin.*, pp. 28–9; *C.P.L.* 1305–42, p. 396: 22 September 1333. In 1329 and 1330 he was licensed to be absent from his (successive) benefices of Aston Ingham and Rock whilst in Orleton's service. The latter he resigned at the Holy See in 1333, at which time he probably became dean of Westbury. *Hereford Reg. Charlton*, pp. 89, 90; *W.R.O.* 2, fo. 55^v^ [945].

99 *C.P.R.* 1327–30, pp. 482–3; *C.P.R.* 1330–34, pp. 42, 277–8.

100 In 1331 a Robert Petit occurs as proctor of M. Thomas de Trillek. He is probably to be identified with the R. Petyt, rector of Souldrop, whom Bishop Burghersh licensed to be absent in Orleton's service. *W.R.O.* 1, fo. 24^r^ [153]; *ibid.* 2, fo. 20^v^ [638: undated]. At Winchester Thomas Petyt, Walter de Masyngton and John de Orleton are named as valets of the bishop: Win.R.O. 1, fo. 69^r^.

101 In 1341 Alice, the widow of John le Rous, granted the manor of Imber ('Immer') to Orleton for her life. He seems to have acted as trustee, regranting it to her two years later. *C.P.R.* 1340–43, pp. 230, 580. This John le Rous could be the man of that name accused of aiding the rebels in 1321: Just. 1/1388/m. 2^v^.

102 *C.P.R.* 1330–34, p. 278. In 1329 Worcester Priory granted him a corrody in return for his professional services to the monks: *Worcester Liber Albus*, pp. 231–3 (from fo. 135^r^).

103 *W.R.O.* 2, fos. 4^v^–5^r^, 8^v^ [508, 542].

Worcester, but as he failed to secure the necessary royal licence Bikerton had to seek pardon for the omission in 1334.[104]

John de Stone, who early in 1328 was holding the manorial courts in the steward's absence,[105] became bailiff of the extensive liberty of Oswaldslow.[106] There are also undated letters, apparently of 1330, for the appointment of John de Hornygwold to that position.[107] The bailiffry of Hanbury, one of the Worcestershire manors, was assigned to John de Baddeby,[108] while Gilbert de Masington became custos of the episcopal palace and prison at Worcester.[109] Oswald Spelly's appointment as superintendent of the five manors of Wick, Whitstones, Hartlebury, Alvechurch and Hanbury could represent some attempt by Orleton at reorganisation.[110]

The administrative system which Orleton encountered on his move to Winchester was somewhat different from either of those he had previously experienced. There was of course a monastic chapter at Winchester, as there had been at Worcester, but the principal officers were the official, his assessor the commissary-general – on the Hereford pattern – and instead of a single sequestrator-general as at Worcester, there were two, one for each archdeaconry. Moreover at Winchester the pattern of triennial visitation was supplemented in the intervening years by general inquisitions, during which the jurisdiction of the archdeacons was suspended, as it was at times of visitation.[111]

The phasing out of the bishop's diplomatic missions meant that at Winchester there were few commissions to vicars-general, only three in fact. Alexander Heriard, the cathedral prior (1328–49), was acting in that capacity in July 1334, apparently because Orleton was unwilling or unable to remain in the diocese without the support of his temporalities.[112] In May of the following year

104 *C.P.R.* 1330–34, p. 554; 23 June 1334; for his appointments as attorney: *ibid.* pp. 277, 373, 472.

105 *W.R.O.* 2, fo. 6r [520]: 14 April 1328. This predates Bikerton's appointment as steward, presumably the first of the episcopate.

106 *W.R.O.* 2, fo. 5v [515]: 13 April 1328.

107 *W.R.O.* 2, fo. 36v [787–8].

108 *W.R.O.* 2, fo. 6r [517]: 13 April 1328.

109 *W.R.O.* 2, fo. 6r [518]: 14 April 1328.

110 *Ibid.* [519]: 14 April [1328].

111 For what follows see Haines, 'Orleton and Winchester', pp. 9–21, which is more detailed.

112 Win.R.O. 2, fo. 45r.

Heriard was reappointed, this time with the official M. John de Usk.[113] The last commission, coinciding with Orleton's final continental journey, is dated 21 July 1336 from Southwark and names the same two persons, but of their operations the episcopal register tells us little.[114]

For once, we know the identity of the diocesan chancellor – M. John de Wolveley. Unlike many contemporary chancellors he was active in the diocese, being associated with the official in various commissions and journeying to Archbishop Stratford's palace at Maidstone to put Orleton's case against the metropolitan's appointment of a prior of Twynham in derogation of the diocesan's rights.[115]

As might be expected, the clerk who figures most prominently in Orleton's Winchester register is once again the official. M. John de Usk is mentioned as such in a commission dated 3 November 1334 in which he is granted additional powers of enquiry, correction and punishment of the bishop's subjects,[116] together with that of insinuating wills, committing the administration of testators' goods to executors and auditing their accounts.[117] It would appear that Usk continued in office for the remainder of the episcopate. His assessor M. Adam Wambergh, the commissary-general, was like Wolveley a man not previously attached to Orleton's *familia*.[118]

No less than eight sequestrators-general can be traced,[119] four in the Winchester archdeaconry: William Gylle of Alresford, Thomas de Meonstoke, Richard de Haylinge and Thomas de Enham; and an equal number in that of Surrey: Gilbert de Kyrkeby, R[oger] Brian, John de Ichenstok and Walter or William atte Brugg. All of these men are entitled *magister* in the records, an indication of the growth in the number of those with

113 Win.R.O. 1, fo. 19r.

114 Win.R.O. 1, fo. 41r.

115 Win.R.O. 1, fos. 93r–95v.

116 Win.R.O. 1, fo. 58v. This commission has been inserted among the entries for 1338. As was made clear by Boniface VIII's regulation (*Sext* 1, 13, c. 2 *Licet in officialem*) such powers were not conferred by a commission of the officiality in general terms.

117 At Worcester, by contrast, commissions to officials at this time never contain clauses authorising them to deal with testamentary matters: this was primarily the business of the sequestrator-general. See *Worc. Admin.*, pp. 112–13 (for a possible case of an official granted testamentary jurisdiction), 114–24.

118 Haines, 'Orleton and Winchester', pp. 14–15.

119 For these men see *ibid.* pp. 16–17.

professional qualifications.[120] Although they were officers of what might be called the bishop's central administration, their concerns were in practice more localised, so it is not surprising to find that most of them were recruited from Winchester diocese.

Other positions were filled by clerks whom Orleton already knew well. We should expect to find M. John de Beautre as registrar, since he severed his Worcester connections by exchanging his benefice in the cathedral city there for Upham, Hampshire, which was a church in Orleton's collation.[121] Several of his notarial instruments were copied into the episcopal register;[122] he was commissioned to induct to benefices on a number of occasions,[123] and witnessed various official processes.[124] He could have been the 'general registrar',[125] but the only person entitled registrar is M. Roger Fraunceys of Breinton, near Hereford, who is called registrar of the Winchester consistory court.[126] This man was possibly a relative of the other Roger de Breynton,[127] archdeacon of Gloucester, who rather than move to Winchester found employment in his native diocese of Hereford with Bishops Charlton and Trillek.[128]

At Winchester Nicholas de Caerwent is again much in evidence. He was made treasurer of the bishop's household and wardrobe[129] and, outliving his patron, died in 1381 at a ripe old age.[130] Another office-holder from Worcester diocese was John de Nibley

120 I have only been able to identify one of the eight, *viz.* Richard de Haylinge, in *Biog. Oxon.* (*s.v.* Wythors de Haillinge) or *Biog. Cantab.*

121 Win.R.O. 2, fos. 48r–49r.

122 Win.R.O. 1, fos. 20r, 55r, 80v; *ibid.* 2, fos. 16v, 22v, 55r.

123 Win.R.O. 2, fos. 74r, 74v, 75v.

124 E.g. Win.R.O. 1, fo. 3r; *ibid.* 2, fos. 46r, 62r.

125 I.e. the bishop's registrar as opposed to the registrar of the consistory court. Cf. Haines, 'John Carpenter', p. 22.

126 Win.R.O. 1, fos. 100Cv–100Dr, 128v; Haines, 'Orleton and Winchester', p. 17. He apparently followed M. William de Alresford in the office.

127 See *Worc. Admin.*, *s.v.* Breynton. Occasionally a scribe may have slipped into designating him *magister*, but despite his absence for study (*H.R.O.*, p. 391, and see above), he appears not to have taken a university degree and is regularly *dominus* in the registers of Bishops Bransford (Worcester) and Trillek (Hereford), as indeed in *H.R.O.*

128 Haines, 'Orleton and Winchester', p. 17; *Hereford Regs. Charlton*, *Trillek*, indices *s.v.* Breynton.

129 He received acquittances as 'receptor denariorum nostrorum pro expensis hospicii et garderobe nostre' between 29 September 1336 and 1 October 1337: Win.R.O. 1, fo. 100Dr; and between 1 October 1338 and 1 October 1339: *ibid.* fo. 85r; and for the same period in the years 1340–1, 1341–2: *ibid.* fos. 110r, 116v. See also *ibid.* fo. 75r.

130 Haines, 'Orleton and Winchester', pp. 17–18.

(Nubbelegh), who acted as treasurer of Orleton's castle-manor of Wolvesey, a short walk from the cathedral church.[131]

Familiar names occur occasionally in the register's folios including those of Adam de Aylton,[132] and Geoffrey de Upton, who secured a benefice in the diocese.[133] There are also some new ones: Adam de Kynsare, termed bishop's clerk,[134] and another domestic chaplain, William de Meone, who followed Caerwent as treasurer of the household.[135] Among the large body of laymen and clerks accompanying Orleton on his last journey to France in 1336[136] are to be found his physician, M. John de Boys,[137] his sometime chancellor, M. John de Wolveley, Robert Petyt, William de Wigton and John de la Lowe, the last soon to leave Orleton's service for that of Wolstan de Bransford, bishop of Worcester, whose official he became.[138]

By the 1340s the bishop's group of faithful clerks had thinned out, but a surprising number survived who had worked with him in previous administrations. In a letter to Bishop Cobham, which has already been quoted, his own words bear witness to a concern for his *familia*[139] and his acts confirm them. Always a man to see that his clerks were in possession of adequate benefices for their support, if not by other means then by his own gift, one of his last acts was successfully to petition the Curia for a large number of dispensations for the holding of canonries and prebends in plurality: for Roger de Breynton, another but less exiguous prebend at Hereford; for his 'secretary' Nicholas de Caerwent, a canonry there; for John de Usk, his long-serving

131 *Ibid.* p. 18. Acquittance was given for the periods Michaelmas–Michaelmas 1336–7: Win.R.O. 1, fo. 100D^r; 1338–9: *ibid.* fo. 85^r; 1340–1: *ibid.* fo. 109^v; and 1341–2: *ibid.* fo. 116^v.

132 E.g. Win.R.O. 2, fos. 46^r, 48^r. As we have seen above, he was dean of Westbury-on-Trym, and in 1335 became rector of Middleton Cheney, Northants., by exchange. William de Edington became dean in his place. See Worcester Reg. Montacute 1, fo. 16^v.

133 Win.R.O. 2, fo. 46^r. He received the collation of East Meon vicarage, which he later exchanged for Candover rectory: *ibid.* fos. 86^v, 89^v.

134 North Waltham rectory was collated to him: Win.R.O. 2, fo. 86^v.

135 He received acquittance 22 November 1344 for the year Michaelmas 1343–4: Win. R.O. 1, fo. 128^r. Compton rectory was collated to him: *ibid.* 2, fo. 86^v.

136 *C.P.R.* 1334–38, p. 306.

137 Rector of Knightwick, Worcs., which he exchanged early in 1337 for Staunton-in-the-Forest (Hereford diocese): Worcester Reg. Montacute 1, fo. 26^v.

138 Haines, 'Orleton and Winchester', p. 19, n. 7: *Worcester Reg. Bransford*, index *s.v.*

139 *Worcester Reg. Cobham*, pp. 80–3.

official, a canonry of Lincoln; for John de Wolveley, a canonry of Salisbury; for John de Boys – skilled in medicine – and John de Nibley, canonries of Chichester; for John de Beautre, a canonry of Exeter; for William de Meone, a canonry in St Mary's, Winchester; and for his chaplain, Adam de Aylton, one in Wherwell.[140]

Having done his best to provide for those who had served him faithfully, the aged bishop died some two years later. Among those who watched over his final hours in Farnham Castle were his nephew John Trillek, bishop of Hereford, Adam de Aylton and Nicholas de Caerwent.[141] Some further duties were required of his friends; the brothers Trillek, Breynton, Carles, Usk and Caerwent were involved as co-executors in the lengthy negotiations necessary to settle Orleton's tangled affairs. The dilapidations at Winchester were considerable and the costs of an expensive lawsuit at the Curia had either to be paid or contested. But both William de Edington, his successor in the bishopric, and Roger de Breynton, the long-suffering executor not only of Orleton but also of Bishop Swinfield, showed their regard for their patron by generous gestures.[142] Moreover, when Edington came to found a chantry in his native township in Wiltshire, he laid down that after commemoration of the founder and his kin the chaplains were to remember Adam Orleton and his friend and colleague Gilbert de Middleton.[143]

ASSESSMENT

If, as is sometimes maintained, medieval biography is impractical, it is scarcely less difficult to determine the qualities of a medieval

140 *C.P.P.* 1342–1419, pp. 57–9. In 1344 he is also said (*ibid.* p. 40) to have petitioned for a canonry of Wells on behalf of 'his chaplain' John Aunger of Hereford diocese, but of this man's connection with Orleton I have so far found no trace. A John Aungier was made deacon by Bishop Charlton in 1335: *Hereford Reg. Charlton*, p. 160.

141 *Hereford Reg. Trillek*, p. 55. The others were John de Middleton, rector of Morestead; Richard de Chelseye, clerk; John de Vinea, surgeon (it is possible that Boys had died by this time); Thomas Fichet and Richard Bishopestone, lay members of the bishop's *familia*.

142 For the executors' activities see *Hereford Reg. Trillek*, pp. 73–5, 77, 123–4, 130, 133–5; H.C.M., no. 1378.

143 *C.P.L.* 1342–62, p. 539. For Edington's career see *Biog. Oxon.*, *s.v.* Edyndon. In 1358 the chantry was converted into a house of Bonhommes: *V.C.H. Wiltshire* 3, pp. 320–4.

bishop as pastor, administrator or judge – but above all as pastor. In many instances there is no lack of documents, but episcopal registers, which incorporate the bulk of these, are largely collections of formal acts and such seemingly unrewarding items as ordination lists, institutions, exchanges of benefices, licences, dispensations and royal writs. At least it can be said that this type of record provides no temptation to emulate those well-rounded portraits derived from the casual or studied observations of chroniclers, often as misleading as they are prejudiced.

An obvious starting-point would be to determine the length of time spent by a bishop in his diocese, on the assumption that the longer he stayed within its borders the more concern he demonstrated for his spiritual obligations. There is some merit in this view, if not taken too far. It is a commonplace, though, that the bishop was a man not only with spiritual responsibilities but with temporal ones as well, both in his particular area and in the country at large. It could be contended that attendance at parliaments, councils and convocations was essential if the Church and realm were to be properly governed, and even that the interests of an individual diocese were not always best served by a bishop who never left it. After all, a criticism advanced against the bishops of Edward II's reign is that after Winchelsey's death they failed to adopt a firm line of policy in the nation's affairs or to produce a leader to whom they and others could rally.

In Orleton's case it was public affairs, mainly in the shape of diplomatic duties, that took him away from his dioceses. As we have seen, in one of his revealing letters to Bishop Cobham, Orleton deplores the fact, as many other bishops involved in temporal affairs were to do both before and after his time, but it is at least possible that the plaint contains an element of truth. When resident, Orleton invariably created a bustle of useful activity and some of the irregularities brought to light at Hereford had certainly been either ignored or overlooked by his much-resident predecessor, Swinfield, who has rightly borne an excellent reputation as a diocesan. However that may be, bishops were the victims of a system which demanded that at least some of them engage regularly in political and diplomatic work. That is not to say, of course, that Orleton and men like him would have wished to shun the world of affairs altogether, even if in moments of stress they sought to convey that impression. That too is probably far from the truth. What is suggested is that once enmeshed in business of this kind it was difficult for bishops to extricate themselves and in such circumstances dioceses, not necessarily by any deliberate choice of theirs, had to take second place. It was one of the burdens of the organised Church. Earlier discussion has shown that it was only at Winchester that Orleton came to play the part of diocesan in the fullest sense and by that time his physical powers were greatly diminished.

Some criteria of episcopal concern and of pastoral care and effectiveness can be tentatively advanced. In general it can be taken as a sign of pastoral responsibility that a bishop undertook regular visitations, since by the thinking of the day that was the means whereby an errant part of the Church could be brought back to pristine purity, with the rooting out of abuses – tares which marred the beauty and order of the Church's garden.[1] Unhappily, details of visitation at this period are without exception scrappy. Much of the material being of short-term interest, such items as visitation rolls and accompanying interrogatories could be discarded after a reasonable interval. What survives is piecemeal and partial. None the less, as this is all that we have, the best must be made of it. At least it can be said that vigorous visitatorial action provides prima facie evidence of greater concern, unless it be argued that such differences arise merely from variations in the quality of recording, which is unconvincing. In Orleton's case there would seem to be clear indications that he took a keen personal interest in the reformation of religious houses in his jurisdiction. It might be that something of this was legalistic – the strict implementation of the law. As a trained canonist this aspect must have weighed with Orleton, though here again it should be remembered that to the medieval mind the implementation of canon law was calculated to restore the Church to that excellence from which it had supposedly fallen. It would be rash to claim on the evidence that we have that the spirit was entirely lacking. Yet even if it be allowed that Orleton was something of a monastic

[1] *Worcester Reg. Bransford*, p. 94, no. 530 (1, fo. 60^r): preamble to mandate for visitation of the cathedral priory in 1342.

reformer, evidence of a corresponding concern for the secular clergy's reformation – at times of visitation, that is – remains singularly sketchy.

A bishop is commonly held to have been a fairly remote figure in the Middle Ages, his personality masked from common men by the dignity of his judicial office or the solemnity of his sacramental one; but the many instances of personal affront to Orleton himself and to members of his *familia* suggest that this was a flimsy façade not calculated to withstand adverse conditions. Yet though there was need for respect and detachment, there was equal need for contact, which leads naturally to another possible criterion of episcopal effectiveness – availability. Apart from times of formal visitation, the bishop could meet clergy and people by moving about his diocese at regular intervals, by personally instituting clerks and celebrating ordinations. The extant documents show Orleton regularly celebrating his own ordinations, even when remote from his diocese; they show him preaching, and so far as his enforced absence allowed, instituting to benefices. We have already glimpsed that tantalising vignette of the dedicated pastor pausing to confirm children brought out to him as he passed along the highway – an episcopal duty seldom recorded, though persistently enjoined. Was it in character? We do not know the answer. But Orleton's attitude to his own clerks demonstrates both approachability and a kindly concern for their welfare – a sentiment which they reciprocated. No lack of mobility is discernible on Orleton's part until ill-health and advancing senility robbed him of his powers. It was then that he chose William de Edington as coadjutor – a man who was to gain an excellent reputation as royal administrator and diocesan bishop, which he enhanced by declining the see of Canterbury.

Lastly, careful examination of Orleton's record in the granting of licences to rectors for absence from their benefices, of his actions with respect to the plurality regulations, and of his enquiries into the irregularities in parishes and their incumbents, serves to create the impression of a diocesan who administered the law with impartial hand, upholding it even when it redounded to the disadvantage of his own *familia*.

Further than that it may not be possible to advance with any assurance. What evidence we have tends to support the more favourable contemporary estimates of his character and abilities. The boast of the legend around his Worcester seal – *Presul translatus sit Adam quia vir tibi gratus* – if lacking in modesty, is not altogether misleading.[2]

[2] *W.R.O.* 2, fo. 20r [634]. For what may be two (more regular) examples of Orleton's seal mottoes as bishop of Hereford see N. R. Ker, introduction to *Facsimile of British Museum MS. 2253, E.E.T.S.* 225, London 1965, p. xxiii.

Chapter 4

POLITICAL INVOLVEMENT

ORLETON AND THE CHRONICLERS

Chroniclers have too readily made or marred the reputations of medieval men; from their folios step forth flesh-and-blood people larger than life, villains or saints. Seldom do we find subtle delineations of character viewed against the background of those circumstances, favourable or unfavourable, in which a man lived out his life.

Adam Orleton provides an example of a man damned by the prejudice and preconception of chroniclers, or to be more exact, of one chronicler in particular. To us he has come down as an unscrupulous ecclesiastical careerist, who abetted rebels in contempt of his oath of loyalty, successfully engineered the escape of a notorious traitor, fanned the smouldering hatred of baronial opposition, fostered the unlawful liaison of a queen, and master-minded a revolution which culminated in the imprisonment of a king, Edward II, whom he had long pursued with an implacable hatred and whose brutal death he contrived by means of a cryptic murder note. Not content with all that he insidiously sacrificed the royal chancellor, Robert Baldock, to a London mob insufficiently satiated by the particularly revolting murder of Bishop Stapledon, another of the king's ministers. Finally he emerged from semi-retirement, senile and half-blind, to fabricate a libellous polemic against his old enemy and ecclesiastical superior, John Stratford, the archbishop of Canterbury. This is a powerful story concocted of elements of truth, half-truth and pure fiction. The chronicler chiefly responsible was an obscure clerk, Geoffrey le Baker.

Two works have been ascribed to Baker: one a substantial *Chronicon*, the other a meagre skeleton of events disparagingly dubbed the *Chroniculum* by E. Maunde Thompson, who edited both towards the end of the nineteenth century.[1] In the *Chroniculum* the author gives his name as Geoffrey le Baker of Swinbrook, *clericus*, and tells us that he wrote the piece at the request of Thomas de la More, knight, [finishing it] on the feast of St Margaret (20 July) 1347 at Osney.[2] When he comes to the reign of Edward II the author is more expansive, but it is noteworthy that he omits any mention of Bishop Orleton and that he describes Isabella (*sub anno* 1325) as 'nobilissima regina Anglie'.[3]

That Baker also wrote the *Chronicon* is to be deduced from the fact that at one point its author addressed the same Thomas de la More, acknowledging his indebtedness to the knight's account of events written in French.[4] Both works are bound up with other material in Bodley MS. 761 and constitute a copy made in the latter part of the fourteenth century.[5] In view of some elementary mistakes[6] and the duplication of material mentioned below, this can hardly have been the autograph of Baker himself as Stubbs tentatively suggested.[7]

A part of the *Chronicon* covering the reign of Edward III only is to be found in B.L. Cotton MS. Appendix LII, which is likewise in a hand of the latter half of the fourteenth century. This manuscript and the two versions for the early part of Edward III's reign, which the scribe of Bodley MS. 761 heedlessly copied one after the other, suggest that there were separate chronicles for the two reigns.[8] Further support for such separation comes from Elizabethan transcripts of the *Vita et Mors Edwardi Secundi*,[9]

1 Oxford 1889. The edition also contains extensive notes from parallel chronicles, particularly the *Brut*, and from Stow's *Annales*. Stow made substantial use of Baker.

2 *Chroniculum*, p. 173.

3 *Ibid*. p. 172.

4 *Chronicon*, p. 27.

5 *Ibid*. pp. xii–xvii. The book comprises 200 leaves of paper of a kind which Maunde Thompson considered (p. xii) to have been in use 'about the year 1360 or immediately afterwards'.

6 Notably the writing of 'mortua matre' for 'mortuo mari' (Mortimer). Orleton is capriciously written 'Torletone' or 'Torltoine' (B.L. Cotton MS. Appendix LII has 'Thorlestone'), forms copied by the Elizabethan transcribers of the *Vita et Mors* (B.L. Cotton MS. Vitellius E. V also has 'Torleron', as has Inner Temple Petyt MS. 47 in the margins). Did the form 'Torletone' arise from a confusion with the Salisbury prebend of 'Torleton' [Tarlton]?

7 *Chronicon*, pp. xvi–xvii; *Chronicles of the Reigns of Edward I and Edward II* 2, p. lxxii: 'Great part of the volume is in the same hand, which, if not Geoffrey le Baker's own, must be in that of an early transcriber'; and cf. *ibid*. p. lviii.

8 *Chronicon*, pp. xii, xvi–xvii.

9 B.L. MSS. Cotton Vitellius E. V and Harleian 310; Petyt MS. 47.

attributed to Thomas de la More but really a version of that part of Baker's *Chronicon* which covers the earlier reign. When Bishop Stubbs came to revise Camden's edition of the *Vita et Mors*, derived from a manuscript no longer extant,[10] he believed in a lost French original composed by Thomas de la More.[11] In fact there seems to be no reason to question Maunde Thompson's argument that the passage in Baker on which this view is grounded refers not to a French chronicle but to some notes in that language on the happenings at Kenilworth, at which time de la More was in the entourage of Bishop Stratford and hence an eyewitness.[12]

If we overlook the colourless *Chroniculum* we are left with a single work, the *Chronicon*, which until 1341 – the furthest we need go, so far as Orleton is concerned – is based on the chronicle of Adam Murimuth.[13] An examination of Baker's text shows that he first mentions Orleton in 1324, frequently thereafter until Edward II's death, but only three times in the rest of the chronicle: when he inserts two passages into Murimuth's account of the treaty with the Scots in 1328, and at the time of Orleton's translations to Worcester and Winchester respectively.[14] If Baker's interpolated passages up to 1328 are taken together they are seen to have a clear-cut purpose: to place the responsibility for Edward II's abdication and death fairly and squarely on the shoulders of Orleton and the queen.[15] Mortimer is a leading actor in the drama – significantly he attracts no vituperation – while Burghersh, the bishop of Lincoln, fills a supporting role. Stratford's part is underemphasised and invokes no personal criticism. As for the plot, the queen's mission to France in 1325, the subsequent despatch of her son to do homage to the French king, the invasion of Isabella's forces and the ultimate fate of Edward all contribute to a preconceived plan, of which Orleton as the queen's evil

10 *Chronicles of the Reigns of Edward I and Edward II* 2, pp. lvii–lix; *Chronicon*, p. vii.

11 *Chronicles of the Reigns of Edward I and Edward II* 2, pp. lviii–lix, lxv–lxvi.

12 *Chronicon*, p. 27. Maunde Thompson writes (*ibid*. p. viii): 'The words "hec vidisti et in Gallico scripsisti" confine the limits of de la More's contribution to what he himself actually saw.'

13 *Chronicon*, pp. x–xi.

14 *Ibid*. pp. 16, 41–2, 54–5.

15 E.g. *ibid*. p. 25: 'Regina . . . apud Herefordiam cum magistro tocius sue malicie, episcopo scilicet istius civitatis, exercitui presidente' (*s.a*. 1326).

genius is the chief architect.[16] There is nothing of this in Murimuth's chronicle.

It is unlikely to be coincidence that Baker, de la More and Murimuth came from neighbouring villages in Oxfordshire, or that the Bohuns, earls of Hereford, were lords of Chadlington hundred in which Swinbrook lay.[17] Baker's precise relationship with de la More is uncertain; he gives no hint of having been his household chaplain. On the other hand, Baker's writing of the minor chronicle at Osney points to a connection with the Augustinian abbey there, though his status was certainly that of a secular clerk rather than a canon. With the publication of the Patent Rolls one more biographical detail has emerged. Our author can be identified as the 'Geoffrey Pachon of Swynebrok, chaplain' who is named among a large group of malefactors pardoned by the panic-stricken Edward on condition that they aided him against the invaders.[18] His offence is not recorded, but it could be that his baronial sympathies had involved him in some fracas or other.

The Bodley manuscript which contains Baker's works was at one time in the possession of the Bohun family.[19] Baker speaks admiringly of Earl Humphrey and knowledgeably of his death at the hands of an unchivalrous opponent at Boroughbridge. At the same time he is reverential towards Edward II, whom he describes as 'amicicie cultor fidelissimus' and 'generosus dominus', but unsparing in his condemnation of the Despensers.[20] Baker's treatment of Stratford is strikingly negative: he does not align him with the queen and deliberately omits Murimuth's description of his dispute with Edward III in 1341, when he was archbishop.[21] These details are revealing of Baker's sympathies but do not readily solve the problem of why or when he made his

16 *Ibid*. pp. 16–17 (*s.a.* 1324), 19 (*s.a.* 1325).

17 *Chronicles of the Reigns of Edward I and Edward II* 2, p. lxxiii; *Chronicon*, pp. viii–x.

18 *C.P.R.* 1324–27, p. 331.

19 *Chronicon*, pp. xv–xvi. There it is suggested (on the basis of art. 9 of the MS.) that it could have been compiled for Thomas de Walmesford, a cleric who benefited from the patronage of John de Bohun, earl of Hereford (*ob*. 1336).

20 *Ibid*. pp. 13–14, 21, 28, 16–17.

21 The 1341 recension of Murimuth contains (*Murimuth*, p. 121) the beginning of the proceedings against Stratford. Baker omits the lengthy passage 'mancipari . . . in suspenso' (pp. 117–20).

politically-inspired additions to Murimuth's circumspect chronicle, converting it from a humdrum account to an outrageously partisan document.

At first glance it might make good sense to adopt a theory advanced by Canon Bannister and interpret the onus placed on Orleton for the events of 1324–8 as counter-propaganda to the *Libellus famosus*, the name given by Stratford to the charges brought against him at the instigation of Edward III in 1341 and ascribed, not without circumstantial evidence, to the aged Orleton, then bishop of Winchester. Yet on closer consideration this appears unconvincing. The *Libellus* does not fasten any responsibility for the revolution on Stratford, and though allegations of the kind that Baker makes might appear calculated to destroy the credibility of the alleged author, they are divorced from the occasion. As a piece of propaganda Baker's version of Edward II's reign would fit more happily into the context of that acrimonious appeal and counter-appeal which accompanied Orleton's promotion to Winchester in 1333. The three charges preferred against the bishop in the following April involved Baldock's death, the political sermon preached at Oxford in 1326, and Orleton's accountability for Isabella's failure to return to her husband for fear of bodily injury.[22] All of these have a place in Baker's narrative. Stratford was chancellor in 1333 and the attack on Orleton, as has been shown, was clearly government-inspired. This incident provided the first opportunity after the fall of Mortimer and Isabella for Orleton openly to be made the scapegoat for what had happened in the previous reign.

As it stands, however, Baker's chronicle includes details of Edward II's captivity which allegedly came to his knowledge after the Black Death. Thus even if the events of 1333 provided the occasion for his prejudiced interpretation, the final recension was made much later. It has already been observed that the small chronicle, written in 1347 (or concluded then), has some independent value merely because it bears no trace of bias against Orleton or the queen. From the discussion so far it transpires that Baker's indictment of Orleton cannot reasonably be accepted

[22] *H.R.O.*, pp. xlviii–xlix; *Responsiones*, cols. 2763–8. Both the appeal and the responses to it are printed from the Winchester cartulary in *Exeter Reg. Grandisson* 3, pp. 1540–7.

without corroboration and this, as we shall see, is conspicuously lacking at some points.

It is significant of Baker's eccentricity that one of the best independent authorities for Edward II's reign, the *Vita Edwardi Secundi*, gives no political prominence to Orleton.[23] This chronicle is believed to be a current compilation, ending in 1325–6 with the failure of Isabella to return from France, and apparently left unrevised.[24] Unlike Baker, the author did not have the benefit of hindsight. Arguing from the manuscript's provenance, the antiquary Hearne attributed authorship to 'a monk of Malmesbury', but the latest editor, following a line of thought initiated by Bishop Stubbs in his introduction to the Rolls Series edition, convincingly postulates that of a secular clerk, John Walwayn the elder. Walwayn had been in the king's service and was seemingly a protégé of the earl of Hereford, Humphrey de Bohun, who is said to have advanced his candidature for the bishopric of Durham in 1316.[25]

It may have been lack of interest, rather than deliberate diplomatic reticence,[26] that led Walwayn, if he was the author, to omit Orleton's name when he came to describe the bishop's confrontation by the king in 1322.[27] More important is his failure to attribute to Orleton any sinister influence on the queen's conduct in 1325. The king's declaration that someone (Mortimer?) was

23 The author, if Walwayn (see below), had died by July 1326. The bishop of Hereford, i.e. Orleton, is mentioned twice (*Vita*, pp. 119, 136–7).

24 The date of authorship was formerly thought to be dependent on that of the *Speculum Regis Edwardi III*, since the *Vita* (pp. xvii, 75, *s.a.* 1316) quotes from a similar complaint about purveyance by 'quidam religiosus'. At one time the *Speculum* was attributed to Archbishop Islip, then to Archbishop Mepham, and most recently (1970), by Leonard Boyle, to William of Pagula (together with the related *Epistola*). The letter in the *Vita* is only partial owing to the loss of leaves at this point in the MS. The coincidence appears striking, but Pagula was of course a secular clerk and the letter in the *Vita* is not specific. Boyle dates both *Epistola* and *Speculum* 1331. See his 'William of Pagula'.

25 *Chronicles of the Reigns of Edward I and Edward II* 2, pp. xliii–xlvii; Denholm-Young, 'Authorship of *Vita Edwardi Secundi*', pp. 189–211; *Vita*, pp. xix–xxviii; *Graystanes*, p. 757; *Biog. Oxon.* 3, app. *s.v.* Walwayn, John senior.

26 As suggested by Denholm-Young, *Vita*, p. xxviii.

27 *Vita*, pp. 119–20. In view of the author's openness about Lancaster on the one hand (pp. 97–9) and Baldock and the Despensers on the other (p. 142) it is unconvincing to ascribe circumspection as the motive behind his failure to name Orleton or that 'quidam miles de partibus Herefordie' (Roger de Elmbridge) who had acted as sheriff of the county and subsequently joined the rebels (*ibid.* pp. xxviii, 119, n. 6). Incidentally, the latter's name is recoverable from various places apart from the *Chroniculum* (p. 171).

behind what he considered to be Isabella's change of attitude towards the younger Despenser is given ample space but not commented upon, although there is a hint that the queen had reason enough of her own.[28]

The *Vita* does provide positive evidence to set against Baker's contention that Orleton continued intransigent. The bishop is shown to have made an approach to Henry of Lancaster in 1325 with a view to securing his mediation with the king. Orleton's itinerary confirms that he was hovering at Middleton in Hampshire within easy reach of Edward II at Winchester. The plan misfired and was to form a constituent of the trumped-up charge of treason brought against Henry in May, but subsequently dropped.[29] This move may have had the boomerang action of precipitating Edward's letter to Pope John, written at the end of May, which urged the removal of Orleton from his bishopric.[30]

Canon Bannister, misled by Blaneforde and Baker, thought that Orleton spent the last three months of 1323 at Shinfield planning the younger Roger Mortimer's escape from the Tower supposedly in the following year.[31] Orleton's participation is a piece of fiction which probably emanates not from Baker himself but from a corruption of his text. A comparison of the *Chronicon* and of the *Vita et Mors* shows that whereas the former has

' 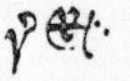 evasionem ',

which the editor rendered ' R[ogeri] evasionem ', the latter more convincingly reads ' R[egis] eversionem '.[32] The date of the escape

[28] *Vita*, pp. 143–5.

[29] *Ibid.* pp. 136–7; *H.R.O.*, pp. 325–7.

[30] *Foedera* 2, ii, p. 137: 28 May 1325.

[31] *H.R.O.*, p. xxvi. Bannister's assertion has been widely adopted: e.g. by McKisack, *Fourteenth Century*, p. 81; Emden, *Biog. Oxon.*, *s.v.* Orleton; and the editors of *G.E.C.* 8, p. 437, n.b.

[32] Compare Bodleian, Bodley MS. 761, fo. 103^{r}; Cotton MS. Vitellius E. V, fo. 264^{r}; Harleian MS. 310, fo. 95^{v}; Petyt MS. 47, fo. 307^{r}. The last has ' eversionem ' added above ' evasionem ' crossed out. The printed *Chronicon* (p. 16) runs: ' quod predictus Adam adesit quondam illis de Mortuo mari, inimicis regis, accomodans eiisdem equos et arma *iuvansque ad dicti R*[*ogeri*] *evasionem* '. The words italicised are interpolated by Baker: cf. *Murimuth*, pp. 42–3. The edition of the *Vita et Mors* (p. 305) has: ' quod predictus Adam adhaesit quondam illis de Mortuomari regis hostibus, eosque equis et armis accomodatis adjuverat ad dicti r[egis] eversionem '. Since Mortimer's ' evasio ' is mentioned only a few lines before, it is easy to see how the confusion with ' eversio ' arose. It remains a possibility that the version in Bodley MS. 761 is what Baker intended, in which case it would have to be placed in the same category as his other unsupported statements about Orleton – constituting a blatant addition to the indictment of 1324 as paraphrased by Murimuth.

is neither 1322, as in Murimuth, nor 1324, as Blaneforde has it, but 1 August 1323 – appropriately the feast of St Peter ad Vincula.[33] If it is accepted that the text of the *Chronicon* is corrupt, then no contemporary source ascribes Mortimer's break from the Tower to Orleton's machinations.

An apocryphal tale found in the *Chronicon*, and of course the *Vita et Mors*, is that Orleton procured Edward II's death by means of an ambiguously-worded message, which could be construed as an instruction to kill the king.[34] This stratagem, as Cassan pointed out in his life of Orleton,[35] was borrowed from Alberic's chronicle, where by the same means the archbishop of Esztergom (Gran) is alleged to have contrived the death of Gertrude, queen of Andrew II of Hungary.[36] Baker's chronology is in any case at variance with Orleton's known movements. To judge from the financial arrangements, Edward's custody was transferred from Henry of Lancaster to Thomas de Berkeley and John Maltravers after 3 April 1327.[37] These men were well-known supporters of Mortimer and it is unlikely that Orleton would have been in a position to give them such orders. As a matter of fact the bishop left London on 30 March and crossed to France less than a week later, not to return until about the middle of January of the following year. The king is believed to have been murdered on 21 September 1327.[38] In his reply to the charges of 1334 Orleton made this very point. To accept Baker's assertion we would have to allow that the issue was determined in France or Avignon, which is to pile fantasy on fantasy.

The coupling of Orleton's name with those of Isabella and Mortimer as promoters of the unpopular Scottish treaty, the 'turpis pax' concluded at Northampton in 1328, is a transparent device to transfer some of the opprobrium to the bishop.[39] There

[33] *Murimuth*, p. 40 (who eccentrically begins his years from the previous Michaelmas); *Blaneforde*, p. 145. See below, 'Years in the wilderness', ch. 4, for further discussion.

[34] *Chronicon*, p. 32; *Vita et Mors*, p. 317.

[35] *Lives* 1, p. 185.

[36] *Chronica Albrici Monachi Trium Fontium*, *M.G.H. SS.* 23, ed. G. H. Pertz, Hanover 1874, repr. 1963, p. 898: 'Reginam interficere nolite timere bonum est.' Baker (*loc. cit.*) writes: 'Edwardum occidere nolite timere bonum est.' This is attributed by Bannister (following Stubbs) to Thomas de la More (*H.R.O.*, p. xlv, n. 1).

[37] See Tout, 'Edward of Carnarvon', pp. 89ff; *Foedera* 2, ii, p. 188.

[38] Tout, *op. cit.* p. 90. For his burial by Abbot Toky see *Hist. Glouc.*, pp. 44–5, and for Westminster Abbey's abortive claim see W.A.M., no. 20344.

[39] *Chronicon*, p. 41. It was part of Lancastrian propaganda to suggest that a treaty

is no reason to believe that he was engaged in the diplomatic negotiations – though Burghersh was; indeed there is positive evidence to the contrary. At the time Orleton, on account of his translation to Worcester, was persona non grata with the government. We have already seen that he returned from the Curia to answer at the York parliament of February 1328 for his presumption. This was certainly the meeting at which preliminaries for the treaty were settled, but Orleton arrived under such a cloud that his advice is unlikely to have been sought.[40] The Lanercost chronicler, who is conspicuously well informed on Scottish affairs, puts the blame on Mortimer and the queen alone, as did Murimuth prior to Baker's gratuitous insertion.[41]

Removal of these palpably fictional elements in Orleton's biography still leaves a number of uncorroborated statements which, in the light of Baker's overall intentions, need to be treated with scepticism or even discountenanced altogether. For instance, no other chronicler alleges that Orleton fomented baronial hatred after Boroughbridge,[42] nor do other sources supply the defect. Indeed, the notion is somewhat unrealistic and hardly necessary as an explanation of events. The contention that it was the bishop who fostered the queen's liaison with Mortimer and drove a wedge between her and her husband by imagining a danger from the younger Despenser is scarcely more credible. Isabella's fear of Despenser and her anger at his conduct needed no arousing; both are well attested.[43] Baker's concept of a long-term plot to overthrow Edward II is explicable only in terms of perverted hindsight informed by a consistent animosity towards Orleton.[44] Yet

with the Scots left Mortimer's hands free to attack Earl Henry (*Cal. P.M.R.*, p. 80). Baker avers that the intention was to isolate Edward III in the same manner as his father.

40 He was at York on 22 January: E.101/309/38. The royal letter warning him not to infringe the rights of the crown by claiming the Worcester bishopric is dated 12 December 1327: on 26 December he was summoned to answer in parliament. *Foedera* 2, iii, pp. 3–4. Cf. *C.C.R.* 1327–30, pp. 208, 217.

41 *Lanercost*, pp. 261–2. For modern accounts see Stones, 'English Mission to Edinburgh', pp. 121–32; *idem*, 'Treaty of Northampton', pp. 54–61 – where it is claimed that in fact the treaty was a good one; Nicholson, *Edward III and the Scots*, ch. 4, 'The Shameful Peace'.

42 *Chronicon*, p. 16.

43 See Blackley, 'Isabella', and the discussion below, 'Years in the wilderness', ch. 4.

44 The animosity is exemplified by the constant use of derogatory epithets and the manner in which they have been interpolated into Murimuth's recital of events.

for the time of the revolution there is one insinuation that requires examination at greater length – Orleton's supposed connivance at the ill-treatment and death of Robert Baldock, Edward II's unpopular chancellor.[45]

The story is briefly told. Baldock was among those captured with the king in Wales and brought back to Hereford, there to be claimed as a clerk by Orleton and lodged in his episcopal gaol.[46] When Orleton went to London he took Baldock with him and kept him in captivity at his house there. But the bailiffs and a crowd of Londoners, asserting the city's jealously-guarded privilege with respect to maintaining a prison, dragged Baldock off to Newgate. There he was miserably abused, dying on 28 May 1327 exactly two months after Orleton's departure for Avignon.[47] Murimuth suggests that the bishop secretly gave assent to the Londoners' action,[48] and this is latched onto by Baker with much elaboration of Baldock's innocence and expatiation on the shocking nature of a crime against a priest of God. No suspicion of Orleton's connivance is voiced in the account of the chronicler presumably in a very good position to know, the Pauline annalist.[49] Orleton's refutation, delivered in response to the appeal of 1334, is to the effect that he brought Baldock to London at the command of Isabella and her son, and at the instance of Stratford, then treasurer,[50] so that he could appear before the provincial council summoned for January 1327.[51] The burden of the charges would doubtless have been the chancellor's support for Edward II's ecclesiastical policy – his ill-treatment of certain bishops and of the English Church in general.[52] In his own defence Orleton

45 *Chronicon*, pp. 25–6.

46 *Knighton*, p. 437, telescopes the events and writes: 'Dictus Robertus adjudicatus est perpetuo carceri apud Newgate.'

47 *Responsiones*, col. 2763; *Annales Paulini*, pp. 320–1. Among the chroniclers, the Pauline annalist gives by far the clearest and seemingly most objective report of the incident.

48 *Murimuth*, p. 50: 'Ubi Londonienses ipsum de custodia episcopi conniventis rapuerunt.' Cotton MS. Nero D. X omits the word 'conniventis'. Baker inserts (*Chronicon*, p. 26) 'non sine dissimulante consensu episcopi'.

49 *Chronicon*, p. 26. The passage 'Tanti sceleris . . . innocentum' is entirely Baker. Cf. *Annales Paulini*, pp. 320–1.

50 *Responsiones*, col. 2763.

51 This met on 16 January 1327 at St Paul's.

52 According to the Pauline annalist (*op. cit.* p. 320) he was indicted by William Trussell 'omnibus criminibus quibus dominus Hugo [Despenser] accusatus erat; et omnis facultas respondendi vel allegandi sibi fuit inhibita'. For details of clerical

argues, somewhat naively, that despite the meeting of parliament, at which there ought to have been nothing to fear, the citizens dragged off his prisoner by force lest friends should secure his release by begging or bribery.[53] That Orleton brought Baldock from Hereford with malicious intent is incapable of proof. It could indeed be argued that Baldock's life was as much at risk from hostile mobs in the bishop's cathedral city, where there were many old scores to be settled, as it was in London.[54] Perhaps the nub of the charge is that once in the capital Orleton either incited the citizenry to carry off Baldock or failed to resist the attempt, the implication being that Orleton's supposedly high concept of clerical immunity extended only to his own skin. At a more realistic level the most that can fairly be said to his discredit is that he failed to take proper account of the predictable threat to his prisoner in a London which had recently provided ample evidence of disorder and murderous anti-clericalism. The Guildhall oath of 13 January 1327 re-emphasised Baldock's reputation as the principal public enemy left alive.[55]

A little help to Orleton's reputation is given by the parallel case of William Irby, the prior of Hereford, who if anything had made himself more objectionable to the bishop than had Baldock – always assuming that Orleton did hold the latter responsible for much of his wrongs, which seems likely. Irby was brought with others to Hereford where, being a clerk, he was handed over by the justices for confinement in Orleton's prison.[56] With the bishop's translation he was removed to the gaol attached to the episcopal palace in Worcester and there lived out the six years of Orleton's episcopate. No sooner had Simon de Montacute succeeded Orleton at Worcester than he was directed by a writ of privy seal to bring Irby to London. Montacute commissioned Wolstan de Bransford, the cathedral prior, to see to this.[57] In due

complaints see the *gravamina* presented to the January 1327 parliament (*Rot. Parl. Inediti*, pp. 106–10) and other petitions presented there (e.g. *ibid.* p. 118). The *gravamina* should be viewed against the background of similar clerical complaints over a long period. See Jones, 'Bishops, Politics and the Two Laws'.

53 *Responsiones*, col. 2764.

54 *Knighton*, for instance, gives a glimpse of the ill-treatment accorded to the captives, p. 437.

55 *Annales Paulini*, p. 323; *Cal. P.M.R.*, p. 11.

56 'Missus est in carcerem . . . eo quod male gesserat contra pacem regis.' *Knighton*, pp. 436–7.

57 Worcester Reg. Montacute 1, fo. 4^{r-v}. Montacute as bishop-elect received the mandate

course Irby was produced before various persons, including M. John de Hildesle, a baron of the Exchequer, in the house of Roger Northburgh, bishop of Coventry and Lichfield, which was situated in the Strand. As a temporary arrangement – until the feast of All Saints (1 November 1334) – Irby was placed in the custody of a certain John Portreve of Tewkesbury, under oath not to leave the realm without licence.[58] Shortly before the expiration of this term Montacute entrusted him to the care of the abbot of St Peter's, Gloucester, the house of his profession, on the understanding that he could resume custody should he wish to do so.[59] The timing of this investigation coincides with the general attack on Orleton following his translation to Winchester. The royal letter to Montacute speaks of Irby's detention being 'saunce cause resonable', a debatable point, but there is no accusation of ill-treatment. In the event the authorities did not consider it wise to release him and so far as is known he spent the rest of his days at Gloucester; he was not restored to his former position as prior of Hereford.[60] The lack of a sensational outcome may explain why the affair escaped Baker's attention; his usual practice was to associate Orleton with some happening which had attracted a degree of notoriety.

Only three items remain in Baker's catalogue of vituperation. The first of these, Orleton's careerism, may be omitted here, since it has already been argued that his promotions should be viewed more rationally in the light of papal policy and the long-term trend.[61] Consideration of the other two items – the armed assistance which the bishop is supposed to have rendered to Mortimer in 1321–2 and his allegedly cruel and heartless behaviour in 1326–7 – must be postponed until they can be dealt with as part of the wider problem of Orleton's involvement in political events.

to produce Irby on 15 April 1334. The following day he wrote to the cathedral prior, directing him to take Irby to the king as ordered in the writ. Not long before (*ibid.* 1, fo. 2r: undated) the prior had received Montacute's instruction to treat Irby 'honorifice iuxta exigenciam religionis sue'. The rubric reads significantly: 'per consilium domini archiepiscopi Cant'. Irby's licence to go on pilgrimage (*ibid.* 1, fo. 5r) may not have been implemented in view of the king's writ.

58 *Ibid.* 2, fo. 5r.

59 *Ibid.* 2, fo. 7v.

60 Neither Irby nor a prior of Hereford (by name) is mentioned in *Hereford Reg. Charlton*. In 1348 Br. John Mangeaunt was prior: *Hereford Reg. Trillek*, p. 129.

61 See above, 'Worcester, 1327–1333', ch. 3.

Meanwhile we shall turn to chroniclers other than Baker who have something to say about Orleton, and initially to two who have already received some attention.

Denholm-Young in his introduction to the *Vita* remarks that the author is by implication favourable to Orleton. Certainly he has nothing to say to his discredit, although one wonders how a man so passionately opposed to papal intervention would have reacted to Orleton's triple promotion by such means. A feature of the chronicle is the way it expands towards the end, which has been interpreted as an indication of the author's greater leisure on retirement from an active career. Despite such expansion and the likelihood that the author came from the west of England there is no reference to Orleton's political variance, which serves as a negative argument to set against Baker's unsupported statements for the crucial period 1324–5.[62]

We know much more about Adam Murimuth's career than was known in Stubbs's day.[63] In many respects his working life is comparable to that of John Walwayn, the suggested author of the *Vita*, and indeed up to a point similar to that of Orleton himself. As a secular clerk who did not reach the topmost rungs of the ladder of ecclesiastical promotion he is sharply critical of those who achieved their advancement with papal assistance, but concerning Orleton, whom he knew well and in whose debt he certainly was, he proves surprisingly reticent. He records Orleton's promotion to Hereford without comment; [64] for the translation to Worcester he merely adds the conceivably barbed statement that the bishop was then at the Curia on the king's business. The final move to Winchester is given lengthier treatment and incorporates Edward III's angry retort that the bishop had given more satisfaction to the king of France than to himself.[65] But it is doubtful if even this goes much, if at all, beyond the official reaction in the heat of the moment; no personal opinion is overtly expressed, though it could be taken as implied by the very fact of the record. Two other mentions of Orleton are purely factual: the accusation against him in the parliament of 1324 and his preaching of a political sermon at Oxford in 1326. However with

62 *Vita*, p. xxi.

63 For a summary life see *Biog. Oxon.*, *s.v.*

64 *Murimuth*, p. 25; cf. *Flores* 3, p. 177.

65 *Murimuth*, p. 70.

respect to Baldock's removal from the bishop's custody he does venture the damaging insinuation commented upon earlier, seemingly on his own initiative.[66] Finally, at the time of Orleton's death in 1345, the aged chronicler stoops to deliver a parting thrust, particularising the twenty-eight years and two months that the bishop had occupied his three sees – the fruits of ambition.[67] Can we recognise here one of those 'emuli' who proved so destructive of contemporary reputations?

The remaining chroniclers who have something derogatory to say about Orleton's doings are all parti pris: William Dene, a notary, because he writes in the *Historia Roffensis* as a champion of the local bishop, Hamo de Hethe, who was reluctant to fall in with the revolutionary proceedings of 1326–7 in which Orleton played a large part;[68] Robert of Avesbury, the registrar of the Court of Canterbury, on account of his favourable disposition towards Archbishop Stratford;[69] and the author of Stratford's biography, formerly credited to the Canterbury monk Stephen Birchington, for the same reason.[70] With regard to Avesbury and 'Birchington' the matter at issue is Orleton's participation during 1341 in the conflict between Edward III and the archbishop. This will have to be dealt with later; at present it may be said of Birchington that his vocabulary and use of derogatory epithets recall Baker's practice. Thus Orleton is 'caecus, tanquam amator discordiae, tunc dicti regis consiliarius principalis', and William Kilsby 'principalis incentor discordiae'.[71] Avesbury is content to affirm that Orleton had always been hostile to Stratford, 'domino archiepiscopo semper infestus',[72] but this is surely too sweeping and one-sided a generalisation to carry conviction. As we shall see later, there is good reason to believe that such hostility first made its appearance at the time of Orleton's promotion to Winchester,

66 *Ibid.* pp. 42–3, 47, 50.

67 *Ibid.* pp. 172–3.

68 *Anglia Sacra* I, pp. 356–83. This is a 'selective' edition and I have used Cotton MS. Faustina B. V throughout.

69 The best MS. of the 'De gestis mirabilibus regis Edwardi tertii' is Harleian MS. 200, used as the basis of Maunde Thompson's edition in the Rolls Series. It is prefaced by a rubric in which the author names himself and his occupation. The preliminary sketch of Edward II's reign does not mention Orleton.

70 *Anglia Sacra* I, pp. 1–48. The ascription to Stephen Birchington is repudiated by Tait in his introduction to *Chronica Johannis de Reading*, pp. 63–75.

71 *Birchington*, pp. 22, 40.

72 *Avesbury*, p. 330.

that it was as much of Stratford's making as Orleton's, and that it manifested itself at particular times rather than constantly.

It remains to make brief mention of two chroniclers who have something to say in Orleton's favour. They are the St Albans chronicler, Henry de Blaneforde,[73] and the Westminster annalist responsible for the relevant portion of the *Flores Historiarum*.[74] Blaneforde is valuable because he gives by far the longest account – a sympathetic one – of Orleton's arraignment in 1324.[75] The author of the *Flores* writes of Orleton in the same glowing terms as of Cobham: both are men of learning worthy of the episcopal dignity.[76] Unlike that of many other chroniclers of his time, his attitude was that papal provision helped to curb the injurious promotions made by the king.[77] Strongly in favour of Thomas of Lancaster and the barons, he is markedly critical of Edward II and of his treatment of the Church.

Apart from purely personal antipathy, the chroniclers' animus against Orleton appears to arise from a variety of factors: dislike of papal provision, jealousy of a successful clerk, anti-French feeling at a time of sustained tension between the English and French monarchs,[78] the anxiety of some ill-defined group to defend Stratford or to launch a counter-attack on his behalf, as well as the desire, possibly the need, to find a scapegoat for the deposition and death of Edward II.

73 On the basis of the rubric on fo. 210r of Cotton MS. Claudius D. VI (see the frontispiece of Riley's edition in the Rolls Series), the portion of the St Albans chronicle for 1307–23 is attributed to John de Trokelowe, that for 1323–4 to Henry de Blaneforde.

74 For the authorship of the chronicle see Tout, 'Westminster Chronicle', pp. 289–304.

75 *Blaneforde*, pp. 140–2. At the same time this chronicler praises Stratford highly: *ibid*. pp. 147–8.

76 *Flores* 3, p. 177.

77 *Ibid*.: 'Ac sic deliberatio dispensativa summi pontificis insolentiarum regis acerbitatem, ecclesiis injuriose saepius illatam, pro magna parte in cinerem sufflavit.' Cf. the anti-papal diatribe following Cobham's rejection as archbishop of Canterbury in 1313: *Vita*, pp. 45–8.

78 Papal and French influence were alleged in the promotion of Ayrminne to the see of Norwich (*Vita*, p. 141; *Sempringham*, p. 353), in that of Burghersh to Lincoln (*Vita*, p. 105), and of course, in that of Orleton to Winchester (*Murimuth*, p. 70). In the case of Louis de Beaumont's provision to Durham the newly-elected John XXII is said to have acted 'Ad rogatum regum et reginarum Franciae et Angliae' (*Graystanes*, pp. 757–8).

THE PATH OF THE MEDIATOR 1317–1321

During the first two-thirds of Edward II's reign, as we have already seen, Adam Orleton was mainly occupied – his diocese of Hereford apart – with diplomatic duties. It would be misleading, though, to assume too rigid a distinction between diplomatic and political affairs. Virtually all of those closely involved in politics at home served at one time or another in some foreign embassy or less formal mission. It was in such a milieu that Orleton must have become intimately aware of the tensions which were to culminate in the baronial revolt of 1321–2.

The author of the *Flores* who besmirches – with what degree of justice we may never know – the reputations of Walter Reynolds and his appointee to the Gloucester archdeaconry, M. William de Birston,[1] yet almost in the same breath speaks glowingly of the new bishop of Hereford, was either unaware of Orleton's earlier association with both of these men, or not concerned to make a point of it.[2] As a royal agent at the Curia Orleton may even have been in part responsible for advancing Reynolds's promotion to Worcester; we know he was in the bishop's entourage soon afterwards and with him at Avignon when Reynolds was entrusted with the king's 'secret negotiations' on Gaveston's behalf.[3] He continued under the bishop's aegis – though simultaneously in royal service – at least until 1312. But there is no need to emphasise the point that one cannot deduce from such an association that Orleton was particularly sympathetic towards Reynolds himself or the king's policy which he was engaged in carrying out. However, the connection does imply patronage, and when in 1313, or thereabouts, Orleton fell into partial disgrace it was Reynolds, by then archbishop, who wrote to Cardinal Arnaud with warm commendation of the envoy's past services to the pope.[4] The archbishop would seem to have been instrumental in rescuing him from the comparative obscurity of diocesan administration, with the result that from the spring of 1314 until his pro-

1 *Flores* 3, pp. 155–6. For a re-examination of the chroniclers' view of Reynolds see Wright, 'Supposed Illiteracy of Archbishop Reynolds', pp. 58–68.

2 *Flores* 3, p. 177.

3 See above, 'In Edward II's service', ch. 2.

4 Canterbury Reg. Reynolds, fos. 33^r, 44^r.

motion to the episcopate in May 1317 Orleton was more or less permanently resident at the Curia as a royal agent.

Until recently historians have accepted the view of Bishop Stubbs that during Edward II's reign there existed a ' middle party ' between the baronage and the king – ' a party of *politiques* '.[5] T. F. Tout, followed by J. Conway Davies, saw its embryonic form in the gathering of the king's curial agents and members of the embassy which reached Avignon in March 1317.[6] Copies of a letter apprising these agents of the embassy's advent were directed to, among others,[7] Orleton himself, Adam Murimuth, William Melton, archbishop-elect of York, Alexander Bicknor, archbishop-elect of Dublin, Thomas de Cobham, shortly to become bishop of Worcester, and M. John de Ross, archdeacon of Shropshire in Hereford diocese and future bishop of Carlisle.[8] The embassy comprised John Salmon, bishop of Norwich, John Hothum, bishop of Ely, Aymer de Valence, earl of Pembroke, and Bartholomew Badlesmere. Here, with some additions, are the names of those who have been credited with exercising a moderating influence in political affairs and forming the nucleus of the ' middle party '.

Stubbs's theory as refined and modified by Tout and Conway Davies was in its main elements accepted by J. R. Maddicott in his book on Thomas of Lancaster,[9] though he looked upon the mission to Pontefract in 1317 for mediation between Edward and Lancaster as marking the ' coming into being ' of the party. From that time until the so-called treaty of Leake nearly a year later he felt that ' the bishops formed the core of the middle party, greatly outnumbering the few lay magnates – Pembroke and Badlesmere in particular – who were similarly anxious for a settlement '.[10]

5 *Chronicles of the Reigns of Edward I and Edward II* 1, pp. cxiii–cxiv.

6 Tout rev. Johnstone, *Place of the Reign of Edward II*, pp. 86 n., 110 n., 320; Tout, *Chapters* 3, pp. 3–4; Davies, *Baronial Opposition*, ch. 5, 'The Middle Party and Its Activities' (esp. p. 429). The historiography of the concept is given in detail by Phillips, *Pembroke*, ch. 5.

7 Among whom were M. Andrea Sapiti, the king's permanent proctor at the Curia, and Gaucelme d'Eauze, appointed with his fellow cardinal, Luca Fieschi, to go to Britain in 1317. Murimuth grumbled about the number of English benefices which Gaucelme acquired. See *Murimuth*, p. 27; Mollat, *Popes at Avignon*, p. 340.

8 *Foedera* 2, i, p. 106; *C.P.L.* 1305–42, pp. 443–4.

9 E.g. *Lancaster*, p. 228: 'The existence of a middle party during these months is not in doubt (though " party " perhaps suggests a degree of organisation and a unity of aim which were not always present).' Cf. *ibid.* p. 215.

10 *Lancaster*, p. 214.

Kathleen Edwards in her study of the political activity of Edward II's episcopate likewise adopted the concept, dividing Reynolds's archiepiscopate into two stages: an initial period of collaboration with the government, marked by the rise of the middle party, and a further one from about the end of 1320, when in her view bishops aligned themselves with one or other extreme – king or barons – or were afflicted with indecision.[11] Miss Edwards, like Dr Maddicott subsequently, did not accept Tout's chronology of the party's genesis, regarding it as just as likely to have arisen from the many gatherings of barons and bishops which took place between 1315 and 1317.[12]

Recently the whole concept of a middle party has been impugned by J. R. S. Phillips in his biography of Aymer de Valence, earl of Pembroke, long considered its paramount lay figure.[13] According to Phillips's argument, at the very moment of the supposed inception of such a party in 1317 the magnates 'far from being openly hostile to the king or sullenly neutral' were on the contrary 'co-operating loyally with him'.[14] This bouleversement of accepted theory, coupled as it is with a pungent critique of the constitutional emphasis given to the reign by earlier interpreters,[15] can expect to encounter opposition, though much will depend on the precise meaning given to the term 'party'.[16] Yet even so fundamental a revision does not materially alter the nature of the participation of the episcopate which Phillips continues to regard as a 'neutral group for the purpose of mediation between the king and Lancaster'.[17]

According to Maddicott this mediatory role was for the period September 1317 to August 1318 undertaken by twelve bishops:

11 'Political Importance of English Bishops', p. 327.

12 *Ibid.* pp. 331–2.

13 *Pembroke*, ch. 5; also *ibid.* pp. 270, 277–9.

14 *Pembroke*, p. 148.

15 E.g. *Pembroke*, pp. 149, 287–8. Both Maddicott and Phillips reject the former orthodoxy of a baronial opposition consistently striving to control the administration.

16 Phillips argues (*op. cit.* p. 176) that the magnates' behaviour was not 'that of a political party under the leadership of Pembroke or anyone else, but was rather that of a community of like minds'. For a critique of such 'reassessment' of Edward II's reign see the review by B. Wilkinson (one of Tout's pupils) in *Speculum* 49 (1974), pp. 752–3.

17 *Pembroke*, p. 123. Cf. *ibid.* pp. 174–5: 'It is safe to say that, without the prelates as a neutral body which could be trusted by both sides, negotiations would never have been started in 1318 and would not have succeeded as far as they did.'

the metropolitans of Canterbury and Dublin, Reynolds and Bicknor, and Bishops Cobham of Worcester, Hothum of Ely, John Langton of Chichester, Walter Langton of Coventry and Lichfield, Monmouth of Llandaff, Martival of Salisbury, Richard de Newport of London, Orleton of Hereford, Salmon of Norwich, and John Sandale of Winchester. Of these he picks out Bicknor, Hothum, Salmon, Sandale and Langton of Chichester as being specially prominent.[18] This choice is determined by the nature of the documents, from which these bishops emerge as spokesmen; only opinions can be hazarded as to the relative influence exerted by individuals during the course of particular discussions and negotiations. Thus the fact of Orleton's participation, rather than its nature or significance, is discoverable by tracing his movements during these critical years.

With his elevation to the episcopate Orleton, from being little more than a capable agent of royal policy, achieved a position by means of which he could influence its formulation. One of the earlier entries in his Hereford register is a copy of a summons to the king's council dated 16 October 1317.[19] Anticipating some time-consuming business he appointed a vicar-general twelve days later and abandoned his diocese for the capital.[20] Edward, recently returned to London from the north and smarting from the insults which accompanied his confrontation with Lancaster, who was protected by the walls of Pontefract Castle,[21] proceeded to bolster his position by means of a series of indentures binding Pembroke and others to his service.[22] The clergy did their utmost to stabilise the situation. According to the Pauline annalist they met in the cathedral towards the end of November, for it was on the feast of St Andrew (30th) that Cardinal Luca Fieschi promulgated the bull for a truce between the English king and Robert Bruce. The following day Archbishop Reynolds excommunicated all breakers of the peace and those who encroached upon ecclesiastical pro-

[18] *Lancaster*, pp. 214–15. Bishop Newport died on 24 August 1318, shortly after the sealing at Leake, Stephen Gravesend being elected in September in his stead. Sandale died on 2 November 1319 and Rigaud d'Assier succeeded him.

[19] *H.R.O.*, p. 50. It is also printed in J. F. Baldwin, *The King's Council in England during the Middle Ages*, Oxford 1913, p. 92.

[20] *H.R.O.*, pp. 43–4.

[21] *Flores* 3, p. 181. Cf. the later accusation against the defeated Lancaster: *Trokelowe*, p. 117. Pembroke is alleged to have urged peace on the king: *Vita*, p. 82.

[22] Phillips, *Pembroke*, pp. 142–3, 148–9.

perty.[23] It is a reasonable assumption that Orleton was at St Paul's: his register shows him to have been in the capital on 6 November and at Highbury for the beginning of December. In fact he is to be found at either Highbury or London for most of December and for the first half of January 1318,[24] which would allow for consultation with those bishops who came together for a council at Westminster on 30 December at which the king was persuaded to prorogue parliament until a more settled time.[25]

His business in London concluded, Orleton spent the latter part of January and the first fortnight of February in his diocese, mainly at his manor of Bosbury.[26] An entry in the Hereford register shows that he was back in London by 27 February, doubtless for attendance at the council which Reynolds had summoned to St Paul's for the 23rd.[27] The bishops on this occasion are credited with securing the postponement of parliament from 12 March to 19 June so as to allow time for reconciliation with Lancaster before the king mustered his forces against the Scots.[28] Orleton continued in London until the second week in March, when he hastened back to conduct his primary visitation.[29] Proceedings were soon interrupted by a journey to Leicester, where the bishop transacted some business on 12 April[30] – the date of the preliminary settlement reached with Lancaster. The king's representatives and others present promised that the baronial Ordinances would be observed and 'evil councillors' removed; royal grants of land were to be resumed and their recipients held to account at the next parliament, while Lancaster and his

23 *Annales Paulini*, p. 281.

24 *H.R.O.*, pp. 45, 47, 50–7.

25 *Vita*, p. 84; *C.C.R.* 1313–18, p. 586; *Pembroke*, p. 154. There is no indication that Orleton actually attended the council, but he could have done so. About this time (January 1318) he was prosecuting a suit in chancery against Hugh Audley the elder, who was detaining lands belonging to the bishopric. *C.C.R.* 1313–18, p. 588; S.C.8/203/10138 (cf. *Calendar of Ancient Petitions relating to Wales*, p. 343).

26 *H.R.O.*, pp. 57–63.

27 *Ibid.* p. 63; *H.B.C.*; Phillips, *Pembroke*, pp. 154–5.

28 Phillips, *Pembroke*, p. 155, nn. 1, 2, gives the references for this meeting. The clergy were directed not to do anything in derogation of royal authority but to leave matters concerning the king for the parliament summoned to Lincoln. *C.P.R.* 1317–21, p. 104; *Foedera* 2, i, p. 146.

29 *H.R.O.*, pp. 63–70.

30 *Ibid.* fo. 19^{v}. Cf. the printed edition, p. 70: 'Verum quod nos, per instantem tractatum apud Leicestriam habendum, cui nos oportet unacum quibusdam aliis prelatis et proceribus interesse.'

followers were to be pardoned their offences.[31] The length of Orleton's stay at Leicester is not known, but he reappears in his diocese on 26 April 1318.[32] A mere fortnight later he set out for London. We catch a glimpse of him on the way crossing Port Meadow between Godstow and Oxford, where he was accosted by a M. John de Lugwardyn brandishing a papal grace for the next benefice in his collation; four days afterwards, 18 May, he is to be found once more in Highbury.[33]

At the beginning of June a meeting of the council took place at Westminster under the leadership of Archbishops Reynolds and Bicknor and the earl of Pembroke.[34] This concerned itself with the urgent need to concert measures against the Scots, and to effect this purpose it tried to conciliate Lancaster while at the same time threatening him with sanctions should he continue to hold armed assemblies. Orleton's name is among those of nine provincial bishops entered on the dorse of the document incorporating these arrangements.[35] Shortly afterwards, on 8 June, Edward confirmed the Leicester agreement.[36] This was followed up by the issue of a safe-conduct for the earl of Lancaster, at the bishops' instigation. The document is dated 11 June from Westminster and Orleton was one of those who sealed it;[37] the following day he received letters of protection for his mission to France, the object of which was to proffer Edward's homage for Aquitaine to the new king, Philip V.[38]

[31] The fullest chronicle account is in *Bridlington*, pp. 54–5. Cf. *Flores* 3, p. 85; *Vita*, p. 85. For articles said to have been agreed at Leicester between Earl Thomas and the prelates see *Knighton* 1, pp. 413–21. The most recent discussion of this meeting, which was attended by (apart from Orleton) Archbishop Reynolds and Bishops Salmon of Norwich, John Langton of Chichester, Sandale of Winchester, Cobham of Worcester (omitted by *Bridlington*) and Monmouth of Llandaff, is that of Phillips, *Pembroke*, pp. 155–60. He stresses the 'vital part' played by the prelates.

[32] *H.R.O.*, pp. 70–1.

[33] *Ibid.* pp. 74–5.

[34] Salisbury, 'Political Agreement', pp. 78–83; Phillips, *Pembroke*, pp. 161–4; Maddicott, *Lancaster*, pp. 217–18.

[35] Two copies of the agreement have been printed: Salisbury, *op. cit.* from C.49/4/26, and Phillips, *Pembroke*, app. 4, pp. 320–1, from C.49/4/27. The latter document is endorsed with the names of the subscribing bishops (apart from the two convening archbishops): Salmon of Norwich, Walter Langton of Coventry and Lichfield, John Langton of Chichester, Newport of London, Martival of Salisbury, Sandale of Winchester, Hothum of Ely, Cobham of Worcester and Orleton himself.

[36] Maddicott, *Lancaster*, p. 218; Phillips, *Pembroke*, pp. 163–4.

[37] Printed in Phillips, *Pembroke*, app. 4, pp. 321–2, from S.C.1/63/183.

[38] *C.P.R.* 1317–21, p. 162; *Foedera* 2, i, p. 153.

The precise time of his return from this abortive embassy is uncertain, but he was at Rue in Ponthieu – within striking distance of the channel – on 29 July, and his letters of protection expired two days later.[39] His presence at Leake makes it clear that he entered England in the first week of August.

Much had happened in the interval. Although Lancaster voiced his distrust of royal safe-conducts, and also of the one issued under the auspices of the bishops and of Cardinals Gaucelme d'Eauze and Luca Fieschi, negotiations continued throughout July. The outcome was a meeting at Loughborough on 7 August between the king and Lancaster, who exchanged the kiss of peace.[40] Finally the 'treaty' of Leake was sealed on 9 August. It was drawn up in the form of an indenture, to one part of which the archbishops of Canterbury and Dublin and eight provincial bishops, Orleton among them, appended their seals.[41] The most important feature of the treaty was the naming of a body of eight bishops, four earls, four barons and a banneret – to represent Lancaster – from which a standing council was to be chosen for permanent attendance on the king. This was to comprise two bishops, an earl, a baron, and a banneret of Lancaster's choice, each of whom would serve a three-month stint.[42]

It has been shown that Lancaster first put forward the idea of a standing council,[43] but the remarkable prominence of the clergy as a constituent element suggests that the bishops forwarded the plan as a means of continuing their moderating influence. Some conclusions drawn from the composition of the episcopal component need to be treated with caution. There would seem, for example, to be little justification for the opinion that 'certain of the bishops now most active politically were no longer working in

[39] *H.R.O.*, pp. 77–8.

[40] The *Bridlington* chronicler cautiously observes (p. 55): 'Sicut astantibus apparuit, concordati sunt.'

[41] *Foedera* 2, i, pp. 156–7. See J. G. Edwards, 'Negotiating of the Treaty', pp. 360–78; Wilkinson, 'Negotiations preceding the "Treaty"', pp. 333–53. For a re-examination of the evidence see Maddicott, *Lancaster*, pp. 218–29; Phillips, *Pembroke*, pp. 165–77.

[42] The bishops were: Salmon of Norwich, John Langton of Chichester, Hothum of Ely, Martival of Salisbury, John de Halton of Carlisle, Cobham of Worcester, David Martin of St David's and Orleton. Halton and Martin replace two of the signatories of Leake, Walter Langton of Coventry and Lichfield and Sandale of Winchester.

[43] J. G. Edwards, *op. cit.* pp. 371, 377. Cf. Maddicott, *Lancaster*, p. 226.

such friendly cooperation with the king as their predecessors during the critical years of Reynolds' pontificate '.[44] Only two elderly bishops, David Martin (St David's) and John de Halton (Carlisle),[45] were newcomers; the remainder had already laboured long and hard for a compromise between the king and Lancaster.[46] Cobham and Orleton have been cited as being unfavourable to Edward on account of his opposition to their advancement.[47] Cobham had been rejected as archbishop in favour of Reynolds in 1313, but it would be out of character for him to have borne a grudge for so long. His attitude towards the king was avuncular;[48] even in 1326 he was reluctant to acknowledge the drift of events. It is also true that not much more than a year had elapsed since Edward's verbal castigation of Orleton for accepting provision to Hereford contrary to his wishes, yet since that time the bishop had been sent on diplomatic missions, apparently with the king's full support.[49] There is no sign of a rift between the two until the winter of 1321.

Emphasis has also been placed on the number of bishops from the Welsh Marches or adjacent areas who were active in political matters.[50] So far as the council nominated at Leake is concerned there were three out of eight – Cobham at Worcester, Martin at St David's and Orleton at Hereford. Cobham, though, came from knightly stock in Kent and had no family ties in the border area.[51] The opposite contention may be more tenable – that the bishoprics were fairly well spaced: two in the south and south-

44 K. Edwards, ' Political Importance of English Bishops ', p. 333.

45 Martin was bishop from 1296 (elected 1293) until 9 March 1328; Halton from 1292 until 1 November 1324. Martin was one of the Ordainers in 1310: K. Edwards, *op. cit.* pp. 318–20, 333.

46 In particular, Hothum of Ely, Salmon of Norwich, John Langton of Chichester and Sandale of Winchester.

47 K. Edwards, *op. cit.* p. 333.

48 This is very noticeable in his comments on the royal behaviour at the Westminster parliament of 1320: *Worcester Reg. Cobham*, p. 97, and see below. It is however true that Earl Thomas had written to the pope in favour of Cobham at the time of the latter's promotion to Worcester. *C.P.L.* 1305–42, pp. 414, 441.

49 K. Edwards (*op. cit.* p. 334) considered that Bishops Assier, Orleton, Hothum, Melton, Halton and Cobham undertook diplomatic missions in support of the ' middle party '. There is nothing to suggest that Orleton was in fact being sent at the behest of persons indifferent or hostile to the king's wishes.

50 K. Edwards, *op. cit.* pp. 333–4.

51 For him see the uncritical biography by Pearce, *Thomas de Cobham*, and *Biog. Oxon.*, *s.v.*

west (Chichester, Salisbury), two in the east (Ely, Norwich), one in the north (Carlisle), one in the extreme west (St David's) and two (Hereford, Worcester) in the west midlands. It must be allowed that the earlier argument would be more satisfactory, from a purely topographical point of view, if Walter Langton, bishop of the sizeable diocese of Coventry and Lichfield and a signatory of the Leake indenture, were to be added to the list; though this would be self-defeating as a measure of Marcher pressure, since he was one of Edward's loyal supporters. The other episcopal signatory not included in the council is John Sandale, bishop of Winchester, whose reappointment as treasurer in November 1318 would in any case have entailed proximity to the king. He too has been classified as one of Edward's friends.[52]

Of the three bishops actually accused of involvement in the baronial revolt of 1321–2 – Droxford of Bath and Wells, Burghersh of Lincoln and Orleton of Hereford – Droxford prior to Leake had taken an inconspicuous part in the negotiations and Burghersh was not appointed until 1320, which leaves Orleton as the only one of the three who was either a member of the council or a signatory of the Leake indenture.[53]

It is therefore difficult not to come to the conclusion that the bishops nominated to the council, rather than being opposed to the king, were intent on continuing their established policy of moderation. Leake, it has been said, marked the high point of their achievement.[54] But the Leake agreement had still to be worked out in detail in the parliament which met at York in October 1318.

We have already noted Orleton's unavoidable absence from the important gatherings which immediately preceded Leake: he scarcely arrived there in time to append his seal to the indenture. The fact of his choice as a member of the council indicates the favourable impression he had made on his episcopal colleagues. There are no specific grounds for thinking that at this time he was acting in the Mortimers' interest, even though as the local diocesan he would have been fully aware of their concerns and attitudes. Diplomatic duties were also to prevent Orleton's partici-

52 Sandale died 2 November 1319.

53 See n. 42 above.

54 K. Edwards, *op. cit.* p. 332, writes of 'the paramountcy of the bishops' position'.

pation in the aftermath of Leake. On 26 August at Nottingham he was appointed an envoy to France to deal with Gascon affairs and must have left the country shortly afterwards.[55] Summonses for the York parliament are dated 24–5 August and the bishop, not expecting to be back in time, deputed a proxy.[56] As it turned out he was in London on 18 October, two days before the opening.[57] Having reported on his mission he made his way back to his diocese and worked there without interruption for the next three months.[58] His behaviour at this point is all the more surprising when we consider that the York parliament has been described as 'the most important gathering held during the reign'.[59] Further, his own obligations as a member of the standing council were to go by default: the canonisation of Cantilupe and other diplomatic business at the Curia and the court of France were to keep Orleton abroad – apart from a flying visit to report to the home government – between March 1319 and the end of July in the following year. He was granted expenses until 22 July 1320, the day the king himself arrived at Dover on his return journey from Amiens.[60]

Back in England the political situation gave the impression of being reasonably stable, despite the continued ill-feeling between the king and Lancaster. Orleton did not delay much more than a week in London before journeying to his diocese by way of Shinfield, where the rectory was in process of being appropriated to the Hereford chapter, and Thame, the prebendal seat of Gilbert de Middleton, with whom he was on good terms. The remainder of August 1320, the whole of September and the first week of October were spent in the diocese.

The Westminster parliament opened on 6 October 1320. Exactly a week later Orleton arrived in London and was appointed

55 *Foedera* 2, i, p. 159.

56 The list of those present at the parliament is given by Davies, *Baronial Opposition*, p. 450, from *Documents of English History*, p. 11. Cf. *Rot. Parl. Inediti*, pp. 64–80. K. Edwards, *op. cit.* p. 334, n. 2 cites Orleton's proxy: S.C.10/6/260. This is dated 20 October 1318 from London, M. Richard de Burton being named.

57 *H.R.O.*, pp. 78–9.

58 *Ibid.* pp. 80–98.

59 Davies, *Baronial Opposition*, p. 450 (and ch. 6 in general). See also Maddicott, *Lancaster*, pp. 229–39; Phillips, *Pembroke*, pp. 176–7. The roll of parliament is printed in *Documents of English History*, pp. 1–54.

60 *Foedera* 2, ii, p. 4; B.L. Add. MS. 17362, fo. 11^r.

a receiver of petitions for Ireland, Gascony and the Isles, in association with Bishops Droxford and Cobham, among others.[61] This parliament has traditionally been regarded as 'the last occasion upon which the middle party was in a position to exert any influence'.[62] Be that as it may, it certainly provided a lull before the storm. The absence of Lancaster was ominous, but he did send representatives, and after the assembly's dispersal two bishops[63] took part in a delegation to the earl, thus continuing the role of mediation.[64] Orleton was occupied in London until mid-November,[65] so it is fairly certain that he was called in for the discussions which led to this initiative.

It so happens that Bishop Cobham in letters to Pope John XXII and Cardinal Vitale Dufour has given us an eyewitness account of Edward's conduct at the Westminster parliament, which was attended, he says, by the archbishop of Canterbury and seventeen suffragan bishops. Edward created a most favourable impression by his early rising and friendly attitude towards prelates and nobles alike. He was regular in his attendance and personally volunteered some ingenious suggestions for the modification of a number of measures, all of which augured well for his future behaviour and the harmony of the realm.[66] It was not long before the bishop was to be sadly disillusioned.

While the bishops were engaged in their conciliatory errand and the still hopeful Cobham reluctantly prepared for negotiations with the Scots,[67] Orleton was immersed in the business of his diocese. He continued to be so until February 1321, on the 7th of

61 *H.R.O.*, pp. 136–46, 151–5; *Rot. Parl.* 1, p. 365. The same receivers of petitions seem to have been appointed at the parliament of July 1321: *Rot. Parl. Inediti*, pp. 92–3.

62 Davies, *Baronial Opposition*, p. 472.

63 *Annales Paulini*, p. 290. Stephen Gravesend, the new bishop of London (consecrated 14 January 1319), and Rigaud d'Assier, bishop-elect of Winchester, were sent from parliament in line with a papal suggestion. Assier was consecrated at St Albans on 16 November; the bishops of Ely and Rochester assisted.

64 According to the Pauline annalist (*loc. cit.*) they were delivering a bull to Lancaster. John XXII had been urging the earl to come to a peaceful settlement. Gravesend fell ill at Northampton and whether the mission actually reached its objective has been questioned, perhaps unnecessarily. *C.P.L.* 1305–42, p. 442; Phillips, *Pembroke*, p. 198.

65 He is last recorded there 11 November; on the 15th he was at Shinfield. *H.R.O.*, pp. 156–8.

66 *Worcester Reg. Cobham*, pp. 97–8.

67 *Ibid.* p. 97: 'Per dominum nostrum regem et ceteros regni magnates humeris meis impositum onus magnum.' Cf. *Foedera* 2, ii, p. 14.

which month he reappeared in London. A fortnight later he was embarking at Dover for a crossing to France.[68] On his return in the last week of April there was some confusion in government circles arising from the Marchers' attack on Despenser property in Wales. Hastening back to London, the king summoned a council of prelates and magnates to discuss what should be done. One outcome was that Orleton was sent with two other bishops – their names are not disclosed – to rally their friends in the Marcher area in order to mitigate the disturbance. Later Orleton seems to have returned to London.[69] He was not detained there much longer; for most if not all of June and for the early part of July he is to be found in his diocese.[70] For the latter part of July and the whole of August his diocesan register is a blank.

During the interval between the Westminster assembly of autumn 1320 and the parliament which met at the same place on 15 July 1321 developments took place which permanently upset the precarious political balance which the bishops had striven to maintain: the rise of the Despensers in the king's affection, their insupportable behaviour, and the grasping policy of the younger Despenser in the Gower peninsula and the Marches in general. This last had led to the devastation of his lands in May 1321 – the situation which had faced Orleton on his return.[71] It is of this 'bellum intestinum' that Cobham writes in an undated letter of the latter part of May: a deadly poison ('venenum insanabile') which the pope alone could remove from the land.[72] Disorder became so rampant that even the shrine of St Oswald in Cobham's cathedral at Worcester was broken into and rifled.[73]

This period also marks the rise of the baronial coalition. Lancaster's biographer summarises the earl's intention thus: 'he set out to secure the support of the north, to build a great confedera-

68 *H.R.O.*, pp. 180–3; Add. MS. 9951, fo. 9v.

69 S.C.1/54/139. For summonses to answer for the disturbances see *Reports touching the Dignity of a Peer* 3, app., pp. 303–6.

70 He is mentioned as being at Bromyard on 13 June: *H.R.O.*, fo. 52v. The number of entries is sparse at this period.

71 For the background see particularly Davies, 'The Despenser War in Glamorgan', pp. 21–64; Maddicott, *Lancaster*, pp. 260–8.

72 *Worcester Reg. Cobham*, p. 101. Speaking of his efforts for peace in Scotland – the periphery – he continues: 'Et dum regni circumferenciam purgare curamus, pestis pessima, familiaris hostilitas, et ad bellum intestinum preparacio latenter irrepsit in centro.' The editor of the register dated this 13 x 30 May.

73 *Worcester Reg. Cobham*, p. 100.

tion of northerners, Marchers and his own forces, and to present – with more than his usual skill – a coherent political programme '.[74] But the adhesion of the northerners was not effected by the ' quasi-parliaments ' of Pontefract and Sherburn-in-Elmet.[75] The three northern prelates – Melton of York, Halton of Carlisle and Beaumont of Durham – responded to the earl's summons to come to Sherburn on 28 June, but after considering the schedule of grievances put before them they judiciously answered that although willing to aid in resisting the Scots, they felt the other matters should be left for deliberation in the next parliament. They cannot be said to have acted in derogation of the king's authority.[76] The barons for their part determined on the exile of the Despensers, and it could be that a draft indictment was actually drawn up at Sherburn, as the St Albans chronicler states.[77]

While Lancaster remained at Pontefract, the Marcher barons moved to St Albans where, to the consternation of the monks, they stayed for three days round about 22 July ' cum maxima pompa et strepitu armorum '. Meanwhile, on 21 July, the anxious Reynolds issued a forty days' indulgence for the peace of the realm. During this time parliament was in session in London and the St Albans chronicler tells us that Bishops Gravesend of London, Martival of Salisbury, Hothum of Ely, Orleton of Hereford and Langton of Chichester, who were sent north as peacemakers, carried back the baronial demands for the Despensers' exile.[78] The *Historia Roffensis* continues the story: the bishops and the earls of Richmond, Arundel, Warenne (Surrey) and Pembroke met the baronial leaders on 27 July at Clerkenwell, where the earls agreed to join them but the bishops declined. At a later stage another conference took place in the Carmelite Friary, where Badlesmere denounced the younger Despenser as a traitor, producing a spurious document to prove the point, but Hamo de Hethe, the bishop of Rochester, promptly exposed its real nature

74 Maddicott, *Lancaster*, p. 268.

75 See Wilkinson, ' The Sherburn Indenture ', pp. 1–28, and more recently, Maddicott, *Lancaster*, pp. 268ff.

76 The Bridlington chronicler gives what purports to be the answer of the clergy to articles put to them by the barons (pp. 64–5). The MS. evidence is fully examined by Maddicott, *loc. cit.*

77 *Trokelowe*, pp. 107–8.

78 *Blaneforde*, p. 109; *Concilia* 2, p. 507.

and would have nothing more to do with the business.[79] The Pauline annalist gives a lively impression of the bishops' proceedings.[80] According to him they came together on various occasions, both in the New Temple and in the Carmelites' house, carrying on their deliberations both before and after dinner and visiting king and barons in turn in an attempt to secure a compromise.[81]

The barons persisted in their course and, having failed to secure the king's assent to a statute for the Despensers' banishment, they proceeded by way of an 'award', as it was technically called.[82] Parliament, it has been argued, provided the occasion for the sentence against the Despensers, but it was not in a strict sense parliamentary.[83] Above all, the prelates seem to have taken no part in the formal proceedings, but to have remained in the great chamber of the palace while the indictment was read in nearby Westminster Hall. Their failure to assent was soon to be put forward as an argument for the illegality of the award.[84] All of which was not accomplished without a warning that if the Despensers were not removed the king would be deposed; a threat which the author of the *Vita* puts into the mouth of Pembroke. Bowing to this pressure, Edward came to Westminster Hall on 14 August and consented to their banishment and disinheritance.

79 B.L. Cotton MS. Faustina B. V, fos. 35^v–36^r. The 'homage e serment' declaration of 1308 attributed to Despenser is printed by Richardson and Sayles, *Governance of Mediaeval England*, pp. 467–9. The incident is treated at length by Maddicott, *Lancaster*, pp. 278–87.

80 *Annales Paulini*, pp. 294–5.

81 The bishops involved were said to be Reynolds and his suffragans of London (Gravesend), Ely (Hothum), Salisbury (Martival), Lincoln (Burghersh), Exeter (Stapledon), Bath and Wells (Droxford), Chichester (John Langton), Rochester (Hethe) and Hereford (Orleton). Cf. *Vita*, pp. 112–13; *Trokelowe*, pp. 109–10; *Brut*, pp. 213–14.

82 Maddicott points out (*Lancaster*, pp. 285–6) that despite statements to the contrary a statute was not enacted (cf. *Vita*, p. 114); it was in fact an 'award' and not entered on the statute roll. The process is in *C.C.R.* 1318–23, pp. 492–5; *Bridlington*, pp. 65–9.

83 Maddicott, *Lancaster*, p. 288, argues: 'The judgement on the Despensers was in no sense a parliamentary one: parliament merely offered an occasion for the delivery of the sentence, and the records make it plain that neither the commons nor the prelates took any part in the proceedings.' But contemporaries were not necessarily so precise. Cobham, for instance, urged that as the process had taken place in parliament the 'processus revocacio' – if that was what the king wanted – ought ('videtur mihi') to be likewise effected 'in pleno parliamento propter hec et alia convocando'. *Worcester Reg. Cobham*, p. 119. Cf. Stapledon's response in similar vein: *Concilia* 2, p. 510; *Exeter Reg. Stapledon*, pp. 442–3.

84 Cotton MS. Faustina B. V, fo. 36^v; *C.C.R.* 1318–23, p. 543; *Bridlington*, p. 70. The younger Despenser's petition urged that there was error 'in that the award was made without the assent of the prelates, who are peers in parliament'.

The barons were pardoned for their attacks on the fallen favourites and parliament dispersed.[85]

Having played his full part in these proceedings, Orleton found time to look to his diocese; he seems to have remained there for the whole of September and October.[86] Only intermittent references to his whereabouts occur thereafter, but these suggest that the bishop was mainly at Bosbury during November and December.[87]

The Despensers' exile was to prove a hollow victory for the barons. According to one chronicler,[88] whose suggestion makes good sense, it was by Edward's design that on 13 October 1321 Queen Isabella sought entry to Leeds Castle, held by the wife of Bartholomew Badlesmere, and was refused entry as anticipated.[89] The promptness of the king's reaction bespeaks some forethought. Within a short time a substantial besieging force was collected – 30,000 men, the Pauline annalist thought – and on the last day of October the castle fell.[90] Meanwhile the Marcher barons had taken up position at Kingston-on-Thames, poised for intervention. There they were offered mediation by Archbishop Reynolds, Stephen Gravesend, bishop of London, and the earl of Pembroke, but would only consent to surrender the castle after a meeting of parliament.[91] As it turned out, they were rendered powerless to raise the siege by Lancaster's veto, imposed because of his hatred of Badlesmere.[92]

85 *Vita*, pp. 113–14.

86 *H.R.O.*, pp. 199–204; *ibid.* fos. 53^v–54^r: Orleton was mainly at his manors of Bosbury and Sugwas. See Maddicott, *Lancaster*, pp. 286ff.

87 The bishop was at Bosbury on the 16th (*H.R.O.*, fo. 55^v) and still there on the 29th (*ibid.* pp. 204–9).

88 Continuator of Trivet: Cotton MS. Nero D. X, fo. 111^r. Cf. *Murimuth*, p. 34: 'Isabella ex ordinatione domini regis venit ad castrum de Ledes', and for the king's preparations, *Lit. Cant.* 3, pp. 403–4. Trokelowe prefaces his remarks on the subject with the statement that the queen was 'semper nutrix pacis et concordiae inter dominum suum, regem, et barones' (p. 110).

89 See Phillips, *Pembroke*, p. 216.

90 *Annales Paulini*, p. 299. *Sempringham* (p. 339) has 60,000!

91 *Murimuth*, p. 34; cf. *Melsa* 2, p. 339. Reynolds had summoned Cobham to London for 16 October (the letter arrived on the 9th), but the bishop declined to come on account of the distance and the shortness of notice. *Worcester Reg. Cobham*, pp. 107–8.

92 *Melsa* 2, p. 339: 'Sed Thomas Lancastriae comes ne hoc facerent per litteras suas eis omnino dissuasit.' Haskins, 'Chronicle of the Civil Wars', p. 78, n. 1, puts down the earl's dislike of Badlesmere mainly to the fact that his claim as steward to appoint the steward of the household was disregarded at the time of Badlesmere's appointment to the latter office in 1318.

Encouraged by his success, Edward determined on further military measures – though careful not to declare a state of war – and set off for Cirencester where he spent Christmas. In the meantime he hit on a plan to rehabilitate the Despensers: Reynolds was directed to summon a provincial council for that purpose. But in thinking that the bishops would be amenable Edward made a miscalculation. The archbishop's mandate summoning the council is dated 14 November from Lambeth, that of the bishop of London as dean of the province the following day from Stepney. As Cobham was quick to point out, scarcely ten days intervened between the receipt of the mandate and the meeting itself.[93] Orleton received his copy about the same time, the evening of 21 November, but it was not until the 29th that he nominated his proctors, Adam Murimuth and Roger de Breynton.[94] He was always willing, he responded, to give help and advice in matters touching the peace and tranquillity of the realm, but in this instance he was prevented from doing so by much urgent business.[95] The king seems to have written personal letters to some or all of the bishops; Cobham received his on 25 November and replied that although he wished to obey the royal command he could by no means reach London in the time available – quite apart from the exceptional perils of the journey. It was of course the depth of winter.[96] Murimuth says much the same when he explains that few came to the council because of the brevity of notice (which would have rendered void any ordinary ecclesiastical summons) and the 'horrorem et viarum discrimina', but oddly enough, considering he was Orleton's proctor, he is unable to give the precise date of the assembly.[97] The Pauline annalist is more informative: not only does he supply

[93] *Worcester Reg. Cobham*, p. 112.

[94] *H.R.O.*, pp. 205–8; *Concilia* 2, pp. 507–9.

[95] *H.R.O.*, p. 205: 'Licet ad pacem regni et tranquillitatem procurandam et firmiter tenendam consilium et auxilium parati semper simus'; p. 208: 'Propter temporis brevitatem et inundacionem acquarum insolitam clerus nostre diocesis cum ea quam mandastis celeritate non potuit congregari', so that he could not certify by 1 December what he had done. This accords with Cobham's statement. It is dangerous on that account to draw a political inference from the absence of the remoter bishops.

[96] *Worcester Reg. Cobham*, pp. 111–12. The letter is dated 25 November 1321 by the editor.

[97] *Murimuth*, p. 35. Stubbs (*Bridlington*, p. 71, n. 1) thought that Murimuth's date (*c.* 10 December) referred to that of the bishops' declaration in favour of the Despensers' recall.

the correct date, he also names the bishops who attended. There were only four in addition to the archbishop: Hothum of Ely, Gravesend of London, Martival of Salisbury and Hethe of Rochester. This rump did what was required of it and on the feast of the Circumcision (1 January) Reynolds obediently declared that the younger Despenser was not lawfully exiled.[98]

The plan had misfired for want of adequate preparation. Edward sought to salvage the situation by urging the absentee bishops to give their opinion of the decision taken by their colleagues. Orleton's reply is not extant, but Cobham, after confessing himself neither able nor sufficiently rash to speak out on his own, concurred in the opinion, going so far as to add that as the Despensers' exile had been decreed by parliamentary process, so should its revocation.[99] Stapledon, bishop of Exeter and a loyal servant of the king to the end, made the same point but more strongly. His response has been interpreted, almost certainly correctly, as not hostile to the Despensers, but indicative of his respect for the authority of parliament – a principle often invoked by the episcopate.[100] Bishop Droxford did not grasp the nettle, contenting himself with an acceptance of the conclusion reached by the king's advisors.[101] As individuals the bishops were obviously vulnerable. Their desire for revocation in parliament did not materialise until May 1322 in the vastly different atmosphere following the king's victory at Boroughbridge.[102]

Much has been said in criticism of Reynolds, but perhaps not enough with respect to his unfortunate concurrence with this particular wish of the king's. It may not be quite right to state that thereafter the episcopal bench was split into 'moderate', 'self-seeking' or 'undecided' bishops – such labels are too simplistic – but it is true that there was never again to be the same opportunity for a united front on matters which fundamentally affected the nation's political welfare.[103]

98 *Annales Paulini*, p. 300; *C.C.R.* 1318–23, p. 543; *Bridlington*, pp. 71–2.

99 *Worcester Reg. Cobham*, p. 119, and see n. 83 above. The pope's bull to dissolve the oaths of those who conspired against the Despensers is dated 5 May 1322: S.C.7/25/5.

100 *Exeter Reg. Stapledon*, pp. 442–3, and see the comments of K. Edwards, 'Political Importance of English Bishops', p. 339.

101 *Bath & Wells Reg. Drokensford*, pp. 199–200.

102 *C.C.R.* 1318–23, pp. 541–6; *Bridlington*, pp. 70–3.

103 See K. Edwards, *op. cit.* pp. 326ff.

YEARS IN THE WILDERNESS 1322–1326

The king's journey to Cirencester marked the prelude to his attack on the Marcher barons.[1] Lancaster remained stubbornly at Pontefract, so Edward grasped the chance to deal separately with the Marchers – notably the earl of Hereford and the two Roger Mortimers, uncle and nephew. About 6 December the barons captured Gloucester, which forced the royal army to turn northwards towards the next bridge over the River Severn, at Worcester.[2] There the barons held the further bank, and rather than force the issue Edward sent a small force to secure the Bridgnorth crossing. There too he was unsuccessful; a rebel force in anticipation of his arrival fired much of the town and broke down the bridge. But at Shrewsbury Edward's forces were able to cross the Severn unmolested, because by that time the Mortimers were reluctant to undertake the responsibility of a large-scale campaign without Lancaster's support. There was another factor; the successful attacks of Sir Gruffydd Llwyd on the castles of Chirk and Holt and the capture of Bromfield Castle by the mercurial Robert Ewer adversely affected the Mortimers' power in their own locality.[3] Thus Edward experienced no difficulty in taking the Marchers' strongholds. It was all over by 23 January, when the Mortimers were taken prisoner – not without suspicion of trickery – and lodged in the Tower.[4]

[1] Edward reached Cirencester on 20 December and spent Christmas there. For his subsequent movements see Maddicott, *Lancaster*, pp. 303–12 (The Boroughbridge Campaign).

[2] Bodleian, Laud MS. Misc. 529, fo. 106v (Evesham version of Higden's *Polychronicon*). Worcester Priory in a petition of 1313 for the appropriation of Dodderhill church made the point that Worcester had the only bridge over the Severn between Gloucester and Bridgnorth: *Worcester Liber Albus*, pp. 124–6 (from fo. 54v).

[3] The continuator of Trivet (B.L. Cotton MS. Nero D. X, fo. 111v) is the chief chronicle source for this explanation of the Mortimers' action. The Meaux annalist (*Melsa* 2, p. 340) put it down to lack of money and the earl of Lancaster's delay (cf. *Vita*, p. 119), the passage being repeated almost verbatim in the *Polychronicon* (p. 310). See J. G. Edwards, 'Sir Gruffydd Llwyd', pp. 589–601, and Parry, 'Note on Sir Gruffydd Llwyd', pp. 316–18, who somewhat modifies the earlier view. I owe the latter reference to Maddicott, *Lancaster*, p. 306, n. 2.

[4] The *Wigmore Chronicle* (p. 352) states that the Mortimers 'gratiam inde sperantes, regi se subdiderunt', which is echoed by a phrase of *Avesbury* (p. 280). *Murimuth* (p. 35) and the 'Evesham chronicler' (Laud MS. Misc. 529, fo. 107r) tell the same story: the Mortimers gave themselves up on the 'fraudulent mediation' of the earl of Pembroke, the Earl Marshal, and the earls of Richmond and Warenne 'qui multa eis promiserunt sub qua forma nescitur'. Cf. *Annales Paulini*, p. 301, and for the

The author of the *Vita* remarks that on arrival at Hereford the king fiercely upbraided the bishop ('episcopus loci') for supporting the barons against their natural lord, and confiscated many of his goods by way of revenge.[5] This would suggest that Edward learned whatever there was to learn of Orleton's disloyal activities. However, it was not until two years later that formal charges were laid. According to the indictment of 1324 the forces of Roger Mortimer the nephew advanced from Bromyard towards Ledbury, pausing on their way at Bosbury, Orleton's manor. The bishop, being 'de concordia et adherentia predicti Rogeri', held a secret conference with the Marcher before the rebel army moved off to Ledbury, where Mortimer awaited the reinforcements – nine armed men including the bishop's marshal are named – which Orleton despatched to his aid the following day. As soon as they arrived, so runs the indictment, the rebels set off for Gloucester.[6]

There is no good reason to doubt the allegation that a meeting between Orleton and Mortimer took place. It could be that the bishop himself alludes to the occasion in a letter to someone close to the king in which he upholds his right 'dey oyer confessiones et conseils de salutz des almes, dont nul seculer justice ne nulle homme terrien ne deit ne ne poet avoir conissance'.[7] If so, this constitutes a defence against pressure to divulge what transpired between the two men. The date is fairly easy to determine: it must have been shortly before the fall of Gloucester, probably during the latter half of November. Orleton was at Bosbury then and during the first week of December.[8]

There remains the question of the degree of Orleton's guilt,

assertion that a safe-conduct was violated, *Melsa* 2, p. 340; *Flores* 3, p. 202. Two safe-conducts and an extension are entered on the patent rolls: *C.P.R.* 1321–24, pp. 48–51; *Parliamentary Writs* 2 (app.), pp. 174–6. According to the *Flores* it was on the third occasion that the barons were attached.

5 *Vita*, p. 119. Cf. Continuator of Trivet (Cotton MS. Nero D. X, fo. 111v), who also omits the bishop's name: 'Redarg[uit] autem rex durius civitatis huius episcopum pro eo quod parti adverse adhibuit se fautorem.'

6 Just.1/1388/mm. 2v (marked 'vacat hic quia alibi'), 5r; K.B.27/255/Rex m. 87v. *Rot. Parl.* 2, pp. 427–8 is an *inspeximus* of the King's Bench record. Cf. *Foedera* 2, ii, p. 177. For an examination of this and other evidence see Haines, 'A Defence Brief for Bishop Adam de Orleton', forthcoming in *B.I.H.R.*

7 H.C.M., no. 1373 D.

8 *H.R.O.*, fos. 55v (16 November), 56v (4 December), *ibid.* (18 January 1322). In the printed edition, pp. 205–6 (20, 29 November).

or even his innocence – a possibility not previously envisaged. Sympathy with Mortimer and the temper of the neighbourhood is understandable, perhaps in part excusable, but did the bishop actually *send* armed assistance from his household? [9] That he did so is specifically denied in what purport to be copies of a certificate found amongst papers in Orleton's ' defence brief '.[10] We cannot identify the authors, but they wrote in answer to questions posed by someone in a position of authority. They give the impression of having local knowledge of Mortimer's ' raising war ' (the wording of the indictment) [11] and conducting an armed *chevauchée* ' par nostre pais '. The admission that the bishop was ' de lacord et de la bone voilance le dit sire Roger ' gives an authentic touch, but the notion of Orleton's having countenanced the pillaging of towns is flatly rejected. Obviously the respondents were men of substance in the area: could the sheriff have been one of them? The sheriff at the time of the revolt was Roger de Elmbridge, who is alleged to have ridden with the king's enemies and to have adopted their livery. For treachery of this order he was hanged when Edward reached Gloucester in February 1322.[12] It could not have been he. His successor, Roger de Chaundos, pricked sheriff in January 1322, was certainly in a position to know the facts of the case and may have been favourably disposed towards Orleton.[13] Further than that it is impossible to go.

Although the certificate is undated, it appears to have emanated from an inquisition on at least two counts, such as might have

9 Maddicott, for instance, writes (*Lancaster*, p. 304, citing Smith, *Episcopal Appointments*, pp. 130–4): '[the earl of] Hereford, his forces strengthened by an alliance with Adam de Orleton, Bishop of Hereford '.

10 Haines, ' Defence Brief '; H.C.M., nos. 1373 G, H. In my interpretation I have been aided by discussion of a number of points with the late Mr C. A. F. Meekings, to whom I am very grateful.

11 Just. 1/1388/m. 5r (printed in part in Smith, *Episcopal Appointments*, p. 134).

12 Laud MS. Misc. 529, fo. 107r. But the author of the *Flores*, a baronial supporter, regarded him (3, p. 203) as one of the ' incliti milites digni honore ' whom the king put to death unjustly. Denholm-Young (*Vita*, p. 119, n. 6) relied on Baker's *Chroniculum* (p. 171) for the identification of Elmbridge as the ' miles de partibus Herefordie ' of his text, but there are other chronicle references, e.g. Haskins, ' Chronicle of the Civil Wars ', p. 80 (Cotton MS. Cleopatra D. IX, fo. 85r); *Brut*, p. 224.

13 P.R.O. Lists and Indexes 9, p. 59. Chaundos (Chandos) had his own lands taken into the hands of the sheriff of Somerset and Dorset ' under the belief that Roger adhered to the king's contrariants ': *C.C.R.* 1318–23, p. 422. For the pressure put on Chandos to join Mortimer, an illustration of the latter's methods, see Just. 1/1388/m. 6v. It is to be noted that the respondents make no defence of Mortimer: they are not members of a ' Mortimer faction '.

taken place between the time of Edward's arrival at Hereford (Denholm-Young calculates that he was there between 29 January and 4 February) and the restoration of Bishops Castle to Orleton on 6 February – followed two days later by a grant of protection for one year.[14] Of course it is arguable that such matters may not have been formally raised until the summer of 1322 or even as late as 1323, during the preliminaries to Orleton's arraignment; but surely the king could not have avoided doing so long before. In any case Orleton was too intelligent, too legally-minded perhaps, to have calculated on exonerating himself by means of a forgery capable of instant repudiation by its putative authors.[15] If a genuine document does lie behind the copies, as seems likely, there is no escaping the conclusion that Edward chose to suppress or at any rate ignore it during the process against Orleton. Such an original, if dated early in 1322, would serve to explain the partial but mysteriously swift rehabilitation of the bishop.

Two other members of the episcopate were implicated in the baronial rebellion: John Droxford, bishop of Bath and Wells, and Henry Burghersh, bishop of Lincoln.[16] During 1322 and much of 1323 Edward's letters to the papal court give the impression that he was more incensed against their conduct than Orleton's. Virtually nothing can be discovered about the details of Droxford's offence, except that the king regarded it as less heinous than that of Burghersh. Edward first gave vent to his feelings about the rebellious bishop of Lincoln in a letter to John XXII dated 25 February 1322 from Weston-Subedge in Gloucestershire.[17] This was closely followed by an order to provision the episcopal castle at Sleaford for royal use – that of Banbury being already in the king's hand.[18] A few months later Edward wrote

14 *Vita*, p. 119 n. 3. Thomas de Hastang (Hastings) was appointed custodian of Bishops Castle 20 January 1322: *C.P.R.* 1321–24, p. 51. He was ordered to surrender it to Orleton on 6 February and two days later the bishop was granted protection for a year: *ibid.* pp. 53, 50.

15 Admittedly forgeries were common enough at the time and the one directed against the younger Despenser, which the bishop of Rochester denounced, provides a case in point. See above, ' The path of the mediator '.

16 See ' The Bishops and the Rebellion of 1321–22 ' in Smith, *Episcopal Appointments*, pp. 130–5.

17 *Foedera* 2, ii, pp. 38–9: ' qui dicto Bartholomaeo, nostro rebelli, totis viribus adhaeret, et nobis contrariatur '.

18 A writ of 3 January 1322 directed the sheriff of Oxfordshire to seize Banbury Castle and to deliver it to Robert Ardern: *C.P.R.* 1321–24, p. 46. Robert Darcy was commissioned (7 February) to raise the county forces against the Lincolnshire insurgents

another letter to Pope John in which he complained of Burghersh's 'crimina notoria', following it up on 2 February 1323 with a demand that both he and Droxford be removed from the realm.[19] He declared that he had issued a safe-conduct for the bishop of Lincoln to make the journey to Avignon with his familiars and goods.[20] Rumours of the king of France's intervention were current and Edward's letter could scarcely have reached Avignon before he learned definitively from his agents there that Burghersh had indeed asked Charles to intercede with the pope and with the cardinal-bishops of Ostia and Palestrina. He besought his fellow monarch to revoke any such letters that had already been issued.[21] In mid-September John XXII replied that he could not accede to Edward's wish for the bishops' removal from office or their translation without satisfactory evidence that they had been guilty of substantial faults.[22] Before this rebuff reached him Edward had reiterated his request for Droxford's removal, coupling it with a proposal that the abbot of the Premonstratensian house at Langdon be appointed in his place.[23]

It will be noticed that in none of this correspondence is Orleton mentioned. Why then, it may be asked, were the charges against him revived late in 1323? To try to answer that question it is necessary to follow his career in the interval, as well as to trace some happenings which may have influenced the king's mind or those of his close advisors, notably the Despensers. True, the handing back to Orleton of Bishops Castle in February 1322 did not represent complete rehabilitation, for ten days afterwards both he and Bishop Burghersh were specifically exempted from Edward's summons to Tickhill prior to the offensive against the earls of

and on 1 March was granted a writ of aid for provisioning Sleaford Castle: *ibid.* pp. 69, 76. See also *C.C.R.* 1318–23, pp. 425, 427, 437.

19 *Foedera* 2, ii, pp. 51–2, 60–1. The earlier letter is dated 3 August 1322 from Newcastle-on-Tyne.

20 *Foedera* 2, ii, p. 61. The safe-conduct for Burghersh to travel to the Curia at the pope's bidding is dated 30 January 1323: *C.P.R.* 1321–24, p. 235.

21 *Foedera* 2, ii, p. 66. Edward expressed astonishment that Burghersh should seek the aid of Charles: 'maxime cum ipsae preces et literae in nostrum vituperium et displicentiam, ac coronae dispendium videantur graviter redundare'.

22 *Ibid.* p. 85: Avignon, 17 September 1323; S.C.7/24/16.

23 *Foedera* 2, ii, p. 86: 10 October 1323. Edward wrote of Droxford: 'Qui nostris inimicis et rebellibus, tempore turbationis, in regno nostro dudum exortae, contra nos adhaesit, se cum eis partem faciendo et cujus mora in dicto regno, propter ipsius multiplicia demerita, absque gravi scandalo, non valemus tolerari.'

Hereford and Lancaster – an understandable omission.[24] In mid-July both bishops were required to render service at Newcastle for the abortive Scottish expedition, though at least in Burghersh's case this was indicative of the king's need rather than a restoration of confidence.[25]

Orleton was mainly in his diocese or at his nearby Gloucestershire manor of Prestbury from the end of January until the last day of April 1322. Early May saw him at the York parliament which assembled less than two months after the royalist triumph at Boroughbridge on 16 March.[26] At York the sentence against the Despensers was formally nullified, the Ordinances revoked and the elder Despenser created earl of Winchester.[27] Edward's victory was complete. Orleton must have contemplated the proceedings with chagrin, more particularly the official interpretation, misleading as it was, of the bishops' part in the Despensers' recall.[28] The author of the *Flores* castigated the prelates as dumb dogs, who could not even raise a bark. But the time for barking had passed and by that stage there was nothing the bishops could do.[29]

24 *Ibid.* pp. 37–8; *C.C.R.* 1318–23, pp. 514, 523.

25 *Foedera* 2, ii, pp. 46–7. A writ of 15 July 1322, issued on the advice of Philip de Middleton, constable of Montgomery Castle, directed Orleton to levy a hundred foot-soldiers: *C.P.R.* 1321–24, p. 179.

26 On 18 and 31 January he appears to have been at Hereford (*H.R.O.*, fo. 56^{v}). He was still there for the first week of February (*ibid.* p. 209). This means that he was in the city for the duration of Edward's stay. An isolated entry (*ibid.* p. 210) points to his having been at Shinfield on 27 February (*anno predicto*), though this seems doubtful. A commission was issued from Bibury on 19 February (*ibid.*) and a charter sealed at Hereford on the 23rd (*ibid.* pp. 220–1). A litigant claimed that Orleton was at his manor of Ross on 2 March (K.B.27/255/m. 23^{r}); he was certainly outside the diocese at his Prestbury manor, near Cheltenham, for the greater part of that month. By the end of March he was at Bosbury, where he remained for the whole of April (*ibid.* fos. 58^{r}, 59^{r-v}, 61^{r}; pp. 211–25, 242). For the York parliament he stayed at Rufforth to the west of the city (*ibid.* fo. 61^{r}; pp. 225–6).

27 See McKisack, *Fourteenth Century*, pp. 71–4; Davies, *Baronial Opposition*, pp. 483, 489–92, 516–17, 582–3; *Foedera* 2, ii, pp. 40–2; *C.C.R.* 1318–23, pp. 541–6.

28 There is, of course, no mention of the fact that a mere handful of bishops attended the provincial council of December 1321 (see above, 'The path of the mediator'), or of the pressures which the king brought to bear against individual diocesans. Hugh Despenser the younger's petition claimed that the award against him (August 1321) was in error as 'made without the assent of the prelates, who are peers in parliament'. It also alleged that the bishops had unanimously counselled the king to annul the award and that they had never assented to it in the first place. *C.C.R.* 1318–23, p. 543, and cf. pp. 510–11). For an equally prejudiced view on the other side see the Commons' petition of 1327: *Rot. Parl. Inediti*, p. 116.

29 'Accersivit rex parliamentum suum apud Eboracum, in quo comparuerunt praelati

While he was at York various persons broke into Orleton's manors of Ross and Upton, did substantial damage to standing timber and drove away stock.[30] As soon as he heard of the inroad Orleton took advantage of his situation at the temporary seat of government[31] and secured three writs for the apprehension of the malefactors, among whom were Thomas and Richard Irby, presumably relatives of William Irby, prior of Hereford, who was to prove such a thorn in the flesh of the diocesan.[32] Once back in his manor of Sugwas the bishop instructed all the officers of his diocese to declare the perpetrators of these outrages ipso facto excommunicate.[33] The date of his mandate, 4 June 1322, is significant in the light of subsequent events.

Orleton's opponents hit back vigorously with wide-ranging allegations against both him and a number of others. These were incorporated about this time in a petition to the king. The petitioners, who are unnamed, begged Edward to authorise Robert de Aston, Prior William Irby and Richard de Scholle – known to be hostile to Orleton – to enquire about clerics in the dioceses of Hereford and Worcester who had rebelled against him or abetted his enemies, as well as to discover the names of such as were guilty of ' horribly excommunicating ' those who, while the king was in the March of Wales, had rightly removed property from the woods and parks of the bishop of Hereford, he being the king's avowed enemy. The petitioners also indicted the constable of the Forest of Dean, Walter de Nasse (Nasshe?), as a waster of the king's substance and principal counsellor of Roger Damory and Thomas de Berkeley. In addition, John de Lynton, Howel le Waleys and Orleton's marshal, Tristram, who like Waleys was to be named in the 1324 indictment as having been ' sent ' by the bishop to Mortimer, were stated to have escaped from Boroughbridge and to be abroad in the locality harassing the royal forces.

totius fere regni, *canes muti non valentes* [Isa. 56.10], immo verius nolentes, *latrare*, qui nec pro jure ecclesiae nec domo Dei murum tanquam veri se opponere curarunt pastores, sed potius lupis exponentes oves Christi.' *Flores* 3, p. 209.

30 *H.R.O.*, pp. 227–8, 231–3.

31 By writs of February 1322 the Exchequer was ordered to move to York and the justices of the common bench to adjourn pleas there. See Broome, ' Exchequer Migrations ', pp. 291–300, where the removal of 1322 is described in detail.

32 *H.R.O.*, pp. 231–3. The writs were tested ' me ipso ' at Rothwell, 3 June.

33 *H.R.O.*, pp. 227–8. For an earlier fracas at Ross (2 March 1322) which allegedly involved Orleton himself see K.B.27/255/m. 23r.

Edward wrote to the bishop, confining his remarks to what he had heard about the excommunication and demanding an explanation. The royal mandate was sent under privy seal from York, but the dating clause is now partly indecipherable: it probably read 23[?] June 1322.[34] Orleton replied at length, recounting the circumstances in which his excommunication had been published. His sentence, he explained, did not concern his *parks* but his *manors* of Ross and Upton in the Forest of Dean; it was pronounced *en généralité*, without naming specific persons, certainly none who had acted on royal authority. To press home the point, he denied denouncing anyone who had come into his parks while Edward was in the Hereford area. As for the summons, he craved to be excused from making the long and hazardous journey to a scene of war, but affirmed that he had done nothing against the state of Holy Church or the laws and customs of the realm, in conformity with which he was fully prepared to answer.[35] Meanwhile the king issued a further summons for Orleton to appear before him – wherever he might be – on 16 August. The bishop failed to respond since by that time Edward was at Alnwick in the Scottish war zone, though no allowance was made for the fact in the official record of his non-appearance. Instead he presented himself at York on 21 August before the king's chancellor, Bishop John Salmon, and two days later before him and the treasurer, Bishop Walter Stapledon. On the second occasion he handed over his written explanation, containing the argument outlined above, but the chancellor dared do no more than acknowledge its receipt, endorsing the document to that effect.[36]

Determined not to let the matter drop, the king again summoned Orleton to his presence. As a result the bishop appeared before Edward and his council at York towards the end of

34 S.C.8/232/11584 (for an English version see *Calendar of Ancient Petitions*, pp. 384–5); S.C.1/32/117. Although the petition is undated it can hardly be coincidence that the king's summons takes up the matter of excommunication. My feeling would be to date it tentatively 4 x 23 June 1322.

35 S.C.1/34/151.

36 *Ibid*. fo. 151ᵛ. The endorsement is headed: 'Coram domino . . cancellario'. The latter part runs: 'Episcopus Hereford' venit in cancellaria regis apud Ebor' et presente ibi domino W[altero] Exon' episcopo thesaurario regis liberavit ista pro excusacione sua de premissis, et dictus cancellarius ea recepit ut valeant quatenus valere poterunt set pro finali excusacione ipsius episcopi Hereford' ea admittere non audebat. per . . episcopum Herefordensem'.

November. Geoffrey le Scrope's presentation of the royal case helps to fill in some of the gaps in the story. The incident referred to dated back to 27 January 1322 – the close of the Marcher revolt – when Edward and his half-brother Edmund, earl of Kent, went hunting in the bishop's parks, perhaps in a fit of euphoria not untainted by revenge. Allegedly the bishop had taken offence, and without respect for the royal dignity excommunicated them. Orleton, conducting his own defence, replied that he had fulminated no excommunication for transgressions in his parks following the royal visit and was prepared to put himself on the country to prove it.[37] The Curia Regis rolls show that for want of a jury prepared to convict the case was adjourned from one term to another until virtually the end of the reign.[38]

The momentum of events was about to transform a local contrivance to embarrass the bishop into an affair of national importance. This escalation is attributable partly to Edward's gullibility and readiness to think the worst of Orleton, partly to a confounding of the real and alleged excommunications. With respect to the last, Orleton's explanation is fully supported by documents in his register, whereas the indictment gives no details of any earlier excommunication. Had any such sentence been promulgated copies of it would have been available. Alternatively, the indictment (though not the petition) may imply that Orleton's denunciation of the devastators of Ross and Upton was designed to extend retrospectively to the hunting incident as well. In his initial reply to the charge Orleton repudiated such an interpretation, and there is certainly no ambiguity about the mandate in his register. These considerations make it difficult to avoid the conclusion that the prosecution was a malicious one.

It is not this incident but Orleton's supposed undercover activity in aid of the imprisoned Mortimers that has provided the traditional explanation of the resurgence of royal anger. Without citing his authority Canon Bannister ascribes the commutation of the death sentences on these men to life imprisonment to the 'strenuous efforts' of Orleton, supported by the bishop of Dur-

[37] K.B.27/250/Rex m. 16^v; S.C.1/32/118.

[38] K.B.27/251/Rex m. 6^r; 252/Rex m. 12^r; 253/Rex m. 13^r; 254/Rex m. 25^v etc. Some account of the case is to be found in Smith, *Episcopal Appointments*, pp. 131–2, together with a transcript of S.C.1/32/118 (*ibid*. p. 133).

ham, Louis de Beaumont.[39] If this could be substantiated it would indeed constitute an important piece of evidence; the likelihood is remote. From what we now know of Orleton's position at the time it is clear that his influence in the king's counsels was minimal or non-existent; any intervention of his in the Mortimers' affairs could only have been counter-productive. His itinerary vouches for the fact that he made no personal approach to Edward, who was at York.

We have already found reason to reject the notion that Orleton spent the last few months of 1323 at Shinfield, plotting the younger Mortimer's release. Misled by Blaneforde, Bannister placed that event a year too late.[40] At the time of the flight, 1 August 1323, the bishop was in his diocese: in all probability he had been resident for the whole of the previous month.[41] That he was in any way cognisant of the plan of escape is improbable, for it had to be concerted at short notice.[42] It is to be admitted that the Marcher area was rife with plots and rumours of plots, as the revelations of the self-confessed Mortimer agents Fernhale and Newbiggin attest, but even they did not incriminate the bishop.[43] All the same, since Orleton was a known sympathiser

39 *H.R.O.*, pp. xxv–xxvi. The date of commutation is given as 22 July 1322, as in *G.E.C.* 8, p. 436 (from *Parliamentary Writs*). But in C.49/roll 12 and Davies, *Baronial Opposition*, p. 565 (transcript of E.163/24/12), the 'pronunciacio et reddicio iudicii' delivered by the justices at Westminster is dated 2 August 1322. Cf. *Parliamentary Writs* 2 (app.), pp. 213, 215–7; *Foedera* 2, ii, pp. 86–7.

40 *H.R.O.*, pp. xxv–xxvi; *Blaneforde*, pp. 145–6. For further details see above, 'Orleton and the Chroniclers'.

41 The bishop was at his manor of Sugwas near Hereford on 3 August and at his Prestbury manor (Gloucs.) on the 22nd. *H.R.O.*, fo. 70^{r-v}.

42 According to the *Brut* (p. 231) Mortimer, learning that his death was planned for the morrow of St Lawrence (i.e. 11 August), escaped the night before. The Wigmore annalist ascribes the escape to the eve of St Peter ad Vincula (31 July–1 August): *Wigmore Chronicle*, p. 352; the *French Chronicle* (pp. 46–7), *Sempringham* (p. 349), and *Annales Paulini* (p. 305) to the following night; Bodleian, Bodley MS. 956, fo. 203^r (Lichfield Chronicle), has 2 August. Confusion about the year was cleared up by Stones, 'Roger Mortimer's Escape', pp. 97–8. For the official enquiry see K.B.27/254/Rex m. 37^r.

43 Thomas de Newbiggin, described in the *French Chronicle* (p. 47) as 'un mauvais ribaud clerk', subsequently became an official agent, informer and blackmailer. Details of his activities and those of Fernhale are in *Parliamentary Writs* 2 (app.), pp. 244–9, and see *ibid.* 2, iii, pp. 838, 1223. The abbot of Wigmore and the priors of Leominster and Wormsley allegedly received letters from Mortimer and succoured his *servientes*. Early in 1326 Margaret, mother of the younger Mortimer, was removed to Elstow nunnery (near Bedford) for holding meetings of 'suspected persons' at Radnor and Worcester. *C.P.R.* 1324–27, p. 206.

of Mortimer's the very fact of the flight may have served to stimulate the king's antagonism towards him.

Various chroniclers dwell with horror on the carnage which followed the baronial defeat at Boroughbridge,[44] yet barely eighteen months later Edward determined to mete out punishment to those of the contrariants who were still at large, including the men who had marched with the barons to London and Kingston in 1321 and those who had subsequently aided the Mortimers with men or money. By a writ dated 1 October 1323 from Skipton, Yorkshire, royal justices were empowered to act in the counties of Lancaster, Derby, Stafford and elsewhere.[45] More detailed are the commissions issued from Kenilworth (28 December) and Worcester (10 January 1324), which specify west-midland counties, including Herefordshire. These commissions, together with a writ of privy seal for the making of fines (Kenilworth, 1 January), preface the assize roll which records the inquisition before Hervy de Staunton and his associated justices.[46]

The assize court opened at Hereford on 23 January 1324. The presentment of the local jurors has already been outlined. To recapitulate briefly: Orleton was alleged to have held secret parley with Mortimer at Bosbury and afterwards to have sent certain named men to him as reinforcement. Orleton did not attempt a rebuttal; to have done so would have been to recognise the court's authority. Instead he made a formal declaration to the effect that he was bishop of Hereford by God's will and that of the pope. As such, he ought not to reply to matters of that kind, nor could he do so without offence to God and Holy Church.[47] To this the justices responded that he had been brought into court by attachment and distraint, not by corporal arrest. As a bishop he was one of the king's barons, holding the lands of his bishopric by barony. Were he to be impleaded for trespass (' transgressio ') by someone

44 For the number of those who suffered see Haskins, ' Chronicle of the Civil Wars ', pp. 73–5 (text of Cotton MS. Cleopatra D. IX, fos. 83^r–85^r at pp. 75–81). But not all those listed in this MS. died *after* Boroughbridge.

45 K.B.27/255/Rex m. 87^v; *Rot. Parl.* 2, p. 427. See also Tupling, *South Lancashire.*

46 Just. 1/1388/mm. 1a, 1b, 2^r.

47 *Ibid.* mm. 2^v, 5^r; K.B.27/255/Rex m. 87^v: ' Ipse est episcopus Hereford' ad voluntatem Dei et summi pontificis et quod materia predictorum articulorum sibi impositorum adeo ardua est, quod ipse non debet in curia hic super predictis sibi impositis respondere nec inde respondere potest absque offensa divina et sancte ecclesie.'

other than the king, he would have to reply in the king's court and therefore could not be of superior status, especially vis-à-vis the king. To this Orleton responded by reiterating his previous statement.[48]

According to the Coram Rege roll Orleton next appeared before the king at Westminster on 24 February 1324, the day after the assembly of the Lenten parliament, when the same accusation was made. This time however Roger Mortimer is termed traitor (' proditor ') and Gilbert atte Nasshe, named as one of those with Orleton at Bosbury, is stated to have been convicted by a local jury of giving him assistance.[49] Once again Orleton repeated his original declaration, whereupon he was claimed for the Church by Archbishop Reynolds, who was ordered to produce him before the king on 19 March – the day after parliament dispersed. For the occasion another jury was empanelled and sent up from Hereford. Only three of the twelve jurymen had been members of the previous panel,[50] and it was stiffened by a group of knights. The jurors found the bishop guilty on the same indictment,[51] the sheriff being instructed to seize his goods, chattels and lands.

Henry de Blaneforde's account of the final stage in this judicial process differs markedly from that of the official record. According to his detailed description, the bishops were alerted by a rumour that the king had called Orleton before him:[52] in other words he had not been given, in proper form, a day to appear before the justices. Ten suffragans, headed by the metropolitans of Canterbury (Reynolds), York (Melton) and Dublin (Bicknor), hastened to the place of summons, where they found Orleton

48 *Ibid.* m. 2^{v}: 'Et se tenet prescise ad huiusmodi racionem suam absque alia responsione in hac parte facienda.' Orleton's 'extra-judicial' rejoinder to the justices' argument is given in H.C.M., no. 1373 D.

49 K.B.27/255/Rex m. 87^{v}; *Rot. Parl.* 2, p. 427. Nasshe was indicted as an adherent of Mortimer: 'Et missus eidem Rogero per Adam episcopum Hereford' ad equitaturam et sumptus ipsius episcopi in auxilium ipsius Rogeri.' He replied that he had only gone because of threats and to avoid death. The jurors rejected the plea and he made a fine of 100s: Just. 1/1388/m. 3^{r}. His lands were quickly restored and he was granted custody of those of Gilbert Talbot (also a contrariant). See *C.P.R.* 1321–24, pp. 17, 191; *C.C.R.* 1318–23, p. 433.

50 Adam de la Linde, Adam Halfnaked and Roger de Poston.

51 There do not seem to have been 'further details of Orleton's alleged treasons' as stated by Usher, 'Career of a Political Bishop', p. 39.

52 'Rex . . . episcopum praedictum convenit. Quo rumore ad aures episcoporum perlato': *Blaneforde*, p. 141.

standing alone – desolate. They immediately took the bishop into their protection and under pain of anathema warned those present not to lay violent hands on him. It was only then, *after* Orleton had been led away,[53] that the king ordered the inquisition to be held in which the jury, who are said to have feared the vengeance of the earthly rather than the heavenly king, swore that he was guilty of all the offences of which he stood indicted. Edward then confiscated his lands and worse than that, allowed his goods to be thrown into the street and ransacked. The bishop, we are told by the sympathetic Blaneforde, following Job's example endured all with fortitude and remained with the archbishop until there should be some sign of royal grace. Writing to Pope John Orleton complained bitterly of this unjust judgement (' iniquum iudicium '). In doing so he clearly intended to imply that it was faulty in law, but also in fact; for in this letter he speaks of his innocence and, with much elaboration, of his unwarranted harassment by the king and others in his service.[54]

Despite his (somewhat superficial) resemblance to Job, Orleton did not abandon the idea of legal redress. It could have been in 1324 that he petitioned against the decision on the ground of errors in the process,[55] but it was not until the following reign that parliament annulled the judgement. At that time (1327) the mandate for the restoration of the Hereford temporalities gave as the chief source of error the fact that the justices proceeded to hold the inquisition at Westminster in Orleton's absence,[56] a finding which accords with Blaneforde. The record of the process delivered to chancery, which includes Orleton's objections, reveals a basic defect destructive of the whole of the justices' proceedings: in the indictment they had admitted a statement that the bishop adhered to Roger Mortimer ' qui levavit de guerra '. It was not a

[53] Thus the inquisition was held irregularly in the bishop's absence (' absentem episcopum '), the king proceeding ' quasi ex officio judicis '. *Ibid.* pp. 141–2.

[54] Cotton MS. Vitellius E. IV 9. This letter is very difficult to read having been much damaged, presumably in the fire at Ashburnham House. Part of it is summarised by Usher, ' Career of a Political Bishop ', p. 42. See below nn. 77, 79, 85.

[55] S.C.8/161/8043. The petition to the king and his council is mutatis mutandis identical with that which prefaces the annulment process of 1327. It is endorsed: ' Veniant recordum et processus coram consilio.'

[56] *Rot. Parl.* 2, p. 429; *C.C.R.* 1327–30, pp. 44–5; *Foedera* 2, ii, p. 177: ' Et licet idem episcopus in inquisitionem aliquam, inde faciendam, se non posuisset, nichilominus praefati justiciarii ad inquisitionem praedictam capiendam processerunt.'

time of war – both sides had been careful to maintain that convention – and in any case Hervy de Staunton's commission did not extend to those who made war, or their adherents, but merely to felonies, robberies and trespasses.[57] Most of the other objections concern the failure of the justices to appoint days for Orleton's appearance in accordance with recognised practice; so that, for instance, the final stage of the process took place 'ac si habuisset diem coram eis'.[58] The adoption of this strategy by a trained lawyer should not be taken as an indication of guilt, or of an inability to mount a cogent defence on the principal issue: it could be said to follow contemporary practice.

Other elements of the procedure are suspect. The Hereford jurors swore to the truth of an indictment, packed with circumstantial detail, two years after the event. This is not to claim that such a lapse of time was unprecedented, but that in view of it the jury can hardly be considered a reliable indicator of Orleton's guilt or innocence. Herefordshire was rife with disaffection, and as has been argued elsewhere, some jurors were known to be antagonistic to Orleton;[59] at least one, Adam Halfnaked, benefited from the confiscation of his temporalities.[60]

Long ago the case attracted the attention of Vernon Harcourt,[61] who was struck by the divergence between the official record of the Coram Rege roll on the one hand, and Orleton's legal objections and Blaneforde's chronicle on the other. The procedural errors were so glaring, he thought, as to suggest that the king himself was virtually conducting the prosecution. As for Orleton,

57 The record of the process as delivered to chancery (1327) is C.49/6/5. An *inspeximus* from the patent roll (1329) is printed in *Rot. Parl.* 2, pp. 427–9; cf. *C.P.R.* 1327–30, p. 365, and *Winchester Chartulary*, p. 185, no. 441 (partial).

58 *Rot. Parl.* 2, p. 428.

59 Usher, 'Career of a Political Bishop', p. 40. Halfnaked had earlier been entrusted with the temporalities of St Guthlac's by the king, apparently in Irby's interest: *C.P.R.* 1321–24, p. 49. In August 1324 Richard de Scholle and Halfnaked were among those warned by Orleton not to associate with the excommunicated Irby (*H.R.O.*, p. 306). Scholle was one of the prior's witnesses for his appeal to the Court of Canterbury (*ibid.* p. 276) and was suggested as a commissioner to act against Orleton and others in S.C.8/232/11584.

60 For his account as custodian see E.372/170/48; E.352/126/38. He was accused of aiding and abetting the slayer of John de Northgrave. Henry de Vorteye, the principal in this affair, was outlawed for failing to respond to the charge, which was eventually withdrawn. K.B.27/250/Rex m. 12v; 252/Rex m. 11r etc. Orleton later farmed the Northgrave lands: *C.C.R.* 1330–34, pp. 429–30.

61 *His Grace the Steward*, pp. 304–7.

he seemed to be demanding 'trial by his peers according to Magna Carta' – what the constitutional lawyers would come to describe as claiming benefit of clergy.[62]

Thanks to the survival of a gathering of documents in Hereford Cathedral Library, Orleton's 'defence brief',[63] and to the procedural objections on the close and patent rolls, we now know a good deal about the theoretical and practical basis of the bishop's defence, even though he refused to plead in court. In the first place he stood firmly on the ground of clerical immunity from secular jurisdiction and the sole right of the apostolic see to determine the case of a 'criminous bishop'.[64] To support this stance he extracted a pertinent passage from the *Decretum* which purports to retail an apposite remark of Constantine himself, derived from Rufinus's translation of Eusebius, as well as a battery of quotations from the papal books, *Extra* and *Sext*, and their commentators Pope Innocent IV and Cardinal Hostiensis.[65] Another ecclesiastical prerogative, the inviolability of the confessional and of spiritual counsel, was justified (we can confidently deduce) in the context of whatever discussion he may have had with Mortimer. To others this could only be of a political character; Orleton defended his action on the ground that the baron was in the first place his 'parishioner'.[66]

What has not so far been remarked upon is that Orleton was indicted not for 'high treason' but for 'trespass' (*transgressio*) – a comprehensive term often used of the armed *chevauchée* so common in lawless times. This is made clear by the record of the process on the assize roll and Orleton's legal objections, in particular by a letter directed to someone in the king's confidence in which the bishop expressly defends himself from the charge of being an accessory to trespassers.[67] It was to the same question

62 *Ibid.* p. 307. Cf. *Blaneforde*, pp. 141–2, and n. 53 above.

63 H.C.M., nos. 1373 A–H. See Haines, 'Defence Brief'.

64 H.C.M., no. 1373 C.

65 H.C.M., no. 1373 A: Decretum C.11, q. 1, c. 41.

66 H.C.M., no. 1373 D: 'Sire. Merveillouse chose et estraunge est que vous me aresonez de ceo qe iay este en privyte ou en counseil de graunt ou de petit ou de nully de sicomme qe ieo suy tant comme il plest a dieu evesqe et prestre et dey oyer confessiones et conseils de salutz des almes, dont nul seculer justice ne nulle homme terrein ne deit ne ne poet avoir conissance.'

67 *Ibid.* (second part): 'Et sire, ceo qe vous me avez dit qe ieo suy mene aresponse par attachement et par destresce arespondre de trespas et de ceo qe ieo duysse avoir envoie gentz en eyde de trespassours, ieo croi qe nulle manere de ley ne chacera

that the unknown commissioners addressed themselves.[68] At this stage the bishop could have settled the matter by making a fine, as did many others.[69] He rejected such a course because he considered it unlawful; an encroachment on ecclesiastical liberties and property.[70] It was a short step to his next conclusion: if ecclesiastical property were not subject to secular power, a fortiori the ecclesiastical person must be immune.[71]

The Coram Rege roll, after stating that Orleton had been summoned before the justices 'de die in diem', goes on without a break to describe the proceedings of 24 February in parliament.[72] Orleton argued that no day had been given for his appearance before that assembly. As recounted above, the official version of what happened there is that the original indictment was read, coupled with the declaration that Mortimer had been adjudged a traitor and one of the bishop's *familia* convicted for helping him. This could be regarded as tantamount to a charge of treason, but it must be remembered that treason was inadequately defined before the statute of 1352 and that precedents were lacking for the arraignment of a bishop in parliament on such a charge. The indictment itself, on the justices' own showing, was concerned with trespass[73] and it was on the indictment (with the added

arespondre del envoy en cas de trespas qest un accessorye qi depent dun principal qi nest mye attache en ma persone.'

68 H.C.M., no. 1373 G.

69 For example, a much less exalted person, albeit a chancery clerk, Robert de Clider-hou, rector of Wigan. He was alleged to have sent two mounted men and four foot-soldiers to Lancaster's aid and to have preached that his parishioners owed him their help as liegemen. He denied the charge and put himself on the country, the jurors finding against him. He was imprisoned and bailed at 1,000 marks, and later made a fine of £200. Smith, *Episcopal Appointments*, pp. 134–5 (from K.B.27/254/Rex m. 19^{r}); cf. *Parliamentary Writs* 2 (app.), pp. 240–1.

70 H.C.M., no. 1373 B: 'Non videtur quod dictus episcopus licite possit per finem exactum pacem transitoriam querere et aliquibus acquiescere absque divine maiestatis offensa et libertatis ecclesiastice lesione.'

71 *Ibid.*: 'Et sicut non debet res ecclesie subicere, submittere vel supponere potestati seculari multo minus debet personam submittere gracie opprimentis.'

72 *Rot. Parl.* 2, p. 427. Hence the objection that the justices assigned to hear the case should not have appointed a day for the hearing 'nisi coram semetipsis etc. et ipsi dederunt ei diem quod esset personaliter coram rege ubicumque' (*ibid.* p. 428).

73 Just. 1/1388/m. 2^{v}. Although this is marked 'vacat hic quia alibi', the later entry at m. 5^{r} does not repeat the justices' argument about 'transgressio', nor is it contained in the recension on the Curia Regis roll. It runs: 'Quod ipse vocatus est ad curiam hic per attachiamentum etc. et per districcionem etc. [gap in MS.] et non per arestacionem corporis sui, et ex quo idem episcopus est baro domini regis et tenet tenementa episcopatus sui de domino rege per baroniam, et si idem episcopus

observation that Roger Mortimer was ' inimicus regis convictus ') that the jury convicted Orleton in absentia when it convened on 19 March.[74]

It may be surmised that Edward, angry at the bishop's staunch resistance to the justices, and further exacerbated by Mortimer's successful flight, tried to manipulate the proceedings so as to give the offence a more sinister look. Faced with this turn of events the bishops at last showed a united front. Orleton, it may be added, was looking not so much to the judgement of his peers as to that of the pope, whom he regarded as the supreme arbiter in matters of this kind. At the same time he was prepared to contend, though not in court, that the process was irregular by the tenets of the law it was supposedly implementing.

Edward II's version of the affair is contained in a letter to the pope of 8 April in which he states, somewhat ingenuously, that the offence came to his notice ' fidedigna relacione ', without a hint of his having known about it in substance, and probably in detail, for more than two years. For taking the part of the king's enemies, he writes, Orleton was accused of the crime of *lèse majesté* (treason), and on his failure to respond to the charge an inquisition was held in accordance with the law and custom of the realm.[75] John XXII is unlikely to have been impressed by this exposition; a few years before, he had asked the king to refrain from summoning his collector, Rigaud d'Assier, before any lay court or subjecting him to that ' custom or rather corruption ' whereby laymen abide by the decision of twelve witnesses to the prejudice of ecclesiastical liberty.[76] Orleton was to give his own account of the tribulations which followed.[77]

ad sectam alterius quam domini regis esset implacitatus de transgressione necessario responderet querenti in curia regis, unde idem episcopus melioris condicionis esse non debet precipue penes dominum regem quam alium etc.'

74 *Rot. Parl.* 2, p. 428.

75 *Foedera* 2, ii, p. 96.

76 *C.P.L.* 1305–42, p. 434.

77 Cotton MS. Vitellius E. IV 9. The general purport of this mutilated copy of a letter is that Orleton had done everything in his power, within the bounds of episcopal liberty and without falling into sin, to accommodate himself to the king, but there was a certain detractor [Baldock or the younger Despenser?] who like another Sinon passing between the Greeks and Trojans, said one thing in secret and another openly (' homo ille qui nos iniuste persequitur . . . velut alter Sinon inter Dan[a]os et Dardanos discurrens . . . et replicans sic et non, unum in occulto et aliud in patulo corde et corde locutus est '). He had so dissuaded the king from a belief in Orleton's innocence that contrary to justice and equity, as well as what was due to

After the sentence the bishop stayed on in London at least until the end of the first week of April 1324. Slightly later he reappears in his diocese.[78] The account of his governance of Hereford has shown how his friends rallied to his support, even to the extent of driving off the stock from his manors to deprive the royal custodians of its benefit. The bishop himself was subjected to gross interference in the performance of his spiritual functions and his register and vestments were carried off.[79]

In an undated letter to Cardinal Vitale Dufour, probably written about the end of March 1324,[80] Bishop Cobham gives his impressions of the situation of those bishops who still lingered under royal displeasure. Orleton continued very much an object of the king's wrath, but this, Cobham hoped, was more in the nature of intimidation than punishment ('spero hoc pocius ad terrorem fieri quam ad penam'). In pursuance of papal letters he had approached the king on behalf of John Stratford – provided to the see of Winchester despite Edward's opposition – and the king had promised to act favourably in the matter. The outcome was to be the restoration on 28 June of Stratford's temporalities. As for Burghersh, Cobham continued, he had been received back into favour and the temporalities of his bishopric of Lincoln were to be released.[81] The record of this restoration on the close rolls concludes with a memorandum that the chancellor, Robert Baldock, admonished Burghersh to give no occasion for their resumption.[82]

his calling, he could not have obtained [favour?] unless he had subordinated himself to lay power and subjected both himself and his church to an illegal obligation of £10,000 ('regalem ani[mum?] . . . ex eius dependet arbitrio, sic pervertit et contra meam innocenciam adeo inflammavit quod . . . [non] potui optinere episcopalem preeminenciam iniquis obligacionibus [etc.] contra fas et equ[u]m et mee professionis debitum potestati laice subegissem et me et ecclesiam . . . decem milibus librarum sterlingorum dampnabiliter obligassem'), though the Hereford bishopric was worth much less than £1,000 [a year]. The resources of the see had been exploited for the advantage of the man for whom no riches were enough ('homo ille cui nullorum successuum copia sufficit') to the detriment of the poor and others for whom they were intended. Because he had not submitted ('et quia non adquiesco perverse hominis voluntati') injury on injury had been heaped upon him.

78 *H.R.O.*, fos. 75^{v}, 76^{r-v}; pp. 277–9, 281.

79 See above, 'Hereford 1317–1327', ch. 3. Orleton in his letter to Pope John (n. 77 above) declared that [Edward] in his Herodian rage ('Herodiana namque sevicia') had forbidden the dean of Hereford and his other subjects to communicate with him or to render him assistance.

80 Written after the dispersal of parliament on 18 March and before Cobham heard of the restoration of the Winchester temporalities by writ of 28 June.

81 *Worcester Reg. Cobham*, pp. 168–70.

82 *C.C.R.* 1323–27, p. 86.

Since Droxford is no longer mentioned as a source of irritation in Edward's letters to the pope,[83] Orleton's position was temporarily one of complete isolation. This is emphasised at the time of the arrival early in November 1324 of the papal nuncios William, archbishop of Vienne, and Hugh, bishop of Orange.[84] They were met, Cobham informed the pope, by four bishops of his creation: those of Winchester (Stratford), Lincoln (Burghersh), London (Gravesend) and Worcester (Cobham himself). These prelates escorted the nuncios to their lodgings and on the following morning to the royal palace at Westminster. Orleton, though in London at the time and likewise a provisee, was conspicuously excluded. None the less, it is possible that he made an unsuccessful attempt to have some private discussion with the visitors.[85]

After the nuncios' departure we know almost nothing of Orleton's movements for the next four months: December 1324 to the end of March 1325.[86] During April he was preoccupied with his diocese, dedicating altars and perhaps carrying out some makeshift visitation.[87] Then, at the very end of the month, he surprisingly appears at Middleton in Winchester diocese, where he received John Stratford's licence to confer the first tonsure on a man from his own diocese.[88] The *Vita* reveals his purpose: he was seeking to come to some accommodation with the king through the agency of Henry of Lancaster.[89]

83 Edward, under papal pressure, replied on 19 February 1324 that he intended to deal favourably ('agere graciose') with Burghersh and others. Both Droxford and Burghersh were summoned (30 December) to a 'colloquium' for discussion of the king's proposed journey to Gascony. *Foedera* 2, ii, pp. 120, 123. Orleton's name was omitted from summonses to parliament etc.: *Reports touching the Dignity of a Peer* 3, app., pp. 346ff.

84 The *Annales Paulini* (p. 308) state that they arrived on 8 November and left on the 21st.

85 *Worcester Reg. Cobham*, pp. 173–4: letter of 17 November 1324. The nuncios had earlier been instructed to take up the cases of the bishops of Lincoln and Hereford with the king: *C.P.L.* 1305–42, pp. 465–6. Orleton apparently refers to his efforts to meet the nuncios in Cotton MS. Vitellius E. IV 9. He goes on to describe how at the king's command pressure was put on the London Minorites, in whose house he had sought refuge, to eject him, and how an attempt was subsequently made to force him to leave the city altogether. He stayed on because he could not go elsewhere in safety.

86 He was at Hereford 20 December, Kingston 9 January 1325, and possibly at Stepney 1 March. The episcopal register has no entry for February. *H.R.O.*, fo. 84^r; pp. 312, 325.

87 *H.R.O.*, fo. 88^v; pp. 313, 324, 339.

88 *H.R.O.*, pp. 326–7.

89 *Vita*, p. 136; *C.P.R.* 1324–27, pp. 120ff. The *Annales Paulini* (p. 308) state that the king received a French embassy there.

During this period, March and April 1325, John XXII was bombarding the king, the papal nuncios, the bishop of Ely (Hothum), the younger Despenser and Queen Isabella with exhortations to intervene on Orleton's behalf, as well as that of Burghersh, who was once again out of favour. Edward had delayed the return of some of the bishop of Lincoln's goods as a means of forcing him to accept royal promotions to benefices in his collation.[90] As emerged during our discussion of the chroniclers, not only did Lancaster fall under suspicion because of Orleton's overtures, but they may also have prompted a further royal letter to the pope (28 May) reaffirming the bishop's treachery and renewing the demand for his removal.[91] Before its arrival Pope John had written cautioning Orleton to behave with humility towards the king, in his own interests and those of his see, and for the avoidance of scandal.[92]

So far as can be ascertained, Orleton was at his rectory of Shinfield for virtually the whole period from the end of May 1325 until August of the following year. This exile was forced upon him by the confiscation of the manors of his see, and meant that he was effectively prevented by distance from attending personally to his spiritual duties.

Meanwhile important events were taking place elsewhere. Queen Isabella sailed for France on 9 March 1325 and with deceptive alacrity came to an agreement with her brother, King Charles IV, for the restoration of Edward II's French possessions with the exception of the Agenais and La Réole, the fate of which was to be settled at a later stage.[93] The treaty was drawn up at Paris on 31 May and confirmed by Edward on 13 June.[94] In compliance with its terms the king was planning to leave for France to perform homage, but at the last moment pleaded illness.[95] Instead Prince Edward, the king's thirteen-year-old son, was invested with the duchy of Aquitaine and the county of Ponthieu and sent to

90 The pope complained to Edward in a letter of 1 April 1325: *C.P.L.* 1305–42, p. 469. See also *ibid.* pp. 465–70, 472, 475, 478.

91 *Foedera* 2, ii, p. 137. In another letter of 1 July 1326 (*ibid.* p. 161) the bishops complained of are not named, but doubtless Orleton was one of them.

92 *C.P.L.* 1305–42, p. 472.

93 *Foedera* 2, ii, pp. 132, 134–6.

94 *Foedera* 2, ii, pp. 137–8.

95 *Foedera* 2, ii, pp. 139–41. His letter to King Charles pleading illness is dated 24 August from Langdon Abbey near Dover.

France in the charge of Bishop Stapledon, among others. He sailed on 12 September and performed homage at Bois-de-Vincennes twelve days later.[96]

Hindsight makes Edward's conduct appear completely irrational: it sealed his fate. This assumption has been strongly challenged on the basis that Edward knew nothing of Isabella's estrangement or her reported fear of the younger Despenser until much later, so that he saw no reason not to send his son to France while she remained there.[97] This, of course, is Edward's own explanation of what happened, as given in a letter to the French monarch.[98] It is not entirely convincing: it could be that his own misgivings were overcome by the self-interested urgings of the Despensers, who had no wish to be left to the tender mercies of their enemies and were equally nervous about leaving the country in Edward's entourage.[99]

Baker, long after the event, saw the 'alumpni Iezabele', Burghersh and Orleton – but particularly Orleton – as puppeteers who contrived the whole show from the queen's departure to negotiate the French treaty, until her return with an invading army. This is fanciful, but provides the basis of a modern argument that the two bishops were 'among the leaders of a second court party, which seems gradually to have come into existence from about 1324 onwards to support the claims of Isabella and her son'.[100] A corollary of this idea is that the queen had 'been trying to build up a party favourable to herself in the episcopate'.[101] Thus she sought the promotion of Louis de Beaumont, whose French idiom was said by the censorious to be closer to his lips than the Latin one.[102] But Burghersh's elevation cannot be explained by the same

96 *Foedera* 2, ii, pp. 141–3; *C.P.R.* 1324–27, pp. 173–5; *The War of Saint-Sardos*, pp. 241–5, where (p. 243, n. 1) the date is corrected from 14 to 24 September. See also Hunter, 'Mission of Queen Isabella', p. 251.

97 Grassi, 'William Airmyn', p. 555.

98 *Foedera* 2, ii, pp. 147–8.

99 *Murimuth*, p. 44: 'Qui nec audebant mare transire nec rege transeunte, in Anglia remanere.' Cf. *French Chronicle*, p. 48. In an imaginary conversation in the *Brut* (p. 234) the younger Despenser attributes the sending of Isabella to his father's counsel.

100 *Chronicon*, pp. 16–19; K. Edwards, 'Political Importance of English Bishops', p. 343.

101 K. Edwards, *op. cit.* pp. 341–2.

102 Details of his promotion and of the queen's part in it are given by *Graystanes*, pp. 757–8, as also an unfavourable view of his appearance, character and relationship with the cathedral priory of Durham (*ibid.* pp. 761–2).

argument; the pressure of his uncle Bartholomew Badlesmere, and of Edward himself are clearly discernible.[103] As for William Ayrminne, it has been shown that he was more the king's candidate than Isabella's, and that the pope, having failed to promote him to Carlisle, which see had already been reserved, provided him to Norwich instead on the false assumption that this would gratify the king, and before the arrival of the queen's recommendatory letters.[104] There is no denying Isabella's interest in such appointments or her forceful advocacy of particular candidates, but with the exception of Beaumont the bishops named were as much in her husband's 'interest' as her own, until circumstances dictated otherwise.

Burghersh's alienation from the king is readily comprehensible. His uncle, Bartholomew Badlesmere, who was so anxious to help him to a bishopric, went over to the barons in 1321. The most probable reason for this was the excessive influence exercised upon Edward by the Despensers.[105] Burghersh's brother, also named Bartholomew, was captured on the surrender of Leeds Castle and sent with his wife to the Tower,[106] while Badlesmere after escaping from Boroughbridge was snatched from his refuge, the bishop's manor of Stowe Park in Lincolnshire, and hanged at Canterbury together with his nephew Sir Bartholomew de Ashburnham.[107] These family tragedies provide reason enough for the bishop of Lincoln's attitude.[108] It is possible that Burghersh was suspected of conspiracy following the temporary restoration of his

103 On Sandale's death in 1319 Badlesmere had asked the king to give the Winchester bishopric to his nephew: S.C.1/33/10. See Smith, *Episcopal Appointments*, pp. 33–6.

104 Grassi, 'William Airmyn', pp. 550–3, 556–8. Cf. Smith, *op. cit.* pp. 41–5. The king wanted Norwich for his chancellor, Baldock.

105 Maddicott, *Lancaster*, pp. 294–5, who also points out Badlesmere's ties of kinship with the Marchers through his wife Margaret de Clare (aunt of Roger de Clifford) and his daughter Elizabeth, wife of Roger Mortimer's eldest son, Edmund. Cf. *Wigmore Chronicle*, p. 352; *G.E.C.* 8, p. 441, n. e.

106 *Annales Paulini*, p. 299. Badlesmere's wife and sister were incarcerated at Dover. Bartholomew Burghersh was released by the Londoners in October 1326. *French Chronicle*, p. 54 and cf. p. 55 n. (extract from Cotton MS. Faustina A. VIII, fo. 163). McKisack, *Fourteenth Century*, pp. 84–5, states that the bishop of Lincoln was among the prisoners, but this must be an error for his brother. For the charges against Badlesmere and Ashburnham see C.49/roll 10.

107 *Brut*, p. 221; *French Chronicle*, p. 44; *Melsa* 2, p. 343. Roger de Clifford (see n. 105 above) was hanged at York: *Murimuth*, p. 36.

108 One suspects that an open-minded examination of Burghersh's career would reveal more justification for his actions than allowed by Stubbs or Tout.

temporalities in 1324, but the more likely explanation of Edward's sustained malignancy is the bishop's vigorous defence of the rights of his see, particularly his own patronage.[109] Edward's encroachments were censured time and again by the indefatigable Pope John.[110] John de Schalby, who as Lincoln diocesan registrar is admittedly not an unbiased witness, may none the less be near the mark with his claim that Burghersh was subjected to persecution.[111]

William Ayrminne provides no better example of a 'queen's bishop'. The king's imputation to him of responsibility for the French treaty of 1325, which turned sour once Charles declined to negotiate the return of the Agenais and La Réole, his refusal to restore the Norwich temporalities[112] and his unwarranted pursuit of the bishop's relatives[113] left two courses open to Ayrminne: concealment or exile. It is generally thought that he made common cause with Isabella in France and came back with her.[114] That he stayed abroad for many months is substantiated; the precise moment of his return remains conjectural. During 1326 a series of writs required his attendance on the king. The last of these, dated 12 September, is directed to the sheriff of Norfolk and Suffolk, who was instructed personally to seek out the bishop and to convince him that his fears of journeying to the king were unfounded.[115] Naturally enough, Ayrminne stayed where he was.

109 Smith, *Episcopal Appointment*, pp. 86–94; *C.P.L.* 1305–42, pp. 468ff. In 1327 Burghersh petitioned for redress: his temporalities had been detained for three years and he had been amerced for refusing to admit the king's presentees. *Foedera* 2, ii, p. 183; *Rot. Parl. Inediti*, pp. 169–70.

110 *C.P.L.* 1305–42, pp. 465–6.

111 *Giraldus Cambrensis* 7, ed. J. F. Dimock (R.S. 1877), app. E (Lives of the Bishops of Lincoln), p. 215: 'Episcopalem dignitatem licet ad instantiam dicti regis fuisset assumptus, plurimas voluntarias persecutiones perpessus, quas cum patientia sustinuit commendanda.'

112 Grassi, 'William Airmyn', pp. 558–60; *The War of Saint-Sardos, p.* 277, n. 1; *C.P.L.* 1305–42, pp. 475–8. Instructions to restore his temporalities and personal goods were given only after Isabella's arrival. Their retention was blamed on Baldock and the younger Despenser. The royal custodians appear to have exceeded their sede vacante rights. *C.C.R.* 1323–27, p. 621; *C.C.R.* 1327–30, p. 24; *Foedera* 2, ii, p. 173; Grassi, *op. cit.* p. 561.

113 *C.C.R.* 1323–27, pp. 554–5.

114 Ayrminne was in France at the beginning of 1326 when summoned before the King's Bench: *The War of Saint-Sardos*, p. 277, n. 1 (quoting K.B.27/265/Rex m. 23^{v}). Grassi, *op. cit.* p. 560, implies that he returned to England but rejoined the queen (who moved to the Low Countries) about June 1326 (*Lit. Cant.* 1, pp. 184–9, cited by Grassi, suggests that he was in England during that month and possibly in July).

115 *C.C.R.* 1323–27, p. 646. Other sheriffs in the home and eastern counties were instructed likewise, but with the omission of the clause about going to the bishop

Another prelate regularly associated with Isabella's 'party' is Alexander Bicknor, the archbishop of Dublin. His misdeeds are retailed by Edward in a complaint to the pope of 28 May 1325. The chief one is that, being in a position of trust, he advised the earl of Kent to surrender the castle of La Réole to the French. In addition he is said to have publicly preached that the younger Despenser, the king's chamberlain and most secret counsellor, was a traitor to king and crown. He is also credited with the boast that only his dignity and order prevented him from putting the matter to the proof of a duel.[116] The determining factor in Bicknor's disaffection was apparently not a partiality for Isabella, but rather a strong dislike of Despenser and his doings.

That Orleton himself was in any substantive sense a 'queen's bishop' is incapable of proof. The argument of Ayrminne's apologist is that his defection was justified by the king's ill-treatment.[117] The same argument would have even more force with respect to Orleton, for he suffered greater hardship at Edward's hands and for a longer period. Despite this, he neither left the country nor surrendered hope of a measure of reconciliation with the king. He did what he could to defend his rights and those of his see, but was reduced to a largely passive resistance by the pressures of the king and his officers. There is no evidence that Orleton knew Isabella personally, had a particular attachment for her, or gave her any indication of support prior to the landing of 1326.[118] The unbalanced assertions of Baker do not at present evoke echoes elsewhere, and are for that reason unreliable as a guide to Orleton's behaviour. Because it was part of his scheme to brand Orleton and Burghersh as fomentors of discord and originators of Isabella's long-term strategy, Baker chose to ignore the awkward fact that it was Stratford who urged the queen's embassy to

in person. This writ seems to indicate that Ayrminne was thought to be in his diocese. For the earlier summonses see *ibid*. pp. 537 (3 January 1326), 549 (6 March).

116 *Foedera* 2, ii, pp. 136–7: 'Hugoni le Despenser juniori camerario et secretissimo nostro, falso et malitiose, crimen falsi, et proditionis, in nos et coronam nostram, imposuit, ea de ipso publice praedicando.' The usual royal demands for his removal and papal remonstrances on his behalf follow. E.g. *C.P.L.* 1305–42, pp. 474, 480; *Foedera* 2, ii, p. 158. See also *Rot. Parl. Inediti*, pp. 94–8, where the editors consider the charge of treachery against the archbishop to have been precipitate.

117 Grassi, *op. cit.* pp. 551, 561.

118 Blackley, 'Isabella', p. 227, expresses the same opinion. The letter of Bishop Cobham 'dated March 1324' is in fact undated (*ibid*. n. 35).

France.[119] As both Orleton and Burghersh were in disgrace their opinions, even if covertly insinuated, could not have had the impact upon which the chronicler insists. The papal envoys, Stratford and the Despensers were all in agreement that the queen should go, and subsequently that Prince Edward should follow her.[120]

Two further ' queen's bishops ' have yet to be considered: John Hothum of Ely and John Stratford of Winchester. The canon of Bridlington, alone among the chroniclers, after recording the fall of Leeds Castle in 1321, mentions that Hothum was attached, summoned to London, and fined for some unnamed offence.[121] The circumstances are obscure. Hothum had been replaced as chancellor in January 1320, but this has been interpreted as a consequence not of royal disfavour but of a ' mere reshuffle within the ruling group '.[122] It may well have been more than that. Blame was attached to the former chancellor for counselling the removal of the Exchequer and other courts to York, where they were in danger from Scottish marauders. The débâcle at Myton served to emphasise the unwisdom. Hothum and the archbishop of York, Melton, entrusted with the raising of the Yorkshire levies, had to flee ignominiously from the skirmish. Once the king reached York the Exchequer and other records were promptly shipped back to London.[123] Hothum subsequently joined Orleton as one of the prelates at St Albans negotiating between the king and his barons.[124] Whether a political offence was imputed to him as a consequence of these or other actions it is impossible to say, but his reaction to this punitive treatment appears to have been an anxiety to fall in with the king's wishes, for he was one of the very few bishops to attend the convocation which approved the recall of the Despensers.[125] Hothum did not

119 *Foedera* 2, ii, p. 132. The originator of the policy is likely to remain undetermined. Isabella herself is an obvious choice, but the pope clearly advocated it as a means of resolving the dispute between the kings and his nuncios were prominent in the negotiations. Cf. Blackley, *op. cit.* p. 228; Lowe, ' Considerations ', p. 540.

120 *Brut*, p. 234; *Foedera* 2, ii, pp. 132, 135; Grassi, *op. cit.* pp. 554–5; Blackley, *op. cit.* p. 228.

121 *Bridlington*, p. 73.

122 Maddicott, *Lancaster*, p. 254.

123 *Flores* 3, p. 189; *Annales Paulini*, pp. 286–7; Broome, ' Exchequer Migrations ', pp. 291–2. William Ayrminne, then ' capitalis clericus cancellariae ', was captured and had to be ransomed.

124 *Trokelowe*, p. 109.

125 *Annales Paulini*, p. 300.

hold office again until the revolution, but he continued to be involved in diplomatic negotiations.[126] On 17 July 1326, with other ecclesiastics, he was granted protection for a year,[127] and almost immediately afterwards, when frantic military preparations against the anticipated invasion were under way, was named advisor for appointing the earl marshal – as it turned out, one of the earliest recruits to Isabella's standard – to superintend the array in the counties of Norfolk and Suffolk.[128] Hothum's episcopal register has not survived, which means that we know very little of his ecclesiastical activities or even his whereabouts, but if the allegations later made against the younger Despenser are true, his temporalities had been encroached upon by the secular authorities and his goods treated in the same manner as Orleton's.[129]

Though he chose to conceal them for the time being, Stratford's grievances against the king and his close advisors were substantial. His promotion to the see of Winchester by papal provision (20 June 1323) while he was at the Curia on royal business brought a particularly virulent response from Edward.[130] Only after a prolonged process of examining the envoy's diplomatic credentials and his actions by virtue of them[131] were the temporalities released, and then not before the bishop had entered into a recognisance with the king for the enormous sum of £10,000.[132] Later on this act was to be laid at the door of Chancellor Baldock, whose own elevation was pre-empted by the pope's partiality for Stratford.[133] The king required £2,000 on demand; the rest was apparently intended to be a bond for Stratford's good behaviour, though after his fall Edward disclaimed any intention of exacting it.[134] Once Stratford had taken the usual oath of fealty to the king

126 E.g. for the Scottish negotiations in 1324: *Foedera* 2, ii, p. 118.

127 *C.P.R.* 1324–27, p. 298.

128 *C.P.R.* 1324–27, p. 302. One need not ascribe sinister motives to Hothum; the appointment was doubtless routine.

129 Taylor, 'The Judgment on Hugh Despenser', pp. 70, 75. See also C.49/roll 11.

130 *Foedera* 2, ii, pp. 82–3.

131 *Foedera* 2, ii, pp. 89–91.

132 *Foedera* 2, ii, p. 101; *C.C.R.* 1323–27, pp. 117, 198–9, 203; *C.P.R.* 1324–27, p. 4.

133 *Foedera* 2, ii, p. 174; Laud MS. Misc. 529, fo. 108r; Smith, *Episcopal Appointments*, pp. 39–41.

134 *C.C.R.* 1323–27, p. 198; *Foedera* 2, ii, pp. 174–5. Apparently Edward made his disclaimer to the bishops of London (Gravesend) and Hereford (Orleton) while he was at Kenilworth. The date of the cancellation of the recognisances is given as 9 February 1326 [*recte* 1327] in *C.C.R.* 1323–27, p. 199. A similar recognisance was demanded from Orleton (n. 77 above).

he was forced to acknowledge a highly inflated obligation of £2,460 5s 10d for the growing crops on his estates.[135] The payment of debts due to him from the king was dilatory: it was February 1325 before authorisation was given for settlement of his expenses while at the Curia in 1322–3.[136] Despite such treatment, Stratford played a considerable part in political affairs during 1325, and was associated with Bishop Stapledon and Henry de Beaumont as companions of the young prince on his journey to France to perform homage.[137] Together with Droxford, bishop of Bath and Wells, he gave advice for the appointment of a surveyor of the local Wiltshire levies as late as 23 July 1326.[138]

It has been tacitly assumed that a number of bishops joined the queen as exiles on the continent and returned with her.[139] The chroniclers do not mention the landing of any bishops in her company, and they could well be right, though Archbishop Bicknor seems a likely exception. The matter requires further investigation.[140]

What has been seen as a conspiracy of self-centred, unscrupulous bishops appears on closer examination to be something quite different. The bishops who were quick to join Isabella[141] were those who had been partly or wholly prevented from exercising their episcopal functions and who had suffered from a sustained policy of financial extortion at the behest, it was generally believed, of Robert Baldock and the younger Despenser, and

135 *Foedera* 2, ii, p. 174. This despite the 'reasonable appraisement' specified in the writ: *C.C.R.* 1323–27, p. 203.

136 *C.C.R.* 1323–27, p. 256.

137 *C.P.R.* 1324–27, p. 174.

138 *C.P.R.* 1324–27, p. 303.

139 McKisack, *Fourteenth Century*, p. 82 (Stratford and Ayrminne said to be in Paris); Grassi, 'William Airmyn', p. 560, writes of Ayrminne joining Burghersh and Orleton abroad.

140 According to *Murimuth* (p. 46) Bicknor (though 'Dunelmensis', i.e. Louis de Beaumont, is an unlikely MS. variant), Burghersh, Orleton and Hothum adhered to Isabella in the early stages. By implication they did not arrive with her. A writ of 12 May 1326 for military preparation against invasion was directed to the archbishops of Canterbury and York, four Welsh bishops, and thirteen English ones, including Beaumont, Burghersh, Droxford, Hothum and Stratford, but not Ayrminne or Orleton – both without their temporalities. *Foedera* 2, ii, p. 156.

141 At Bristol, where on 26 October 1326 Bicknor, Stratford, Hothum, Burghersh, Orleton and Ayrminne were all present for the appointment of the duke of Aquitaine as custos of the realm, his father being technically outside it. *Foedera* 2, ii, p. 169.

perhaps to a much lesser extent of Bishop Stapledon.[142] About Stratford and Ayrminne one cannot be certain, since their diplomatic work in France brought them into close contact with the queen, but the other English bishops cannot justifiably be accused on the available evidence of having concerted anything against the king. The reality seems to have been a grim hanging on in poverty and isolation in the hope that eventually there must be a return to normal life.

As for Orleton himself, it is hard to countenance Baker's contention that he was at the centre of a treasonable plot and hence apprised of the queen's every movement. If such were the case his behaviour in the late summer and autumn of 1326 would be inexplicable. Isabella landed at Orwell in Suffolk on 24 September.[143] At the end of July and perhaps in August he was still keeping a tenuous hand on diocesan affairs from Shinfield; on 8 September he was at Oxford, on the 14th and 15th at Wigmore and Bromfield, and on the 27th at Hereford.[144] In other words he was moving *away* from the scene of operations. The reason was a pastoral not a political one: on 3 August the elder Mortimer had died after four and a half years of incarceration in the Tower. His body was taken by cart to Wigmore, where Orleton buried it in the abbey which the Mortimers had founded.[145] Once this task was accomplished it could only have been a matter of a fortnight or so before news of the queen's successful arrival reached him at Hereford. His years of persecution were over.

ISABELLA'S TRIUMPH 1326–1327

Definite intelligence of the queen's landing probably took rather less than a week to reach Orleton. It was known in Canterbury by 28 September, the date of Prior Henry Eastry's letter to Archbishop Reynolds suggesting a possible course of action. Three bishops, he advised, should be sent to probe the intentions of the

142 Covetousness is alleged against the bishop both by the *Brut* (p. 238) and by the author of the *Vita* (p. 139), though both at Exeter and at Oxford he is accounted a notable benefactor. He has been praised as an administrative reformer of independent mind: Davies, *Baronial Opposition*, pp. 529–37.

143 *Annales Paulini*, pp. 313–14.

144 *H.R.O.*, fos. 79v, 101v, 102r; pp. 370–1; *Wigmore Chronicle*, p. 351.

145 *Wigmore Chronicle*, p. 351.

armed foreigners, the count of Hainault and his men, and to exhort them not to disturb the peace of the Church and realm. In his opinion the archbishop ought to refrain from sending armed men anywhere, except such as might be required to maintain his status or that of his church, and to bear in mind the pope's desire for a peaceful reconciliation with Isabella.[1]

The chronicler Murimuth, at this point echoed by the author of the *Flores*, states that the response of the disaffected was immediate.[2] Thomas of Brotherton, earl marshal and half-brother of the king, and Henry earl of Lancaster,[3] with various barons and knights and almost all the prelates, but particularly the archbishop of Dublin (Bicknor) and the bishops of Lincoln (Burghersh), Hereford (Orleton) and Ely (Hothum), rushed to join the insurgents, who remained for some time at Walton-on-the-Naze in Brotherton's lands.[4] 'Almost all the prelates' is a gross exaggeration, but one wonders why Ayrminne is not named among them, the River Orwell being at the south-eastern extremity of his diocese of Norwich.

In the *Historia Roffensis* William Dene describes [5] the activities of another and slightly larger group intent on mediation in the manner prevalent during the earlier part of the reign. But first of all Archbishop Reynolds, with the support of Bishops Gravesend and Stratford and the abbots of Westminster and Waltham, tried the bizarre stratagem of publishing at St Paul's (on 30 September) a seven-year-old bull of excommunication directed against the Scots, in the hope that appropriate modifications would make it appear a sentence against Isabella and those coming with her.[6]

[1] *Lit. Cant.* 1, p. 194; cf. pp. 195–6.

[2] *Murimuth*, pp. 46–7; *Flores* 3, p. 233.

[3] His title was formally restored on 3 February 1327, though some chroniclers designate him earl of Lancaster well before that time.

[4] Brotherton, fifth son of Edward I, was earl of Norfolk (created 16 December 1312). He had been deputed as 'captain and principal surveyor of the army' in the counties of Norfolk and Suffolk, Essex and Hertford. *C.P.R.* 1324–27, p. 302.

[5] William Dene was a secular clerk and a notary. He later became archdeacon of Rochester. For other details of him see *Rochester Reg. Hethe*, intro. and index *s.v.* The chronicle ascribed to him survives in a single MS., B.L. Cotton MS. Faustina B. V (fos. 2–101) and is printed with significant omissions by Wharton.

[6] *Annales Paulini*, p. 315; E.159/93/77; and see above, 'In Edward II's service', ch. 2. It has been suggested that this was a riposte to the claim of the invaders that the pope had absolved the English from their oath of fidelity to the king and that he would excommunicate all who bore arms against Isabella. According to Baker two cardinals with the queen's forces upheld the story. See *Chronicon*, p. 196 (nn.).

When this provoked hostile murmurings among the citizens Reynolds tried another tack; he would summon to St Paul's those of his suffragans who were available so that they could select envoys to treat with the queen. Hamo de Hethe, bishop of Rochester, objected to the choice of meeting-place because he feared the ugly mood of the Londoners. As a result, it was in the achiepiscopal manor of Lambeth on the safer southern bank of the Thames that the bishops of London, Winchester, Exeter (Stapledon), Worcester (Cobham) and Rochester came together on 14 October. Only Stratford could be prevailed on to volunteer his services as a delegate, and then on condition that he did not go alone. Hamo de Hethe resisted pressure to accompany him, so for want of support the plan fell through.[7] If Murimuth is to be trusted, and he was no friend of the archbishop, Reynolds was attempting to keep in with both sides by secretly sending money to the queen.[8]

On 15 August, the day after these abortive discussions, occurred the brutal murder of Bishop Walter Stapledon, one of Edward II's most loyal servants. Archbishop Reynolds, on receiving warning of the murderous intentions of the Londoners, fled to Kent, but Hamo de Hethe only learned of the danger from the tumult itself, and as Reynolds had taken his horses, he was forced to flee on foot.[9] Such was the ignominious confusion of those who sought to temporise.

In an undated letter sent to Orleton shortly afterwards[10] the ailing and unhappy Cobham bemoaned the negative outcome of his journey to London. His intention had been fivefold: to attend a meeting of the clergy to forward papal business,[11] to join with other bishops in bringing peace between Edward and Isabella, to

7 Cotton MS. Faustina B. V, fo. 47v (*Anglia Sacra* 1, p. 366).

8 *Murimuth*, p. 47; *Flores* 3, p. 233. It is suggested that others did much the same.

9 Cotton MS. Faustina B. V, fo. 48v.

10 It was probably written in the latter half of October, some time after the meeting at Lambeth on the 14th. There is no mention of the summons to parliament issued on 28 October, despite the bishop's hopes in that direction. He was at his Hillingdon manor.

11 Later (20 November) a writ issued at Ledbury in the king's name directed that aid be given to the papal nuncios, the archbishop of Vienne and John Grandisson (later bishop of Exeter). On 16 January 1327 the nuncios asked the clergy assembled at St Paul's to contribute a subsidy for use against the emperor (Louis of Bavaria), but nothing was done and they left in some trepidation within three days. *Foedera* 2, ii, p. 170; *Annales Paulini*, p. 324.

press litigation in the royal court and that of Canterbury, to seek out more efficacious medical treatment than was available in his own area, and finally to perform an overdue vow of pilgrimage at the shrine of St Thomas of Canterbury. The programme was a total failure: the meeting of the clergy lacked the necessary authority, the king abandoned the capital,[12] the legal suits were lost in both courts, there was too much turmoil to secure medical treatment, and as for the pilgrimage to Canterbury, his illness made travel on horseback impossible and even in a carriage it was a painful business. Faced with such problems the much-lauded Cobham, who but for Edward's insistence would have been primate, set the same course as his supplanter Reynolds, going over to Isabella's side.[13] He asked Orleton to make excuses to the queen for his absence and to offer her the use of his houses and goods, should she need them. He did also drop the hint that the whole matter might be regularised by an early summoning of parliament.[14]

While these ineffective manoeuvres were in process, Orleton travelled from Hereford to join the queen. Nothing is known of his itinerary because the Hereford register is blank for the month of October. Though the supposition is based on the unsupported testimony of Baker, it is not inherently improbable that some time after the landing the bishop was deputed to address the 'conspirators' to the effect that it would be as well for the realm were the king to be ruled by their counsel.[15] Naturally, Baker's anxiety to saddle Orleton with the responsibility for political events makes it difficult not to suspect attributions of this kind.

At this juncture, however, we have only Baker to guide us. On reaching Oxford, he states, Orleton preached publicly before the university[16] on the theme *Caput meum doleo* – 'My head is sick' – to make the point that it might be necessary to remove a

[12] On 2 October.

[13] The Canterbury prior, Henry Eastry, gave somewhat unrealistic advice to Reynolds: *Lit. Cant.* 1, pp. 194–5. In a subsequent more practical letter (of early December?) he suggested that the archbishop approach the queen before her letters of invitation arrived. *Ibid.* pp. 202–3. Dene says that on 7 December at Maidstone Reynolds tried to persuade Bishop Hethe to accompany him to Isabella at Wallingford: Hethe refused but had already sent an emissary. Cotton MS. Faustina B. V, fo. 49^r.

[14] *Worcester Reg. Cobham*, pp. 204–5.

[15] *Chronicon*, p. 21: 'Qui pleno conspiratorum parliamento peroravit.'

[16] *Chronicon*, p. 23.

failing head from the kingdom – one that did not respond to the ministrations of Hippocrates.[17] This looks like a false attribution, for both the *Historia Roffensis* and the Lanercost Chronicle, quite independent authorities, agree that this was the text taken by Bishop Stratford at the time of the 1327 parliament.[18] That Orleton preached at Oxford, but in November, is alleged by the author of the *Libellus* of 1334. In his reply to the charge, some eight years after the event, the bishop gives his version of what happened. It was in October – correcting the *Libellus* – that as an introduction to the proclamation of intent, which the queen had first published at Wallingford on 15 October, he took for his text Genesis 3.15, 'I will put enmity between thee and the woman, and between thy seed and her seed; it shall bruise thy head . . .' This, he pointed out, had come to be maliciously interpreted as an attack on the relationship between Edward and Isabella, but the head referred to was not the king's but that of the younger Despenser, and he conceived the enmity as being between Despenser and the queen and her seed – the young Prince Edward. No sane man, in his view, could maintain that the words applied to the king. In the context of the proclamation, which was directed against the younger Despenser and the chancellor, Robert Baldock, this contention is not unreasonable.[19]

Bishop Stubbs thought that the *Responsiones* indicated that the queen travelled from Oxford to Wallingford – backwards in the direction of London.[20] It is much more likely that Isabella was at Wallingford on 15 October and at Oxford somewhat later. Edward halted at Wallingford on the 7th, and having attempted to make the castle defensible, departed in the direction of Gloucester. On leaving Oxford Isabella's forces also made their way to Gloucester, where Baker says that Stapledon's head was brought as an offering to 'Diana', and then to Bristol, defended by the elder Despenser. Edward himself must have crossed the Severn at or near Gloucester, proceeding along the further bank to Chepstow. There he appointed the elder Despenser to lead the forces

17 Stow was guilty of a malapropism at this point: 'Neither ought it to be bound with any hurtfull bands of an hypocrite.' See *Chronicon*, p. 198 (nn.).

18 *Lanercost*, pp. 257–8. Dene gives Stratford's text as *Cuius capud infirmum cetera membra dolent*. Cotton MS. Faustina B. V, fo. 49v.

19 *Responsiones*, cols. 2763–6; *Foedera* 2, ii, p. 169.

20 *Chronicles of the Reigns of Edward I and Edward II*, p. xciv; *Chronicon*, p. 23.

of the south-western shires against the invaders, a meaningless gesture.[21] Bristol soon fell and on 26 October Orleton with Archbishop Bicknor and four other bishops – Stratford (who must have joined the queen overtly shortly after the 15th),[22] Hothum, Burghersh and Ayrminne – witnessed the proclamation of Prince Edward as custos of the realm.[23] The elder Despenser underwent a form of trial on the following day and was sentenced to death.[24]

The army then moved northwards and crossed the Severn to Hereford, where Isabella spent much of November, at least part of the time in Orleton's palace.[25] A force under Henry of Lancaster was detached to find the king and his few remaining adherents – a task accomplished on 16 November at Llantrissant, Glamorgan.[26] Orleton, sent from Hereford to secure the Great Seal, met the returning party at Monmouth.[27] The official account relates how the king gave custody of the seal to Sir William Blount, a member of his household, who came back with Orleton and delivered it to the queen and her son at 'Martleye' on 26 November.[28] Professor Tout identified this place as Martley in Worcestershire,[29] but it is more likely to have been Much Marcle, Herefordshire,[30] since four days later, on the feast of St Andrew, the queen was present at Cirencester Abbey when the seal was placed in the custody of William Ayrminne, bishop of Norwich.[31]

Meanwhile important happenings were taking place in Hereford, though the dates given for them do not dovetail with those of the exceptionally detailed story of the fortunes of the Great

21 *C.P.R.* 1324–27, p. 332.

22 In the early morning of the 15th he tried unsuccessfully to persuade the bishop of Rochester (Hethe) to go with him to the queen on behalf of the episcopate. It was to be the day of Stapledon's murder. Cotton MS. Faustina B. V, fo. 48r (*Anglia Sacra* 1, p. 366 omits this).

23 *Foedera* 2, ii, p. 169.

24 *Annales Paulini*, pp. 317–18.

25 *C.P.R.* 1324–27, p. 337; *C.C.R.* 1323–27, p. 620. On St Cecilia's day (22 November) chancery records, brought from Swansea Castle, were delivered to Isabella in the palace.

26 See, for instance, *Annales Paulini*, pp. 318–19.

27 There he delivered a message about the seal in accordance with his instructions (' omnia, sic sibi injuncta, eidem domino regi exposuit per ordinem ').

28 *Foedera* 2, ii, p. 169; *C.C.R.* 1323–27, pp. 655–6.

29 *Chapters* 3, p. 3, n. 1.

30 As suggested by Canon Bannister (*H.R.O.*, p. xxxvii). It would indicate an intention to cross the Severn at Gloucester rather than Worcester, which is consistent with the livery of the seal at Cirencester.

31 *Foedera*, *loc. cit.*

Seal. It is possible that Orleton was in his cathedral city on 9 November when he gave John de Bromfield charge of the Despenser manor of Beaumes, the first-fruits of Isabella's gratitude.[32] We know that he dated a commission there on the 17th.[33] He is supposed to have left Hereford to collect the seal on 20 November and to have delivered it to the queen six days later, a surprisingly long interval. There is evidence that he was back in Hereford on the 27th.[34] The principal authorities for what happened in the meantime are the Pauline annalist and the Leicester chronicler, Knighton. The latter gives a graphic description of the ill-treatment of the captives, the younger Despenser, Robert Baldock and William Irby, prior of St Guthlac's, on their arrival at Hereford.[35] Both accounts agree that judgement was pronounced against Despenser on 24 November, the Pauline annalist adding that Baldock was brought before the same judges immediately afterwards, denied the right to reply to the charges against him, and claimed as a clerk by the bishop *ibidem praesens*.[36] The annalist does not specify Irby's fate, but Knighton tells us that he was gaoled at Hereford for actions against the king's peace.[37] On the face of it, Orleton's itinerary in quest of the seal would preclude his being at Hereford for these judicial proceedings; at the time he was supposedly somewhere between Monmouth and 'Martleye'.[38]

We do not know how much longer Orleton stayed at Hereford after the last mention of his being there on 27 November.[39] What is clear is that during December he rejoined the queen at Wallingford, where Walsingham records the celebration of Christmas 'cum summo gaudio et honore'.[40] According to Orleton's later apologia it was at Wallingford that a number of bishops, himself, Reynolds, Stratford and Ayrminne, discussed with the

32 *H.R.O.*, p. 371.

33 *H.R.O.*, pp. 372–3.

34 *H.R.O.*, p. 371.

35 *Knighton*, pp. 436–7. Cf. *Brut*, p. 240.

36 *Annales Paulini*, pp. 319–20.

37 *Knighton*, p. 437: 'Eo quod male se gesserat contra pacem regis.'

38 *Foedera* 2, ii, p. 169.

39 There are no further entries in his register until 30 January: *H.R.O.*, fo. 102^r. At that time Orleton was in London.

40 *Walsingham*, p. 185 (from B.L. Royal MS. 13 E. IX). Cf. *Ypodigma Neustriae*, p. 264, where Walsingham states that two archbishops and six bishops were present. The author of the *Flores* has 'Exoniam' (3, p. 235), apparently an error for 'Oxoniam'.

earls of Lancaster and Kent as well as other nobles of their counsel the problem of preserving the queen's reputation.[41] In consequence he was allotted the task of explaining in public that the queen was unable to return to her husband because of his vicious anger ('saevitia'). This, Orleton claimed, was precisely what he did, adding nothing of his own: [42] the accusation that he acted in derogation of the sacrament of marriage was therefore a falsehood.[43] In support of this contention he gave the text of a letter which purported to be one sent to Archbishop Reynolds by the queen while she was at Paris. In it she expressed her fear of Despenser and her belief that if she returned to the king her life would be in danger.[44] This letter apart, there is plenty of evidence to support Orleton's argument that the queen's attitude had been formed long before he could have been in a position to exert influence.[45]

The discrepancies between the chroniclers' accounts of what happened in the 'parliament' which assembled at Westminster early in January 1327 [46] defy reconciliation.[47] Of the two major ones it has generally been felt that the Lanercost chronicler's version is the more reliable, despite the fact that William Dene, who is credited with the authorship of the *Historia Roffensis*,

[41] *Responsiones*, col. 2766.

[42] *Ibid*. cols. 2766–7: 'Nichil addens de proprio vel minuens de injuncto.' This accords with Dene who says (Cotton MS. Faustina B. V, fo. 47v) that the queen passed from Oxford to Wallingford Castle where 'in nataliciis Domini pro victoria potita' she had it publicly preached 'per episcopum Herforden' Adam de Orleton quod metu mortis quam rex ei intemptaverat marito adherere non audebat'.

[43] *Ibid*. He made the further point that the danger was not removed by the younger Despenser's death 'Quem rex immoderato et inordinato amore dilexit, et propter hoc magis fuit ejus saevicia accensa ad vindicandum ipsius mortem.'

[44] *Ibid*. cols. 2767–8. The letter is dated 5 February 1326.

[45] The author of the *Vita* (pp. 143–5) states that at the parliament of November–December 1325 the king spoke of Isabella's reluctance to return. He gives the text of the speech Edward is supposed to have made and of the common form letter which was to be sent by the bishops. Cf. Edward's own letter to Isabella in *Foedera* 2, ii, p. 148 (1 December 1325). This and other evidence is reviewed by Blackley, 'Isabella'. The king's denial that he had banished his wife and son or that there had been any danger to the papal nuncios seeking audience with him was circulated by the bishop of London (Fulham, 6 May 1326), on behalf of the archbishop, and is duly entered in Orleton's register. *H.R.O.*, pp. 357–9; *Concilia* 2, p. 529 (Otford, 25 April 1326).

[46] This met on 7 January and writs *de expensis* were issued on 9 March. See *Rot. Parl. Inediti*, pp. 99–179.

[47] Compare Wilkinson, 'Deposition of Richard II', pp. 223–30; Clarke, 'Committees of Estates', pp. 27–45. Both writers were content to use Wharton's text of the *Historia Roffensis*.

obviously had close contact with the events he describes, especially where they concern his own diocesan, Hamo de Hethe.[48]

The Lanercost chronicler states that the bishops of Winchester and Hereford, that is Stratford and Orleton, were sent to the king at Kenilworth to ask him to come to parliament. The idea behind this move appears to have been to afford Edward an opportunity of hearing the charges against him, although his actual appearance could have proved embarrassing for those who were manipulating the change of kingship. It so happens that this preliminary mission of two bishops is confirmed both by the Pipewell Chronicle and by a letter of Henry Eastry, the Canterbury prior. In the first case the bishops are identified as those of Hereford and London (Gravesend), for which there is confirmation elsewhere, but Eastry mentions no names.[49] The Lanercost chronicler goes on to describe how the envoys returned to Westminster on 12 January and there announced the king's negative reply ' to the clergy and people '. Three days of sermons ensued, though perhaps ' political addresses ' would be a more appropriate designation. On the first day, 13 January, Orleton took as his text *Rex insipiens perdet populum suum* [50] and dwelt upon the king's stupidities and puerilities as well as the misfortunes which emanated from them. When he had finished, the people with one voice shouted that they did not wish the king to reign over them any longer. This has been taken to mark the time when the deposition was agreed upon,[51] but the chronicler himself

48 The chronicle runs from 1315 to 1350. Dene apparently came from Winchester diocese. Hamo de Hethe secured the archdeaconry of Rochester for him (by papal provision). He is last mentioned in Hethe's register (not as archdeacon of Rochester) on 1 January 1349. See *Rochester Reg. Hethe*, p. 889 (cf. pp. 119–21); *C.P.L.* 1305–42, p. 234; n. 5 above.

49 *Lanercost*, pp. 257–8; Pipewell Chronicle (Cotton MS. Julius A. 1, fo. 56^{r-v}) in Clarke, *op. cit.* n. A, pp. 44–5; *Lit. Cant.* 1, pp. 204–5. Identification of the bishops as those of London and Hereford is supported by incidental mention of their journey in *Foedera* 2, ii, pp. 174–5. McKisack, *Fourteenth Century*, p. 89, gives the bishops as Lincoln (apparently from Baker's account of the later mission) and Winchester.

50 Ecclus. 10.16.

51 E.g. by the *French Chronicle* (p. 57), the Lichfield Chronicle (Bodleian, Bodley MS. 956, fos. 205–6: quoted Clarke, *op. cit.* p. 36, n. 3), and *Thorne* (col. 2039). Higden (*Polychronicon* 8, p. 322) may have regarded 13 January as the date of deposition. What he actually says is that a parliament was held in London on that day ' Ubi de communi ordinatione missi sunt solemnes nuncii ad regem incarceratum . . . ipsumque pro domino ulterius non haberent.' However, in view of the lateness of the chronicler his opinion is not very significant.

scarcely implies that it was, for he prolongs the proceedings for a further two days without any sense of anti-climax. On the 14th Bishop Stratford is said to have taken up the theme *Caput meum doleo*, to show that the kingdom had endured an ailing head for many years. Finally, on 15 January, Archbishop Reynolds preached on the rabble-rousing saw *Vox populi vox Dei*, ending with a declaration that by the unanimous consent of all the earls and barons, of the archbishops and bishops, and of the whole clergy and people, Edward was deposed from his dignity and would no longer reign. Thereupon the magnates with the consent of the whole community are said to have sent envoys to the king at Kenilworth to renounce their homage and to declare Edward's deposition. The precise composition of this 'embassy' need not concern us here, but according to the chronicler it contained twenty-four persons, including two bishops – Stratford and Orleton.[52]

It is certainly remarkable that this lengthy narrative is so much at variance with the equally circumstantial account of the *Historia Roffensis*. According to this, the parliament opened on 7 January with a speech by Orleton, who thereby seems to have performed a function usually exercised by the chancellor.[53] Supported by 'many bishops' he contended that if the queen were to return to the king she would be killed by him: this looks like the brief handed out to Orleton at Wallingford.[54] Eventually the bishop asked whether those assembled wished the king or his son to rule over them. As this was a momentous decision he suggested that they should all return to their lodgings and come back the following day after they had breakfasted.[55] When they did reassemble on 8 January there was a division of opinion, fear of the consequences being an important factor.[56] At last it was agreed that

[52] Cf. Wilkinson, *op. cit.* p. 225, n. 4, who argues: 'There is little doubt that the agreement to depose Edward was reached on 13 January, but the Lanercost chronicler has stated this quite clearly.' But has he? It was only on the 15th at the end of his sermon that the archbishop declared 'rex Edwardus fuit depositus', and it was then that the (second) mission to Kenilworth was despatched. See *Lanercost*, pp. 257–8.

[53] The point is made by Stubbs, *Constitutional History* 2, p. 361, but others might make the opening speech: see, for instance, Plucknett, 'Parliament', p. 107.

[54] *Responsiones*, col. 2766.

[55] Cotton MS. Faustina B. V, fo. 49^{v}: 'Et in crastino post sumpcionem cibi et potus omnes potati redirent et questioni episcopi responderent.'

[56] *Ibid.*: 'Quidam ex habundancia cordis, quidam metu ducti, nonnulli tacite propter metum London' questioni respondere nolentes.'

the young Edward should be king and after the performance of homage he was led into the great hall at Westminster with the words 'Ecce rex vester'. Only then, by Dene's account, were the three sermons preached, though telescoped together, in the reverse order, and with a variation of texts. Reynolds is said to have spoken first on the theme *Vox populi vox Dei*, Stratford next on *Cujus caput infirmum, caetera membra dolent*, while Orleton concluded with an exposition of the text *Vae terrae, cujus rex puer est.*[57] There was a shout of 'Ave rex', followed by the chanting of *Gloria, laus et honor*. Since he refused to join in either, the bishop of Rochester was jostled and threatened with death. Both he, the archbishop of York (Melton) and the bishops of London and Carlisle (Ross) withheld their consent. Hethe, though refusing to take the oath of fealty to the new king, sent Reynolds to answer for him. It is at this juncture that Wharton's text is defective, omitting Dene's record of the (second) mission to Kenilworth, which will be discussed below.[58]

The chronology of both these versions is far from convincing. It is arguable that the bishops' initial mission to Kenilworth could scarcely have been accomplished between the opening of parliament and 12 January – less than five full days for the journey to Kenilworth and back.[59] If the bishops did return by the 12th, and there is some reason for believing that the Lanercost chronicler is correct in this, then it looks as though they left before parliament assembled, as Prior Eastry implies in an undated letter.[60] In any case, what was the assembly doing between the 7th and the 12th? The Lanercost chronicler does not say; for him the proceedings only begin to take shape on the envoys' return. Dene, however, states that parliament was listening to Orleton's arguments and as early as 8 January being brought to some form of consensus in favour of deposition.[61] Undoubtedly he has telescoped events:

57 The same text was to be found apposite in Richard II's time.

58 Cotton MS. Faustina B. V, fo. 49^{v}.

59 The round trip would have been about 160 miles. Forty miles a day was possible, but it is unlikely that the bishops proceeded at such a pace. For the timing of fifteenth-century journeys see Armstrong, 'Distribution and Speed of News', pp. 429–54.

60 *Lanercost*, p. 257; *Lit. Cant.* 1, pp. 204–5.

61 Cotton MS. Faustina B. V, fo. 49^{r-v}: 'Et tandem quesitum fuit quem mallent regnare patrem regem vel filium, et hoc primo die parliamenti. Et congregatis in parliamento per eundem episcopum iniunctum fuit quod quilibet ad suum hospicium iret et in crastino . . . redirent et questioni episcopi responderent.' See n. 55 above.

far too much is crowded into the opening days of the session. On the other hand, the Lanercost chronicler seems to have thought that the deposition occurred on 15 January. Yet there is strong evidence to suggest that the real date was the 13th[62] and that envoys left the scene in time to reach Kenilworth seven days later.[63]

The feast of St Hilary, 13 January, was also the date of the Guildhall oath to maintain the cause of the queen and her son, to uphold the City of London's privileges, and to support the ordinances of the parliament in session made to the honour of God and Holy Church and for the benefit of the whole people.[64] Dene treats of the oath *after* the second mission to Kenilworth, remarking that all the bishops subscribed to it except for Archbishop Melton of York and Bishops Gravesend of London and Ross of Carlisle. Hamo de Hethe, the hero of the narrative, swore saving his order and the provisions of Magna Carta and had a notarial instrument drawn up to that effect.[65] The list given in the City of London's Plea and Memoranda Roll substantially confirms Dene, though it omits the bishop of Durham (Louis de Beaumont) from the oath-takers. Beaumont's sympathies were however not in doubt. Thus the occupants of twelve of the seventeen English sees are recorded to have taken the oath – Exeter being vacant owing to Stapledon's murder – and three demurred.[66] The city records, confirmed by the French Chronicle, show that a further oath was taken by Archbishop Reynolds and other bishops on 20 January, by which time the young Edward is described as 'now king'.[67] The form of oath given by the Pauline annalist is mistakenly attributed to the earlier occasion.[68] The Lanercost chronicler omits this oath-taking altogether.

62 See nn. 51–2 above. It hardly needs to be stated that Orleton could not both have gone on the initial mission and addressed parliament on the 8th.

63 The Pipewell chronicler (Cotton MS. Julius A. 1, fo. 56ᵛ: Clarke, *op. cit.* p. 44) gives the 20th as the date of the deputation's arrival at Kenilworth. Wilkinson (*op. cit.* p. 225, n. 4) not unreasonably tries to square this with *Lanercost* (p. 257) by suggesting that the deputation could have left Westminster on the 16th, the day after Reynolds's speech, and still have been in time to reach Kenilworth on the 20th.

64 *Cal. P.M.R.*, pp. 12–14. Listed among the oath-takers are the archbishops of Canterbury and Dublin and twelve diocesan bishops, including Orleton, Burghersh and Stratford.

65 Cotton MS. Faustina B. V, fo. 50ʳ. For Nicholas North, the notary concerned, see *Rochester Reg. Hethe*, index *s.v.*

66 *Cal. P.M.R.*, p. 13.

67 *Ibid.* p. 11; *French Chronicle*, p. 58.

68 *Annales Paulini*, pp. 322–3. Those named are the archbishops of Canterbury and Dublin and the bishops of Salisbury, Lincoln, Ely, Bath and Wells, Coventry and

A feature of both these chronicles is their failure to mention any justificatory ' articles of deposition '. Orleton in his apologia gives a list of what purport to be the formal reasons for deposition, arguing that they were devised by Stratford and on his authority incorporated in a public instrument by his ' secretary ' William Mees.[69] That Archbishop Reynolds did publish some articles of the kind in parliament is well attested.[70]

Before attempting to assess Orleton's participation in these proceedings it is necessary to have a closer look at the later mission to Kenilworth and in particular Baker's account of it, upon which excessive reliance may have been placed.[71] Baker, we have already seen, was following Murimuth, and the latter continues to provide the skeleton for the narrative at this point. From Murimuth, for instance, Baker adopted the statement that three bishops went on the mission.[72] He named them (Murimuth does not) as Stratford, Orleton and Burghersh. Now, he is the only chronicler to include Burghersh and it is hard to escape the conclusion that this was done to maintain Baker's thesis of the bishops' joint conspiracy. Historically it is almost certainly unsound. According to Baker two of the bishops, Stratford and Burghersh, went on ahead to join Edward's custodian, Henry of Lancaster, in persuading the king to resign.[73] This assent, we are told, was obtained before the arrival of Orleton, whom Baker dubs ' infandus imbassiator '. His version suggests that on reaching Kenilworth Orleton lent solemnity and decorum to the occasion by marshalling the members of the delegation in order of rank.[74] On emerging from an inner room the king, overcome by grief, fainted. The earl of Leicester [75] and Bishop Stratford raised him to his feet. When he had more or less recovered his senses, Orleton proceeded to acquaint him with the purpose of the deputation. In this, so Baker

Lichfield, Chichester and Rochester. This apparently confirms the ' archbishop of Canterbury and seven bishops ' of the *French Chronicle*.

69 *Responsiones*, cols. 2765–6.

70 E.g. *French Chronicle*, p. 57; Cotton MS. Julius A. I, fo. 56r (Clarke, *op. cit.* p. 44); Bodley MS. 956, fos. 205–6 (Clarke, *op. cit.* p. 36, n. 3).

71 *Chronicon*, pp. 26–8.

72 *Ibid.* pp. 26–7; *Murimuth*, p. 51.

73 *Chronicon*, p. 27.

74 *Ibid.*: ' Nuncios ceteros . . . quos in regis camera secundum suas dignitates ordinice collocavit.'

75 It is interesting that Baker calls Henry of Lancaster ' comes Leicestrie ' at this date. In *Murimuth* (p. 49) he is ' comes Lancastrie ' even in 1326.

says, he acted ' mira impudentia ', in no way deterred by the state of Edward's mind, though to him he was the most odious of men.[76] Orleton then urged the king to resign in favour of his son, lest someone else (Mortimer?) should be chosen in his place. The following day the members of the deputation renounced their homage through William Trussell on behalf of the whole nation, and Thomas le Blount, the king's steward, signified the dissolution of his household by breaking his staff of office. After that the deputation made its way back to London.[77]

The corresponding portion of the *Historia Roffensis* was edited out by Wharton and so has been ignored by commentators. Of course this chronicler was also biased against Orleton, not however in person, so far as we can judge, but as a member of the group dedicated to the king's overthrow. According to Dene it was Bishops Gravesend of London, Hothum of Ely and Orleton who were sent to Kenilworth. He confirms Edward's abject behaviour, but puts it in a somewhat different light. The former monarch is said to have fallen on his knees, to have craved pardon for his misdeeds, and to have begged for his life; to all of which Orleton returned a cruel and unyielding answer.[78]

It will now be evident that Orleton's responsibility for implementing the abdication was shared among the clergy, principally by Archbishop Reynolds and Bishop John Stratford. Reynolds, as primate, was clearly in a position to influence events by virtue of his office, and as has been recounted already, he passed from a simulated excommunication of the ' invaders ', possibly balanced by a conciliatory gesture, through a mediatory phase to full-blooded support of Isabella, even to the point it would seem of reading the ' articles of deposition '. In all this he shows no sign of

[76] *Chronicon*, p. 28: ' Mira impudencia non confusus regis animum attrectare, cui se putavit pre ceteris mortalibus exosum fuisse.' Stratford's sympathetic gesture (though perhaps genuine) is in line with Baker's favourable rendering of his conduct.

[77] *Ibid.* and cf. C.49/roll 11.

[78] Cotton MS. Faustina B. V, fo. 49^{v}: ' Cui Herfordensis penitenti et veniam petenti severum durum et crudelem inrespondendo se ostendit.' If the bishop of Ely (Hothum) did take the oath in London on 20 January (nn. 63, 68 above) then Dene could be mistaken in the statement that he went to Kenilworth. But in Dene's account the Guildhall oath comes *after* the deputation's return (*ibid.* fo. 50^{r}), though his use of the word ' interim ' leaves the order of events in doubt. Clarke, by relying on Wharton's text, failed to note Dene's version of the delegation's composition. See app. 2 d. below.

acting on principle, but every indication of being swayed by each turn of events, even seeking to placate the Londoners by an untimely gift of wine.[79]

Stratford adopted a cautious approach from the very beginning, despite his previous contact with the queen on the continent. He had plenty of justification for turning the tables on Edward II's councillors, but his initial reaction was not to join the invaders but to temporise by at least going through the motions of mediation. The flight of the king and the rising of the Londoners in Isabella's favour made Edward's cause look hopeless: Stratford gravitated to the queen. At once he became one of the prime movers of policy. By mid-November he was acting-treasurer[80] and on a mission to London with the queen's letters requiring the election of a mayor. Hamo de Chigwell was removed from office and Richard de Bethune, suspected of complicity in Mortimer's escape from the Tower, was elected in his stead.[81] Stratford is supposed to have accompanied Orleton on the initial journey to Kenilworth and on the later one. If Baker is to be taken literally, he performed a more vital if less spectacular task than Orleton. One chronicle, that of Lanercost, gives him even greater prominence than Orleton in the procedings of the January 1327 parliamentary assembly, but the balance is more than redressed by the *Historia Roffensis*. We are not likely to discover which is nearer the truth.

What then is to be said of Orleton's participation in these affairs? Unlike both Reynolds and Stratford he was firmly for the queen and those with her from the moment he knew of their arrival in England; what, if anything, passed between them before that time it is impossible to say.[82] Orleton's own explanation of his activities is that he was working against Edward's evil councillors, notably the younger Despenser, as executor of a common

79 *Op. cit.* fo. 50^r: 'Ubi Walterus archiepiscopus Cant' obprobia et convicia multa sustinuit a London' et vadiavit eis .l. dolia vini pro concordia habenda.'

80 *Annales Paulini*, p. 318; Davies, *Baronial Opposition*, p. 568 (transcript of appointment).

81 *Annales Paulini*, *loc. cit.* Stratford and Thomas Wake are recorded to have visited the Guildhall at Christmas, when the bishop promised to supply lead for the roof of the chapel there, and Wake the necessary timber. *Calendar of Letter Books E*, p. 215.

82 Blackley, 'Isabella' (pp. 221, 227), is equally sceptical about the traditional assumptions that have been regarded as fact.

policy for their removal from the king's side. Thus it was that he came to give an exposition of the reasons for the queen's coming: the damage done to the Church and realm by tainted counsel, the despoiling of the prelates, and the disinheritance, imprisonment, banishment and exile of the great men of the land – all because Despenser had interposed himself between the king and his subjects.[83] Subsequently, in parliament, he sought to justify the queen's failure to return to her husband. At first this was a question of political expediency: if the queen were to be reconciled to Edward the projected revolution would be pointless, since before parliament assembled the 'evil councillors' were all either dead or imprisoned. Later, with the accession of the new king, it became a matter of propriety – the queen's public reputation – and Orleton states that it was among the items discussed at the council which met at Stamford in April 1327, by which time he was abroad.[84] Among the articles of accusation against Mortimer following his arrest in 1330 is one to the effect that he brought discord between Edward II and Isabella and put it about that the queen would be killed if she approached her husband.[85] The origin of this 'discord' lies further back than the political necessity of 1326–7; it has even been claimed that Isabella's reluctance to return to her husband may have preceded her association with Mortimer.[86]

The manipulation of parliament to bring round those who hesitated to accept the king's deposition and still hankered after some form of reconciliation between Isabella and Edward is to a greater or lesser degree attributed to Orleton, but by far the major cause of the odium heaped upon him is the firmness amounting to cruelty which he is said to have displayed when he confronted the demoralised and despairing king at Kenilworth. It should be recalled, though, that there is no one to give his side of the story. Orleton's surviving letters and his apologia give scant trace of the acerbity, let alone the viciousness, which some chroniclers ascribe to him. Modern historians, impressed by Edward's pitiable situation and his belated show of penitence, are forgetful of the appal-

83 *Responsiones*, cols. 2764–5.
84 *Ibid*. col. 2767.
85 E.g. *Knighton*, p. 457. The articles in the edition (pp. 454–8) are somewhat shorter than those in *Rot. Parl.* 2, pp. 52–3.
86 By Blackley, *op. cit*.

ling character of the latter part of the reign and have far too readily accepted the strictures of Baker. Orleton certainly had reason for rancour; that he showed it in the manner suggested cannot be accepted without qualification. The chroniclers concerned were not in favour of Edward's deposition; Orleton, on the contrary, had worked since the queen's return for the replacement of an impossibly tyrannical government.[87]

At the beginning of the reign of Edward III the well-ventilated but hardly successful precedent of a standing council was revived. Orleton was one of the four bishops – the others were the metropolitans Reynolds and Melton, and Stratford of Winchester – named in a council of twelve ' without whom nothing should be done '.[88] Professor Tout was of the opinion that this was not intended to be an effective instrument, but merely represented ' another attempt to exploit the name of Lancaster and the traditions of the last reign, in the interests of the dominant party '.[89] All the same, it was to be the initial article of accusation against Roger Mortimer that he had set up such a council and that nothing was permitted to be done without the assent of four of its members: a bishop, an earl and two barons.[90] The councillors are said to have been nominated at or before Edward III's coronation, but it may have been before 28 January, the date of Orleton's appointment as treasurer and that of Hothum as chancellor.[91]

On the eve of the coronation the new treasurer released to

87 Davies, *Baronial Opposition*, p. 509, says of Edward II: ' He was not a tyrant, but merely inefficient, hence he did not arouse any deep hostility in the people.' The logic of the general desertion of his subjects in the autumn of 1326, including ' every section of the official class ' (Tout, *Chapters* 3, p. 4), points to a conclusion closer to that of Phillips who summarises the aftermath of Boroughbridge (*Pembroke*, p. 214) thus: ' The result was a total victory for the king, the ascendency of the Despensers, a massacre of the English magnates unsurpassed even in the fifteenth century, and the creation of a regime supported only on fear and military force.' See also the confirmatory opinion of Williams, *Medieval London* (pp. 290–2), who regards Despenser, Arundel and Baldock as ' notorious for cynical abuse of power '.

88 Baldwin, ' The King's Council ', p. 132, quoting Cambridge, Corpus Christi College MS. 174, cap. 216; Barnes, *History of Edward III*, p. 4 (who also made use of this MS.); *Rot. Parl.* 2, p. 52. The laymen were the earls of Lancaster, Norfolk (earl marshal), Kent and Warenne and an equal number of barons: Sir Thomas Wake, Sir Henry Percy, Sir Oliver Ingham and John de Ros. Cf. Tout, *Chapters* 3, pp. 10–11, 13. Baldwin reiterates the conventional view of Orleton as ' guiding spirit of the revolution ', friend of Mortimer, and ' self-seeking ' prelate (*op. cit.* pp. 130, 133 and n. 1, 136).

89 *Chapters* 3, p. 13.

90 *Knighton*, p. 454; *Rot. Parl.* 2, p. 52. The individual members are not named.

91 Baldwin, *op. cit.* pp. 132–3.

Robert de Woodhouse, keeper of the wardrobe, a number of precious articles – one worth almost £50 was a gift to the former king from the elder Despenser – for use during the ceremonies.[92] The coronation took place at Westminster Abbey on 1 February, the Sunday after the feast of the Conversion of St Paul.[93] The official record states that it was attended by nine bishops of English sees, including Orleton,[94] and by the bishop of Llandaff, John de Eaglescliff.[95] The bishop of Rochester, Hamo de Hethe, is omitted from the list. Dene, however, gives some seemingly authentic details of the coronation and attributes to his diocesan an important part in the proceedings, despite Hethe's earlier reticence in accepting the new monarch. As one might expect, Archbishop Reynolds actually crowned the king, assisted by the bishops of London and Winchester who helped to support the crown on the young Edward's head. In response to the question put by Sir John de Suly, Hamo de Hethe is said to have declared that the king could not be crowned unless he took an oath to uphold the laws.[96] Subsequently, in concert with William Ayrminne, bishop of Norwich, he chanted the litany.[97]

After this we know something about Orleton's routine administration as treasurer,[98] but very little about his political activities. One aspect in evidence is the redress of his own grievances, as well as those of numerous others implicated in the recent 'quarrel' of the earl of Lancaster. With the annulment of the process against him, the way was clear for the formal restitution

92 B.L. Cotton Charter IV 9.

93 *Foedera* 2, ii, p. 172; *Annales Paulini*, pp. 324–5; *Murimuth*, p. 51. For the order of the coronation see C.49/roll 11 (dorse). After the archbishop had offered the prayer 'Deus humilium' there was to be a sermon by one of the prelates 'si le temps le soffre'.

94 The others, apart from Archbishop Reynolds, were Hothum (Ely), Stratford (Winchester), Beaumont (Durham), Cobham (Worcester), Langton (Chichester), Burghersh (Lincoln) and Ayrminne (Norwich).

95 The only Welsh bishop in attendance and the only one who took the Guildhall oath (*Cal. P.M.R.*, p. 13). The pope translated him from Connor on 20 June 1323 (S.C.7/56/13), but his temporalities were only restored on 13 August 1324. *C.P.L.* 1305–42, p. 232; *C.P.R.* 1324–27, p. 11.

96 Cotton MS. Faustina B. V, fo. 50^r: 'Dominus Johannes de Suly miles Roff' episcopum requisivit an rex legem quam populus suus elegit custodire vellet. Episcopus querenti respondens quod alioquin non coronabitur nisi prius prestito iuramento de servando leges.'

97 *Ibid.*: 'Norwycen' et Roffen' letaniam canebant'. Cf. C.49/roll 11 (dorse).

98 E.403/266 (issue rolls, pells); *Calendar of Memoranda Rolls*, index *s.v.*

of his much-abused temporalities.[99] Authority was also given for the payment of allowances and expenses due to him for diplomatic service before the start of the troubles.[100] Among the petitions to parliament was one which affected both him and a number of other bishops; it was for the revocation of royal presentations made after Lancaster's death to the detriment of prelates who had espoused his cause or were considered to have done so.[101] Already Orleton had received a measure of compensation for his substantial losses of goods and income. The Despenser manor of Beaumes was followed by custody of those of Ashchurch and Temple Guiting in Gloucestershire and goods and chattels there belonging to the Despensers and Baldock.[102] He was also to become custodian of the manor of Rosamund, formerly held by John de Benstede, and warden of Feckenham Forest in Worcestershire.[103]

The ruling group in the country early in 1327 is delineated by the names of those who witnessed the City of London's charter of liberties (sealed 6 March), which was coupled with pardons for offences committed by Londoners during the recent troubles and acquittance of their debts to the former king.[104] Orleton apart, there were three bishops, Reynolds, Chancellor Hothum and Ayrminne, whilst the lay element comprised the earls of Norfolk, Lancaster and Kent, and three barons, Roger Mortimer, Thomas Wake, Lancaster's son-in-law, and John de Ros, steward of the king's household.[105] Shortly afterwards, on 18 March, Orleton

99 C.49/6/5; *Foedera* 2, ii, p. 177 (16 February 1327); *C.C.R.* 1327–30, pp. 44–5. Orleton was also active in securing the cancellation of the many recognisances exacted by those in power during Edward II's reign. The earl of Arundel, shortly before his death (exec. 17 November 1326), confessed to Orleton that he had demanded recognisances of 2,000 marks for a debt of half that sum owed by Henry Nasard of London (for further notice of whom see: E.43/365; *Calendar of Letter Books E*, index *s.v.*) and despite repayment of the debt had refused to withdraw them. Instead a new one for 600 marks had been entered into. The council ordered the justices to cancel it. *C.C.R.* 1327–30, pp. 47, 50. See also other instances in 1331 (*C.P.R.* 1330–34, p. 202) and 1332 (*ibid.* p. 298).

100 *C.C.R.* 1327–30, p. 4: 13 February 1327.

101 *Rot. Parl. Inediti*, p. 118, no. 5 (cf. no. 4); *C.C.R.* 1327–30, p. 102.

102 *C.C.R.* 1327–30, pp. 86, 104, 488; *C.P.R.* 1327–30, p. 103.

103 There is a summary of Orleton's debts and expenses, including the farms paid for various lands of which he had custody, mainly abstracted (*c.* 1341) from the Pipe Rolls, in Win.R.O. 1, fos. 175^r (*al.* 47)–176^r (attached membrane). See also *ibid.* fos. 152^v, 182^r (*al.* 54); E.372/178/19^r; Neilson, 'The Forests', p. 462; *C.F.R.* 1327–37, p. 222.

104 *Annales Paulini*, pp. 326–32.

105 As compared with membership of the standing council (n. 88 above), Melton and

gave up his post of treasurer; twelve days later he left London on a diplomatic mission. To all outward appearances political stability was at last restored.

THE STRATFORD AFFAIR AND ITS PRELUDE 1327–1341

The origins of the animosity which in 1341 flared up between Adam Orleton and John Stratford are not so obvious as has on occasion been implied.[1] By that date Orleton was bishop of Winchester, in the twilight of his life; Stratford, younger by a few years perhaps,[2] had on Simon Mepham's death in 1333 been translated from Winchester to Canterbury, and then, during the king's absence in France, had acted as custodian of the young prince with the title of *dux regis*,[3] thus reaching a pinnacle of achievement denied to Orleton, who after his final diplomatic mission of 1336 to all intents and purposes withdrew from secular affairs. In these circumstances it appears almost inexplicable that Orleton should rally in so determined a manner to an Edward III who was temporarily incensed against one of his chief councillors. The earlier careers of the two bishops provide no satisfactory explanation of this enmity. It is true that while Orleton was in the 'wilderness' during the latter part of Edward II's reign Stratford was co-operating with the government as a diplomatic agent, and that on Queen Isabella's return he for a while played a waiting game; after that, however, the bishops stood side by side until Edward II's deposition was effected. It seems probable,

Stratford are missing from among the bishops and Warenne, Sir Henry Percy and Sir Oliver Ingham (Mortimer's close associate, appointed justice of Chester) from the laymen.

1 Notably by some of the chroniclers: see above, 'Orleton and the chroniclers'. In *Avesbury* (p. 330) Orleton is 'archiepiscopo semper infestus', in *Birchington* (p. 40) 'amator discordiae'. Bannister (*H.R.O.*, p. xlvii) thought that he 'welcomed the invitation to come out of retirement to lead the attack upon the man who, more than any other, save perhaps William de Montacute, was responsible for the death of his dearest friend [Mortimer]'. Usher ('Career of a Political Bishop', p. 47) argued from the raising of questions of 'foreign policy' in 1341 that the two bishops 'were engaged in a continuing debate with each other that arose out of an established feud'.

2 Stratford was D.C.L. by 1312 and received his first benefice in 1316. This suggests that he was born in the early 1280s. He died 23 August 1348 (*Birchington*, p. 41). See *Biog. Oxon.*, *s.v.*

3 The term is used by Dene and quoted by Tout (*Chapters* 3, p. 102, n. 3), who gives (*ibid.* pp. 101–3) a general appraisal of Stratford's position at the time.

then, that it is to the period between 1327 and 1341 that we must look for the evolution, though not necessarily the origin, of what seems to have been a conflict partly of personalities and partly of policies.

During this period Stratford acted first as Lancaster's mouthpiece and then, with Mortimer's fall, as Edward III's chancellor, marking the end of a lengthy interlude during which he had been excluded from office. Canon Bannister explains Orleton's political interventions at this time, as always, in terms of support for Mortimer. But such interventions, as he admits, were now rare. The bishop does not seem to have taken any identifiable part in government at home after 1328, occupying himself (when outside his diocese) almost exclusively with diplomatic negotiations. Among the chroniclers, not even Baker deems it necessary to attribute political decisions to him after the Scottish treaty of that year.[4] At the same time, the bishop's itinerary demonstrates that he was diligent in attending parliaments, though seldom present at less 'representative' assemblies and only on rare occasions at meetings of the king's council.[5] The deduction must be that he was not being regularly consulted, except on foreign relations. We catch a glimpse of him acting in concert with Stratford to calm the parliamentary outcry against the papal collector Itier de Concoreto, whom the hot-blooded sought to expel from the realm, as well as coming to the assistance of Archbishop Mepham, a supporter of Lancaster, when he aroused a hornet's nest at Canterbury.[6] A fuller examination of the actions of both Orleton and

[4] *Chronicon*, p. 41.

[5] Plucknett remarks on the absenteeism of bishops from parliaments ('Parliament', p. 106) and names both Stratford (when bishop of Winchester) and Orleton (as bishop of Worcester) as defaulters. This is mistaken. It takes no account of enforced absence due to the king's diplomatic requirements and in any case is not supported by the extant parliamentary proxies (S.C.10). There is only one proxy for Orleton (S.C.10/6/260: 20 October 1318). His itinerary while at Worcester shows that he was in the vicinity of eight out of the ten assemblies designated parliaments in *H.B.C.* which met between 1328 and 1332. On the other two occasions he was abroad. However, Hamo de Hethe (Rochester) and Louis de Beaumont (Durham) frequently appointed proxies.

[6] *Thorne*, cols. 2043, 2045; Lunt, *Accounts Rendered by Papal Collectors*, pp. xxv–xxvi. The conflict arose from Mepham's attempt in 1329 to visit St Augustine's Abbey in his cathedral city. The archbishop accused the papal judge-delegate, Itier de Concoreto, of citing him in parliament (of 1330: Thorne; of 1331: *Foedera* 2, iii, p. 72) for matters touching the crown rather than the ecclesiastical forum. According to the abbey's proctor, Mepham sought to have Itier punished 'tanquam

Stratford during this time will perhaps help to substantiate what has been said above and to provide a framework for the crisis of 1341.

When Orleton vacated the treasurership early in 1327, Burghersh succeeded him, the principal office of chancellor being filled at the time by John Hothum, bishop of Ely.[7] Stratford held no office but was despatched on a mission to France shortly after Orleton's own departure.[8] In February 1328 Orleton returned to a hostile court, outraged by his acceptance of papal translation to Worcester.[9] Once that matter was settled, he was able to snatch a few moments in his new diocese. His ministrations were cut short by a summons to parliament, which assembled at Northampton on 24 April. The bishop must have arrived about a week later,[10] but soon gravitated to the centre of affairs. The principal ministers were changed shortly after his coming: Bishop Burghersh moved from the treasurership to be chancellor; Thomas Charlton, the new bishop of Hereford, succeeded Burghersh as treasurer; while in the royal household John de Wysham became steward and Sir Thomas Wake chamberlain.[11] Orleton possibly had some say in this ministerial reshuffle; he was certainly present in St Andrew's Priory, Northampton, at the time of the transfer of the Great Seal to Burghersh.[12] The precise political complexion

reum laesae majestatis', but the bishops intervened. Following the fracas (21 March 1331) at the archbishop's manor of Slindon (Sussex), when those who sought to publish a citation on the abbey's behalf were forcibly resisted, Orleton joined the bishops of London (Gravesend), Lincoln (Burghersh), Carlisle (Ross), Norwich (Ayrminne), Chichester (Langton), Salisbury (Wyville) and Ely (Hothum) in a testimonial to Mepham's character. Mepham attempted to visit Exeter but the pope warned him that he had exempted Bishop Grandisson from his jurisdiction. Orleton was one of the executors of the papal mandate. *C.P.L.* 1305–42, p. 369.

7 Appointed 28 January 1327, *H.B.C.*; cf. Tout, *Chapters* 3, p. 8, who regards the appointments of Hothum and Orleton as betokening 'some attempt . . . to carry out the Commons' wishes'.

8 *Foedera* 2, ii, pp. 180–1; Mirot and Déprez, 'Ambassades anglaises', pp. 555–6; E.101/309/39–40.

9 *Foedera* 2, iii, pp. 3–4; *W.R.O.* 2, fo. 4^{r-v} [500–6]

10 On 28 April he was at Bishops Hampton (Warwicks.) and on 2 May at Brockhall (Northants.) and Northampton. *W.R.O.* 1, fo. 16^{v} [40]; 2, fo. 23^{r} [657–8].

11 See Tout, *Chapters* 3, pp. 16–18 for details. Roger Northburgh is listed as treasurer 2 March–20 May 1328 but Tout (*op. cit.* p. 17, n. 4) regards it as 'highly probable' that he did not act. He is also distrustful of the Pauline annalist's claim that these changes took place *in* the Northampton parliament, regarding this as Lancastrian wishful thinking (*Annales Paulini*, p. 340). Cf. *Cal. P.M.R.*, p. 79.

12 *C.C.R.* 1327–30, p. 387. Also present were Roger Mortimer, William la Zouche of Ashby, Oliver Ingham, John de Crumbwell or Cromwell and Gilbert Talbot, king's

of the new appointments is hard to determine, but it looks as though they were not unfavourable to Lancaster,[13] and there seems to have been a concurrent arrangement whereby he was to be on hand to give counsel to the king.[14] Another decision made at Northampton was that Orleton and Roger Northburgh, bishop of Coventry and Lichfield, should go to France to claim the crown on Edward III's behalf.[15] This was an ominous step – one which was to be the subject of criticism by Stratford.[16]

The appearance of political equilibrium was deceptive; when in June 1328 a council was held at Worcester, Lancaster proved unwilling to agree to the sending of a military force to Gascony until the matter had been discussed in a larger assembly.[17] Such an assembly was in due course summoned to York,[18] but the earl excused himself from attendance, thereby postponing a decision once more – or so it was said.[19]

At this point the paths of Orleton and Stratford become widely divergent. The latter was to become the leading ecclesiastical figure in Lancastrian opposition to the domination of the king by Mortimer and Isabella[20] – an opposition joined by Gravesend, bishop of London, and by the archbishop of Canterbury, Mepham. Orleton, by contrast, virtually withdrew from politics. On his return from Paris he went back to his diocese, emerging only for a quick trip to Nottingham – he was there on 23 July 1328 – probably for consultation on the briefing of the archbishop of

chamberlain. The group has a strong Mortimer complexion. Tout (*Chapters* 3, p. 15, n. 3) regards Talbot as a Lancastrian because he was 'of the quarrel of Thomas, late earl of Lancaster'. In fact this is only a general designation; both he and his sons Richard and Gilbert rode with Mortimer's forces in 1321. See Just. 1/1388/mm. 2^v, 7^v.

13 Burghersh was to remain with Mortimer and the queen until their fall in 1330. Wysham may have become more a supporter of Lancaster than Mortimer (Tout, *Chapters* 3, p. 18, n. 3); Wake was Lancaster's son-in-law. Charlton had been Edward II's trusted clerk and his candidate for the see of Hereford in 1317, when Orleton secured it. Tout (*op. cit.* p. 17) looked on him as a curialist seeking his own advancement – but we really do not know the truth of the matter.

14 *Cal. P.M.R.*, p. 79.

15 *Ibid.* p. 78. This was a point made by the 'court group' anxious to show that Lancaster was a party to the arrangement.

16 Stratford argued that he had no influence in the counsels of the king's advisors at that time and hence was not responsible for an act that precipitated the war ('quae quidem legatio maximam guerrae praesentis materiam ministravit'): *Birchington*, p. 29.

17 So runs the *pièce justificative* of the 'court group': *Cal. P.M.R.*, p. 79.

18 31 July 1328: *H.B.C.*

19 *Cal. P.M.R.*, *loc. cit.*

20 *Ibid.* pp. 79–81.

Armagh, who was about to set out for the Curia.[21] He did not attend the assembly at York at the end of July, where contention could be expected but was in fact averted by Lancaster's non-attendance. He did respond in person to the summons for a parliament which assembled at Salisbury on 16 October.[22]

The Salisbury parliament witnessed open conflict between the Mortimer and Lancaster factions. In the previous month Stratford and Sir Thomas Wake had gone as Lancastrian spokesmen to London, where they expounded the earl's case against the prevailing government: the king did not live of his own; certain prelates and barons ought to be in attendance on him as laid down by the Westminster parliament (of 1327), but this was not the case; it was desirable that peace should be maintained in the kingdom.[23] The practical outcome was the sending of a contingent of Londoners to join the forces which Lancaster had mustered in the midlands and moved to the neighbourhood of Winchester.[24] To the Salisbury parliament the earl sent reasons for his non-appearance, to which the prelates were reluctant to reply until Stratford arrived. When he did so, he proceeded to explain that Lancaster was absent because of his quarrel with Mortimer and that the latter had made peace with Scotland to leave his hands free for crushing the earl. He ended with a plea for peace between the contending groups.[25] Mortimer, in the interval made earl of the March, which some considered an unprecedented title,[26] proceeded to defend himself in the king's presence from Stratford's verbal onslaught. According to the court's version of the proceedings the bishops were satisfied with his answers and after Mortimer had taken an oath on the archiepiscopal cross to do nothing to Lancaster's detriment, Stratford and Gravesend were sent to request him to come to the parliament. Lancaster, suspicious of the offered

21 *W.R.O.* 1, fo. 17r [50]; *Foedera* 2, iii, p. 15.

22 He was at Cirencester on 15 October, at South Burcombe, near Salisbury, where he stayed several days, on the 20th. *W.R.O.* 2, fo. 10v [558]; 1, fos. 32r, 34v [224, 289].

23 *Cal. P.M.R.*, pp. 66–8, 79–80.

24 *Ibid.* pp. xxxiv, 73–4, 82–3. According to the *Brut* (p. 260), six hundred men were sent. This was officially denied. An account of happenings in London at this time is given by Williams, *Medieval London*, pp. 301–5. See also Redstone, 'Some Mercenaries of Lancaster', pp. 151–66; Holmes, 'Rebellion of Lancaster', pp. 84–9.

25 *Cal. P.M.R.*, pp. 80–1.

26 E.g. *Annales Paulini*, pp. 342–3: 'Et talis comitatus nunquam prius fuit nominatus in regno Angliae.'

safe-conduct, declined to do so and occupied Winchester.[27] Parliament broke up in disorder, some of the bishops withdrawing without leave, Stratford being one of those later called to account for so doing.[28] If Birchington does not exaggerate, Stratford's fears were well founded: during his flight from Wilton, where he had been staying in the monastery while parliament was in session, only timely warning is said to have saved him on three occasions from murderous ambush by Mortimer's agents.[29]

It has been surmised that at Salisbury Orleton was giving aid and counsel to Mortimer, but there is no evidence to support the theory and the bishop's itinerary makes it clear that he did not subsequently follow the court.[30] He seems to have remained at Salisbury until the end of the parliamentary session, being at Idmiston just north of the city on 1 November, obviously en route to his diocese.[31] Mortimer and the queen travelled in the direction of London.[32] Later on, as we shall see, military considerations dictated their migration to the west, at which time Orleton, if still in his diocese, could have been in contact for a brief while, though by chance rather than prearrangement.[33]

Reynolds's successor as archbishop of Canterbury, Simon Mepham, was a scholarly man of saintly reputation, who none the less in a few years found himself in conflict with the pope, his nuncio, the two major monastic houses in his cathedral city, various of his suffragan bishops, the northern metropolitan and, in the political sphere, the Mortimer interest in control of the king.[34] At Salisbury he took a stand with the opposition; on his return to London he preached at St Paul's and together with Bishops Stratford and Gravesend joined the earls of Norfolk and Kent,

27 *Cal. P.M.R.*, pp. 82–3.

28 *Annales Paulini*, p. 342; Plucknett, 'Parliament', p. 106, n. 2; Tout, *Chapters* 3, p. 23.

29 *Birchington*, p. 19.

30 *H.R.O.*, pp. xiii, xliv. After the Salisbury parliament he seems to have returned to the diocese and to have remained there at least until the middle of December.

31 *W.R.O.* 1, fo. 32r [225]; 2, fo. 10v [561].

32 A 'rough itinerary' of the chancery between 2 November 1328 and 20 January 1329, which fits in with what is known of the king's movements, is given by Holmes, 'Rebellion of Lancaster', p. 84.

33 Between 23 and about 29 December the court was at Gloucester and Worcester.

34 The most detailed (though totally unsympathetic) account of Mepham's part in the Lancastrian 'rebellion' is to be found in the *Historia Roffensis* (B.L. Cotton MS. Faustina B. V, fos. 51v–52v). Cf. *Annales Paulini*, pp. 343–4.

Sir Thomas Wake and other men of Lancaster's persuasion for political discussions.[35] Mortimer, in the king's name, threatened to raise the royal standard against them, but on 23 December the archbishop sent a letter suggesting that Edward desist from the use of force and await the meeting of parliament.[36] After Lancaster reached the capital on the first day of the new year, 1329, the confederates are said to have agreed on ordinances for the benefit of the kingdom,[37] whereupon a deputation, which included Mepham and Gravesend, set out for the court to negotiate a settlement.[38] Lancaster's position collapsed about the third week in January following the desertion of the earls of Norfolk and Kent and the ravaging of his lands by Mortimer.[39] He submitted and was forced to enter into a substantial recognisance, as were his major supporters, while others who had been excepted from the king's grace fled abroad.[40] A cataclysm comparable to that of 1322 had been narrowly averted.

Orleton's movements during this critical time are sparsely documented. He could have been in his diocese during the latter half of December,[41] when Mortimer, anxious to shorten his lines of communication with the March, passed from Gloucester to Wor-

35 According to the *Historia Roffensis* (fo. 51v), at Salisbury 'Archiepiscopus Cant' novus, modum et mores hominum totaliter ignorans, comitibus Kancie et Lancastrie et eorum sequele qui contra reginam et Rogerum de Mortuo Mari regnantes sub colore utilitatis regni se partem facientes cepit adherere, multa locutus est sed parum profecit.'

36 *Cal. P.M.R.*, pp. 84, 85–6; *Lit. Cant.* 3, pp. 414–16 (text of the archbishop's letter with omission of a clause supplied by Holmes, 'Rebellion of Lancaster', p. 87, n. 9).

37 *Annales Paulini*, p. 344. The Lancastrian complaints are set out in *Cal. P.M.R.*, p. 81; cf. *Brut*, pp. 258–9.

38 *Annales Paulini*, p. 344. Dene (*Historia Roffensis*, fo. 52r) describes this deputation in detail, saying that the archbishop went on ahead and too readily revealed the nature of his mission, despite warnings not to do so. The king's council thereupon won him over: 'Ita quod archiepiscopus consilio regis se totaliter dedit et adhesit ut dicitur iuramento se obligavit. Quo facto iniunctum est archiepiscopo ad comites redire et eis dicere quod quotquot gracie regis se submittere vellent exceptis quatuor graciam invenirent. Et factum est quod omnes qui de adventu archiepiscopi spem habuerunt firmam de pace facienda et de eius adventu plurimum gaudebant postea in ridiculum habentem et in fabulam prothdolor ei maledicabant.'

39 *Knighton*, p. 450; Holmes, *op. cit.* pp. 86–7. Dene (*op. cit.* fo. 52v) records the dénouement thus: 'Comites vero Lancastrie, Kancie et ceteri eis adherentes confusi expectabant adventum regis apud Bedeford' ubi regi equitanti pedites occurrerunt et omnes in luto profundo genibus provolutis prostrati gracie regis se submiserunt.'

40 *Cal. P.M.R.*, pp. 85–6; *Knighton*, pp. 450–1; *C.C.R.* 1327–30, pp. 528–30. Holmes in his account of the insurrection did not make use of Cotton MS. Faustina B. V, which provides a useful complement to Knighton and the Pauline annalist.

41 His register gives no assistance for this period or for January 1329.

cester – where the archbishop's letter caught up with him.[42] Mortimer soon pressed on; passing through Leicestershire he eventually confronted his rival at Bedford.[43]

These happenings, momentous though they were, left no obvious mark on the course of ecclesiastical events. Mepham's enthronement took place at Canterbury on the feast of St Vincent (22 January 1329); five days later he presided over his first provincial council at St Paul's.[44] It was at St Paul's that Bishop Ayrminne celebrated a *missa de pace*: after the gospel the murderers of Bishop Stapledon were solemnly declared excommunicate, as were those responsible for firing the abbey of St Edmund.[45] Orleton arrived in London in time for the council, as we know from his participation in the discussion on the financial problems of the University of Oxford, following which he wrote a long letter to his diocese (dated 19 February) urging the collection of money for its relief.[46] He continued in the city for the parliament adjourned from Salisbury to Westminster where an *inspeximus* of the annulment process of 1327 was drawn up.[47] Once parliament had dispersed on 22 February Orleton made his way to Beaumes, remaining there until the end of April. The reason for this is uncertain, but it enabled him to return to London in mid-May,[48] possibly in connection with the king's imminent crossing to France in the company of Bishop Burghersh to do homage to Philip VI in Amiens cathedral.[49]

42 *Cal. P.M.R.*, pp. 84–5.

43 Details of the ravaging of Lancastrian lands are given by the partisan Knighton (p. 450). A royal summons for the mayor and twenty-four citizens of London to appear at St Albans is dated 22 January 1329, which gives a terminus ad quem for Lancaster's submission. The king's council discussed with the delegation the question of punishing those Londoners who had been with Lancaster's men at Winchester or Bedford. *Annales London*, pp. 242–3.

44 *Murimuth*, p. 59; *Annales Paulini*, pp. 344–5, where the council's proceedings are given at some length. The caustic Dene (fo. 52^{v}) was content to comment: 'In concilio antedicto nulla fuerunt expedita sed sicuti prelati et clerus in magnis sumptibus ad concilium venerunt ita vacui sine reparacione gravaminum ecclesie recesserunt.'

45 For this sacrilege see *Cal. P.M.R.*, p. 73 and n. The mayor of London, Hamo de Chigwell, was thought to be cognisant of the affair, but was given protection as a clerk by the bishop of London, Gravesend: *Annales Paulini*, pp. 346–7; Cotton MS. Faustina B. V, fo. 52^{v}.

46 Coventry and Lichfield Reg. Northburgh 3, fo. 102^{r}. See app. 2 b. below.

47 He seems to have been in London for most of February. The *inspeximus* is in *Rot. Parl.* 2, pp. 427–8. Orleton may have felt the need to secure his position.

48 *W.R.O.* 1, fos. 18^{v}–19^{r}, 34^{v} [82–7, 296]; 2, fo. 28^{v} [720].

49 *Foedera* 2, ii, p. 26.

Shortly before the king left the country Orleton made his way back to his Worcester diocese and immersed himself in its affairs. Apart from just over two months in the late summer and autumn of 1329 – spent between Beaumes, Hillingdon and London – he continued to give attention to such matters until January 1330, at which point two consecutive embassies – followed by an extended stay at Beaumes – made him an absentee until the first week of October.[50] They also prevented his attendance at the Winchester parliament of March 1330, which at Mortimer's behest condemned the earl of Kent on a trumped-up charge of conspiracy.[51]

On his return to the diocese Orleton stayed barely a fortnight before setting out for the assembly summoned to Nottingham. It is possible that he had some inkling of the plot being hatched against Mortimer; we know nothing for certain. On 20 October, the day after Mortimer's arrest in Nottingham Castle, Orleton was at nearby Ilkeston in Derbyshire.[52] He then moved off in the direction of Leicester, apparently maintaining contact with the court, but before long returned to his principal Worcestershire manor, Hartlebury.[53] Mortimer was condemned at the parliament which met in London towards the end of November;[54] Orleton was in the capital for its duration.[55]

Contrary to what one might expect, the earl's death and Queen Isabella's 'retirement' had no perceptible effect on the bishop's career.[56] The month of January 1331 saw his departure with Bishop Ayrminne on yet another mission to France – several more

50 See above, 'A career resumed', ch. 2.

51 *Knighton*, p. 452; *Murimuth*, pp. 59–60; *Annales Paulini*, p. 349; *Lanercost*, pp. 260, 265. The last chronicler tells how a friar preacher, Thomas Dunheved, attempted to persuade the earl that Edward II was still alive by alleging that he had raised the devil, who told him so. See Tanquerey, 'Conspiracy of Thomas Dunheved', pp. 119–24. The *Brut* (pp. 263–7) gives a lengthy but conflicting account of the incident. Archbishop Melton, Bishop Gravesend (London) and the abbot of Langdon (Edward II's nominee for Droxford's see in 1323) were implicated: *Rot. Parl.* 2, p. 54.

52 *W.R.O.* 1, fo. 36^v [337]. See Crump, 'Arrest of Roger Mortimer', pp. 331–2.

53 He was there by 4 November: *W.R.O.* 1, fo. 33^r [249].

54 *H.B.C.*: 26 November–9 December.

55 He was there from 27 November to 18 December inclusive. The outside dates are provided by *W.R.O.* 1, fo. 35^r [308]; 2, fos. 37^v–38^r [797].

56 Nor that much on Burghersh's, who resumed office as treasurer in 1334 and remained a royal councillor until his death in 1340. The bishop of Lincoln was with the queen and Mortimer in Nottingham Castle when they were surprised by William de Montacute and his party. See, for instance, *Knighton*, p. 458; *Bridlington*, p. 101. In Thomas de Burton's chronicle Burghersh 'per latrinam evadere conabatur' (*Melsa*, p. 360).

were to follow – and he continued to attend parliaments with his accustomed regularity.[57] Stratford, on the other hand, was to reap substantial rewards from Edward's personal regimen: on 28 November 1330 he succeeded Burghersh as chancellor and three years later followed Mepham in the chair of St Augustine at Canterbury.[58]

It was Stratford's translation to Canterbury that made possible Orleton's migration to Winchester – a move which was to be resisted by the whole weight of government. It also precipitated a public appeal to the Curia, and in view of the presence of John de Scures, the sheriff of Hampshire, and of John de Schordich, the influential diplomatic agent and royal councillor, this has every appearance of official contrivance.[59] The appeal constituted a three-point indictment of Orleton's conduct at the time of the revolution, alleging his responsibility for Baldock's death, his provocation of Edward II's subjects to rebel, imprison and kill him, and his authorship of the calumny that the queen could not return to her husband for fear of the consequences.[60] The individual allegations have been considered elsewhere; here it may be re-emphasised that Orleton's studied response was to counter each accusation by reiterating the facts as he saw them and supplying documentary confirmation wherever possible, finally faulting the whole presentation on a technical point.[61] Such a method provides a potent defence against the accepted practice of defamation by notoriety.[62]

One must not slip into the methods of Orleton's calumniators, but it could be that Stratford, or some over-zealous supporters of his, irked by long years on the fringes of political power, seized

57 He was in London at the time of the September 1331 parliament and for those of January, March and September 1332. He was abroad for the parliament which met in December 1332 at York.

58 *H.B.C.*, pp. 84, 211. He was provided to Canterbury 26 November 1333.

59 *Winchester Chartulary*, pp. 104–5, 105–7, nos. 233–4; see above, 'Winchester 1333–1345', ch. 3.

60 The *Responsiones* were printed by Twysden from Lambeth MS. 1213, pp. [*sic*] 300–6. Both appeal and responses are given in full from the Winchester Chartulary in *Exeter Reg. Grandisson* 3, pp. 1540–7.

61 The appellant perjured himself by claiming that the 'facts' of his appeal (dated 2 April 1334) were known throughout England 'publica voce et fama', and at the same time (elsewhere in the appeal) arguing that two hours before he had known nothing of them. *Responsiones*, col. 2768.

62 Notoriety *per evidentiam facti* was recognised by canon law as proof of guilt.

the opportunity provided by a more critical appraisal of the revolution on Mortimer's arrest to concoct the *Libellus* for the purpose of casting the sole blame for what had occurred on Orleton. This is incapable of proof, but Orleton's responses by their emphasis on Stratford's own responsibility suggest the direction from which he felt the attack had come. Pope John's astringent criticism of Stratford's behaviour at this time points in the same direction.

Vindictiveness has been attributed to Orleton mainly on the dubious authority of Baker, but it is conceivable that in this instance the bishop was sufficiently irritated to store up the memory of his wrongs. If such was the case, an opportunity for turning the tables on Stratford was to present itself in 1341.

The circumstances of the political crisis of 1341 and its course have been the subject of detailed examination from the political and constitutional standpoints;[63] what is intended here is a brief recapitulation of the salient facts, a filling-in of some gaps with the aid of material chiefly from unpublished ecclesiastical sources, and a reappraisal of Orleton's participation.

Since Michaelmas 1339 Stratford had been acting as principal councillor to Edward's son, the duke of Cornwall, keeper of the realm during his father's absence on the continent. The king's warlike activities were the source of increasing concern to the archbishop; they contravened the papal policy of peace[64] and their concomitant was onerous taxation with its accompanying threat to the Church's liberties. Evidently Stratford was finding it more and more difficult to serve two masters.

Matters were brought to a head by the financial measures of 1340. In their London convocation the clergy reluctantly agreed to grant an additional tenth to the king, but only in return for a 'charter of liberties'. This charter accompanied the writ for the collection of the tenth[65] and on 30 May Stratford wrote a private

[63] Notably by Lapsley, 'Stratford and the Parliamentary Crisis', pp. 6–18, 193–215; Wilkinson, 'Protest of the Earls', pp. 177–93; Stubbs, *Constitutional History* 2, pp. 176–87; Tout, *Chapters* 3, pp. 69–142; Hughes, *Early Years of Edward III*, chs. 7–9, pp. 100–81; and most recently by Fryde, 'Edward III's Removal of His Ministers', pp. 149–61.

[64] *C.P.L.* 1305–42, pp. 579–80; Lunt, *Financial Relations* 2, p. 632. Benedict XII's offer of mediation in 1339 is in *Hemingburgh* (pp. 348–50), also Edward's reply (*ibid.* pp. 351–4). See also *Rochester Reg. Hethe*, pp. 650–2.

[65] It is printed from the Exeter register of Bishop Grandisson in *Concilia* 2, pp. 655–6 (dated 16 April 1340).

letter to his suffragans by way of explanation in which he advised them to deposit the document in a safe place.[66] Orleton's registrar had the charter copied into his episcopal register.[67] Stratford's letters also contained a disturbing report: he had learned of the king's intention to take the cardinals' procurations [68] from the collectors by way of loan, if necessary by force.[69] By the time this information reached Orleton he had already experienced the actions of the royal agents. On 23 May two of them appeared at Waverley Abbey and removed the £55 which the abbot, as collector in the Surrey archdeaconry, had been storing there preparatory to delivering it to the cardinals' representatives. Just over two weeks later, on 11 June, a more imposing contingent which included Robert de Popham, the sheriff of Hampshire, arrived at Hyde Abbey, where the contribution of the Winchester archdeaconry, amounting to £144, was stored. This too was appropriated. In recounting these happenings to the cardinals and to his metropolitan Orleton outspokenly categorises the forced levy as a 'novum genus mutui quod sine consensu contractum est'.[70]

More illegality was to follow. In response to the king's urgent demands the parliament of Lent 1340 [71] made a grant of the ninth sheaf, lamb and fleece, on the understanding that it did not extend to the ordinary clergy who neither held lands by barony nor were under obligation to attend parliament, and who had already been taxed for the tenth.[72] The royal collectors proceeded in some cases to ignore these distinctions.[73]

66 *Worcester Reg. Bransford*, pp. 67–8, 511–12. The registrar omitted to record the charter itself. It is alluded to *ibid*. pp. 289–90.

67 Win.R.O. 1, fos. 91^{v}–92^{v}.

68 *Worcester Reg. Bransford*, p. 512.

69 *Ibid*.: 'Eciam si resistant'.

70 Win.R.O. 2, fo. 33^{r-v}, 22 June 1340. The phrase has been scored through. For other instances of action by the king's officers see Lunt, *Financial Relations* 2, p. 632. On 18 June the king directed the bishops to recover the procurations from the collectors of the tenth, an idea adumbrated by the archbishop in his letter of 30 May. *C.P.R.* 1338–40, p. 547; *Worcester Reg. Bransford*, pp. 289, 512; *Winchester Chartulary*, p. 221, nos. 521, 533.

71 This met (*H.B.C.*) 20 January–19 February 1340.

72 The terms of the grant are set out with great precision in the subsequent complaints made by the archbishop. See below, nn. 78–9.

73 See, for instance, the abbot of Reading's complaint in *Rochester Reg. Hethe*, p. 656, and nn. 78–9 below. For the aggrieved reaction at Winchester see *Winchester Chartulary*, pp. 221–2, nos. 522–3. On 13 June 1341 Orleton instructed the prior and convent to retain sufficient of the royal tenth to discharge the cardinals' procurations still outstanding (*ibid*. no. 521).

Despite such irregular devices the king continued chronically short of money, a shortage which compelled him to abandon the siege of Tournai and to agree to a truce. Angry at this dénouement, Edward arrived without warning at Tower Steps on the night of 30 November and proceeded to order the arrest of his chief ministers. The chancellor, Robert Stratford, brother of the archbishop, and the treasurer, Bishop Northburgh, were peremptorily dismissed; only their prelacy saved them from imprisonment.[74]

Archbishop Stratford judiciously retired to Canterbury, where he remained between 2 December 1340 and 17 April of the following year. He was far from inactive. On 31 December he sealed letters for the publication of sentences of excommunication against all who infringed ecclesiastical liberties – the king and his family excepted. These letters were distributed in the normal way by Ralph Stratford, bishop of London and dean of the province. Orleton received his copy on 8 January.[75] Meanwhile, on the first day of the new year, the archbishop wrote to Edward, denouncing his evil councillors and pointing out that those who charged him with treason were ipso facto excommunicate for defamation.[76]

The king reacted by summoning the archbishop to appear before him, and when he expressed fear for his life, issued a safe-conduct on 26 January.[77] This could scarcely have arrived before Stratford despatched a letter to the new chancellor, Robert Bourchier, in which he meticulously delineated the terms under which the clergy had consented to the tenth and the ninth and roundly castigated the proceedings of the royal collectors as contrary to the

[74] Details of the truce reluctantly entered into by the angry king are given in *Knighton*, pp. 19–22. For the king's actions on his return see particularly *French Chronicle*, pp. 83–9; *Avesbury*, pp. 323–4; *Birchington*, pp. 20–1; *Foedera* 2, iv, p. 87; and for comment: Tout, *Chapters* 3, pp. 121–2; Fryde, 'Edward III's Removal of His Ministers'.

[75] Win.R.O. 1, fos. 99^{v}–100^{r}. Copies are in *Hemingburgh*, pp. 375–80; *Walsingham*, pp. 237–40. In the Winchester register the archbishop's mandate to the dean of the province is dated Canterbury 31 December 1340, Ralph Stratford's mandate to Orleton incorporating both it and the articles of excommunication Orsett 3 January 1341. Orleton certified the archbishop of his action from Farnham, 6 March.

[76] *Hemingburgh*, pp. 363–7; *Walsingham*, pp. 231–4; *Avesbury*, pp. 324–7 (original French).

[77] *Birchington*, p. 32; *Foedera* 2, iv, p. 89. Lapsley ('Stratford and the Parliamentary Crisis', p. 15) was unaware of the date of Stratford's mandate forbidding his suffragans to collect the ninth illegally. He suggested that it was 'sometime before 26 January'. In fact it was dated three days *after* the safe-conduct. See n. 79.

recently granted charter and to Magna Carta itself.[78] This letter was followed up with a mandate to his provincial bishops forbidding collection of the ninth from those assessed to the tenth and instructing them to suspend collection of the latter if need be. A report on the action taken was to be returned by 1 May.[79] The archbishop rounded off his measures with a forcibly-worded mandate directed against lay encroachment and the dishonour done to ecclesiastical persons.[80]

This determined, not to say provocative attitude, was embarrassing for the king; in particular it damaged his capacity for resuming the war and tarnished his image abroad. Ever since Edward's return various charges against the archbishop had been bandied about viva voce. Stratford expressed willingness to answer them, but only in parliament. This the king could not allow; the archbishop would be able to count on allies in his opposition to arbitrary taxation. Edward countered by publishing the notorious *Libellus*, and when the archbishop replied at length and with measured argument, he followed it up with a rejoinder.[81]

The faces behind the anti-Stratford manoeuvres are to some extent discernible. Until recently the king's military and diplomatic preparations had been principally in the hands of a caucus of four: Bishop Burghersh, William de Montacute, earl of Salisbury, William Kilsby and Sir Geoffrey le Scrope.[82] The death

78 *Hemingburgh*, pp. 367–9; *Walsingham*, pp. 234–5. It is dated 28 January 1341.

79 Printed *Concilia* 2, pp. 659–60 (29 January 1341) from *Exeter Reg. Grandisson*. The copy in *Hemingburgh* (pp. 371–5) is undated. The Winchester scribe entered the mandate and Orleton's certification (29 April 1341) as follows: 'Nos vero qui parati sumus ex officii debito exacciones illicitas ab ecclesiasticis seu ecclesiasticis personis nobis subditis cohibere, nullos invenimus exactores in nostra diocesi culpabiles in premissis.' However, a writ of 10 February declared that Orleton under penalty of excommunication had inhibited many religious from paying the ninth and other persons from collecting it, to the king's 'preiudicium et dampnum gravissimum'. He was forbidden to fulminate any such sentences, but Edward conceded that those paying the ninth should not pay the tenth also. To what extent this writ is based on specific information from Orleton's diocese is uncertain. A further writ of 20 March authorised the diocesan to recover the sums owing for the cardinals' procurations from the collectors of the tenth. Win.R.O. 1, fos. 100^v–101^r (the folios are not now contiguous), 171^v (*al.* 43^v)–172^r (*al.* 44^r).

80 Dated 30 January from Canterbury: Win.R.O. 1, fo. 100^v; *Concilia* 2, p. 660, from *Exeter Reg. Grandisson*.

81 *Birchington*, p. 32. The *Libellus famosus* is discussed below. Stratford's lengthy *excusaciones* are printed in *Concilia* 2, pp. 663–9; *Birchington*, pp. 27–36. They are not in Orleton's register. For the king's rejoinder of 31 March see *Concilia* 2, pp. 674–5, and *Birchington*, pp. 36–8; also Win.R.O. 1, fo. 173^v (*al.* 45^v).

82 Tout, *Chapters* 3, p. 99, calls this 'a select inner council'.

abroad during December 1340 of both Burghersh and Scrope deprived the king of trusted and experienced advisors at a critical juncture.[83] Kilsby, an unsuccessful candidate for the archbishopric of York on Melton's death, was a younger man and among the chosen few who accompanied the king in his sudden return from the continent.[84] It would be easy, though almost certainly erroneous, to jump to the conclusion that at this point Edward turned to Orleton as a man of great experience – an elder statesman politically at variance with Stratford – and entrusted him with the task of committing the royal case against the archbishop to a formal document. Such a conclusion has commonly been adopted, but needs re-examination in the light of the meagre evidence available.

Birchington's view is that during the parliament of April 1341 Orleton was one of Edward III's confidants.[85] Could he also have been responsible for the *Libellus famosus*, as Stratford dubbed it, composed over two months previously? Both Avesbury and Birchington suggest that he was. The former indicts Orleton on the basis of common report ('prout dicebatur a pluribus'), adding that he had always been antagonistic to the archbishop.[86] Birchington tells the story of Orleton's encountering Stratford during the parliament of 1341 and taking the opportunity to deny authorship of the *Libellus*. This the chronicler takes to be an indication of guilt, on the principle *qui s'excuse s'accuse*.[87] Now the earliest

83 *Ibid.* pp. 123–4. But *Birchington* (p. 21) does not say, as Tout thought, that they both died on 2 December. That is given as the date of Scrope's death; Burghersh's followed on the Monday of the following week, 4 December. *Le Neve* 1, p. 1, following Murimuth, gives the month only.

84 Tout, *Chapters* 3, p. 120. Tout describes (*ibid.* pp. 117–18) how Edward maintained Kilsby's candidature against the canonical election of William Zouche by the York chapter. For the king's return see *Foedera* 2, iv, p. 87.

85 The chief chronicle authority is of course, Birchington, who mentions Orleton only on 27 and 28 April (*op. cit.* pp. 39–40). His account forms the basis of Wilkinson's close analysis, 'Protest of the Earls' (cf. McKisack, *Fourteenth Century*, p. 176, n. 2). The *French Chronicle* (p. 90) has no mention of Orleton; Kilsby is the prime mover. See also *Lit. Cant.* 2, p. 229. Kilsby's position is emphasised by the fact that after the affair had blown over a deputation from the king went to Otford to urge Stratford to receive him back into favour. They embraced and the whole company sat down amicably to dinner. *Winchester Chartulary*, pp. 219–20, nos. 517–18.

86 *Avesbury*, p. 330.

87 The chronicler's phrase is 'Sed se excusavit ore tenus', which Lapsley aptly renders 'Qui s'excuse s'accuse' ('Stratford and the Parliamentary Crisis', p. 194, n. 79). This rendering is adopted by Usher as a pointer to the truth ('Career of a Political

copy of the *Libellus* is dated 10 February and one assumes that its form and content were the topic of much prior discussion.[88] By looking at Orleton's itinerary we find that he was at Farnham until the first week of January, and seemingly at Esher for the remainder of that month and the first few days of February.[89] Esher is admittedly near London, but by no means so convenient for contact with the king's council as the episcopal house at Southwark. Orleton's itinerary is defective at this crucial point, so we cannot say that he did *not* set out for London on 4 February, but it is equally possible that he returned to Farnham, where he is to be found both on 19 and 21 February and at the beginning of March.[90] In any case the time factor seems to preclude his having given other than general advice on the drafting of the document. That he composed it is improbable.[91]

Another factor militating against Orleton's authorship needs to be considered. In the *Libellus* are a number of scurrilous phrases, which some have regarded as consistent with the bishop's supposedly vicious and vindictive character.[92] It so happens that Orleton has left several examples of contentious correspondence in none of which is there any trace of the sort of scurrility to be found in the *Libellus*. Orleton's manner of argument can best be studied in the *Responsiones*, which speak for themselves.[93]

Bishop', p. 46) and serves to show how mud can be made to stick. Neither writer pauses to test the insinuation against the bias of its originator.

88 *Avesbury*, pp. 330–6 (10 February 1341: addressed to the dean and chapter of St Paul's); *Hemingburgh*, pp. 380–8, and *Foedera* 2, iv, pp. 90–1 (12 February: to the bishop of London); *Birchington*, pp. 23–7 (12 February: to the prior and convent of Canterbury). The copy sent to Orleton (10 February) is in Win.R.O. 1, fos. 172^{r} (*al.* 44^{r})–173^{r} (*al.* 45^{r}), with the rubric 'Mandatum regium contra archiepiscopum Cantuar' '.

89 E.g. Win.R.O. 2, fos. 34^{r}, 35^{v}, 86^{v}, 87^{r}. There are some lengthy gaps between the individual dates. The first volume of the register is defective at this point.

90 *Ibid.* 1, fos. 87^{v}, 98^{v}, 99^{r}, 102^{r}. There is little doubt that Orleton was at Farnham for the whole period 19 February–6 April. He could have been there both slightly earlier and slightly later.

91 This is in agreement with Tout, *Chapters* 3, p. 128, n. 1, who makes the practical point: 'It is unlikely that an aged bishop, whose political course was run and who was becoming blind, would have gratuitously taken up the duties of a chancery clerk.'

92 For instance, McKisack, *Fourteenth Century*, p. 171, writes: 'Orleton of Winchester denied responsibility for the *libellus*, but its abusive tone suggests either he or Kilsby was probably the author.'

93 Apart from these we have Orleton's reply to the dean and chapter of Wells rejecting their claim for first-fruits from his nephew's prebend of Yatton (app. 2 a. below) and his response to Archbishop Stratford's suggestion for a compromise following

There is a further point of interest in this connection. Stratford's letter with instructions to publish his arguments in contradiction of the *Libellus* was received by Orleton on 22 March. It was copied into the Winchester register with a note of the diocesan's reply: he had not published anything in derogation of the archbishop's reputation.[94] We may never know whether he was speaking the truth.

From what has been said above it looks as though Orleton may not have been summoned to the king's assistance until the opening of parliament on 17 April 1341, possibly even later than that. Once again the register is not very helpful about the bishop's movements. He was at Farnham on 6 April and his presence in London is not recorded until 27 April. Thereafter he seems to have remained at the seat of government until the last week of May: on the 31st he was at Esher.[95]

Birchington provides a day-to-day account of Stratford's attempts to secure a hearing in parliament. The first mention of Orleton is once again on 27 April when in conjunction with Chancellor Bourchier and John Darcy he approached Stratford on the king's behalf, urging him to obey and humble himself before Edward, so that he could be received back into favour. It was at this meeting that Orleton denied responsibility for the *Libellus*, the archbishop not deigning to reply.[96] On the following day the archbishop, bishops and peers of the realm were in the Painted Chamber, but when Stratford came to talk of peace the king withdrew.[97] It was during this discussion, Birchington informs us, that Orleton, whom he describes as blind and a lover of discord,[98] was caught out in a falsehood in that he imputed to Stratford the fabrication of an oath of homage to the king of

the latter's (allegedly illegal) appointment of the prior of Twynham (Win.R.O. 1, fo. 94^{v}), as well as numerous documents concerning his dispute with the archdeacon of Surrey. The letter in *H.R.O.* (pp. 29–30) about Gilbert de Sedgeford is fairly strongly expressed.

94 It is dated Canterbury 10 March 1341, and apparently accompanied a copy of the *excusaciones*. Win.R.O. 1, fo. 102^{r-v}. A truncated copy from Bath & Wells Reg. Ralph of Shrewsbury is in *Concilia* 2, pp. 670–1. Orleton replied: 'Super quibus scire dignetur vestra paternitas quod nichil est in vestrum opprobrium per nos vel per alios auctoritate nostra hactenus publicatum' (3 May, Westminster).

95 Win.R.O. 1, fos. 99^{r}, 101^{r}, 102^{v}, 103^{v}, 104^{r-v}; 2, fos. 33^{r}, 88^{v}. There appears to be no entry dated between 6 and 27 April.

96 *Birchington*, p. 39.

97 *Ibid*. p. 40: 'Ubi tractatu pacis habito ab eodem archiepiscopo rex Anglie se retraxit.'

98 *Ibid*.: 'Caecus tanquam amator discordie'.

France without proper consultation; in fact he could not have remembered any such thing, being absent in France at the time.[99] It so happens that this statement can to some extent be tested. It refers to the events of 1331, when Edward III (as a minor) did liege homage for Gascony and other French lands, a move which came to be regarded by some as prejudicial to his claim to the throne of France.[100] The precise nature of the rebuttal seems to hinge on the assertion that Orleton could not *in person* have overheard Stratford at the time of the oath's formulation. In that limited sense it could be true, though the case is not quite watertight. The facts are that Orleton's embassy lasted until 25 March 1331, when he reported back to the council at Westminster.[101] He was therefore in England some days before the publication of the text of the oath and well over a week before the king's party sailed from Dover on 4 April.[102] Stratford, who was chancellor at the time, must have been in consultation with the returning ambassador prior to his own departure. Even if Orleton cannot be shown to have been present when the oath was being devised, he certainly arrived on the scene shortly afterwards, when he would surely have learned precisely how its wording had been arrived at, if not from Stratford himself then from some other councillor closely concerned. This incident possibly provides a more reliable clue to the reason for Orleton's involvement than the notion of a long-nurtured grudge. This is not to deny the likelihood that when the two men came face to face old rancours leapt once more to the surface. In this context a less cynical interpretation of Orleton's denial of responsibility for the *Libellus* would be that it was intended as a conciliatory gesture. We have already found reason to suggest that it may also have been a truthful statement.

Birchington makes no further reference to Orleton. He was not one of the four bishops – the episcopal element in a committee of twelve peers chosen to ' advise the king ' about the articles against Stratford – nor among the ten bishops who on 3 May stood with

99 *Ibid.*: ' De falsitate per pares praedictos convictus fuit super eo, quod falso imponebatur dicto archiepiscopo; quod ipse, dum erat regis consiliarius quandam declaracionem homagii regis Angliae faciendam regi Franciae ex capite suo absque consultu fecisse debebat, quod idem Wynton' nichil scivit de tractatu aliquo nec recoluit; quia tunc fuit nuncius regis . . .'

100 *C.P.L.* 1305–42, p. 587, contains the official rejection of this view.

101 See above, ' In Edward II's service ', ch. 2.

102 *Foedera* 2, iii, pp. 61–2.

Stratford when he asked to be received into the king's grace.[103] Orleton's meteoric reappearance on the political scene was over, it could well be that the part he played in this episode was much less important than we have been led to believe.

The Stratford affair constitutes a striking parallel to Orleton's own experience in the previous reign. There was the accusation by an angry king, later magnified into a charge of treason; the sentence of excommunication which the monarch chose to interpret as a personal affront; and a dramatic appearance in parliament. Of course the differences are equally remarkable. Orleton would not admit the right of a secular court to judge him even on the lesser charge of trespass. When treason was broached both men took the same stand, but in Stratford's case the accusation was quietly shelved. The archbishop, who for much of his life was a devotee of St Thomas Becket,[104] may have acted the martyr from time to time; Orleton exhibited no such proclivity, but was none the less of the opinion that he had been grievously wronged. Both stood firm in defence of ecclesiastical liberty, Stratford being forced eventually to compromise. The sequel in Orleton's case was vastly different; Stratford, although his independence in ecclesiastical matters continued to provide a source of friction, recovered a measure of influence in Edward III's counsels.[105]

When everything possible has been said by way of mitigation or explanation Orleton's behaviour in 1341 remains somewhat of an enigma. Whatever his intention, it looks very much as though his opposition to Stratford served to compromise his elevated view of the episcopal dignity as well as to undermine his earlier stand against unlawful taxation. It could be, however, that Orleton considered both the war and the concomitant taxation to have been the consequence of Stratford's policies. He certainly allowed Edward to make use of him and it was this that prompted the chroniclers to charge him with spiteful hostility.

103 *Birchington*, p. 40; Wilkinson, 'Protest of the Earls', pp. 188–9.

104 For his foundation of a chantry in honour of St Thomas in 1331 and its subsequent enlargement see *Worc. Admin.*, pp. 233, 242–4. It was in the parish church (Holy Trinity) of his native Stratford.

105 For his later career see *Biog. Oxon.*, *s.v.*; Fryde, 'Edward III's Removal of His Ministers', p. 161; Bolton, 'Council of London'.

Chapter 5

SUMMING UP

Bishop Stubbs entertained few doubts about Adam Orleton: during Edward II's reign he figures as 'the confidential agent of Mortimer and the guiding spirit of the Queen's party'.[1] In fact for Stubbs the dramatis personae of Edward's decline and fall are singularly uncomplicated: Ayrminne he dubs 'the Queen's creature', Orleton 'Mortimer's confidant'; both are condemned as 'lacking such slender justification as might be furnished by the fears of Stratford or the vindictiveness of Burghersh'.[2] It was to Orleton, he writes, that 'the guilt of complicity with the king's murder was popularly attached'; to which statement he grudgingly adds: 'in so dark and cruel a transaction his own firm and persistent denial must be allowed to qualify the not unnatural suspicion'.[3] The revolution over, Stubbs envisages Orleton as one who 'quitted the field of secular preferment and devoted himself to the attainment of ecclesiastical promotion'.[4]

T. F. Tout was at least as outspoken. According to his analysis of John XXII's appointments to the English episcopate only one bishop, Thomas de Cobham, 'represented a high spiritual type'; his colleagues comprised 'scandalous self-seekers of the official type such as Adam Orleton, John Stratford and William Ayrmyn'.[5] In Tout's opinion Canon Bannister 'makes the best case he can for Orleton's character, but he is more successful in demonstrating his ability than his morality'.[6] There is some force in this observation, for although Bannister rightly dismisses the vituperative inventions of Baker's narrative, he paradoxically rests his case on what he considers a realistic appraisal of the times:

1 Stubbs, *Constitutional History* 2, p. 361.
2 *Ibid*. p. 367. Stratford is dubbed 'somewhat of a statesman'.
3 *Loc. cit*.
4 *Ibid*. p. 384.
5 Tout rev. Johnstone, *Place of the Reign of Edward II*, p. 209.
6 *Ibid*. p. 20. He remarks that Orleton and Stratford were scholars of repute.

Orleton, he remarks, was no ' ideal saint '.[7] But Bannister's apologia includes the incongruous adoption as fact of what were for him the more acceptable of Baker's assertions, and in this way he permits himself to be misled by the very propaganda he condemns elsewhere. In consequence he depicts Orleton as busily directing an underground resistance movement by fomenting the queen's hatred of her husband,[8] planning Mortimer's escape and organising a group opposed to Edward II.[9] The available facts do not sustain such an interpretation. Notwithstanding Orleton's substantial grievances and the king's hostility, amounting to persecution, only Baker and unsupported conjecture point to his connivance at a change of government in anticipation of Isabella's return. Of his latent sympathy for those who suffered there can be no doubt; it is amply demonstrated by the promptitude with which he made common cause with the returning exiles.

There has been a natural tendency to applaud the fidelity of those who initially remained loyal to the king, and rightly so; but something has also to be said on the other side. Granted it was a serious matter to break the episcopal oath of fealty, but against this must be set the ruinous course that Edward had long pursued in defiance of episcopal efforts to avert conflict, and his subsequent harassment of those bishops who showed signs of ' intransigence '. It is less than just to contend that ' the queen's bishops ', as they have been misleadingly styled, were motivated purely by self-interest. As for Orleton himself, his decision to join the queen came when the success of her enterprise was still in doubt: unlike Stratford he had the courage of his convictions.

Various factors have contributed to the disapprobation surrounding those who supported the revolution. Among them may be counted the pitiable condition of the king at Kenilworth when faced with deposition and the revulsion to which his subsequent fate gave rise. As for Isabella, her triumph was associated with the vengeful destruction of personal enemies, and even if these were few and unpopular, the manner of their dying left an unpleasant memory. Worse still, the ' reign ' of Isabella and

7 *H.R.O.*, pp. xxxiii, li.

8 *H.R.O.*, pp. xxxii–xxxiii.

9 *H.R.O.*, p. xxix. Bannister erroneously conjectured that Blaneforde was likening Orleton to the angel who assisted St Peter to escape.

Mortimer, as at least one chronicler described it,[10] went a long way towards revivifying the evils for which Edward II and his chief councillors had been condemned. Only by a hair's-breadth was a repetition of Boroughbridge avoided. Even under Edward III's personal rule there was some danger of sliding back into the old ways and alienating the 'people', as Stratford was bold enough to point out.[11] The rancours of Edward II's unhappy reign outlived him by many years; they were to pursue Orleton to the grave.

Of course Orleton was able and ambitious. The more debatable point is whether his ambition overstepped the accepted canons of behaviour in furtherance of personal interests. There are some who would say that it did. After all, it was in opposition to the government of the day that he secured all three of his bishoprics, taking full advantage, we are led to believe, of his diplomatic position – as both Ayrminne and Stratford are likewise said to have done. But there were legitimate differences of opinion as to the unrestricted nature of the king's right to choose bishops, and there is more to Orleton's promotion than successful opportunism. Pope John XXII marked him out for advancement at an early stage; had he not continued to be impressed by Orleton's quality and reliability no amount of curial manipulation would have prevailed. Yet, even allowing for Orleton's confidence of papal support, it may be too much to jump to the conclusion that in 1327 he was able to calculate with any precision his short-term, let alone his ultimate, chances of promotion. The suggestion smacks of being wise after the event.

This fact of papal patronage does point to a loyalty which has not been given sufficient consideration in analyses of Orleton's motivation. Not only did he express gratitude for his initial promotion at John XXII's wish, he also reaped substantial benefits from successful petitions for himself and his *familia* and consistent support when he fell foul of the home government. When Itier de Concoreto, the papal nuncio, was in danger of maltreatment he was quick to give aid.[12] As a canonist he held a high opinion

[10] B.L. Cotton MS. Faustina B. V, fo. 51v: the earls of Kent and Lancaster are said to have consorted 'contra reginam et Rogerum de Mortuo Mari regnantes'. *Cf. ibid.* fo. 50v and *Melsa* 2, p. 360.

[11] *Birchington*, p. 32.

[12] *Thorne*, col. 2043.

of papal jurisdiction and clerical immunity basing his own defence in 1324 on these twin principles. Nor need it be assumed that he conveniently jettisoned them in Baldock's case, or even in that of Stratford: Birchington does not associate Orleton with the murmurings of treason. None the less, in this latter instance he did to some extent compromise his concept of episcopal immunity and there is an inconsistency in his response to Edward III's summons for help. By opposing Stratford he indirectly furthered the cause of war. Peace was what he had ostensibly sought and it was war which engendered the illegal taxation to which he vigorously objected.

Loyalty to the papacy is probably more fundamental to an understanding of Orleton's career than loyalty to Mortimer, but whatever the relative emphasis given to these two loyalties, it is unrealistic to isolate a single operative principle as explanatory of Orleton's conduct over a working life of some fifty years, especially in view of the volatile character of politics at this time. It is perhaps more useful to consider his career in its successive stages.

It was as bishop that Orleton first came to have a significant impact on internal political decisions. Between 1317, when he assumed the see of Hereford, and 1321, the outbreak of the baronial revolt, there is no reason to believe that he was other than wholeheartedly in favour of the moderating policy of his politically-active colleagues, with whom he made common cause whenever his diplomatic obligations permitted. His 'adherence' to Roger Mortimer the nephew in the winter of 1321, though by no means proven, could have come about for a variety of reasons. First among them would be his long association with the diocese of Hereford, in which the Mortimers were the predominant lay lords. Orleton was a man of independent mind, but he might have gravitated towards the Mortimers partly in response to strong and widespread local feeling, and partly as a reaction against the king's decision to recall the Despensers in defiance of 'moderate opinion': a decision which ended episcopal mediation, a policy successful in staving off armed conflict even if it did nothing to remove underlying differences.

There is another possibility. As the indictments presented before Hervy de Staunton show, the younger Mortimer was quite unscrupulous in persuading men to join him by threat or force.

He may even have determined to compromise a bishop known to be exasperated by the king's abandonment of clerical advice. In view of the disturbed state of the west-midland shires the fact that members of Orleton's household joined the insurgents, and that others on good terms with him did the same, is hardly proof of treasonable intention on his part. Loyalties were divided. Even Richard Irby, apparently the same man who attacked Orleton's manors of Ross and Upton, was convicted of supporting Mortimer and Sir Roger Damory.[13]

Whether in fact Orleton showed more than 'sympathy' with Mortimer must be left to individual interpretation of the evidence. The manner in which the king proceeded against the bishop argues that his case was a weak one, and that Edward was motivated by a degree of aversion amounting to malignity. One thing that cannot reasonably be alleged against the bishop is that he calculated on personal gain from the Mortimer connection. Only a prophet of extraordinary perception could in 1321 have foreseen the strange concatenation of events which was to bring the younger Mortimer to power at the end of 1326. Even then, Orleton received little more than restitution of his temporalities, some few grants of land and goods to offset prodigious losses and the expenses of further diplomacy, and, for a short while, the office of treasurer. In the interval of some four and a half years he subsisted at the whim of a persistently hostile government. Deprived of the king's favour, and from 1324 of the temporalities of his see, he faced a bleak future.

Notwithstanding the contrary arguments that have been advanced, it would be rash to reject out of hand the possibility that during this time of political isolation Orleton was doing nothing more than biding his time in anticipation of some favourable turn of events. It was comparatively easy to ferry letters to and fro across the channel, despite government vigilance;[14] Mortimer's escape and the conspiracy to seize royal castles[15] demonstrate what could be achieved by a handful of resolute men. The country was rife with disaffection and rumour. It must be

13 Just. 1/1388/m. 10v.

14 See, for instance, *Foedera* 2, ii, pp. 163ff; *Lit. Cant.* 1, pp. 172–4, 181.

15 In 1323 enquiries were being made into the conspiracy to seize the Tower, Wallingford, Windsor and other royal castles. E.g. *C.P.R.* 1321–24, pp. 234, 257, 314, 349. For the temporary capture of Wallingford see *Vita*, pp. 129–31

reiterated, however, that the only suggestion of this kind involving Orleton comes from Baker. To John XXII the bishop was expatiating on his injustices and the wrongs done to his see, and at the pope's instigation making attempts at accommodation with the king.[16] If Cobham's interpretation is accurate, Edward II's intention was to terrorise the bishop into inactivity,[17] but there is no proof that he contemplated conspiracy.

Once Isabella had landed in England, Orleton was ready enough to endanger his life for what may have been far more than the amelioration of his own condition – the belief that nothing other than Edward II's removal would bring peace and order to the realm. This, of course, entailed close association with the queen: an association which involved a degree of responsibility for what has been characterised as the viciousness of her actions and the depravity of her conduct towards her husband. This was particularly the case in that he acted as spokesman on a number of occasions. Having said all this, it needs to be remembered that there was no other alternative to Edward's misrule.

The revolution accomplished, Orleton did not follow the path of an ambitious power-seeker. On the contrary, he left the Mortimer and Lancaster factions to engage in a struggle for mastery and his friend and colleague Burghersh to occupy the chancellorship. We can only surmise what was in his mind at this juncture, but it is far from satisfactory to posit ambitious self-interest to fill the vacuum. Admittedly the bishopric of Worcester would shortly fall vacant, but was that a more desirable prospect for an ambitious man than maintaining a position in the government at home? Once the opportunity of moving to Worcester presented itself, Orleton was hardly to blame for welcoming it as a means of leaving behind old enmities at Hereford and the likelihood of further troubles there. Estrangement from the court followed;

[16] Cotton MS. Vitellius E. IV 9: *Vita*, pp. 136–7; *C.P.L.* 1305–42, p. 427.

[17] *Worcester Reg. Cobham*, p. 169: 'Set spero hoc pocius ad terrorem fieri quam penam.' This remark of Cobham's is difficult to interpret. It could mean that he thought Edward wished to deprive Orleton of the capacity to act against him, but (he hoped) it was not for anything he had done already. For the context see above, 'Years in the wilderness', ch. 4. Prior Eastry's comment on the withholding of the temporalities of Winchester, Lincoln, Hereford and Llandaff is picturesque. He writes: 'In suis diocesibus seminant atque metunt, sed manus ad aratrum temporalium non apponunt.' (*Lit. Cant.* 1, p. 165, where it is dated 1325 by the editor, though 1324 seems preferable.)

perhaps Orleton never recovered his influence, since after 1328 evidence for his co-operation with the government of Mortimer and Isabella is extremely meagre.

The rest is aftermath. Like Burghersh and of course Stratford, Orleton survived the fall of Mortimer almost unscathed. Here it is worth remarking that Baker's charges against Orleton recapitulate some of those levelled against Mortimer, but once the appeal against his translation to Winchester had failed they were no longer relevant. No further purpose could be served by discrediting an old and worn-out campaigner.

Orleton's character and motives are likely to remain obscure, yet with the rejection of manifest propaganda and prejudice it should be possible to see the man in truer perspective. The figure is not that depicted either by Baker or by Stubbs; the lines must be more carefully drawn. It was no virulent monster who could remit a sentence on the grounds that it was Christmastide, the season when Christ himself came into the world to save sinners;[18] who faced with a case of adultery commuted the public penance to one less severe, recalling as he did so Christ's action in similar circumstances;[19] or who requested of the royal chancellor that a writ of attachment should not be executed on account of the age and debility of the man concerned.[20] It was Orleton, too, who dedicated the cemetery at Allensmore for the burial of the poor and of children to save the expense of the journey to Hereford.[21]

Orleton was on excellent terms with the Hereford chapter. On his promotion to Worcester he was at the canons' request given papal permission to retain the tithes of Shinfield, originally granted for the duration of his tenure of the see of Hereford. Nine years afterwards, in 1329, as a concession to the urgent needs of the cathedral fabric, Orleton agreed to pay £40 a year for the church, double the original amount. Clearly he was no grasping man.[22]

18 Win.R.O. 1, fos. 29v–29*r.
19 Win.R.O. 1, fo. 2v.
20 S.C.1/39/162. The man referred to is John de Scures, described as a friend who was old (approaching eighty years) and feeble. The name is the same as that of the sheriff of Hampshire in 1334, at the time of the appeal against Orleton.
21 *H.R.O.*, pp. 66–7; *Hereford Reg. Trillek*, pp. iv–v, 105–6.
22 *C.P.L.* 1305–42, p. 280; *Lettres communes Jean XXII*, no. 30267; *Hereford Cathedral Charters*, pp. 207–8, 209–10 (H.C.M., nos. 2269, 1375).

Not surprisingly it is possible to find less favourable indications. For instance, the papal decision in the case of certain lordships formerly belonging to Philip de Middleton argues that Orleton, Bishop Charlton, his successor at Hereford, and the prior of Snead acted high-handedly and with a measure of injustice. However, we know only one side of the case because Charlton's proctor died and it went undefended.[23]

Orleton was a capable lawyer; the quality of judicious argument revealed by many of his letters is in direct contradiction to the impression of scurrility and spitefulness derived from certain chroniclers. The *Responsiones* are dignified and objective in tone, as competently presented as the much-admired *Excusaciones* of Archbishop Stratford, but far more succinct.

It is not easy to strike a balance. Orleton has been denigrated by men of opposing factions,[24] but one ought not on that account to lean too far in the other direction. He was without doubt a painstaking and competent diocesan when duties of state allowed; a forceful man who made life-long friendships and fervent enemies. Among his friends may be numbered the members of an exceptionally stable *familia*, whose interests he had at heart, Gilbert de Middleton, official of the Court of Canterbury, Bishops Burghersh and Cobham, William de Edington, his protégé and successor as Winchester diocesan, Pope John XXII and possibly the younger Mortimer.[25] His enemies were equally diverse: Edward II, William Irby, the vexatious prior of Hereford, Archdeacon Inge, a constant thorn in his flesh at Winchester,[26] and, every now and then, Stratford. Scholars, such as Cobham and Laurence Bruton, he met on equal terms.

The times were rough: Orleton experienced physical assault or the threat of it on several occasions, and in 1324 the possibility

[23] *Hereford Reg. Trillek*, pp. i, 67–75.

[24] The precise make-up of these at any particular time is hard to determine, but after 1327 Mortimer and Lancaster groupings drew apart. Orleton, however, was in 1334 being blamed 'retrospectively', not because he was active in politics at the time.

[25] Such evidence as there is cannot be said to demonstrate strong friendship between Mortimer and Orleton. The bishop was certainly close to the baron in some respects, but that is another matter.

[26] The Inge dispute also brought Orleton into conflict with Stratford, from whose jurisdiction the bishop appealed to the Curia. Edward III complained to the pope and cardinals on Stratford's behalf, extolling the principle that such matters should be settled in England. *Concilia* 2, pp. 584–5; *Foedera* 2, iii, pp. 166–7.

of death. Whatever his faults as politician or prelate he was a man of courage, who recognised tyranny when he saw it and was not afraid to stand up and be counted. In the process of political revolution objectionable things were done; it is these that have irreparably damaged Orleton's image.

Appendix 1

WORCESTER DIOCESE: TABLES ILLUSTRATING ORLETON'S ADMINISTRATION

a. Absence for study from parochial benefices 1302–1349

Diocesan	Years [a]	No. of licences and yearly average	Years involved and yearly average	Benefices affected
Gainsburgh	3⅔	85 (23.2)	166 (45.2)	59
Reynolds	5	79 (15.8)	149 (29.8)	54
Cobham	9	156 (17.4)	226 (25.1)	93
Orleton	4½ +	55 (11.5)	110 (24.4)	47
Montacute	3	54 (18.0)	92 (30.7)	41
Bransford	9	43 (4.7)	62 (6.8)	39

[a] To avoid aberrations the 'years' do not refer to complete episcopates but to periods of more or less 'normal' recording, as follows: Gainsburgh, 13 Oct. 1303–28 June 1307; Reynolds, 6 Nov. 1308–9 Oct. 1313; Cobham, 25 Nov. 1317–20 Sept. 1326; Orleton, 29 Feb. 1328–11 Oct. 1332; Montacute, 19 May 1334–29 April 1337; Bransford, 30 March 1339–30 March 1348.

b. Dispensations for absence from parochial benefices 1328–January 1334 [a]

Purpose	No. of licences	Approx. no. of years involved
Study [b]	56	117
Absence	11 [c]	18 +
Attendance	26 [d]	23½ +
Farm	4 [e]	14
Total	97	172½

[a] There are no licences for 1333 and only two for 1334. The earliest licence is dated 29 February 1328, the latest 30 January 1334, by which time Orleton had been translated to Winchester.

[b] The figures are higher than in the previous table because of a single seven-year licence for January 1334.

[c] One with no stated term.

[d] Eleven for an indefinite term; one from 1334.

[e] In addition, three of the licences for study and two of those for absence specifically permitted farming.

c. Exchanges of benefices 1328–1332 [a]

Year	Within diocese	Outside diocese	Total exchanges	Institutions involved	Total institutions [b]
1328	1	7	8	9	36
1329	2	8	10	12	34
1330	2	0	2	4	23
1331	2	6	8	9	34
1332	5	6	11	16	37
Totals	12	27	39	50	164

[a] Recorded processes of exchange for the whole of Orleton's episcopate total forty-seven, of which two are known to have been abortive. Of the remaining forty-five, three involved an exchange of prebends and one, that of Gloucester archdeaconry, for a cathedral dignity. These are omitted from the table. The other two exchanges date from 1334 – which leaves thirty-nine. Only two chantries were exchanged for parochial benefices.

[b] Including chantries – to which there are eleven institutions (and one more in 1334) – but excluding prebends and archdeaconries.

Appendix 2

LETTERS AND DOCUMENTS

a. *Correspondence about the Trillek prebend in Wells cathedral*

W.R.O. 2, fos. 17^v–18^r

Undated

The dean and chapter of Wells request Bishop Orleton's aid in securing the first-fruits allegedly due from his nephew, Thomas Trillek, prebendary of Yatton.

WELL'

Venerabili patri in Christo domino Ade dei gracia Wygorn' episcopo, sui humiles et devoti . . decanus et capitulum ecclesie Well' honorem cum reverencia debita tanto patri. Reverende paternitati vestre ius et consuetudo ecclesie nostre Wellen' nos excitant et inducunt. Est enim in ea reverende pater obtentum et hactenus observatum quod prebendarum quarumcumque dicte ecclesie nostre vacancium capitulum percipiat primos fructus ac prebenda de Iacton nuper vacante, in qua discretus vir et valens dominus Thomas de Trillek nepos vester prebendarius nunc existit, escaetori nostro taxacionem eiusdem iuxta constitucionem in ea parte editam acceptanti, sibique super ea satisfieri a ministris dicti prebendarii pluries postulanti est expressius denegatum. Super quo reverende paternitati vestre insistimus prece nostra ut placeat vobis ministris et ballivis dicti prebendarii litteratorie precipere ad effectum ut super dicta taxacione que summam continet xxx li. escaetori nostro nostri et ecclesie nostre nomine satisfaciant ut est iuris. Hinc supplicacioni nostre reverende pater velitis condescendere. Advertentes quod ad iura consuetudines et statuta predicte ecclesie nostre observanda sumus astricti sicut et predictus dominus Thomas confrater noster et concanonicus vinculo iuramenti. Super hiis placeat digne dominacioni vestre domino H. de Folham confratri et concanonico nostro [1] presencium portitori exponere et nobis rescribere velle vestrum.

24 January [1330]

Orleton's reply to the above letter

RESPONSIO

Venerabilibus et discretis viris amicis nostris in Christo karissimis dominis . . decano et capitulo ecclesie Well', Adam permissione divina ecclesie

[1] There is no canon of this name in *Le Neve* 8.

Wygorn' minister salutem cum augmento continuo celestium graciarum. Licet ad honores et commoda vestra et ecclesie Well' sinceris desideriis anelemus, tamen nepoti nostro prebendario de Iatton in ecclesia vestra nunc causa studiorum in remotis agenti presertim cum ab eo quod iniustum est petitur adesse nos excitat iusticie debitum et nature. Sane a memoria vestra non credimus excidisse qualiter idem nepos noster ad prebendam de Iatton quam nunc obtinet tanquam vacantem per mortem magistri Roberti de Baldok' post multa impedimenta sibi circa execucionem dicte prebende nimis voluntarie per bone memorie venerabilem patrem dominum Johannem tunc Bathon' et Well' episcopum [2] et vos auctoritate apostolica finaliter est admissus, quodque primi fructus eiusdem prebende a tempore vacacionis huiusmodi provenientes ad manus eiusdem patris vel nepotis sui, cui de facto cum de iure non potuit dictam prebendam contulerat, pervenerunt, et [3] vos insuper litteram obligatoriam dicti episcopi super taxacione quam excaetor vester a nepote nostro nunc exigit a nonnullis dicimini recepisse. Et quidem si fructus ab hiis ad quos pervenerunt exegeritis, vel non exigendo tacite remiseritis forsitan vel expresse, bona fides non patitur ut a nepote nostro iterum exigantur. Nec debet secundum apostolum quod uni est remissio alii esse tribulacio sicut noscis.[4] Placeat igitur vestre providencie premissis pensatis per sapienciam vestram nos instruere quid in hac parte ulterius facere debeamus. Parati enim sumus quecumque amabilia iusta et racionabilia fuerint pro vobis exequi cum effectu. Nos vestris gratis affectibus offerentes et spiritualibus suffragiis suppliciter commendantes. In omni prosperitate vos conservet altissimus et semper dirigat ad eterna. Scriptum Lond' xxiiii[a] die Januarii.[5]

b. Orleton requests aid for Oxford University from his diocese

Coventry and Lichfield Reg. Northburgh 3 (B/A/1/3), fo. 102[r]
19 February 1329

Mandate to the clergy of the Worcester diocese as a result of discussion in the Canterbury convocation.

Adam permissione divina Wygorn' episcopus dilectis filiis . . archidiaconis nostre diocesis et eorum . . officialibus salutem graciam et benediccionem. Oxoniensis universitas velud ager fertilis uberes proferens in quo grana sciencie colliguntur producensque viros virtutum varietate fecundos, sciolos magnificans et ignaros efficiens virtuosos quam quilibet provincie Anglicane in sortem domini vocatus tanquam stellam matutinam preceteris refulgentem fervore intime dileccionis tenetur revereri, et eius comodum affectare pro defensione iurium et privilegiorum suorum quibus ab antiquis

[2] Bishop Droxford or Drokensford died 9 May 1329. His nephew (mentioned below) was Richard Droxford.

[3] *Et* interlined.

[4] 2 Cor. 8.13.

[5] For a summary of the dispute over this prebend see *Le Neve* 8, p. 80.

temporibus fuerat insignita laicorum machinacionibus fraudulentis, qui semper clericis opido sunt infesti, in defessis laboribus et expensis adeo fatigatur hiis diebus, quod nisi eidem que super certo aliquo non existit fundata celeriter succurratur, de enervacione eiusdem et iurium suorum quod dolendum est verisimiliter formidatur, sumptusque et expensas quos occasione premissa in dies facere oportebit non poterit aliqualiter sustinere prout in instanti concilio London' celebrato ostensum extitit satis plane. Nos sicut et ceteri confratres ex deliberato consilio ad premissa nostre intencionis oculum eidemque universitati volentes ne subita dispersio eiusdem imineat aut ruina modis et viis quibus poterimus subvenire, vobis et cuilibet vestrum in virtute obediencie firmiter iniungendo mandamus quatinus singuli vestrum sui archidiaconatus . . abbates . . priores necnon eccelesiarum rectores et vicarios omnes et singulos ad aliquos certos diem et locum specialiter convocantes ipsos cum sollicitudine debita ac circumspeccione provida efficaciter inducatis, ut universitati predicte aliquam certam pecunie porcionem de bonis suis ecclesiasticis velint concedere graciose per quam indigencia eiusdem in tanta necessitate ex causis premissis posite quod veraciter intelleximus et vobis amaricato corde referimus non minus quam in aliis diocesibus valeat relevari. Datum London' xi kalen' Marcii anno domini millesimo CCC^{mo} vicesimo octavo.

c. Correspondence with Archbishop Stratford about the appointment of the prior of Twynham

Win.R.O. 1, fo. 94^{v}

12 August [1340]

Stratford, having appointed Robert de Legh on his own authority, suggests a compromise with Orleton as diocesan.

EPISCOPO WYNTON' PRO DICTA PROVISIONE PER ARCHIEPISCOPUM CANT'.

Frater carissime, vestris patentibus litteris atque clausis quas nuper nobis misistis perpendimus evidenter quod de persona ydonea prioratui Christi ecclesie de Twynham vestre diocesis nos hac vice provideri velletis, ac vir discretus magister Johannes de Wolveleye vester cancellarius nobis sub vestra credencia intimavit quod vestre condescenderet voluntati ut fratrem Robertum de Legh' dicto prioratui alias per nos in priorem prefectum, facta resignacione primitus sui status auctoritate vestra, noviter preficeremus eundem et ut secrecius installaretur in brevi. Nos affectantes dictum consummari negocium sine lite ac tute, vobisque consultis ad plenum quid in hac parte facere intendebamus procedere cupientes, vos requirimus et ex corde an vestre conveniat voluntati si de dicto fratre Roberto quem ceteris canonicis dicti prioratus ad ipsius regimen magis ydoneum reputamus, prout multorum instruccionibus informamur, provideamus de huiusmodi prioratu, nobis velitis ad plenum rescribere per harum baiulum in omnibus velle vestrum. Dominus vos conservet ad regimen gregis sui. Scriptum apud Saltwode xii die mensis Augusti.

14 August [1340]

Orleton states that he has no wish to oppose Legh's appointment by the archbishop provided this is done on his authority as diocesan.

RESPONSUM LITTERE IMMEDIATE PRESCRIPTE.

Reverendo [*sic*] pater et domine precarissime, scire dignetur vestra providencia circumspecta quod non est, fuit aut erit intencionis nostre fratrem Robertum de Legh quem ad regimen prioratus Christi ecclesie de Twynham ydoneum reputatis, si auctoritate nostra eidem prioratui per vos prefectus fuerit, reprobare vel quicquam opponere quod vestre provisionis effectum valeat impedire, sed pocius ad confirmacionem optatam huiusmodi negocii quod ad nostrum pertinet officium vestre dominacionis contemplacione eidem impendere volumus cum gracia et favore. Incolumitatem vestram in longa tempora protendat altissimus ad regimen ecclesie sponse sue. Scriptum apud Farnham sub sigillo secreti nostri xiiii die mensis Augusti.

d. William Dene's account of the second [6] *mission to Kenilworth*

B.L. Cotton MS. Faustina B. V, fos. 49^{v}–50^{r} [7]

Hiis itaque peractis missi sunt ad patrem qui fuit rex London' Elien' et Herforden' episcopi duo comites, duo barones, de communitatibus civitatibus et quinque portibus certi nuncii, vice omnium de regno apud Kelyngworth, ubi rex qui fuit in carcere et custodia comitis Lancastrie detentus fuit, ad reddendum sursum homagia, et reddiderunt. Ubi rex, qui fuit genibus provolutis manibus levatis, peciit veniam de commissis, et ut eum vivere sinerent et non occiderent humiliter peciit. Cui Herfordensis penitenti et veniam petenti severum durum et crudelem inrespondendo se ostendit. Homagiis sursum redditis regi in custodia detento, ad parliamentum London' nuncii redierunt. Mox ad coronandum novum regem dies Dominicus in vigilia Purificacionis statuitur.

6 Dene himself does not record an initial mission to the king.

7 This passage is omitted in Wharton's edition between 'cum aliis non consenserunt' and 'Interim Londonienses'. See *Anglia Sacra* 1, p. 367.

Appendix 3

ITINERARY 1317–1345

No finality is claimed for the following itinerary. For the sake of brevity, only the outside dates of Orleton's stay in a particular place during any one month have been given. For the most part the details noted are intended to illustrate the text rather than to provide a full account of the bishop's activities or a complete list of the meetings of parliament or provincial council. References to Orleton's Hereford register are given by folio number, where the printed edition is defective. His Worcester register is cited by the number of the entry in the forthcoming calendar, the Winchester one by volume and folio number.

Date	Place	Details	Reference
1317			
May 22	Avignon	Consecration as bishop of Hereford	*H.R.O.*, xi
June 30	Canterbury	Profession of obedience to archbishop	*Canterbury Professions*, 93
July 2	Lambeth	Livery of spiritualities	*H.R.O.*, 1
9–16	Yeoveney, Middx		4–7
21	Thurlaston-by-Leicester		7
23	Bonnington, Notts.		7–8
23–4	Nottingham	Livery of temporalities (24th)	16
25	Bonnington		8–9
Aug. 8–25	Thame, Oxon.	Consecrates altars	14–22
27	Ashbury, Berks.	Consecrates altars	18
Sept. 2–9	Edington, Wilts.		19–24
17	Evesham		20
18	Sugwas	Enters diocese	29
21–2	Whitbourne		26–7
24–5	Bromyard	Ordination (24th)	17, 27
27–30	Sugwas		28–30
Oct. 2–3	Hereford	Enthronement (2nd)	31–3
4–27	Sugwas	Murimuth appointed general proctor (13th)	31–42
28	Prestbury, Gloucs.		43–4
Nov. 6	London	Attends royal council	43
26	Highbury		H.C.M., 1368
Dec. 1–19	Highbury		*H.R.O.*, 47–54
20	London		54

Jan.	3–12	London		45, 56–7
	20	Awre		fo. 16r
	25	English Bicknor		fo. 16r
	29	Ross		60
Feb.	2–14	Bosbury		59–62
	16	Gloucester		62
	27	London	Convocation, St Paul's	63
March	2–3	London		64
	4	Westminster		64–5
	7	London	In house of dean of St Paul's	69–70
	18	Sugwas		65
	20	Holme Lacy		fo. 18r
	22	Sellack		65
	25	Kilpeck		66
	26–7	Sugwas		fo. 18r; H.C.M., 1378
	27	Allensmore		66–7
	28	Bosbury		67–8
April	12	Leicester	Meeting for settlement with earl of Lancaster	fo. 19v
	26	Monnington-on-Wye		70–1
May	1	Wormsley		71
	7	Bodenham		71–4
	10	Bosbury		74
	14	Port Meadow, Oxford	M. John de Lugwardine presents papal grace for benefice in bishop's gift	75
	18	Highbury		75

Date		Place	Details	Reference
June	1–10	Highbury		*H.R.O.*, 76; H.C.M., 1369
	11	Westminster	Safe-conduct for earl of Lancaster issued	S.C.1/63/183
post	16	Abroad		
July	29	Rue, Ponthieu	Appoints proctors in Curia	*H.R.O.*, 77–8
Aug.	9	Leake	Seals Treaty of Leake	*C.C.R.* 1318–23, 112–14
Oct.	18–20	London	Parliament at York	*H.R.O.*, 78–9; S.C.10/6/260
	22	Reading		*H.R.O.*, 79–81
	23	Wantage		81
	27	Leominster	Mandate enjoining residence	86
Nov.	7–12	Sugwas		81–3, fo. 21v
	13	Hereford	Cathedral chapter house	84
	15	Bosbury		85
	26	Leominster		fo. 24r
	29	Limebrook		fo. 24r
	30	Shobdon		fo. 24r
Dec.	1	Shobdon		86–7
	3	Hergest		87
	3	Radnor		fo. 24r
	7	Wigmore	Visitation of Wigmore Abbey	85–6
	18	Diddlebury		88–9
	19	Bosbury		98
	22–5	Bromfield		fo. 25r, 89–90, 169
	28–30	Wigmore	Publishes injunctions for Wigmore Abbey: resignation of abbot in	

Jan.	3	Wigmore	Disorderly canon sent to Keynsham Abbey	92–3
	5	Wormsley	Appoints prior	93–4
	6–9	Sugwas		fo. 26^r, 94
	11–13	Bosbury		fo. 26^v, 95–6
	16	Leominster		97
	17–19	Bosbury		97–8
	22	Oxford		fo. 27^r
Feb.	2–19	London	In room of Gilbert de Middleton, official, Court of Canterbury (8th)	102–4, 106–7, 212–13; 216–17
	28	Dover	Sets out for Curia	109
May	4–6	Avignon		110, 113–14
	31	Avignon	Priory of St Rufus-by-Avignon	112–13
June	12–19	Avignon	*Ibid*.	115–16
Sept.	8–15	Avignon	*Ibid*.	118–19
Oct.	1	Avignon	*Ibid*.	fo. 33^r
Nov.	4	Avignon	*Ibid*. Receipt given for borrowed books	120
1320				
Jan.	16–17	Avignon	*Ibid*. Promises pension to cardinal-bishop of Ostia	120–1
Feb.	6	Loughborough	Witnesses *inspeximus* of charters	*H.M.C.R.* 15, app. X, p. 3
	20–9	London		*H.R.O.*, 121–2, 124, fo. 33^v
March	1	London		124, 127–8
	5–19	Canterbury	Borrows cross from priory sacrist (17th)	127–30 S.C.1/49/109, 180^v

Date		Place	Details	Reference
March	19	Canterbury	Grants forty days' indulgence to king (19th)	*H.R.O.*, 129–30
	20	Dover	Commission to confer benefices	130
April	1	Paris		130
	22–4 [1]	Avignon	Issue of Cantilupe's bull of canonisation (17th)	131–4
May	7–31	Avignon		131–2, 133–4, fo. 38^v
June	4–8 [2]	Avignon		134–5
	30	Amiens	Homage performed by Edward II	
July	20	Boulogne	Burghersh's consecration	B.L. Cotton MS. Faustina B. V, fo. 34^r
	22	Dover?	Claims expenses until this date	B.L. Add. MS. 17362
Aug.	4–6	London		*H.R.O.*, 136–8
	8	Shinfield		fo. 38^r
	16	Thame		fo. 37^v
	30	Ledbury		138–9
Sept.	2–3	Bosbury		140, 147–9
	10–11	Sugwas		140
	20	Hereford	Indulgences for penitents at Cantilupe's shrine	142–3, 154
	22	Sugwas		144
	26–7	Abergavenny	Appoints Richard de Bromwich prior	190–2, 151–5
	30	Sugwas		fo. 40^r
Oct.	3–6	Sugwas	Feast (2nd) of the newly-sanctified Cantilupe	fo. 40^r, 144–5
	6	Bosbury		145

			Gascon petitions	146, fos. 40v–42r
Nov.	8–11	London		155–7, fo. 43r
	15	Shinfield	Business of Shinfield appropriation	157–8
	18–19	Wenlock	Bishop admits prior (18th)	168, fo. 46r
	26–7	Bosbury		fo. 45r, 165
	27	Sugwas [?]		179
Dec.	9	Kinlet		fo. 45v
	11	Morehall-by-Kinlet		167
	16–17	Munderfield ('Momerefeld')		fos. 45v–46r
	18	Wigmore [?]		fo. 47v
	18–19	Wenlock	Admits prior of Monmouth (18th)	168
	21–2	Eaton Priors		fo. 46v, 169–70
	25	Bromfield		169
	27	Bishops Castle		172
1321				
Jan.	3	Worthen		172–3
	6–7	Caws Castle		173, fo. 47r
	10	Stretton-in-Strettondale		fo. 47v
	11	Munslow		173
	19–20	Sugwas		fo. 47v
	20–1	Hereford		fo. 47v, 174
	22–4	Sugwas		177–8
	25	Bosbury	Appoints vicar-general	180
	27	Prestbury		182

[1] The earlier date is that of a letter addressed to Orleton.

[2] Both of these entries could belong to 1319, but if so would be out of order.

Date		Place	Details	Reference
Feb.	1–3	Shinfield		*H.R.O.*, 180–2
	7–15	London		183–90, fo. 50^{v}
	21	Dover	Sets out for France	Add. MS. 9951, fo. 9^{v}
March	5	Beauvais		*H.R.O.*, fo. 52^{v}
	20	Paris		S.C.8/237/11825
April	24	Dover		Add. MS. 9951, fo. 9^{v}
		London	Unable to find anyone to whom to report	S.C.1/54/139
June	13	Bromyard		*H.R.O.*, fo. 52^{v}
	15–25	Whitbourne		fo. 53^{r}
July	1–7	Whitbourne		197–8, fo. 53^{r}
	9	Steventon		fo. 53^{r}
	c. 22	St Albans	Mediator with barons	*Trokelowe*, 108–9
	27	Clerkenwell and London	Parliament	Cotton MS. Faustina B. V, fo. 34^{v}
			Exile of Despensers July–August	
Sept.	3–14	Bosbury		*H.R.O.*, fo. 53^{v}, 199
	15	Sugwas		fo. 53^{v}
	16–19	Bosbury		fo. 53^{v}
	23–5	Sugwas		fos. 53^{v}–54^{r}
	26	Bosbury		199–200
	29	Hereford		201
Oct.	3–4	Sugwas		200, fo. 54^{r}
	10	Bosbury		fo. 54^{r}
	16	Sugwas		204
	19–20	Bosbury		202, fo. 54^{v}
Nov.	16–29	Bosbury		fo. 55^{v}, 204–9
Dec.	4	Bosbury	Convocation at St Paul's for Despen-	fo. 56^{v}

Jan.	18–31	Hereford	King upbraids Orleton for association with contrariants	fo. 56^{v}
Feb.	1–6	Hereford	Arrest of Mortimers	209, 220
	18	Sevenhampton, Gloucs.		fo. 57^{r}
	19	Bibury		209–10
	23	Hereford	Orleton confirms site for Dominicans there	221
	27	Shinfield [?]		210
March	2	Ross [?]		K.B.27/255/m. 23^{r}
	6–19	Prestbury, Gloucs.	Battle of Boroughbridge (16th)	*H.R.O.*, 211–18, fo. 58^{r}
	29–30	Bosbury		217–18
April	4–30	Bosbury		fo. 59^{r}, 220, 222–5, fos. 59^{r-v}, 61^{r}
May	11	Sherburn [in Elmet]		fo. 61^{r}
	12–16	Rufforth, Yorks.	Parliament at York	fo. 61^{r}, 225–6
	30	Bosbury		fo. 61^{v}
June	4	Sugwas	Excommunication of violators of manors of Ross and Upton	228
	6	Hereford		227
	8–15	Sugwas		fos. 62^{r}, 63^{r} 228–31
	16–18	Bosbury		233–34, fo. 63^{r}
	25–6	Prestbury		237–8, 241–2
July	6–30	Prestbury		238–43, fo. 65^{r}
Aug.	1–12	Prestbury		244–7, fo. 66^{r}
	13	Evesham		246
	19	Doncaster		fo. 66^{v}
	21–3	York	Responds to royal summons re excommunication	S.C.1/34/151

Date		Place	Details	Reference
Sept.	6–11	Prestbury		*H.R.O.*, 247–8
	17–20	Bosbury		fos. 66^v–67^r
	27	Sugwas		fo. 67^r
	28	Hereford		248–9
	30	Sugwas		fo. 67^r
Oct.	5–9	Sugwas		250–1, fo. 67^{r-v}
	9	Hereford		249–50
	10–16	Sugwas		251–2, fo. 68^r
	18–26	Bosbury		254–5, fo. 68^v
Nov.	29	York	Responds in king's presence to summons re excommunication	K.B.27/250/Rex m. 16v
1323				
June	9	Whitbourne		*H.R.O.*, fo. 79^r
July	14–23	Whitbourne		255–9, fo. 69^r
Aug.	3	Sugwas	Mortimer the nephew escapes from Tower (1st)	fo. 70^r
	22–4	Prestbury		262, fo. 70^v
Sept.	7	Bromyard [?]		263
	8	Whitbourne		263–4
Oct.	21	Shinfield		fo. 71^r
Nov.	7	Shinfield		fo. 71^v
	?	Kensington		264–5
	24–8	Shinfield		265, fo. 71^v
Dec.	1–27	Shinfield		fo. 72^r, 266–7
1324				
Jan.	2–10	Shinfield		fo. 73^r, 268–9
	c. 23–7	Hereford	Appearance before assize court	Just.1/1388

	11–19	Gloucester	Commission to admit new prior of Hereford (19th)	275–7, fo. 74v
	24	Westminster	Indictment at beginning of session of parliament	K.B.27/255/Rex m. 87v
March	8–27	London	Confiscation of temporalities	*H.R.O.*, 277–81, fos. 75v, 76r
April	2–6	London		fo. 76v
	23	Ross	Attack on the bishop by William Irby	285–6
	25	Marcle		fos. 77r, 87v
	26	Hereford		285
	30	Churcham	Visitation of church	288
May	13	Monmouth		287–8
	18	Eaton ('Monketon')		fo. 80r
	26	Hereford		297–8
June	2	Hereford		300–1
	9	B[romyard?]	Ordination	313
	15–26	Wormsley		299–303, 322
July	19	Thame		fo. 82r
Aug.	2	'Wodecride'	Mandate for publication of Irby's excommunication	306
	17	London		307–8
Oct.	31	London	Parliament in session	311
Nov.	11–28	London	Visit of papal nuncios (bishop prevented from seeing them?)	308–9, 312, fos. 83r, 84r
Dec.	20	Hereford		312

Date		Place	Details	Reference
1325				
Jan.	9	Kingston		*H.R.O.*, fo. 84^{r}
March	2	London diocese	Licensed to celebrate orders	325
April	9–12	Hereford		313, 339
	14	Weobley		339
	16	Kings Pyon		339
	17	Wormsley		339
	18	Kington	Dedicating altars in various churches (9th–18th)	339
	19	Wormsley		fo. 88^{v}
	20	Hereford		324
	30	Middleton, Hants	Approach to Lancaster for intervention with king	327
May	6	Middleton		326–7
	16–20	London	Confers orders in church of Augustinian friars (20th)	fo. 90^{r}, 329
	23–9	Shinfield		fo. 90^{r}
June	12–28	Shinfield		329–30, fos. 90^{r}, 105^{v}
Aug.	9–16?	Earley, Berks. (‘ Arleye ’)	[‘ *u.s.*’ dates in MS.]	fo. 90^{v}
Sept.	11–19?	Shinfield	[‘ *u.s.*’ dates in MS.]	fo. 91^{r}
Oct.	22	Shinfield		fo. 91^{r}
Nov.	30	London	Parliament in session, Westminster	332
Dec.	12	London		332
	18–30	Shinfield		319–20, 333

Jan.	4–5	Shinfield		333, fo. 90^{v}
	14	London		333–4
	16–30	Shinfield		321, 343, 346 fo. 91^{v}
	31	Lechlade, Gloucs.		fo. 87^{r}
Feb.	1	Lechlade		351
	2	Coln St Dennis	Reconciles church for Bishop Cobham	346
	9–14	Shinfield		347–8, fos. 87^{r}, 95^{v}, 96^{v}
	15–26	Reading	Ordains in St Mary's church	345, 352, fo. 95^{v}
March	8–17	Shinfield		358–9
April	5–8	Shinfield		357–8
May	10–24	Shinfield		361–2, fo. 99^{r}
June	24	Shinfield		362–3
July	9–28	Shinfield		364–6
Sept.	8	Oxford		fo. 101^{v}
	14–15	Wigmore	Buries elder Mortimer	370–1 *Wigmore Chron.*, p. 351
	15	Bromfield		*H.R.O.*, fo. 101^{v}
	27	Hereford	Landing of Isabella and Mortimer (24th)	fo. 79^{v} *et al.*
Oct.	15	Wallingford	Queen's proclamation	
	?	Oxford	University sermon by Orleton	*Responsiones*, 2764
	26	Bristol		*Foedera*. 2, ii, 169
Nov.	17	Hereford		*H.R.O.*, 373
	20	Hereford		*Foedera*. 2, ii, 169
	?	Monmouth	To collect Great Seal from king	*Ibid.*

Date		Place	Details	Reference
Nov.	24	Hereford [?]	Sentence on Despenser and Baldock	*Ann. Paul.*, 319–20
	26	Marcle	Delivers seal to queen	*Foedera*. 2, ii, 169
	27	Hereford		*H.R.O.*, 371
Dec.	20	Reading	Ordination, St Mary's church	*Hereford Reg. Trillek*, 91
	25	Wallingford	Christmas spent with the queen	Cotton MS. Faustina B. V, fo. 47v
1327				
Jan.	7	London	Parliament	
	20?	Kenilworth	Mission to Edward II re deposition	
	30	London	Appointed treasurer (28th)	*H.R.O.*, 102r
	31	Tower of London	Release of precious articles for coronation	Cotton Charter IV, 9
Feb.	1	Westminster	Attends coronation of Edward III	*Foedera* 2, ii, 172
	16		Temporalities restored following annulment of process against him	*Rot. Parl.* 2, 427–9
March	26	Beaumes	Ceases to be treasurer after 24 March	*H.R.O.*, 376
	28	Westminster		374–5
	30	London	Leaves for France and Avignon	E.101/309/38
April	5	Dover–Wissant		*Ibid.*
Sept.	28	Avignon	Provision to Worcester	*W.R.O.*, 491
			Murder of Edward II (21st)	
Oct.	9	Avignon	Engages to pay curial *servicia*	*H.R.O.*, 381
1328				
Jan.	22	York		E.101/309/38
Feb.	22–9	York	Answers at parliament for accepting promotion	
			Publishes bulls: sets up administra-	*W.R.O.*, 210, 260–2, 498–501, 586

				C.P.R. 1327–30, 245
	6	Etherdwick, Yorks.		*W.R.O.*, 508
	19	Cirencester	Ordination	1
	20	Lechlade		32, 593
	26–30	Beaumes		*H.R.O.*, 376ff *W.R.O.*, 33
	31	Reading	Consecrates holy oil for Bishop Martival	3, 270
April	2–6	Beaumes	Ordination (minor)	2, 211, 266–7
	9–25	Cleeve		34ff, 212, 268ff, 300, 512–24, 644ff
	28	Bishops Hampton		40, 214, 660
May	2	Brockhall, Northants.	Parliament at Northampton	657
	2–15	Northampton	Sent with Bishop Northburgh to claim French crown	41, 215–16, 272ff, 525–6, 658
	16	Dunstable, Beds.		217
	18–19	London		218–19, 279–80
	20	Canterbury		220
	21	Dover		665
	30	Paris		Perroy, *Hundred Years War*, 80–1
June	*c.* 7	Back in England		
	15	Fladbury		*W.R.O.*, 44
	19	Worcester	Enthronement	529
	22–7	Bredon		48, 221, 281, 301, 527, 537, 669

Date		Place	Details	Reference
June	29	Cirencester		*W.R.O.*, 49, 222
	30	Kempsford		6
July	4	Hanbury (*recte* Henbury?)		302
	5–7	Henbury		532, 536, 546
	9	Frampton		539
	9	Gloucester		*H.R.O.*, 380
	10	Llanthony-by-Gloucester	Ordination (minor)	*W.R.O.*, 4, 8
	11	Gloucester		282
	13	Tewkesbury		540, 597
	14–15	Pershore		541, 671
	16	Alcester		672
	23	Nottingham	Court there: archbishop of Armagh sent to Curia	50, 674
	26	Alvechurch		51
	28–9	Hartlebury		542ff, 595
	31	Wick-by-Worcester		52
Aug.	1	Wick-by-Worcester		547
	3	Bredon		53, 533
	4–5	Winchcombe	Visitation of abbey	548–9
	19–22	Beaumes		54ff, 678ff
Sept.	7	Beaumes		58
	16	Bibury		60
	20	Withington		61
	20–3	Barnwood		62, 286, 318
	24	Gloucester	Ordination	9, 283
	24–30	Bredon		63, 68, 284–5,

	7–12	Hartlebury		[illegible]
	13	Kempsey		319
	14	Tewkesbury		288
	15	Cheltenham		73
	15	Cirencester		558
	18	Netheravon, Wilts.	Parliament at Salisbury	223
	20–2	South Burcombe		224, 289
Nov.	1–2	Idmiston		225, 561
	8	Ripple		562
	10–28	Hartlebury		74–5, 226, 290, 563
Dec.	1	Worcester		258
	3	Wick-by-Worcester		320
	8–16	Hartlebury		76–7, 222, 321, 564ff
1329				
Feb.	5–19	London	Convocation, St Paul's; bishop writes on behalf of Oxford University	79ff, 570, 707–12
			Parliament	Lichfield Reg. Northburgh 3, fo. 102r
	28	Shinfield		*W.R.O.*, 83
March	8–10	Beaumes		84–5
	10	Shinfield		86
	12–22	Beaumes		86, 228, 291, 571, 599
				Liber Albus, 84
April	1–8	Beaumes	Ordination (minor)	*W.R.O.*, 10, 11, 229–30, 293

Date		Place	Details	Reference
April	14	London		*W.R.O.*, 717
	18–30	Beaumes	Ordination (minor)	12, 231, 718
May	11–17	London		296, 303, 720
	20	Hillingdon		721
June	4	Beaumes		13, 87
	12–13	Stanton-St-John, Oxon.		232–3, 726
	15–16	Bredon		724–5
	17	Tewkesbury Abbey	Ordination (414 names)	14
	23	Worcester [?]		298
	25	Cookhill		89
	27	Studley		90, 299
	28	Wootton Wawen		91
	30	Bishops Hampton		731
July	1	Warwick		92
	4	Bishops Hampton		572
	9	Hailes		600, 604, 736
	12	Winchcombe	Injunctions for abbey	94, 744
	16	Bredon [?]		603
	17	Hillingdon		97
	21	Beaumes		95
Aug.	18	Beaumes [?]		323
Sept.	18–29	Beaumes		576, 607
Oct.	5–6	London		98, 608
	14	Hillingdon		99
	16	Warwick		609
	17–18	Blockley		105, 750–1, 755–6
	22	Fladbury		

	8	Gloucester		S.C.1/38/115
	13	Hartlebury [?]		*W.R.O.*, 295
	18–25	Henbury		610–11
	29	Bristol	Visitation, St James's Priory	613
Dec.	1	Sodbury		615
	2	Horton		106
	6	Horsley		619
	8	Minchinhampton		107, 618
	11	Cirencester		578
	18	Beaumes [?]		234
	21	Great Rissington		205
	23	Dodderhill	Ordination	16, 19
	26–30	Hartlebury		108ff, 745
1330				
Jan.	2–8	Hartlebury		579–80, 305, 764
	12	Stanton-St-John, Oxon.		111
	16	Beaumes		112, 765
	24–31	London	Commission to go to France with Bishop Ayrminne	18, 325, 623(?) E.101/310/7–8
Feb.	10	Dover		*Ibid.*
March	18	Wissant		*Ibid.*
	25	Reading		*Ibid.*
	28	Southwark		*C.P.R.* 1327–30, 534
April	2	Witney		*W.R.O.*, 625
	3	Woodstock		627
	6–8	Beaumes		328, 626

Date		Place	Details	Reference
April	11	Woodstock	Commission for French marriage negotiations	*W.R.O.*, 113, 716
	11–14	Beaumes		327, 330–1
	21	Dover		E.101/310/14
May	26	Wissant	Bois de Vincennes convention (8th)	*Ibid.*
	30	Hillingdon		*W.R.O.*, 628–9
June	1	Woodstock		E.101/310/14
	11	Witney		*W.R.O.*, 333
				117, 770, 795
	17	Woodstock	[Wrongly July in one entry.] Embassy sent to France at this time	
			Royal *tractatus* at Osney [*Lit. Cant.* 1, 320]	
	22–30	Beaumes		114–15
July	2–30	Beaumes		116, 118, 235–6
Aug.	7–16	Beaumes		119, 306, 335, 340, 775–7
Sept.	1–30	Beaumes		237, 245–7, 581–3, 631ff
Oct.	4	Bishops Hampton		336
	12	Blockley		120–1
	12	Great Barrington		248
	20–1	Ilkeston, Derbys.	Nottingham assembly	122, 337
			Seizure of Mortimer	
	23	Glenfield-by-Leicester	King at Leicester	124
Nov.	4–8	Hartlebury		249, 338, 782ff

	12	[Drakes?] Broughton		339
	13	Pershore		125
	13	Winchcombe		786
	14	Tetbury		253, 342
	15–16	Horton		254–5
	16	Imber, Wilts.		225–6
	27	London	Parliament at Westminster	308
Dec.	1–18	London		132, 309ff, 795, 797
				Liber Albus, 86
	21–9	Beaumes		*W.R.O.*, 799
1331				
Jan.	7	Eynsham	Appropriation of Tetbury	204
	8	Wallingford		130
	14	Beaumes		136
	17–23	London	Mission to France	131, 133–5, 803, 805–7
				E.101/310/16
	28	Dover		*Ibid.*
March	25	Westminster	Treaty of Paris (9th)	
April	1–8	Beaumes		*W.R.O.*, 137, 314, 808, 814ff
	19	Hillingdon		351
	23–27	London		138, 352
May	1	Hillingdon		139
	16	Blockley		822
	19	Beaumes [?]		354
	25	Campden	Ordination (417 names)	21
	25	Blockley		140

Date		Place	Details	Reference
June	4–21	Hartlebury		*W.R.O.*, 206–9, 359–60, 823ff
	26	Blockley		356
July	1–3	Hartlebury		830–1
	4	Worcester, St Oswald's		833
	5	Kempsey		397, 832
	10	Stonehouse		834
	16–26	Henbury		357, 835–6
	27	Hawkesbury		844
Aug.	6–21	Bredon		345, 396, 838–40, 842–3
	21	Blockley		346
	30	Alvechurch		347
Sept.	1–14	Alvechurch		141, 326, 349–50, 846
	15	Alcester	Dedication of altar, mass and sermon	366
	16	Sedgeberrow	Dedication of church, preaches	367
	16–17	Hinton		150, 361, 857
	18–20	Withington		142, 144–5, 362–4
	21	Lechlade	Ordination (minor)	22
	22	Speen, Berks.		143
	25	Beaumes		365
	29	Hillingdon		385–6
	30	London	Parliament at Westminster	146
Oct.	4	Beaumes		152
	9–14	London		147, 369–71,

Nov.	2–3	Beaumes		151, 859ff
	7	Withington		373
	11	Ripple		153
	14–22	Alvechurch		154–7, 374, 864ff
	23	Tardebigge	Visitation	375
	27	Alvechurch		376–7
Dec.	2	Hartlebury		158
	11	Longdon		380
	17–19	Ripple		381–4
	29–30	Hartlebury		159, 353, 387
1332				
Jan.	1–6	Hartlebury	Ordination (minor) and celebration of mass (6th)	23, 388, 392
	11	Withington		161
	15	Cirencester		160
	25	London		391
Feb.	1	Beaumes		163
	25–6	Beaumes		164
March	1	Beaumes		166
	7	Winchester		167
	9	Southampton	Reconcilation of churchyard for Bishop Stratford	128
	11	Beaumes		398
	11–12	Hillingdon		167, 399
	18–26	London	Parliament at Westminster	400–8, 880ff
	29	Beaumes		887

Date		Place	Details	Reference
April	4	Tormarton	Ordination (minor)	*W.R.O.*, 24
	4–6	Pucklechurch		409–12
	7	Berkeley		413
	10–15	Hartlebury		168–70, 886, 888–9
	18	Beckford	Ordination	25, 417
	19	Bredon		416
	19–20	Withington		414–15
	20	Cirencester [?]		172
	20	Hillingdon		171
	23	Beaumes		418
	27	London	Sent to France with Bishop Stratford and others	173, E.101/310/28
May	1	Dover		*Ibid.*
June	6	Woodstock		*Ibid.*
	13	Pershore Abbey	Ordination	*W.R.O.*, 26
	13	Ripple		421
	16	Withington		174, 419
	21–2	Ripple		175, 420
	25	Wick		422
	27	Hartlebury		176
July	2–22	Hartlebury	Election process of abbot of St Augustine's, Bristol	177, 423–7, 899ff
	31	Beaumes		903
Aug.	25	Pilton, Som.		428
Sept.	10–19	London	Parliament at Westminster	430ff, 446, 905, 908

	27	Cirencester		450
	29	Winterbourne		191
	30	Henbury		449
Oct.	1–3	Henbury		192–5, 447–8, 451
	5	Winterbourne		922
	5	Berkeley		452
	6–7	Gloucester		196, 453–9ff
	7–9	Bredon		197, 460
	11	Hartlebury		463
	15	Bromsgrove		198
	17	Alvechurch		465, 923
	23–4	Bishops Hampton		394, 466, 924–5
	28–31	Withington		199, 468–70
Nov.	1	Withington		200
	2–3	Bibury		201–2
	6	Hillingdon [?]		181
	9–11	London	Mission to France and Avignon	179, 189, 203, 930 E.372/178/42
Dec.	19	Paris	Ordination (minor)	*W.R.O.*, 27
1333				
Feb.	22	Paris	Leaves for Avignon	E.372/178/42
	27	Nogent l'Artaud	Ordination (minor)	*W.R.O.*, 28
March	20	Nogent l'Artaud	Ordination (minor)	30
Sept.	10	Avignon	Leaves for Paris	E.372/178/42
Nov.	6	Paris		*W.R.O.*, 180
Dec.	3	Dartford, Kent	Provision to Winchester (1st)	187

Date		Place	Details	Reference
1334				
Jan.	9	Wallingford		E.372/178/42
	11	Islip	Appropriation of Longdon	*W.R.O.*, 935, 947
	15	Bibury		474–5, 477
	19	Blockley		476
	23–6	Bredon		478–80
	26–9	Fladbury		481, 485
	30–1	Hartlebury		482–4, 934
Feb.	7	Shinfield		944
	13	Stanton-St-John, Oxon.		936–7
	13–14	Enstone		184–5, 938–9
	14	Tredington		31
	15–16	Bishops Hampton		186, 486ff
March	2	Haywards Heath, Sussex	Parliament at York	188
	20	Winchester Cathedral Priory		*Win. Chart.*, 109
	21–7	Winchester		Win.R.O. 1, fos. 1^r, 2^r
April	1–27	Winchester	Appeal against bishop's provision (2nd)	*Win. Chart.*, 104–7; Win.R.O. 1, fos. 1^r–3^v; 2, fo. 43^{r-v}
May	1–31	Winchester		*Ibid.* and 1, fo. 4^r
June	2–29	Winchester		1, fos. 4^v–5^r; 2, fos. 43^v–44^rff
July	9	'Manydenne'		1, fo. 5^r

	11	Westminster	Reconciles St James's hospital	1, fo. 5
	14	Coulsdon	Reconciles church	*Ibid.*
	15–16	Chertsey		1, fo. 5^{r}
	17	Shinfield		*Ibid.*
Sept.	7	Shinfield		1, fo. 10^{v}
	23–9	Southwark	Restoration of temporalities (23rd)	1, fo. 6^{v}; 2, fo. 43^{v}
Oct.	1–6	Southwark		1, fos. 6^{v}, 8^{r}
	10–12	Canterbury	Acknowledges (12th) debt of £1,000 to Archbishop Stratford for growing crops	1, fos. 9^{r}, 17^{r}; 2, fo. 44^{r}
	14	Southwark		2, fo. 44^{r}
	19	Sutton		1, fo. 9^{v}
	20–31	Marwell		*Ibid.* and fo. 10^{r-v}
Nov.	2–3	Marwell		1, fos. 27^{r}, 58^{v}
	3–9	Winchester	Commences primary visitation	1, fo. 10^{v}; 2, fo. 45^{r}
	9–11	Wolvesey		1, fo. 10^{v}
	12	Winchester	Preaches in cathedral	*Ibid.*
	14–15	Southwick	Visitation of priory	*Ibid.* and 2, fo. 45^{r-v}
	16	Hambledon	Dedicates high altar	1, fo. 11^{r}
	17–18	Southwick		*Ibid.* and 2, fo. 45^{v}
	18–19	Titchfield		1, fos. 11^{v}–12^{r}
	19–22	Southampton	Visitation of St Denys (22nd)	1, fo. 11^{r-v}
	23	Southwick		1, fo. 14^{r}

Date	Place	Details	Reference
Nov. 24	Southampton		Win.R.O. 1, fos. 11^r, 12^v
26–7	Mottisfont	Visitation of religious houses	1, fo. 11^r; 2, fo. 45^v
28	Romsey		*Ibid.*
30	Marwell		1, fo. 13^v
Dec. 1–14	Marwell		1, fos. 12^r, 13^{r-v}
19	Wolvesey		1, fo. 14^r
23	Marwell		*Ibid.*
28	Clere		1, fo. 11^v
1335			
Jan. 7	Downton		1, fo. 14^r
14–15	Clere		1, fo. 14^v
17–20	Farnham		*Ibid.* and fo. 4^v
26–31	Southwark		1, fo. 15^r; 2, fos. 45^v–46^r
Feb. 3	Esher		2, fo. 46^r
6–21	Farnham		1, fo. 15^v; 2, fos. 46^v–47^r
20–3	Guildford	Visitation of Surrey archdeaconry	1, fo. 15^v; 2, fo. 47^r
25–7	Kingston	Visitation 'clero et populo excellenter predicando'	1, fos. 15^v–16^r
28	Esher		1, fo. 16^r
March 2–4	Esher		*Ibid.*
5–8	Merton	Visitation of priory	1, fo. 16^v; 2, fo. 47^r
8	Esher		1, fo. 16^r

	31	Ilkeston, Derbys.	Parliament at Nottingham	2, fo. 52^{v}
April	1	Nottingham		1, fo. 16^{v}
	2–3	Ilkeston	Acknowledges debt to Geoffrey, son of Geoffrey le Scrope, justice	*Ibid.* and 2, fo. 47^{v}
	9	Adderbury, Oxon.		2, fo. 47^{v}
	13–30	Clere, Highclere and Burghclere		1, fos. 17^{v}–18^{v}; 2, fo. 47^{v}
May	1–14	Highclere		1, fos. 18^{v}–19^{v}, 22^{r}, 28^{r}; 2, fo. 47^{v}
	19	Bishopthorpe, York	Acknowledges debt of £100 to Archbishop Melton	1, fo. 20^{v}
			Parliament at York	
	31	Acaster, Yorks.		2, fo. 48^{r}
June	1–11	Acaster Malbis		*Ibid.* and 1, fos. 19^{v}–20^{r}
	24–5 [3]	Badby, Northants.		2, fo. 48^{r}
	29	Witney, Oxon		1, fo. 20^{v}
July	1 [4]	Wargrave		*Ibid.*
	6–23	Farnham		1, fos. 20^{v}–22^{r}, 48^{v}; 2, fos. 48^{r}–49^{r}
Aug.	1	Esher		1, fo. 25^{r}
	2–23	Farnham		1, fos. 22^{v}–24^{v}, 28^{r}; 2, fos. 48^{r}–49^{r}

[3] 1, fo. 22^{r} has an entry dated 20 June [*sic*] 1335 from Farnham.
[4] 1, fo. 21^{r} has an entry dated 7 July [1335] from York [*sic*].

Date		Place	Details	Reference
Aug.	26–8	Southwark	Royal council in London re defence of the realm	Win.R.O. 1, fo. 24^{v}; 2, fo. 49^{v}
	29	Esher		1, fo. 25^{r}
Sept.	4	Tandridge	Visitation of priory	1, fo. 28^{v}
	2–7	Esher		1, fos. 21^{r}, 25^{r-v}
	8	Newark		*Ibid.*
	8–10	Farnham		1, fos. 21^{r}, 25^{v}; 2, fo. 14^{r}
	12	Cranleigh		1, fo. 25^{v}
	13	Farnham		1, fo. 26^{r}
		Oxenford–Elstead	Fracas on highway caused by Archdeacon Inge	1, fo. 28^{v}
	15	Sutton		1, fo. 29^{r}
	16–21	Marwell		1, fos. 26^{r}, 52^{r}; 2, fo. 49^{v}
	24	Southampton		2, fo. 49^{v}
Oct.	1	Carisbrooke, Isle of Wight		1, fo. 26^{r}
	9	Cheriton		*Ibid.*
	11–22	Farnham		1, fos. 26^{r}, 28^{r}; 2, fos. 49^{v}–50^{r}
Nov.	5–30	Highclere	'Episcopus mutavit sigillum suum ad causas' (10th)	1, fos. 27^{v}–29^{r}; 2, fo. 50^{v}
Dec.	5–6	Farnham		2, fos. 51^{r}, 136^{r}
	10	London	Acknowledges obligation of £50 to Bardi of Florence	1, fo. 29^{r}
	10–13	Esher		1, fos. 29^{r-v};

				2, fo. 51
	25–31	Bishops Waltham		1, fos. 29^{*r-v}ff; 2, fo. 51^{r}
1336				
Jan.	2	Waltham		2, fo. 51^{v}
	4–24	Farnham	Implementation of bull in support of Crusade (12th)	1, fos. 29^{*v}–31^{r}; 2. fos. 14^{r-v}, 51^{v}
Feb.	4–17	Farnham		1, fos. 31^{v}–32^{v}; 2, fo. 52^{r}
	21	Selborne	Visitation of priory	1, fo. 33^{r}
	23	Sherborne	Visitation of priory	*Ibid.*
	26	Wargrave		1, fo. 33^{v}
March	3	Wargrave		2, fo. 52^{r}
	12–28	Southwark and London	Parliament at Westminster	1, fos. 33^{v}–34^{v}; 2, fos. 52^{v}, 53^{r}, 62^{r}
	28	Esher	'quo die dominus episcopus Wynton' devillavit'	1, fo. 34^{v}
April	4	London	With Archbishop Stratford and Bishops Gravesend, Hethe and Burghersh asks pope for postponement of first year of papal tenth	1, fo. 35^{v}
	4–25	Wargrave	Commission for bishop's enthronement (6th)	1, fos. 34^{v}–37^{r}, 39^{r}
	30	Esher	Injunctions for Sherborne Priory	1, fo. 38^{v}
May	4–7 [8?][5]	Southwark	Visitation of priory	1, fo. 37^{r-v}; 2, fo. 53r

[5] The MS. makes the bishop's visitation 7 May 1337 [sic] with corrections on 13th [8th?]: 1, fo. 37^{v}. The entry for Newark which follows, omits the year.

Date		Place	Details	Reference
May	10–14	Esher		Win.R.O., 1, fos. 37^{v}–38^{r}
	14	Southwark	Admits prior of Carisbrooke	2, fo. 53^{v}
	15–16	Newark	Visitation of priory	1, fo. 37^{v}
	16–26	Wargrave	Pension of 200 florins for Cardinal Gaucelme (26th)	1, fo. 38^{r}; 2, fo. 55^{v}
	26	Highclere		1 fo. 38^{r}
June	1–15	Highclere		1, fos. 38^{r}–39^{v}, 42^{r}; 2, fos. 53^{v}ff
	19–20	Wargrave		2, fo. 54^{r}
	28	Northampton	Royal council plans embassy to France	2, fo. 55^{r}
July	2	Kislingbury, Northants.		1, fo. 40^{r}
	3		Licensed by Bishop Burghersh to consecrate high altar of Adderbury, Oxon.	*Ibid.*
	13–14	Brightwell, Berks.		2, fo. 54^{r}
	15	Wargrave		1, fo. 40^{r}
	16	Esher		1, fo. 40^{v}
	18–21	Southwark		1, fos. 40^{r}–41^{v}; 2, fo. 54^{r-v}
	21	London		E.101/311/21
	24	Dover	Final mission to French court	*Ibid.*
Aug.	9–20	Paris	Pension granted to Bernard Sistre jun. (10th)	Win.R.O. 1, fo. 42^{v}
			Receipt given to Peruzzi (20th)	E.43/100
Sept.	5	London		E.101/311/21

	6	Witney		1, fo. 43
	10–12	Highclere		1, fos. 43^{r}, 45^{r}; 2, fo. 56^{r}
	16	Wargrave		2, fo. 55^{v}
	19–25	Esher		1, fos. 44^{v}–45^{r}; 2, fo. 56r
Nov.	2	Esher		*Ibid.* and 1, fo. 45^{v}
	11	Newark		2, fo. 56^{r}
	15–18	Farnham		1, fos. 47^{r}, 50^{r}
	20	Wintney	Appointment of prioress	1, fo. 46^{v}
	28	Newington		1, fo. 47^{r}
	28	Sutton		*Ibid.*
Dec.	5–11	Marwell		1, fo. 48^{v}; 2, fo. 56^{v}
	17–22	Highclere		1, fos. 47^{v}–48^{v}; 2, fo. 57^{r}
	26–9	Wolvesey		1, fo. 48^{r}; 2, fo. 57^{r}
1337 Jan.	3–6	Highclere		1, fo. 48^{r-v}
	15–16	Southwark		*Ibid.*
	18–22	Esher		1, fo. 49^{r}; 2, fo. 57^{r}
	25–30	Farnham		1, fos. 49^{v}, 58^{r}
Feb.	2	Farnham		2, fo. 57^{r}
	6–11	Marwell		1, fo. 49^{v}; 2, fo. 57^{r-v}

Date		Place	Details	Reference
Feb.	9–11	Twynham (Christchurch)	Visitation of priory	Win.R.O. 1, fos. 49^v–50^r; 2, fo. 57^v
	13	Breamore	Visitation of priory	*Ibid.*
	15–18	Downton		1, fo. 50^r
	27	Highclere		1, fo. 50^v; 2, fo. 57^v
March	8–13	Southwark		1, fos. 50^v–52^v; 2, fo. 58^r
	16–25	Esher		*Ibid.* and 2, fo. 58^v
	26–31	Farnham		1, fos. 52^r, 53^r; 2, fo. 58
April	3	Esher		1, fo. 53^r
	5	Lambeth and Southwark		1, fos. 54^r, $100A^r$
	8–12	Esher		1, fos. 53^r–54^r
	15–26	Farnham		1, fo. 54^{r-v}; 2, fo. 59^r
May	2–10 [6]	Farnham		1, fos. 69^v, 141^v; 2, fo. 59^r
	12	Winchester	Second visitation begins	1, fo. 54^v
	13–23	Winchester and Wolvesey	Visitation of St Mary's, Winchester, Hyde Abbey	1, fos. 54^v–55^r; 2, fo. 59^r
	23	Wherwell	Visitation	*Ibid.*
	29	Downton		1, fo. 146^r
June	9–26	Highclere		1, fos. 42^r, 55^v–56^r, 140^r,

July	4–18	Farnham		1, fos. 56^{v}–$57(ii)^{r}$, 142^{v}; 2, fo. 60^{v}
	22–4	Southwark		1, fo. $57(ii)^{r-v}$; 2, fo. 60^{v}
	26–31	Esher		*Ibid.* and 1, fos. 60^{v}, 143^{r}
Aug.	1	Esher		2, fo. 60^{v}
	11	Wolvesey		2, fo. 61^{r}
	12	Cheriton		2, fo. 60^{v}
	27	Newark		1, fo. $100B^{r}$
Sept.	1	Farnham		1, fo. 143^{v}
	8	Marwell		1, fo. $100A^{r-v}$
	11–12	Wolvesey		*Ibid.* and 2, fo. 61^{r}
	17	Farnham		2, fo. 61^{r}
	20	Chertsey	Canterbury convocation at St Paul's	1, fos. 65^{v}, 66^{r}
Oct.	4	Esher		1, fo. $100A^{r}$
	14–24	Wargrave		1, fo. $100A^{r-v}$; 2, fos. 61^{r-v}, 63^{r}
	24	Esher		2, fo. 61^{v}
	27	Wargrave		*Ibid.*
	28	Stockwell		1, fo. $100C^{v}$
Nov.	1–10	Wargrave		1, fos. $100B^{v}$, 144^{r}; 2, fo. 62^{v}

[6] 2, fo. 59^{r} has 1336 for the entry for 10 May.

Date		Place	Details	Reference
Nov.	19	Southwark		Win.R.O. 1, fo. 100D^{v}
	23	Esher		2, fo. 63^{r}
Dec.	3–19	Southwark		1, fos. 66^{v}, 100D^{v}; 2, fo. 63^{r}
	24	Stockwell		1, fo. 100D^{v}
	27	Southwark		*Ibid.*
1338				
Jan.	15–30	Farnham		1, fo. 57^{v}; 2, fos. 19^{v}–20^{v}
Feb.	4–14	Farnham		1, fo. 57^{v}; 2, fos. 63^{v}, 66^{r-v}
	19	Southwark		2, fo. 64^{r}
March	1–11	Esher		1, fo. 57(iii)^{r}; 2, fos. 21^{r}, 64^{r}, 65^{r}
	22	Avington		1, *loc. cit.*
	27–29	Highclere		*Ibid.*
April	3–8	Highclere		1, fo. 57 (iii)^{v}; 2, fo. 66^{v}
	16–24	Farnham		1, fo. 58^{r-v}; 2, fos. 65^{r}, 66^{v}
May	2–11	Farnham		1, fos. 58^{v}, 61^{r}; 2, fo. 67^{r}
	13–23 [7]	Highclere		*Ibid.* and 1,

	11	Farnham		*Ibid.*
	13–14	Downton		2, fo. 67^r
	15	Breamore	Priory directed to obey statute of Council of Oxford	1, fo. 61^{r-v}
	17	Broughton		1, fo. 64^r
	25	Winchester		1, fo. 63^v
July	1–4	Waltham, South Waltham		1, fos. 61^v, 62^v; 2, fo. 67^r
	6	Marwell		1, fo. 62^r
	7–10	Waltham		1, fo. 61^{r-v}; 2, fo. 67^r
	21	Farnham		1, fo. 63^r
Aug.	7–31	Wargrave		1, fos. 63^v–66^v; 2, fos. 22^r, 67^v, 68^r
Sept.	3–9	Wargrave		1, fos. 64^v, 142^v
	14–23	Witney		2, fo. 68^r
	28 [8]	Highclere	Bishop excuses himself from convocation at St Bride's (1 Oct.) on account of infirmity	1, fos. 66^r, 67^r
Oct.	15–30	Marwell		1, fos. 67^r–68^r
Nov.	3	Farnham		*Ibid.* and 2, fos. 24^r, 68^v
	11–23	Esher		1, fo. 68^r, 69^r
	23–8	Farnham	Bishop instructs religious to give spiritual and temporal help to ward off invasion	*Ibid.* and 1, fos. 148^r–149^r

[7] 1, fo. 59^v has Ashbury 16 May 1338.

[8] 1, fo. 66^r has 1337.

Date		Place	Details	Reference
Dec.	12–31	Farnham		Win.R.O. 1, fos. 66^{v}–69^{r}, 149^{v}; 2, fo. 24^{r}
1339				
Jan	7	Winchester		H.C.M., 1376
	8–31	Farnham	Bishop excuses himself from assembly summoned by cardinals prior to the parliament of 3 Feb. 1339	Win.R.O. 1, fos. 70^{r}, 151^{r}, 157^{r}; 2, fos. 25^{v}, 69^{r}–70^{v}
Feb.	3–22	Farnham		1 fos. 69^{v}–70^{r}, 151^{v}; 2, fos. 68^{v}–69^{r}
March	3–28	Farnham		1, fos. 70^{v}, 75^{r}, 153^{r}ff; 2, fos. 69^{v}–72^{r}
April	13–26	Waltham		1, fos. 74^{r}, 156^{v}; 2, fos. 26^{r}, 72^{v}
May	4–30	Waltham		1, fos. 74^{r-v}, 77^{r}; 2, fos. 71^{v},72^{v}
June	3–23	Waltham		1, fos. 70^{r}, 75^{r-v}; 2, fos. 33^{v}, 73^{r}
July	5–28	Waltham		1, fos. 77^{v}–78^{r}, 158^{r-v}; 2, fos. 31^{r}, 73^{v}–74^{r}
Aug.	2–30	Waltham		1 fos. 78^{r}–80^{r}; 2, fos. 31^{r},

				2, fos. 76^{r-v}, 83^{r}
Oct.	11–28	Highclere		2, fos. 77^{r-v}, 79^{v}
Nov.	5–30	Farnham	Election process of prior of Merton in presence of Bishops Robert Stratford (Chichester) and Richard Francis (Waterford) (5th)	1, fos. 80^{v}–83^{r}, 85^{r},160^{v}; 2, fos. 78^{r}, 79^{r}
Dec.	2–30	Farnham	On death of Bishop Bentworth of London (8th) Orleton, acting as dean of Canterbury province, summons convocation for January 1340	1, fos. 83^{v}–85^{r}, 161^{r-v}; 2, fos. 79^{v}–80^{v}
1340				
Jan.	2–28	Farnham		1, fos. 84^{v}–86^{r}, 162^{r}; 2, fos. 80^{v}–82^{r}
Feb.	6–25	Farnham		1, fos. 85^{v}–86^{v}, 162^{r}; 2, fo. 82^{r}
March	3–31	Farnham		1, fos. 86^{v}–87^{r}; 2, fo. 82^{r-v}
April	10–28	Farnham		1, fos. 86^{v}–88^{r}; 2, fo. 82^{v}
May	1–21	Farnham		1, fos. 88^{r}, 90^{r}; 2, fos. 34^{v}, 83^{r}, 85^{v}
June	6–30	Waltham	Writ tested at (28th) by Edward, duke of Cornwall, asking prayers for the king's success in Flanders	1, fos. 25^{r}, 88^{v}–90^{v}, 164^{r-v}; 2, fos. 83^{v}–84r

Date		Place	Details	Reference
July	1–12	Waltham		Win.R.O. 1, fos. 90^{r-v}, 158^{r}, 165^{v}
	24–30	Farnham		1, fos. 90^{v}, 93^{v}, 94^{r}; 2, fo. 84^{r}
Aug.	1–28	Farnham	King thanks Orleton for gift of 30 sacks of wool	1, fos. 91^{v}–99^{r}, 167^{v}–168^{r}; 2, fos. 84^{v}–85^{r}
Sept.	1–29	Farnham		1, fos. 96^{r}–99^{r}, 171^{v}; 2 fo. 85^{v}
Oct.	2–31	Farnham		1, fos. 97^{v}–98^{r}, 169^{v}; 2, fos. 85^{v}–86^{v}
Nov.	1–28	Farnham		1, fos. 98^{r-v}, 170^{v}; 2 fo. 86^{v}
Dec.	2–22	Farnham		1, fo. 98^{r-v}; 2, fos. 35^{v}, 86^{v}
1341				
Jan.	1	Farnham		2, fo. 34^{r}
	10–28	Esher		1, fos. 108^{r}, 110^{v}; 2 fos. 35^{v}, 86^{v}
Feb.	1–7	Esher		1 fo. 110^{v}; 2, fos. 34^{r}, 87^{r}
	19–27	Farnham		1, fos. 98^{v}–99^{r}
March	3–26	Farnham		1, fos. 99^{r}–102^{r}, 111^{r}; 2, fo. 87^{v}
April	1–6	Farnham		1, fo. 99^{r};

			17th; Stratford refused entry	103^v *Birchington*, 39ff
May	3–24	Westminster		Win.R.O. 1, fos. 99^r, 102^v–104^v; 2, fo. 88^v
			Approbacio of the will of Hugh de Courtenay, earl of Devon (27th)	
	31	Esher		1, fo. 99^r
June	3–16	Esher		1, fos. 104^{r-v}, 108^r; 2, fos. 37^r, 88^r
July	4–30	Farnham	Amicable settlement of dispute with Archbishop Stratford about Twynham election	1, fos. 99^r, 104^v–105^r, 108^v; 2, fos. 37^r, 88^v–89^r
Aug.	2–26	Farnham		2, fo. 89^r
Sept.	7	Farnham		*Ibid.*
	13–30	Waltham		1, fo. 106^r–109^r; 2, fo. 89^v
Oct.	3–11	Waltham		1, fo. 106^r; 2, fo. 89^v
	15–22	Wolvesey	Bishop appoints proctors for convocation at St Paul's: too ill to attend	1, fos. 107–108^r, 111^v; 2, fos. 89^v–90^r
	26–9	Farnham		2, fo. 90^{r-v}
Nov.	3–23	Farnham		1, fos. 109^r–110^r; 2, fo. 90^v

Date		Place	Details	Reference
Dec.	4–30	Farnham		Win.R.O. 1, fo. 110r; 2, fos. 90^{v}–91^{r}
1342				
Jan.	7–28	Farnham		1, fo. 110^{r}; 2, fo. 91^{r-v}
Feb.	6–28	Farnham		*Ibid*. and 2, fo. 92^{r}
March	6–29	Farnham		1, fos. 110^{r}–111^{r}; 2, fos. 41^{r}, 92^{r-v}
April	1–20	Farnham		1, fo. 111^{v}; 2, fos. 93^{v}, 94^{r}
May	2–3	Farnham		2, fo. 93^{v}
	15–24	Wargrave		1, fo. 111^{v}; 2, fo. 94^{r}
June	5–25	Wargrave		*Ibid*. and, 2, fo. 94^{v}
July	4–22	Wargrave		1, fo. 112^{r}; 2, fo. 95^{r-v}
Aug.	18–21	Farnham		*Ibid*.
	26	Marwell		1, fo. 112^{v}
Sept.	3–20	Marwell		1, fos. 113^{v}, 114^{v}, 118^{v}, 179^{r}; 2, fos. 96^{r}, 97^{v}
Oct.	3–17	Marwell	Canterbury convocation at St Paul's	1, fos. 115^{r}–117^{v}; 2,

	28–30	Waltham	1, fo. 115^{r-v}; 2, fo. 97^{r}
Nov.	6–27	Waltham	1, fos. 115^{r}–116^{v}; 2, fos. 96^{v}, 97^{r}
Dec.	1–31	Waltham	1, fo. 117^{r-v}; 2, fos. 39^{r}, 97^{v}, 98^{r}
1343			
Jan.	4–18	Waltham	1, fos. 117^{v}–118, 180^{v}
	26	Farnham	2, fo. 98^{v}
Feb.	11–20	Farnham	1, fo. 118^{v}; 2, fo. 98^{v}
March	1–29	Farnham	1, fos. 118^{v}–119^{v}
April	1–21	Farnham	1, fos. 119^{v}–120^{r}
May	18–23	Yately	1, fo. 120^{r-v}
	23	Farnham	*Ibid.*
	26–9	Wargrave	*Ibid.*
June	14–24	Wargrave	1, fo. 121^{r}; 2, fo. 99^{r}
July	1–25	Wargrave	*Ibid.*
	30–1	Wolvesey	1, fo. 121^{r-v}
Aug.	7	Wolvesey	1, fo. 122^{r}
Sept.	6–23	Highclere	1, fos. 121^{v}–123^{r}; 2 fo. 99^{v}

Date		Place	Details	Reference
Oct.	4–13	Highclere		Win.R.O. 1, fos. 121^{v}–122^{r}; 2, fo. 100^{r}
Nov.	10–24 [9]	Farnham		1, fo. 122^{r}; 2, fo. 42^{v}
Dec.	2–28	Farnham		1, fo. 122^{r-v}; 2, fos. 100^{r}–101^{r}
1344				
Jan.	2–30	Farnham		1, fos. 122^{v}–123^{v}; 2, fos. 42^{v}, 101^{r}
Feb.	2–10	Farnham		1, fos. 123^{v}–124^{r}; 2, fo. 101^{v}
	13	Winchester		2, fo. 102^{r}
	13–19	Farnham		1, fo. 124^{r}; 2, fos. 101^{v}–102^{r}
March	1–30	Farnham		1, fos. 123^{v}–124^{v}; 2, fo. 102^{r-v}
April	8–15	Farnham		1, fo. 125^{r}; 2, fo. 102^{v}
May	2–29	Farnham		1, fos. 125^{v}–126^{r}; 2, fos. 102^{v}–103^{r}
June	5–28	Farnham		1, fo. 126^{r}; 2, fo. 103^{v}
July	1–28	Farnham	Appoints prior of Newark by devolution (1st)	1, fos. 126^{r}–127^{r};

				127^v
	29	Waverley Abbey	Consecration of Orleton's nephew, John Trillek, as bishop of Hereford	*Hereford Reg. Trillek*, 21
Sept.	2–21	Farnham		Win.R.O. 1, fos. 127^r–128^r
Oct.	2	Farnham		1, fo. 127^v
Nov.	20–4	Farnham		*Ibid.* and 1, fo. 128^r; 2, fo. 42^v
Dec.	19–28	Farnham		1, fo. 127^v; 2, fos. 102^r, 105^r
1345				
Jan.	10–30	Farnham		1, fo. 128^{r-v}; 2, fo. 105^r
Feb.	3–24	Farnham		*Ibid.*
March	3–29	Farnham		*Ibid.* and *Win. Chart.*, 59
April	2–29	Farnham		1, fo. 128^v; 2, fo. 106^v
May	17	Farnham		2, fo. 107^r
June	3–15	Farnham		2, fos. 106^v–107^r
July	12	Farnham		*Ibid.*
	18	Farnham	Death of Adam Orleton in Farnham Castle	2, fo. 107^{r-v}; *Hereford Reg. Trillek*, 55

[9] 2, fo. 42^v gives 11th year of translation, but 10th is more likely.

BIBLIOGRAPHY

Note: Certain items included in the list of abbreviations are not repeated here.

I MANUSCRIPT SOURCES

CAMBRIDGE

University Library

Gg 1 15: Brut Chronicle.

Ely Diocesan Records G/I/1: Register of Simon de Montacute (1337–45).

CANTERBURY

Register of Archbishop Walter Reynolds (*See* London, Lambeth Palace Library).

HEREFORD

Cathedral Library

1373 A–H: Orleton's 'defence brief' (1324).

1378: Roger de Breynton's claim against Orleton's executors.

1443: Details of the process leading to Cantilupe's canonisation.

1445: *Inspeximus* in Orleton's presence of Pope John XXII's bull for Cantilupe's canonisation.

Other manuscripts which concern Orleton or his relations and *familia* are too numerous to list. In the footnotes they are cited by the numbers of the typescript catalogue: B. G. Charles and H. D. Emanuel, 'A Calendar of the Earlier Hereford Cathedral Muniments' 2, N.R.A. 1955. Indexes are kept at Hereford and in the National Register of Archives, Chancery Lane.

Diocesan Registry

Register of Richard Swinfield (1283–1317).

Register of Adam de Orleton (1317–27).

Bibliography

LICHFIELD

Joint Record Office

Register of Walter Langton (1296–1321), B/A/1/1.

Register of Roger Northburgh (1322–58), B/A/1/1 (ordinations), B/A/1/2–3.

LINCOLN

Lincolnshire Archives Office

Register of Henry Burghersh (1320–40). [Owing to the temporary closure of the record office I was unable to see this MS. in situ and the microfilm arrived too late for me to make as much use of it as I should have liked.]

LONDON

British Library

Add. MSS.:

9951: Wardrobe Book 14 Edward II.

17362: Wardrobe Book 13 Edward II.

24509: Abstracts.

24511: Abstracts.

Detached seal, CXLVI 21 (Orleton's as bishop of Worcester).

Cotton Charters:

II. 26. 27: Letter from Mortimer to the king mentioning the bishop of Hereford.

IV. 9: Indenture of release by Orleton as treasurer of precious articles for use at Edward III's coronation.

Cotton MSS.:

Claudius D. VI: St Albans Chronicles, Trokelowe and Blaneforde.

Claudius E. VIII: Murimuth's chronicle.

Cleopatra D. III: Chronicle of Hales to 1314; Brute Chronicle to Edward III.

Cleopatra D. IX: *Fragmenta de bellis et causis bellorum civilium tempore Edwardi Secundi; Speculum Regis Edwardi* attributed to Archbishop Islip.

Domitian D. XII: Anonymous chronicle.

Faustina B. V: *Historia Roffensis.*

Julius A. 1: French Chronicle (Pipewell).

Julius E. 1: Gascon documents.

Nero C. VIII: Wardrobe Book 4 Edward II.

Nero D. X: Continuator of Nicholas Trivet.

Vitellius E. IV. 9: Letter of Orleton to Pope John XXII.

Vitellius E. V: Elizabethan transcript of the *Vita et Mors Edwardi Secundi.*

Appendix LII: Damaged fragment of Baker's *Chronicon* for the reign of Edward III.

Harleian MSS.:
310: Elizabethan transcript of the *Vita et Mors Edwardi Secundi.*
1240: Mortimer cartulary.
3836: Murimuth's chronicle.
Royal MS. app. 88: Leaves from Orleton's Winchester register of papal bulls.
Stowe MS. 533: Wardrobe Book 15–17 Edward II.

Inner Temple Library
Petyt MS. 47: Elizabethan transcript of the *Vita et Mors Edwardi Secundi.*
Various transcripts in the Petyt collection mention Orleton: see *Catalogue of Manuscripts in the Library of the Honourable Society of the Inner Temple*, ed. J. C. Davies, 3 vols. London 1972.

Lambeth Palace Library
Register of Archbishop Walter Reynolds.
MS. 1213: *Diversi Tractatus.* Includes Orleton's *Responsiones* and letters of Pope John XXII written on his behalf in 1334.

Public Record Office
Chancery:
C.47: Miscellanea. Bundles 27–32 diplomatic documents.
C.49: Parliamentary and Council Proceedings.
C.70: Roman Rolls.
C.81: Warrants for the Great Seal.
Exchequer:
E.30: Diplomatic Documents.
E.43 W.S.: Ancient Documents with Seals from Wardrobe Debentures. [In conjunction with card catalogue of seals.]
E.101: Various Accounts. Includes those of *nuncii* and of the Wardrobe and Household [P.R.O. 'Descriptive List of Wardrobe Books Edward I – Edward IV', comp. E. W. Safford, typescript 1932].
E.159: Memoranda Rolls, King's Remembrancer.
E.163: Exchequer Miscellanea.
E.352: Chancellor's Rolls (Pipe Office).
E.368: Memoranda Rolls, Lord Treasurer's Remembrancer.
E.372: Pipe Rolls.
E.403: Issue Rolls.
E.404: Wardrobe Debentures.
Justices Itinerant:
Just.1/1388: Inquisitions by Hervy de Staunton and his associates, 1324.
Just.3/116: Hereford Gaol Delivery 18 Edward II.
King's Bench:
K.B.27: Coram Rege Rolls.
Special Collections:

S.C.1: Ancient Correspondence.
S.C.7: Papal Bulls.
S.C.8: Ancient Petitions.
S.C.10: Parliamentary Proxies.

Transcripts:
P.R.O. 31/9/17A: Register of Petitions by Andrea Sapiti.

Society of Antiquaries

MS. 120: Wardrobe Book 10 Edward II.
MS. 121: Wardrobe Book 11 Edward II.
MS. 122: Chamber Account Book 18 Edward II.
See also W. St J. Hope, 'Seals of English Bishops', listed below.

Westminster Abbey Muniment Room

20344: Claim by Br. Robert de Beby on behalf of the Westminster monks for the body of Edward II.
21256–70: Documents concerned with the appropriation of Longdon church to Westminster Abbey and the ordination of the vicarage there, temp. Bishops Orleton and Montacute of Worcester.

NORWICH

Norfolk Record Office

Register of John Salmon (1299–1325).
Register of Robert Baldock, bishop-elect and confirmed (1325).
Register of William Ayrminne (1325–36).

OXFORD

Bodleian Library

Bodley MS. 761: Baker's *Chronicon* and *Chroniculum*.
956: Lichfield Chronicle.
Laud MS. Misc. 529: Evesham version of Higden's *Polychronicon*.
Tanner MS. 197: Wardrobe Book 4–5 Edward II.
[Deposited] New College MS. 187: Copy of Decretals of Gregory IX made for Orleton at Vienne.

WINCHESTER

Hampshire Record Office

Register of John Stratford (1323–33).
Register of Adam Orleton (1333–45).
Register of William de Edington (Edyndon) (1345–66).
Winchester Pipe Rolls (1334–44), nos. 159346–54, 159361, 159451.
Handlist of the Episcopal Records of the Diocese of Winchester, ed. A. J. Willis, 1964 (typescript).

WORCESTER

Cathedral Library

Liber Albus.

Registrum Sede Vacante.

Hereford and Worcester Record Office, St Helen's

Register of Godfrey Giffard (1268–1302).

Register of Walter Reynolds (1308–13).

Register of Walter Maidstone (1314–17).

Register of Thomas de Cobham (1317–27).

Register of Adam Orleton (1327–33).

Register of Simon de Montacute (1333–7).

II PRINTED SOURCES

1 CHRONICLES

Annales London.: *Annales Londoniensis*, see *Chronicles of the Reigns of Edward I and Edward II* 1.

Annales Paulini: See *Chronicles of the Reigns of Edward I and Edward II* 1.

Avesbury: *Robertus de Avesbury, De Gestis Mirabilibus Regis Edwardi Tertii*, ed. E. Maunde Thompson, R.S. 1889.

Baker, Chronicon: *Chronicon Galfridi le Baker de Swynebroke;*

Baker, Chroniculum: *Chroniculum Galfridi le Baker de Swynebroke*, ed. E. Maunde Thompson, Oxford 1889.

Birchington: *Stephani Birchingtoni monachi Cantuariensis Historia de Archiepiscopis Cantuariensibus*, ed. H. Wharton, *Anglia Sacra* 1, London 1691.

Blaneforde: See *Trokelowe.*

Bridlington: *Gesta Edwardi de Carnarvon auctore Canonico Bridlingtoniensis*, see *Chronicles of the Reigns of Edward I and Edward II* 2.

Brut: *The Brut or Chronicles of England*, 2 vols. (cont. pagination), E.E.T.S. o.s. 131, 136, London 1906, 1908.

Chronicles of the Reigns of Edward I and Edward II, ed. W. Stubbs, 2 vols., R.S. 1882, 1883.

Chronicon, Chroniculum: See *Baker.*

Civil Wars' Chronicle: [Extract] ed. G. L. Haskins, 'Chronicle of the Civil Wars' (see below), pp. 75–81 (B.L. Cotton MS. Cleopatra D. IX, fos. 83^r–85^r).

Flores: *Flores Historiarum* 3, ed. H. R. Luard, R.S. 1890.

French Chronicle: *Croniques de London*, ed. G. J. Aungier, Camden Soc. o.s. 28, London 1844.

Graystanes: *Roberti de Graystanes Dunelmensis Episcopi Historia de Statu Ecclesiae Dunelmensis*, ed. H. Wharton, *Anglia Sacra* 1, London 1691. (*Cf. Historiae Dunelmensis Scriptores Tres*, ed. J. Raine, Surtees Soc. 9, London–Edinburgh 1839, pp. 35–123.)

Guisborough: *The Chronicle of Walter of Guisborough, Previously Edited as the Chronicle of Walter of Hemingford or Hemingburgh*, ed. H. Rothwell, Camden 3rd ser. 89 (1957).

Hemingburgh: *Chronicon domini Walteri de Hemingburgh, vulgo Hemingford nuncupati*, ed. H. C. Hamilton, Eng. Hist. Soc., London 1849.

Hist. Glouc.: *Historia Gloucestriae*, in *Historia et Cartularium Monasterii Sancti Petri Gloucestriae* 1, ed. W. H. Hart, R.S. 1863.

Historia Roffensis: *Willielmi de Dene Historia Roffensis*, ed. H. Wharton, *Anglia Sacra* 1, London 1691. (B.L. Cotton MS. Faustina B. V.)

Knighton: *Chronicon Henrici Knighton*, ed. J. R. Lumby, 2 vols., R.S. 1889, 1895.

Lanercost: *Chronicon de Lanercost*, ed. J. Stevenson, Bannatyne Club, Edinburgh 1839.

Lichfield Chronicle: [Extracts] M. V. Clarke, 'Committees of Estates' (see below), pp. 33, 36 (Bodleian, Bodley MS. 956).

Melsa: *Chronicon Monasterii de Melsa auctore Thoma de Burton, abbate* [continuation to 1406] 2, ed. E. A. Bond, R.S. 1867.

Murimuth: *Adae Murimuth, Continuatio Chronicarum*, ed. E. Maunde Thompson, R.S. 1889.

'Peterhouse Chronicle': [Extract] J. F. Baldwin, 'The King's Council' (see below), p. 132. (Cambridge, Corpus Christi College MS. 174.)

Pipewell Chronicle: [Extracts] M. V. Clarke, 'Committees of Estates' (see below), n. A, pp. 44–5 (B.L. Cotton MS. Julius A. I, fo. 56^{r-v}); J. Taylor, 'Judgment on Hugh Despenser' (see below), pp. 73–5 (fos. 54^{r}–56^{r}).

Polychronicon: *Polychronicon Ranulphi Higden Monachi Cestrensis* 8, ed. J. R. Lumby, R.S. 1882.

Sempringham: *Chroniques de Sempringham* [continuation of *Le Livere des Reis de Engletere*], ed. J. Glover, R.S. 1865.

Thorne: *Chronica Guillelmi Thorne Monachi Sancti Augustini Cantuariae*, ed. R. Twysden, *Historiae Anglicanae Scriptores Decem*, London 1652.

Trivet: *Nicolai Triveti Annalium Continuatio*, ed. A. Hall, Oxford 1722.

Trokelowe: *Johannis de Trokelowe et Henrici de Blaneforde . . . Chronica et Annales*, ed. H. T. Riley, R.S. 1866.

Vita: *Vita Edwardi Secundi*, ed. N. Denholm-Young, London 1957.

Vita et Mors: *Vita et Mors Edwardi II conscripta a Thoma de la Moore*, see *Chronicles of the Reigns of Edward I and Edward II* 2.

Walsingham: *Chronica Monasterii Sancti Albani, Thomae Walsingham . . . Historia Anglicana* 1, ed. H. T. Riley, R.S. 1863.

Wigmore Chronicle: Ed. W. Dugdale, *Monasticum Anglicanum*, London 1817–30, 6i.

Ypodigma Neustriae: *Chronica Monasterii Sancti Albani, Ypodigma Neustriae, a Thoma Walsingham* 7, R.S. 1876.

2 COLLECTIONS OF DOCUMENTS AND CALENDARS

Acta Sanctorum mensis Octobris 1 (Bollandistes), Antwerp 1765, pp. 539–705.

Anglia Sacra, ed. H. Wharton, 2 vols., London 1691.

Bath & Wells Reg. [*John*] *Drokensford*, 1309–29, ed. E. Hobhouse, Somerset Record Soc. 1887.

Bath & Wells Reg. [*Ralph of*] *Shrewsbury*, 1329–63, ed. T. S. Holmes, Somerset Record Soc. 1897.

Calendar of Ancient Petitions relating to Wales, ed. W. Rees, Cardiff 1975.

Calendar of Chancery Warrants 1, 1244–1326, London 1927.

Calendar of Letter Books of the City of London, D (1309–14), *E* (1314–37), *F* (1337–52), ed. R. R. Sharpe, London 1902–4.

Calendar of Memoranda Rolls (Exchequer) Michaelmas 1326 – Michaelmas 1327, London 1968.

Canterbury Professions, ed. M. Richter, C.Y.S. 1973.

Cartularium Gloucestriae: Historia et Cartularium Monasterii Sancti Petri Gloucestriae, ed. W. H. Hart, 3 vols., R.S. 1863–5.

Catalogue of Manuscripts in the Library of the Honourable Society of the Inner Temple, ed. J. C. Davies, 3 vols., London 1972.

Chartularium Universitatis Parisiensis 2, ed. H. Denifle and E. Chatelain, Paris 1891.

Collectanea 2nd ser., ed. M. Burrows, O.H.S. 16 (1892).

Concilia Magnae Britanniae et Hiberniae 2, ed. D. Wilkins, London 1737.

(Sacrorum) Conciliorum Nova et Amplissima Collectio 25, ed. J. D. Mansi, rev. J. B. Martin and L. Petit, Paris 1903.

Councils and Synods, ed. F. M. Powicke and C. R. Cheney, 2 vols., Oxford 1964.

Documents Illustrating the Activities of the General and Provincial Chapters of the English Black Monks, 1215–1540, ed. W. A. Pantin, Camden 3rd ser. 45, 47, 59 (1931–7).

Documents Illustrative of English History in the 13th and 14th Centuries, ed. H. Cole, London 1844.

Encomium Emmae Reginae, ed. A. Campbell, Camden 3rd ser. 72 (1949).

Exeter Reg. [*John de*] *Grandisson*, 1327–69, ed. F. C. Hingeston-Randolph, London–Exeter 1894–9.

Exeter Reg. [*Walter*] *Stapledon*, 1307–26, ed. F. C. Hingeston-Randolph, London–Exeter 1892.

Hereford Cathedral Charters: *Charters and Records of Hereford Cathedral*, ed. W. W. Capes, Hereford 1908.

Hereford Reg. [*Thomas de*] *Cantilupe*, 1275–82, ed. R. G. Griffiths and W. W. Capes, Cantilupe Soc. Hereford and C.Y.S., London 1907.

Hereford Reg. [*Thomas*] *Charlton*, 1327–44, ed. W. W. Capes, *ibid.* 1912.

Hereford Reg. [*Adam de*] *Orleton*, 1317–27, ed. A. T. Bannister, *ibid.* 1908.

Hereford Reg. [*Richard de*] *Swinfield*, 1283–1317, ed. W. W. Capes, *ibid.* 1909.

Hereford Reg. [*John de*] *Trillek*, 1344–61, ed. J. H. Parry, *ibid.* 1910–12.

Letters from Northern Registers, ed. J. Raine, R.S. 1883.

Lettres communes des papes d'Avignon: *Jean XXII* (*1316–34*), ed. G. Mollat, *Bibliothèque des Écoles Françaises d'Athènes et de Rome*, 3rd Ser., 16 vols., Paris 1904–47.

Liber Albus of Worcester Priory, ed. J. M. Wilson, W.H.S. 1919. See also: *Worcester Liber Albus* (extracts).

London Regs. [*Ralph*] *Baldock*, 1304–13, [*Gilbert*] *Segrave*, 1313–16, [*Richard*] *Newport*, 1317–18, [*Stephen*] *Gravesend*, 1318–38, ed. R. C. Fowler, C.Y.S. 1911.

Parliamentary Writs, ed. F. Palgrave, Record Commission, 2 vols. in 4, London 1827–44.

Reports . . . Touching the Dignity of a Peer, 5 vols., London 1920–9.

Rochester Reg. [*Hamo de*] *Hethe*, 1319–52, ed. C. Johnson, C.Y.S. 1914–48.

Rotuli Parliamentorum, ed. J. Strachey *et al.*, 6 vols., London 1767.

Rotuli Parliamentorum Anglie Hactenus Inediti, ed. H. G. Richardson and G. O. Sayles, Camden 3rd ser. 51 (1935).

Salisbury Reg. [*Simon de*] *Gandavo*, 1297–1315, ed. C. T. Flower and M. C. B. Dawes, C.Y.S. 1914–34.

Salisbury Reg. [*Roger*] *Martival*, 1315–30, ed. K. Edwards, C. R. Elrington and S. Reynolds, C.Y.S. 1959–65.

The Gascon Calendar of 1322, ed. G. P. Cuttino, Camden 3rd ser. 70 (1949).

The War of Saint Sardos, ed. P. Chaplais, Camden 3rd ser. 87 (1954).

Treaty Rolls 1, 1234–1325, ed. P. Chaplais, London 1955.

Treaty Rolls 2, 1337–1339, ed. J. Ferguson, London 1972.

Winchester Chartulary: Chartulary of Winchester Cathedral, ed. A. W. Goodman, Winchester 1927.

Winchester Reg. [*John de*] *Pontissara*, 1282–1304, ed. C. Deedes, C.Y.S. 1915.

Winchester Reg. [*John*] *Sandale*, 1316–19, and [*Rigaud de*] *Asserio*, 1319–23, ed. F. J. Baigent, Hants. Record Soc. 1897.

Winchester Reg. [*Henry*] *Woodlock*, 1305–16, ed. A. W. Goodman, C.Y.S. 1940–1.

Worcester Liber Albus, ed. J. M. Wilson, London 1920. See also *Liber Albus of Worcester Priory* (Calendar).

Worcester Reg. [*Wolstan de*] *Bransford*, 1339–49, ed. R. M. Haines, H.M.S.O./W.H.S. 1966.

Worcester Reg. [*Thomas de*] *Cobham*, 1317–27, ed. E. H. Pearce, W.H.S. 1929–30.

Worcester Reg. [*William*] *Gainsburgh*, 1302–7, ed. J. W. Willis Bund, W.H.S. 1906; *Introduction*, R. A. Wilson, W.H.S. 1928.

Worcester Reg. [*Godfrey*] *Giffard*, 1268–1302, ed. J. W. Willis Bund, W.H.S. 1898–1900.
Worcester Reg. [*Adam de*] *Orleton*, 1327–33, ed. R. M. Haines, H.M.S.O./W.H.S. [in press].
Worcester Reg. [*Walter*] *Reynolds*, 1308–13, ed. R. A. Wilson, W.H.S. 1927.
Worcester Reg. Sede Vacante, 1301–1435, ed. J. W. Willis Bund, W.H.S. 1893–7.

Typescript

Calendar of the Earlier Hereford Cathedral Muniments, ed. B. G. Charles, and H. D. Emanuel, 3 vols. and indexes, N.R.A. 1955.
Handlist of the Episcopal Records of the Diocese of Winchester, ed. A. J. Willis, Hampshire Record Office, 1964.

3 SECONDARY WORKS

Armstrong, C. A. J., 'Some Examples of the Distribution and Speed of News in England at the Time of the Wars of the Roses', in Hunt *et al.* eds., *Studies*, pp. 429–54.
Baldwin, J. F., 'The King's Council', in Willard and Morris eds., *English Government at Work* 1, pp. 129–61.
Bannister, A. T., *The Cathedral Church of Hereford*, London 1924.
Barnes, J., *The History of . . . Edward III*, Cambridge 1688.
Behrens, B., 'Origins of the Office of English Resident Ambassador in Rome', *E.H.R.* 49 (1934), pp. 640–56.
Bellamy, J. G., *The Law of Treason in England in the Later Middle Ages*, Cambridge 1970.
Blackley, F. D., 'Isabella and the Bishop of Exeter', in *Essays in Medieval History Presented to Bertie Wilkinson*, eds. T. A. Sandquist and M. R. Powicke, Toronto 1969, pp. 220–35.
Bolton, B., 'The Council of London of 1342', in *Councils and Assemblies,* S.C.H 7 (1971), pp. 147–60.
Boyle, L. E., 'William of Pagula and the *Speculum Regis Edwardi III*', *Mediaeval Studies* 32 (1970), pp. 329–36.
'The Constitution *Cum ex eo* of Boniface VIII: Education of Parochial Clergy', *Mediaeval Studies* 24 (1962), pp. 262–302.
Broome, D. M., 'Exchequer Migrations to York in the 13th and 14th centuries', in Little and Powicke eds., *Essays*, pp. 291–300.
Cam, H., *Law-Finders and Law-Makers in Medieval England*, London 1962.
Cassan, S. H., *Lives of the Bishops of Winchester*, 2 vols., London 1827.
Cerchiari, E., *Capellani Papae . . . seu Sacra Romana Rota* 2, Rome 1920.
Chaplais, P., 'English Arguments concerning the Feudal Status of Aquitaine in the 14th Century', *B.I.H.R.* 21 (1948), pp. 203–13.

'Le Duché-Pairie de Guyenne: l'hommage et les services féodaux de 1303 à 1337' (pt 2), *Annales du Midi* 70 (1958), pp. 135–60.

Charles, B. G. and H. D. Emanuel, 'Notes on Old Libraries and Books', *National Library of Wales Journal* 6 (1949–50), pp. 353–71.

Churchill, I. J., *Canterbury Administration*, 2 vols., London 1933.

Clarke, M. V., *Fourteenth Century Studies*, Oxford 1937.

'Committees of Estates and the Deposition of Edward II', in *Historical Essays in Honour of James Tait*, ed. J. G. Edwards *et al.*, Manchester 1933, pp. 27–45 (also in Clarke, *Medieval Representation and Consent*, London–New York 1936, repr. New York 1964, pp. 173–95).

Clementi, D., 'That the Statute of York Is No Longer Ambiguous', *Album Helen Cam* 2, Louvain–Paris 1961, pp. 93–100.

Colledge, E. [Intro. to] *The Latin Poems of Richard Ledrede O.F.M.*, Toronto 1974.

Cristofori, F., *Storia dei Cardinali di Santa Romana Chiesa*, Rome 1888.

Crump, C. G., 'The Arrest of Roger Mortimer and Queen Isabel', *E.H.R.* 26 (1911), pp. 331–2.

Cuttino, G. P., *English Diplomatic Administration 1259–1339*, 2nd edn, Oxford 1971.

'A Memorandum Book of Elias Joneston', *Speculum* 17 (1942), pp. 74–85.

'Another Memorandum Book of Elias Joneston', *E.H.R.* 63 (1948), pp. 90–103.

Davies, J. C., *The Baronial Opposition to Edward II*, Cambridge 1918.

'The Despenser War in Glamorgan', *T.R.H.S.*, 3rd ser., 9 (1915), pp. 21–64.

Davis, H. W. C., ed., *Essays in History Presented to R. L. Poole*, Oxford 1927, repr. New York 1969.

Denholm-Young, N., 'The Authorship of the *Vita Edwardi Secundi*', *E.H.R.* 71 (1956), pp. 189–211.

'The Mappa Mundi of Richard of Haldingham at Hereford', *Speculum* 32 (1957), pp. 307–14.

Collected Papers, Cardiff 1969. (Reprints the above at pp. 267–89 and 74–82 respectively.)

Denholm-Young, N., ed., *Liber Epistolaris of Richard of Bury*, Roxburghe Club, Oxford 1950.

Déprez, E., *Les préliminaires de la Guerre de Cent Ans, Bibliothèque des Écoles Françaises d'Athènes et de Rome* 96, Paris 1902.

See also Mirot and Déprez.

Douie, D. L., 'The Canonisation of St Thomas of Hereford', *Dublin Review* 229 (1955), pp. 275–87.

Edwards, J. G., 'The Negotiating of the Treaty of Leake, 1318', in Davis ed., *Essays*, pp. 360–78.

'Sir Gruffydd Llwyd', *E.H.R.* 30 (1915), pp. 589–601.

Edwards, K., *English Secular Cathedrals*, 2nd edn, New York 1967.
'The Political Importance of the English Bishops during the Reign of Edward II', *E.H.R.* 59 (1944), pp. 311–47.
'Bishops and Learning in the Reign of Edward II', *Church Quarterly Review* 138 (1944), pp. 57–86.

Emanuel, H. D., 'Notaries Public and Their Marks Recorded in the Archives of the Dean and Chapter of Hereford', *National Library of Wales Journal* 8 (1953–4), pp. 147–63.
See also Charles and Emanuel.

Emden, *Biog. Cantab.*, see Abbreviations.
Biog. Oxon., see Abbreviations.

Fowler, K., *The King's Lieutenant: Henry of Grosmont, First Duke of Lancaster, 1310–1361*, London–New York 1969.

Fryde, E. B. and E. Miller, eds., *Historical Studies of the English Parliament 1: Origins to 1399*, Cambridge 1970.

Fryde, N. M., 'Edward III's Removal of His Ministers and Judges, 1340–1', *B.I.H.R.* 48 (1975), pp. 149–61.

Galbraith, V. H., 'The Chronicle of Henry Knighton', in *Fritz Saxl, a Volume of Memorial Essays*, ed. D. J. Gordon, London 1957, pp. 136–48.
'The *Historia Aurea* of John, Vicar of Tynemouth, and the Sources of the St Albans Chronicle (1327–1377)', in Davis ed. *Essays*, pp. 379–98.
'The Tower as an Exchequer Record Office in the Reign of Edward II', in Little and Powicke eds., *Essays*, pp. 231–47.

Grassi, J. L., 'William Airmyn and the Bishopric of Norwich', *E.H.R.* 70 (1955), pp. 550–61.

Graves, E. B., *A Bibliography of English History to 1485*, Oxford 1975.

Haines, R. M., 'Adam Orleton and the Diocese of Winchester', *J.E.H.*, 23 (1972), pp. 1–30.
'A Defence Brief for Bishop Adam de Orleton', *B.I.H.R.* (in press).
'Wolstan de Bransford, Prior and Bishop of Worcester, *c.* 1280–1349', *University of Birmingham Historical Journal* 8 (1962), pp. 97–113.
'The Education of the English Clergy during the Later Middle Ages: Some Observations on the Operation of Boniface VIII's Constitution *Cum ex eo* (1298)', *Canadian Journal of History* 4 (1969), pp. 1–22.
'The Appropriation of Longdon Church to Westminster Abbey', *Trans. Worcs. Archaeological Soc.* 38 (1961), pp. 39–52.
'Aspects of the Episcopate of John Carpenter', *J.E.H.* 19 (1968), pp. 11–40.

Harcourt, L. W. V., *His Grace the Steward and the Trial of Peers*, London 1907.

Haskins, G. L., 'The Doncaster Petition, 1321', *E.H.R.* 53 (1938), pp. 478–85.
'A Chronicle of the Civil Wars of Edward II', *Speculum* 14 (1939), pp. 73–81.

Hill, M. C., *The King's Messengers 1199–1377: A Contribution to the History of the Royal Household*, London 1961.

Holmes, G. A., 'Judgement on the Younger Despenser', *E.H.R.* 70 (1955), pp. 261–7.

'The Rebellion of the Earl of Lancaster, 1328–29', *B.I.H.R.* 28, (1955), pp. 84–9.

Hope, W. St J., 'The Seals of English Bishops', *Procs of the Soc. of Antiquaries*, 2nd ser., 11 (1887), pp. 271–306.

Hughes, D., *A Study of . . . the Early Years of Edward III*, London 1915.

Hunt, R. W., W. A. Pantin and R. W. Southern, eds., *Studies in Medieval History Presented to F. M. Powicke*, Oxford 1948, repr. 1969.

Hunter, J., 'Journal of the Mission of Queen Isabella to the Court of France and of Her Long Residence in That Country', *Archaeologia* 36 (1855), pp. 242–57.

Johnstone, H., *Edward of Carnarvon*, 1284–1307, Manchester 1946.

Jones, W. R., 'Bishops, Politics and the Two Laws; the Gravamina of the English Clergy, 1237–1399', *Speculum* 41 (1966), pp. 209–45.

Kirsch, J. B., 'Andreas Sapiti, Englischer Prokurator an der Kurie im 14 Jahrhundert', *Historisches Jahrbuch* 14 (1893), pp. 582–95.

Knowles, D. and R. N. Hadcock, *Medieval Religious Houses*, Cambridge 1953.

Langlois, C.-V., 'Documents relatifs à l'histoire du xiiie et du xive siècle', *Revue Historique* 87–8 (1905), pp. 55–79.

Lapsley, G. T., 'Archbishop Stratford and the Parliamentary Crisis of 1341', *E.H.R.* 30 (1915), pp. 6–18, 193–215 (repr. in *Crown, Community and Parliament*, ed. H. M. Cam and G. Barraclough, Oxford 1951, pp. 231–72).

Larson, A., 'English Embassies during the Hundred Years War', *E.H.R.* 55 (1940), pp. 423–31.

'Payment of 14th-Century English Envoys', *E.H.R.* 54 (1939), pp. 403–14.

Leland, J., ed. L. T. Smith, *Itinerary* 5, London 1907–10.

Little, A. G. and F. M. Powicke, eds., *Essays in Medieval History Presented to T. F. Tout*, Manchester 1925, repr. New York 1967.

Lizerand, G., *Clément V et Philippe IV le Bel*, Paris 1910.

Lowe, W. I., 'The Considerations Which Induced Edward III to Assume the Title King of France', *Annual Rept, American Historical Assn for the Year 1900* 1, Washington 1901, pp. 537–83.

Luard, H. R., 'Adam of Orlton', *D.N.B.* 1.

Lucas, H. S., 'The Machinery of Diplomatic Intercourse', in Willard and Morris eds., *English Government at Work*, 1, pp. 300–31.

Lunt, W. E., *Financial Relations of the Papacy with England to 1327, 1327–1534*, 2 vols., Cambridge, Mass. 1939, 1962.

Lunt, W. E., ed. E. B. Graves, *Accounts Rendered by Papal Collectors in England 1317–78*, Philadelphia 1968.

McKisack, M., *The Fourteenth Century 1307–1399*, Oxford 1959.
Medieval History in the Tudor Age, Oxford 1971.
Maddicott, J. R., *Thomas of Lancaster 1307–1322: a Study in the Reign of Edward II*, London 1970.
Michelmore, D. J. H., 'The Expenses of Adam Orleton, Bishop of Worcester, on a Mission to France, 1332', *The Mariner's Mirror* 58 (1972), pp. 177–8.
Mirot, L. and E. Déprez, 'Les ambassades anglaises pendant la Guerre de Cent Ans: catalogue chronologique (1327–1450)', *Bibliothèque de l'École des Chartes* 59 (1898), pp. 550–77.
Mollat, G., *The Popes at Avignon 1305–1378*, New York 1965.
'L'élection du Pape Jean XXII', *Revue d'Histoire de l'Église de France* 50 (1910), pp. 34–49, 147–66.
Morris, W. A. [Intro. to] Willard and Morris eds., *English Government at Work* 1.
Müller, E., *Das Konzil von Vienne 1311–1312*, Münster in Westfalen 1934.
Neilson, N., 'The Forests', in Willard and Morris eds., *English Government at Work*, 1, pp. 394–467.
Nicholson, R., *Edward III and the Scots*, Oxford 1965.
Parry, B. P., 'A Note on Sir Gruffydd Llwyd', *Bulletin of the Board of Celtic Studies* 19 (1962), pp. 316–18.
Pauli, R., *Geschichte von England* 4, Gotha 1855.
Pearce, E. H., *Thomas de Cobham*, London 1923.
Perroy, E., *The Hundred Years War*, London 1951.
Phillips, J. R. S., *Aymer de Valence, Earl of Pembroke 1307–1324*, Oxford 1972.
Plucknett, T. F. T., 'Parliament', in Willard and Morris eds., *English Government at Work* 1, pp. 82–128 (also in Fryde and Miller eds., *Historical Studies*, pp. 195–241).
'The Origins of Impeachment', *T.R.H.S.*, 4th ser., 24 (1942), pp. 47–71.
Putnam, B. H., *The Place in Legal History of Sir William Shareshull . . . a Study of Judicial and Administrative Methods in the Reign of Edward III*, Cambridge 1950.
Queller, D., *The Office of Ambassador in the Middle Ages*, Princeton 1967.
Redstone, V. B., 'Some Mercenaries of Henry of Lancaster', *T.R.H.S.*, 3rd ser., 7 (1913), pp. 151–66.
Richardson, H. G. 'The *Annales Paulini*', *Speculum* 23 (1948), pp. 630–40.
Richardson, H. G. and G. O. Sayles, *The Governance of Mediaeval England*, Edinburgh 1963, repr. 1964.
Robo, E., *Mediaeval Farnham: Everyday Life in an Episcopal Manor*, Farnham 1935, repr. 1949.
Safford, E. W., 'An Account of the Expenses of Eleanor Sister of Edward III on the Occasion of Her Marriage to Reynald, Count of Guelders', *Archaeologia* 77 (1928), pp. 111–40.

Salisbury, E., 'A Political Agreement of June, 1318', *E.H.R.* 23 (1918), pp. 78–83.

Sayles, G. O., 'The Formal Judgement on the Traitors of 1322', *Speculum* 16 (1941), pp. 57–63.

See also: Richardson and Sayles.

Smith, W. E. L., *Episcopal Appointments and Patronage in the Reign of Edward III*, Chicago 1938.

Stones, E. L. G., 'The Date of Roger Mortimer's Escape from the Tower', *E.H.R.* 61 (1951), pp. 97–8.

'The English Mission to Edinburgh in 1328', *Scottish Historical Review* 28 (1949), pp. 121–32.

'The Treaty of Northampton, 1328', *History*, n.s. 38 (1953), pp. 54–61.

Stubbs, W., *The Constitutional History of England*, 3 vols., Oxford 1874–8.

Tait, J., ed. [Intro. to] *Chronica Johannis de Reading et anonymi Cantuariensis*, Manchester 1914.

Tanquerey, F. J., 'The Conspiracy of Thomas Dunheved, 1327', *E.H.R.* 21 (1916), pp. 119–24.

Taylor, J., 'The Judgment on Hugh Despenser, the Younger', *Medievalia et Humanistica* 12 (1958), pp. 70–7.

Templeman, G., 'Edward III and the Beginnings of the Hundred Years War', *T.R.H.S.*, 5th ser., 2 (1952), pp. 69–88.

Thomas, W., *Survey of the Cathedral Church of Worcester*, London 1737.

Titow, J. Z., *Winchester Yields: A Study in Medieval Agricultural Productivity*, Cambridge 1972.

Tout, T. F., *Chapters in Medieval Administrative History*, 6 vols., Manchester 1920–33.

Collected Papers, 3 Vols., Manchester 1932–4, including:

'The Westminster Chronicle Attributed to Robert of Reading', vol. 2, pp. 289–304 (*E.H.R.* 31 (1916), pp. 450–64);

'John of Halton, Bishop of Carlisle, an Introduction to the *Registrum Johannis de Halton*', vol. 2, pp. 101–42 (cf. *Carlisle Reg. Halton*, 1292–1324, C.Y.S. 1913);

'The Captivity and Death of Edward of Carnarvon', vol. 3, pp. 145–90 (*B.J.R.L.* 6 (1920), pp. 69–113).

Tout, T. F., rev. H. Johnstone, *The Place of the Reign of Edward II in English History*, Manchester 1936.

Tupling, G. H., *South Lancashire in the Reign of Edward II*, Chetham Soc., 3rd ser., 1 (1949).

Usher, G. A., 'The Career of a Political Bishop: Adam de Orleton (*c.* 1279–1345)', *T.R.H.S.*, 5th ser., 22 (1972), pp. 33–47.

'Adam de Orleton', unpublished M.A. thesis, University of Wales 1953.

Wilkinson, B. *The Chancery under Edward III*, Manchester 1929.

Studies in the Constitutional History of the 13th and 14th centuries, Manchester 1937.

'The Negotiations preceding the "Treaty" of Leake, August 1318', in Hunt *et al.* eds., *Studies*, pp. 333–53.

'The Protest of the Earls of Arundel and Surrey in the Crisis of 1341', *E.H.R.* 46 (1931), pp. 177–93.

'The Sherburn Indenture and the Attack on the Despensers, 1321', *E.H.R.* 63 (1948), pp. 1–28.

'The Deposition of Richard II and the Accession of Henry IV', *E.H.R.* 54 (1939), pp. 215–39 (also in Fryde and Miller eds., *Historical Studies*, pp. 330–53).

Willard, J. F. and W. A. Morris, eds., *The English Government at Work 1327–1336* I, Cambridge, Mass. 1940.

Williams, G. A., *Medieval London: From Commune to Capital*, London 1963.

Wright, J. R., 'The Supposed Illiteracy of Archbishop Walter Reynolds', *The Church and Academic Learning*, S.C.H. 5 (1969), pp. 58–68.

Yates, W. N., 'The Fabric Rolls of Hereford Cathedral 1290/1 and 1386/7', *National Library of Wales Journal* 18 (1973), pp. 79–86.

INDEX

Aylton or Aylington, Adam de, dean of Westbury, chaplain of Orleton as bp of Hereford, 92, 97
Ayrminne, William, bp of Norwich (1325–36), keeper of the Great Seal (Nov. 1326): alleged determinants of his promotion, 37, 116 n.78; attends coronation of Edward III and chants litany, 178 & n.94; celebrates *missa de pace* at convocation (1329), 187; chancery clerk and keeper of the seal, 14 n.39, 158 n.123, 166; diplomatic missions, 31, 33, 39, 188, 233; estimates of, 156, 199; integrity impugned by Edward II, 37, 201; omitted from writ for resisting invasion (1326), 160 n.140; one of the 'queen's bishops', 156ff; question of his whereabouts in 1326, 156, 160 n.139, 162; seals (with Orleton) convention of Bois de Vincennes (1330), 33; spoliation of goods of, 51; temporalities restored (1326), 156 n.112; testimonial to Abp Mepham's character (1330), 182 n.6; witnesses City of London charter (1327), 179; witnesses proclamation as *custos regni* of Prince Edward (1326), 160 n.141, 166

Badby (Northants.), 243
Baddeby, John de, bailiff of Hanbury, 93
Badlesmere, Bartholomew, steward of the household (1318–Oct. 1321): at alleged inception of 'middle party' (1317), 118; capture and death following Boroughbridge (1322), 155; charges against, 155 n.106; diplomatic missions, 16–17, 23, 24 n.85; joins barons against the king (1321), 155; Lancaster's hatred of, 131; messengers of kept waiting at Hereford (1317), 44; produces spurious document to incriminate younger Despenser (1322), 129; promotes interests of his nephew, Henry Burghersh (*q.v.*), 24, 155; ties of kinship with Mortimer, 155 n.105; wife, 155 n.105, holds Leeds Castle against king, 131, incarcerated at Dover, 155 n.106
Badyngton, Roger de, proctor of Orleton, 5 n.24
Baker, Geoffrey le, clerk, of Swinbrook, chronicler, 102ff; account of second mission to Kenilworth (1327), 173–4; attributes to Orleton responsibility for Scottish treaty (1328), 39, and vindictiveness, 190; authority for statement that Orleton addressed the insurgents (1326), 164; claims that Orleton plotted Edward II's death and deposition, 102, 104–5, 108ff, 203–4, and plotted the queen's journey to France (1325), 104, 154; pardoned as malefactor (1326), 105; praises Queen Isabella in *Chroniculum*, 103; regards Orleton's mission of 1328 as being on his own behalf and the queen's, 27 n.5; sympathetic towards Stratford, 104, 174 n.76; views Burghersh and Orleton as fomentors of discord, 154
Baldock, Ralph, bp of London (1306–13), member of delegation to Vienne (1311), 13
Baldock, M. Robert, chancellor (1323–6), 165; allegedly abuses power, 177 n.87; criticised by author of *Vita*, 107 n.27; death, 102, 106, 189, events leading up to, 111–12; diplomatic missions, 21–2; elevation to bishopric pre-empted by Ayrminne, 155 n.104, by Stratford, 159; 'extortions', 160; keeper of privy seal (1320–3), 22; king's letter to at time of Vienne council, 13 n.29; and Orleton: claimed as clerk by, 167, receives goods and chattels of, 179, unable to report to (1321), 26; treatment of (1326), 167, 228; warns Bp Burghersh to behave, 151
Baldwin, J. F., reiterates traditional view of Orleton, 177 n.88
Banbury Castle, 137
Bannister, Canon A. T.: assumes Orleton's loyalty to and dependence on Mortimers, 2, 200, 202; attributes to Orleton commutation of Mortimers' death sentences (1322), 142–3, and escape of younger Mortimer, 108–9, 143; defence of Orleton, 199–200; view of Orleton's part in the 1341 crisis, 106, 180 n.1
Barcheston (Warwicks.), church of, 77
Barcheston or Bercheston, John de, rector of Esher, 77
Bardi, the, merchants of Florence, 24 & n.89, 244
Baret, Richard, vicar of Bromyard, 47 n.41
Barewe, M. Hugh de, 47 n.41
Barnwood (Gloucs.), 230
Bath and Wells, bps of, *see* Droxford, John; Haselshaw; Shrewsbury, Ralph of

Baysham (Herefs.), church of, 45 n.24
Beaumes (Berks.), elder Despenser's manor of (from 1326 held by Orleton), 33, 53, 57, 85, 167, 179, 187–8, 229–38; *see also* Shinfield
Beaumont, Henry de, brother of Bp Louis de Beaumont (*q.v.*), accompanies Prince Edward to France (1325), 160
Beaumont, Louis de, bp of Durham (1318–33): absences from parliament, 181 n.5; allegedly responsible with Orleton for commutation of Mortimers' sentences (1322), 142–3; letters from Orleton transmitted to (1320), 22–3; name omitted from those taking Guildhall oath (1327), 172; present at Edward III's coronation, 178 n.94; promotion: sought by Queen Isabella, 154, influenced by English and French kings, 116 n.78; responds to summons to Sherburn (1321), 129; whereabouts at time of Isabella's landing, 160 n.140
Beaumont, Br. Richard de, prior of Hamble, 77 n.122
Beautre, John de, notary public, rector of St Helen's, Worcester, later of Upham, 77, 97; possibly in Hereford registry, 85 & n.31; registrar of Worcester diocese, 90–1, of Winchester diocese, 95
Beauvais (Oise), 222; death of Bp Gainsburgh at, 9
Becket, St Thomas, abp of Canterbury (1162–70): rules on reiteration of profession to a superior, 55; Stratford's devotion to, 198
Beckford (Gloucs.), 238
Bedewynde, Walter de, treasurer of York, 10
Bedfont (Middx.), church of, 47 n.45
Bedford, submission of Henry of Lancaster at, 187
Bedhampton (Hants.), 66
Bello, Richard de, canon of Hereford, reputed author of the *Mappa Mundi*, 7
Benedict XII, Pope (1334–42), 190 n.64
Benstede, John de, king's clerk, 179
Bentworth or Bintworth, M. Richard, D.C.L., bp of London (1338–9), 80, 253; with Orleton on diplomatic mission, 38
Bercheston, *see* Barcheston, John de
Berde, Richard, called, of Ledbury, notary public, registrar of Bp Montacute, 85 n.31, 91
Berkeley (Gloucs.), 238–9
Berkeley, Thomas de, 140
Bermondsey (Surr.), Cluniac priory, 68
Bertrand, Cardinal, *see* Montfavèz
Bethune, Richard de, mayor of London, 175
Bibury (Gloucs.), episcopal manor, 139 n.26, 223, 230, 239–40
Bicknor, *see* English Bicknor
Bicknor, Alexander, abp of Dublin (1317–49): at Avignon (1317), 118; claims Orleton for the Church (1324), 145–6; complained of by Edward II (1325), 157; joins Isabella's forces (1326), 160 & n.141, 162; mediatory role, 120; takes Guildhall oath (1327), 172 n.68; witnesses proclamation of Prince Edward as *custos regni* (1326), 166
Bikerton, Richard de, steward of Orleton at Worcester and his attorney, 92, 93 n.105; granted lands at Northwick, 92–3
Bintworth, Richard, *see* Bentworth
Birchington, Stephen, chronicler (attributed): derogatory attitude to Orleton, 115, 196, in 1341, 194ff; describes Stratford's flight from Wilton (1328), 185; his authorship repudiated by Tait, 115 n.70
Birston, M. William de, archdeacon of Gloucester, 9, 117
Birthou, W. de, scribe, 13 n.33
Bisham (Berks.), Augustinian priory, 75
Bishopestone, *see* Bishopstone
Bishoprics, process of election to, 29ff, 30 n.17, 37–8 n.61
Bishops: alleged unscrupulousness of, 160, 199–200; dubbed *canes muti* by author of *Flores* (1322), 139; forbidden by Stratford to collect ninth from those paying tenth, 192–3; interest in standing council, 123–4; mediatory role, 118ff, at Leicester (1318), 122 n.31, at St Albans and London (1321), 129–31; notion of 'queen's bishops' examined, 154ff; reasons for joining Isabella, 160ff, 200; sympathies at time of 'Treaty' of Leake (1318), 124ff
Bishops Castle (Salop), 50, 138, 221
Bishops Hampton (Hampton Lucy, Warwicks.), episcopal manor, 182 n.10, 229, 232, 234, 239–40
Bishops Waltham (Hants.), episcopal manor, 64, 245, 251–5, 257

Index

Edward II, king of England—*cont.*
that he banished his wife and son, 168 n.45; denounces: Orleton for revealing counsel at the Curia, 18, Burghersh for asking aid of French king, 138, Stratford as *pseudo nuncius*, 37; deposition, 26, 62, 169ff, 228, part played by Orleton and Stratford in, 180–1; estimates of nature of reign of, 118ff, 177 n.87, 199ff; flight (1326), 85, 165ff; forbids Orleton to accept Hereford bishopric (1317), 17–19, demands his removal from (1325), 108; *Herodiana sevicia* (Orleton), 51 n.75, 151 n.79; homage performed by (1320), 25, 220; hunts in Orleton's parks (1322), 140–2; 'inordinate love' for younger Despenser, 168 n.43; insists on Reynolds as primate, 164; involvement in Orleton's trial (1324), 144ff; marches to Cirencester (1321), 132, 134; pleads illness rather than go to France (1325), 153–4; praises Orleton for diplomatic efforts (1312), 14; promises to observe Ordinances (1318), 121, secures absolution from oath (1320), 24; rumoured to be alive in 1328, 188 n.51; secures Gaveston's absolution from excommunication, 9, and Despensers' recall (1321), 132–3; supports canonisation of Cantilupe, 5, 8; upbraids Orleton at Hereford (1322), 135, 137, 223

Edward III, king of England (1327–77)
as prince (created duke of Cornwall 1312): appointed *custos regni* (1326), 160 n.141, 166; enmity between him and younger Despenser preached by Orleton, 165; invested with duchy of Aquitaine, 153
as king: abandons siege of Tournai (1340), 192, and returns unexpectedly to London, 192; attends Cantilupe's translation, 25 n.95; brother, *see* Eltham; conflict with Stratford (1341), 190ff; coronation, 177–8, 228; gives way on issue of liege homage (1331), 34; letter to Bp Montacute re Irby, 113; marriage to Philippa of Hainault (1328), 27–8; opposes Orleton's translation to Winchester (1333–4), 61ff, piqued by French king's forwarding of, 36; publishes *Libellus famosus* (1341), 194ff; reign, 7, 177, 180ff; supports Kilsby's candidature for York, 194 n.84; supports Abp Stratford against Orleton, 206 n.26; taxation enforced by despite clerical opposition (1340–1), 190ff

Edward, duke of Cornwall (1337–76), eldest son of Edward III, 180, 253

Edwards, Kathleen, her views on Edward II, the episcopate and the 'middle party', 119

Eleanor, sister of Edward III, marriage to Reginald II, count of Guelders, 32–3

Elmbridge, Roger de, sheriff of Hereford, 107 n.27, 136

Elstead (Surr.), 80, 244

Elstow (Beds.), Benedictine abbey (nuns), 143 n.43

Eltham, John of, brother of Edward III, earl of Cornwall (1328–36), 32 n.28, 35

Ely diocese, 125; bps of, *see* Hothum; Montacute, Simon de

Emma, Queen, wife of Canute, legend of, 65

Empshott (Hants.), 76 n.119

English Bicknor (Gloucs.), 42 n.7, 217

Enham, M. Thomas de, sequestrator-general in Winchester archdeaconry, 94

Enstone (Oxon.), 240; appropriation of church of, 57

Esher (Surr.), episcopal manor, 195, 242–51, 254–5; rector of church of, 77

Esztergom (Gran), Hungary, abp of, 109

Étampes (Essonne), 17

Etherdwick (Yorks.), 229

Eu, Joan, daughter of count of, 35

Euze or Duèse, Jacques d', cardinal-bp of Albano, bp of Avignon, 16, *and see* John XXII

Evesham (Worcs.), 216, 223; Benedictine abbey, 54 n.7, 56

Ewell deanery (Surr.), 71

Excusaciones of Abp Stratford, xiii, 193 n.81, 196 n.94, 206

Exeter diocese, Mepham's attempted visitation of, 182 n.6; bps of, *see* Grandisson, John de; Stapledon

Eynsham (Oxon.), 235; Benedictine abbey, 58 n.32

Fairford (Gloucs.), appropriation of church of, 58 & n.34, 59

Farges, Cardinal Raymond de, dean of Salisbury, 17 n.54

Faringdon (Berks.), 239

Farndon, Hugh de, Orleton's proctor, 2 n.6

Farnham (Hants.), castle-manor of, 195, 214, 242–5, 247–59; alterations for Orleton at, 65; Orleton's final hours spent at, 97, 259
Felde, John de la, canon of Hereford, 87
Fernhale, Richard de, 143
Fichet, Thomas, lay member of Orleton's *familia*, 97 n.141
Fieschi, Cardinal Luca, 16, 22, 43, 118 n.7, 120, 123
FitzAlan, Edmund, earl of Arundel (1306–26), 129; alleged abuse of power, 177 n.87; at Clerkenwell with barons (1326), 129; confesses to demanding illegal recognisances, 179 n.99
Fladbury (Worcs.), 229, 232, 240
Flaxley (Gloucs.), Cistercian abbey, monk of, *see* Cays
Flores Historiarum, Westminster chronicle: attitude to Orleton, 116; besmirches reputations of Birston and Reynolds, 117; castigates bps as *canes muti* (1322), 139; description of Isabella's landing, 162, of safe-conducts issued to the Mortimers (1322), 134
Folham, H. de, canon of Wells, 211
Foliot, Gilbert, bp of Hereford (1148–63), of London (1163–87), 55
Ford (now Fordingbridge) (Hants.), church of, 66
Ford, John de, subprior of Winchester, 82 n.2
Frampton (Gloucs.), 230
Francis, Richard, bp of Waterford (1338–*c.* 1349), suffragan of Orleton at Winchester, 80, 253
Fraunceys, M. Roger, of Breinton, registrar of Winchester consistory court, 95
Frédol, Cardinal Bérenger, papal penitentiary, 14
Frome (Herefs.), rural dean of, 48 n.47
Froyle (Hants.), appropriation of church of, 75 n.107, 76, 78 n.129
Frye, William, of Merrow, 67
Fulham (Middx), bp of London's manor, 168 n.45
Fykys, M. Henry, *see* Peters

Gaetani, Francesco, claimant to treasurership of York, 10 n.11
Gainsburgh, William, bp of Worcester (1303–7), 9, 209
Galeys, Philip le, abbot of Wigmore, 46, 218
Gascony, duchy of, 9ff, 32ff; encroachment by Philip V's officials in, 20; Edward II's proposed visit to, 152 n.83; seneschals of, *see* Craon; Pecche; *see also* Aquitaine
Gaucelme, Cardinal, *see* Jean
Gaveston, Piers, earl of Cornwall (1307–12), 9–10, 14, 117
Geoffrey, abbot of Quarr, 68
Geoffroi, lord of Mortagne-sur-Dordogne, 26 n.96
Gertrude, queen of Hungary, 109
Ghent, Simon de, bp of Salisbury (1297–1315), 4
Giffard, Godfrey, bp of Worcester (1268–1301), 1 n.8, 3–4
Glenfield-by-Leicester, 234
Gloucester, 134–5, 165, 185 n. 33, 186, 217, 225, 230, 233, 239; St Mary's church (de Lode), 57 n.29; St Peter's Benedictine Abbey, 45–6, 50, 113, abbots of, *see* Toky; Wigmore, John de
Gloucester archdeaconry, 56, 210 n.a
Gloucester, John of, abbot of Hailes, 21
Gloucester, Laurence of, *see* Bruton, Laurence
Gloucester, M. Robert of, relative of M. Robert le Wyse of, 2 n.11
Gloucester, M. Robert le Wyse of, *see* Wyse
Godshill (I.O.W.), church of, 66, 69 n.47
Gore, M. Nicholas de, prebendary of Westbury, 56
Gower Peninsula (South Wales), 128
Grandisson, John de, bp of Exeter (1327–69), 59, 80 n.140, 182 n.6, 190 n.65
Grandisson, Otto de, diplomatic envoy at Vienne, 13
Gravesend, Stephen, bp of London (1319–38), 159 n.134, 168 n.45, 245; acts as mediator (1321), 129ff; assists at Edward III's coronation, 178; attends Lambeth assembly (1326), 163; attends provincial council for Despensers' recall (1321), 133; implicated in 'Dunheved conspiracy', 188 n.51; joins opposition to Mortimer and Isabella (1328), 183–6, accompanies Mepham as negotiator (1329), 186; member of delegation to Lancaster (1319), 127 n.63, falls ill at Northampton, 127 n.64; protects Hamo de Chigwell, 187 n.45; publishes bull against Isabella (1326),

Index

Loughborough, William de, royal *nuncius*, 13 n.29
Louis IV, of Bavaria, emperor (1314–47), 163 n.11
Louis IX, St, king of France (1226–70), 25 n.93
Lowe, John de la, official of Worcester diocese, 96
Lucy, Godfrey de, bp of Winchester (1189–1204), 76 n. 119
Ludlow (Salop), Orleton family in, 2
Ludlow, Richard de, 47 n.37
Lugwardine or Lugwardyn, M. John de, 122, 217
Lynton, John de, 140

Maddicott, J. R.: his views on the 'middle party', 118, on mediation of bps, 119–20
Magna Carta, proceedings of royal collectors said to contravene, 192–3
Maidstone (Kent), archiepiscopal palace, 94, 164 n.13
Malden (Surr.), ordination of vicarage at, 76 n.119
'Manydenne', 240
Marcle, *see* Much Marcle
Marie, daughter of Philip VI of France, 32 n.28
Martin, David, bp of St David's (1296–1328): member of council nominated at Leake (1318), 123 n.42, 124; one of the Ordainers, 124 n.45
Martival, Roger, bp of Salisbury (1315–30), 52 & n.78, 81, 229; associated with Orleton re Oxford University dispute, 60–1; attends provincial council for Despensers' recall (1321), 133; issues indulgence for Cantilupe's shrine, 48 n.51; mediates in 1321, 129; seals conciliatory document (1318), 122 n.35; signatory of Leake (1318) and member of council, 122 n.42; takes (second) Guildhall oath (1327), 172 n.68
Martley (Worcs.), 166
'Martleye', probably Much Marcle (Herefs.), *q.v.*
Marwell (Hants.), episcopal manor, 241–2, 244, 247, 249, 251, 256
Masington, Gilbert de, custos of Orleton's palace and gaol at Worcester, 93
Masington or Masyngton, Walter de, valet of Orleton at Winchester, 92 n.100
Meaux (Yorks.), Cistercian abbey, chronicler of, *see* Burton, Thomas de
Mees, William, secretary of John Stratford, 173
Melton, William, abp of York (1317–40), 18, 22–3, 243; at Avignon in 1317, 118; attends Lancaster's quasi-parliament at Sherburn (1321), 129; claims Orleton for Church (1324), 145; considered to have undertaken missions in support of 'middle party', 124 n.49; implicated in Dunheved conspiracy, 188 n.51; issues indulgences for Cantilupe, 48 n.51; member of standing council (1327), 177, 179–80 n.105; raises Yorkshire levies and is defeated at Myton (1319), 158; refuses to take Guildhall oath (1327), 172; withholds consent to proclamation of new king (1327), 171
Meone, William de, treasurer of Orleton's household at Winchester, 96–7
Meonstoke, M. Thomas de, sequestrator-general in Winchester archdeaconry, 94
Mepham, Simon, abp of Canterbury (1328–33), 180–1; attempts to visit Exeter diocese, 182 n.6; attribution to of *Speculum regis*, 107, n.24; death, 36; demands renewal of Orleton's profession, 55; joins Lancastrian group, 183, 185–6; mandate concerning elevation of York primatial cross, 61; preaches at St Paul's (1328), 185; presides over provincial council (1329), 187; quarrel with Itier de Concoreto, 181–2 n.6
Mere, John de, chaplain of Orleton at Worcester, 91–2
Merrow (Surr.), 66
Merton (Surr.), 242; Augustinian priory, 71–3, 242, 253, prior of, *see* Kent, Thomas de
Merton College, *see* Oxford University
Meysey, John de, 56
Middle party, historiography of, 118ff
Middleburgh (Zeeland), 28
Middleton (Hants.), 108, 152, 226
Middleton Cheney (Northants.), 96 n.132
Middleton, M. Gilbert de, canon of Hereford, official of Court of Canterbury, 4, 6–7, 18, 41 n.2, 42, 126, 206, 219; commemorated (with Orleton) in Edington chantry, 97; deputed to fill episcopal benefices at Hereford, 87
Middleton, John de, rector of Morestead, 97 n.141

Index